Studies in Eighteenth-Century Culture

Volume 37

Studies in Eighteenth-Century Culture

Volume 37

Studies in Eighteenth-Century Culture

Volume 37

Published by The Johns Hopkins University Press for the American Society for Eighteenth-Century Studies

The Johns Hopkins University Press
Baltimore and London
2008

Printed in the United States of America on acid-free paper.
9 8 7 6 5 4 3 2 1

The Johns Hopkins University Press
2715 North Charles Street
Baltimore, Maryland 21218-4363
www.press.jhu.edu

ISBN 978-0-8018-8795-6
ISBN 0-8018-8795-X
ISSN 0360-2370

Articles appearing in this annual series are abstracted and indexed in *Historical Abstracts* and *America: History and Life*.

Contents

Editor's Note

While the intellectually diverse essays that constitute *SECC* 37 testify to the impressive range of scholarship in our period, the question of how eighteenth-century writers make sense of the past—how they interpret it, give it meaning and form, and deploy it for their own practical, aesthetic, and ideological purposes—emerges as a resonant, if unintentional, theme of this volume. And as our contributors remind us, constructing narratives of the past was a high-stakes enterprise with influential cultural, social, and political effects, including the emergence of new disciplines and codifications of knowledge; the (often punitive) assessment and treatment of foreign cultures and peoples; and the articulation of resistance to dominant hierarchies of values and the social structures they support. Although varying widely in their focus, topics, and scope, the essays in this volume share a common concern with investigating Enlightenment categories of historical understanding and determining how these categories helped shape Enlightenment culture. Another shared concern is their awareness of the prejudices and predilections that we as scholars bring to our interpretation and use of history.

The three essays that begin this volume turn their attention to a discussion of origins. In his study of conjectural history's influence on the emerging discipline of sociology, Frank Palmeri argues that both discursive forms exhibit common narrative features. Eighteenth-century conjectural history, as practiced by Ferguson, Condorcet, Hume, Kant, and others, is defined by a naturalistic rather than providential explanation of social organization; an emphasis on the organic, interdependent relations among law, religion, kinship, and other social structures; an insistence on the unplanned development of social institutions; and a conception of societies as progressing through distinctive stages from primitivism to sophistication. As Palmeri demonstrates, the founding sociologists of the nineteenth century, Comte and Spencer, adopted the principal features and narrative patterns of the genre of conjectural history, for it provided a template for mapping the social life of cultures from whom few material traces survive—a method that proved attractive to other social sciences as well. The problem of origins also informs Stuart Peterfreund's essay on natural theology. Resting on the argument from design, which attributed the order of nature to God the creator made manifest in his creations, natural theology experienced a radical shift as early eighteenth-century science attempted to explain the workings of inanimate phenomena: the God of Boyle and Newton revealed himself not through his creatures but through the mechanisms by which they functioned. At the end of the eighteenth century, as scientific inquiry moved from physiology toward investigating the origins of life, the location of design moved as well, this time situating itself in the system–such as Darwin's theory of evolution—which is regulated by laws of energy and matter. As Peterfreund notes, whether this particular argument from design requires belief in a designer remains one of our most heated cultural debates. The difficulty of locating a creator is a theme in Tony C. Brown's essay on the mounds of the Ohio Valley and the particular interpretive challenges they posed to their late Enlightenment observers. In their apparent ability to resist identification and comprehension, the mounds mystified Europeans, whose attempts to imagine a history for them, and a civilization capable of producing them, ended in defeat. As Brown argues, only excavation—and the concomitant destruction of the mounds themselves–makes a narrative of the earthworks possible, and thus comprehensible to European thought.

A focus on the production of knowledge likewise informs Shane Agin's work on Diderot's campaign for a program of sex education in France. Agin examines how Diderot's concern for his daughter's transition to marriage and motherhood intensified his interest in creating a discursive space–or an educational forum—in which sexual beliefs and practices could be discussed and assessed apart from the influence of the established church on the one hand and the libertine subculture on the other. Proclaiming the importance of anatomy lessons for young men and women alike, Diderot insisted that knowledge unconnected to the confessional or to libertinage would ensure the happiness of couples in marriage, and through their successful reproduction, the overall health, welfare, and strength of the French nation. The creation of domestic intimacy is also the subject of Suzanne R. Pucci's essay on the textual and pictorial strategies that create the concept of family unity in Bernardin de Saint-Pierre's *Paul et Virginie*. According to Pucci, the early modern period experienced a shift in conceptions of the family from the diachronic model of lineage to the spatial model of domestic attachment, with intimacy being represented and articulated as synchronic relations among kin positioned within an enclosed interior space. The tableau of family togetherness produced in fiction such as *Paul et Virginie* not only helped define the boundaries of domestic life, but also foreshadowed the present-day photograph in its simultaneous rejection of and dependence upon readers and viewers outside the frame.

Turning from France to Spain, the following two essays also analyze the construction of a conceptual framework dividing insiders from outsiders. First, Ana Hontanilla examines how the descriptions featured in eighteenth-century British travel narratives functioned to exclude Spain as part of a civilized, enlightened Europe. Employing a stadial view of historical progress, these travelers determined that the people of Spain, hampered by the superstitions of Catholicism, the ideological repression of the Inquisition, a despotic government, and the absence of a commercial spirit, more closely resembled the natives of colonized territories than the citizens of developed, advanced European states like Britain. Producing this image of a backward and barbaric Spain allowed the British to celebrate their own political, cultural, and economic development while legitimizing their attempts to exploit the resources of Spaniards, whose supposed intolerance, tribalism, and indolence presumably justified their subjugation. As Mark R. Malin's essay shows, depictions of natives in novels from the Spanish Enlightenment follow a similar representational logic and serve similar ends. Projecting both Enlightenment ideals (sympathy for others, selfless commitment to the public good, disdain for absolutism) as well as European taboos ("barbaric" lawlessness, sexual licentiousness) onto the natives enabled Spanish novelists and translators to critique customs and mores prevalent in their own society while at the same time justifying Spain's persecution and control of native peoples. The debate over the figure of the native is in essence a dispute over the tensions dividing Spain itself, with the natives serving as the embodiment of both reformist and traditionalist ideologies.

The next set of essays takes us back to Britain, yet continues to focus on the intersections between emergent and residual forms of cultural life. Categorizing eighteenth-century literary production into two main blocs–one attuned to the commercial marketplace and dominated by the book trade, the other composed of gentleman authors centered in the established church–Simon During argues that the exchanges between these two shaped the conceptual and ethical structures of literature during this period. Analyzing works by the market-oriented printer John Nichols and by the authors associated with William Warburton, bishop of Gloucester, During examines how the complicated interactions among political, religious, and commercial institutions challenge previous narratives of literature's modernization, and call into question their stress on the prevailing influence of market forces over genteel literary culture. Julia Rudolph's account of Giles Jacob's abridgments of law books similarly identifies the continuities between two seemingly divergent techniques of legal study, one based on manuscript practices and the other based on print. Rudolph maintains that far from perverting the goals of humanistic learning (as contemporary critics charged), Jacob's abridgements helped aspiring lawyers handle the "information overload" of eighteenth-century legal practice both by imitating the familiar structure of the manuscript commonplace book and providing a useful model for students's construction of their own individual books. Paradoxically, printed abridgements like Jacob's employed the devices of manuscript practices to manage the profusion of print itself, while their physical format of wide margins and interleaved pages blurred distinctions between readers and authors, composition and consumption, by encouraging students to amend and add to the text itself. As Rudolph reminds us, the organization and codification of knowledge was a foundational Enlightenment project—and one which Jacob was instrumental in advancing.

The complexities involved in making sense of the past surface as a theme among eighteenth-century writers themselves. Anne H. Stevens's essay analyzes the emergence of literary forgery and historical fiction in Britain as imaginative articulations of a growing skepticism toward positivistic historical methods: literary historians's increased interest in and confidence about reconstructing the past provoked the very forgeries that blurred the distinctions between authenticity and falsity. Examining texts produced during the period from Macpherson to Scott, Stevens traces the connections that developed among histories of literature, forgery, and fiction, connections that continue to resonate in the genre of historical novels. Jennifer Thorn's contribution likewise performs a revision of literary history by illuminating the radical political stance within Phillis Weatley's poem *Niobe*. Traditionally considered an exercise in imitating Ovid, *Niobe* holds the reputation of a competent if unexceptional rendition of a classical text. But as Thorn demonstrates, when placed in its contemporary discursive context—which includes American suspicion of the classics's moral effects, the cultural preoccupation with motherhood, slavery's subversion of the black family, and the growing colonial resentment toward tyrannical authority—the poem articulates Wheatley's intellectually complex, emotional response to the conditions of her life with a clarity and force that unsettle more conventional images of her. Providing a richly historical framework for revisionist interpretation is also the goal of Hilary Englert's work on object-narrated fiction before and after the publication of Laurence Sterne's *Tristram Shandy*. According to Englert, contemporary literary history distorts both Sterne's fiction and the mid-eighteenth-century culture of object narratives by dissociating his novels from rhapsodical writing, and from the questions such writing raised about the fluidity of boundaries between original genius and collective composition, creativity and compilation, and elite literature and market-driven ephemera. Restoring a sense of Sterne's involvement with popular fiction of his time allows for a better assessment of how his writing responds to, and bears the marks of, the conflicts among the various forms of literary production.

No editor must be reminded that producing a volume of essays is a collaborative enterprise. My predecessor Jeffrey N. Ravel has graciously continued to provide his counsel, and my co-editor Downing A. Thomas has offered invaluable assistance from start to finish. The industry and expertise of editorial board members Claire Baldwin, James Carson, Lisa Cody, Lisa Freeman, Anne C. Vila, and Johnson Kent Wright were essential for the production of this volume, which benefitted greatly from their generous offerings of time and advice. As always, Vickie Cutting in the ASECS office served as a model of efficiency and good guidance in all things relating to *SECC*; her diligence, and the consummate professionalism of Myrta Byrum at The Johns Hopkins University Press, made the publication process go forward without a hitch. Lydia McDermott, a doctoral student in Composition/Rhetoric at Ohio University, proved herself the best imaginable editorial assistant; I am also grateful to Benjamin Ogles, Dean of Ohio University's College of Arts and Sciences, and Joseph McLaughlin, Chair of the English Department, for their support of my work on *SECC*. Byron R. Wells, Executive Director of ASECS, and William Briechner of The Johns Hopkins University Press responded quickly and favorably to my request to include *SECC* as part of Project Muse; their encouragement of this venture has resulted in the digitization of volume 37 and all subsequent volumes, making excellent scholarship in the eighteenth century available to a wider audience of our colleagues. The vitality and success of *SECC* depend upon these colleagues—the scholars who submitted their essays for consideration as well as the scholars who served as readers and critics—and their collective contributions deserve the highest regard.

Linda Zionkowski
Ohio University

Conjectural History and the Origins of Sociology

FRANK PALMERI

Among the individuals or groups of thinkers who influenced sociology as the new discipline took shape in the middle and late nineteenth century, those most frequently named as precursors have included Montesquieu and the Scottish social thinkers such as Adam Ferguson, Adam Smith, John Millar, and Henry Home, Lord Kames.[1] Ferguson in particular has figured prominently, beginning with an early study by William Lehmann which considered him the father of sociology.[2] Associated thinkers too have been named as the crucial influence on the formation of sociology, especially the Scottish Enlightenment figures as a group. Without undervaluing the importance of such figures, we may look for the origins of the discipline not only in antecedent individuals or schools, but also in a genre of historical narrative, in this case, the form that has been known as conjectural, theoretical, or speculative history ever since Dugald Stewart discussed it under those terms in his life of Adam Smith.[3]

Shifting emphasis away from an approach based on a history of individual ideas or motifs may suggest an account of the emergence of the new discipline based on a genealogy of narrative forms. Such a method traces not so much the occurrence and reiteration of ideas as the transformation and recombination of features of form. For example, because eighteenth-century conjectural history exhibits, among other features, a stadial view of history and an organic understanding of society, changes in the conception of historical stages and in the extent of a thinker's organicism will have dramatic effects on the shape of the genre in his hands. Thus, when Comte argues that not only has the history of western society fallen into three stages, but also that each science must proceed through the same stages before the highest period of scientific knowledge is reached, then the stages of conjectural history have been transformed, moved beyond designating merely the means of subsistence and reconceived as forms of intellectual, scientific, and institutional life that are not even bound to a single chronology. Similarly, when the implicit or metaphoric organicism of most of the conjectural histories becomes in Spencer's *Principles of Sociology* a recurring assertion of detailed parallels between processes in various organs and organisms and social processes exemplified by different cultures in different times and places, then the parallels have moved from being metaphoric to being metonymic—instances of the same processes in different registers—and again, the pattern from the earlier genre has been both retained and significantly altered.

The elaboration of the methodological approach sketched here may not appear entirely unfamiliar because the form is to a certain extent a generalization of the ideas or content it expresses. That is, conjectural history and the discipline of sociology both seek to explain the origins and developmental history of religion, languages, and forms of political organization, but divergent theses or emphases on some or all of these subjects account for the differences between the two discursive forms. Nonetheless, beneath dissimilarities and incommensurabilities, a focus on conjectural history holds the possibility of bringing into focus continuities that remain obscure when tracing the influence of individual figures, single ideas, or national schools of thinkers.

We may consider as conjectural histories not only narratives by Scottish thinkers of the late eighteenth century, but also similar accounts from other national cultures and contiguous periods. Among early examples of such histories could be included works by Bernard Mandeville (especially the second volume of the *Fable of the Bees* [1729]), Giambattista Vico (*The New Science* [1725 & 1744]), and A.-R.-Jacques Turgot ("Philosophical Review of the Successive Advances of the Human Mind" [1750]). Jean-Jacques Rousseau's *Discourse on the Origins and Foundation of Inequality* (1755), David Hume's *Natural History of Religion* (1757), and Adam Ferguson's *Essay on the History of Civil Society* (1767) constitute classic instances of the form. Many of Adam Smith's works incorporated conjectural histories, including "Considerations Concerning the First Formation of Languages" (1761), and the "History of Astronomy" (1795), as well as parts of the *Wealth of Nations* (1776). John Millar's *Origin of the Distinction of Ranks* (1771, 1773, 1779) and the *Sketches of the History of Man* (1774) by Henry Home, Lord Kames, must be mentioned in any account of this genre. Johann Gottfried Herder's chapters concerning the early history of mankind in *Ideas for a Philosophy of the History of Mankind* (1784–1791) and Immanuel Kant's "Speculative Beginnings of Human History" (1786) give evidence of the currency of the form among German thinkers. M.-J. Antoine-Nicolas Caritat, marquis de Condorcet's *Sketch of a Historical Picture of the Progress of Mankind* (1795) and even the second book of Thomas Malthus's *Principle of Population* (first edition, 1798; second book originally published, 1803) give evidence of most conventional features of the form, and help constitute a bridge between the often progressive Enlightenment thinkers and nineteenth-century political economy of scarcity.

Conjectural histories sought to develop naturalistic narratives of the course of human societies, including especially the earliest stages of human social life. To provide a means of understanding early periods for which no documentary or material evidence remains, and also to offer accounts of the transitions and gaps between eras represented in the historical record, these thinkers had recourse to psychologically plausible narratives of what could or must have happened in order for human beings to develop the use of articulate language, or the institutions of kinship, religion, and authority. Many conjectural histories carry their narrative forward so that it overlaps with recorded history, and they discern the same pattern of progressive improvement in both historic and pre-historic times. Pursuing their ambition of providing a universal secular history of civilization, conjectural histories turn away not only from providential history with a biblical basis, but also from political and antiquarian history, which remained national or local in their focus.[4]

Apart from the distinctive arguments, positions, and emphases adopted by different thinkers, almost all conjectural histories exhibit certain features that give them a family resemblance to each other, and define them as belonging to the same form. Among the significant traits both for an understanding of the genre and for the later development of sociology (and other social sciences), the most important are: (1) a naturalistic approach that avoids recourse to a deity or providence for the explanation of social organization and development; (2) an organic conception of society in which laws, religion, customs, and manners are interrelated and interdependent; (3) an emphasis on the unplanned, unforeseen, and noncontractual development of institutions; and (4) a conception of the stages through which most or all societies develop, though at different rates and with local variations, in the natural course of things. These stages are usually cast either in terms of their means of obtaining subsistence (hunter-gatherer, pastoral, agricultural, commercial), or in terms of their level of civilization (savage, barbarian, civilized).

One or two of the conjectural histories among those just named do not give evidence of one of these characteristics or concerns. Kames, for instance, does not adopt a fully naturalistic perspective, but instead often quickly traces the development of social institutions back to providence as a cause and explanation. He repeatedly ascribes the wonderful aptness of arrangements in the society and the natural world to a primary cause, not to secondary causes. For example, he writes that "the wisdom of Providence is in no instance more conspicuous than in adjusting the constitution of man to his external circumstances . . . So barbarian hunters are great and gross feeders."[5] Similarly, Herder does not believe that all cultures follow the same path through the same three or four stages of development; he does however, believe that cultures and peoples are born, grow, mature as they realize their potential, and then become moribund, like individual organisms. To take a third example, Rousseau does not stand outside but among those in the natural law tradition who consider society to be founded upon a contract; he diagnoses a corrupt contract in the *Discourse on Inequality*, while in the *Social Contract* he envisions a proper or ideal form of foundational agreement. Despite its contractualism, which Rousseau both accepts and critiques, the *Discourse on Inequality* still employs a naturalizing, loosely stadialist, and organicist approach in its narrative of the early stages of human social life. It is true that his account serves to provide a platform for his political and social critique, but the same can be said for other exemplars of the form, including Hume's *Natural History of Religion,* Millar's *Origin of the Distinction of Ranks*, and Condorcet's *Sketch*.

Aside from Kames (and, to a lesser extent, Vico), a naturalistic approach is a defining trait of most conjectural histories. These authors make inferences backwards from where the historical trail leaves off and speculate on the earliest forms of social institutions precisely because recourse to divine causation does not constitute for them an adequate explanation. In this way, the genre reveals continuities with the line of political thought that includes Locke, Hobbes, and the natural law theorists. Although Hobbes and Locke adopt a naturalistic approach to the analysis of the origins of social and political institutions, their thought is neither organicist nor stadial, and in both cases it continues to be centered on a founding contract. A distinctive exception within this natural law tradition, Pufendorf's thought shares a noncontractual mechanism with the later conjectural histories;

deriving commerce from an inherent sociability in humankind eliminates the need for an appeal to an originary social contract. In this theoretical history, commercial activity develops within and alongside earlier stages of society before becoming the dominant form.[6] Nevertheless, aside from this example, the emergence of social order from unplanned human action remains generally absent from the speculations on social origins by thinkers in the natural law tradition, as does a universal set of stages through which all varieties of humankind develop.

Rousseau makes it clear in the introduction to his *Discourse on Inequality* that he proposes setting to one side the claims made by religious texts and authorities in order to develop what he himself calls his conjectures or hypotheses.[7] When Hume offers the first natural history of religion, a study of religious phenomena from outside a religious perspective, he initiates a project that will be extended by E. B. Tylor in *Primitive Culture* (1871), a founding work of cultural anthropology, and by Emile Durkheim in *Elementary Forms of Religious Life* (1912), a crucial early work for the discipline of sociology. Moreover, all of the conjectural historians conceive of society as a complex whole in which customs, forms of thought, laws, and domestic arrangements reinforce each other and are of a piece. Such an understanding is especially clear in the works of Vico, Smith, Ferguson, and Millar, and it underpins the central notion of the organic nature of society and culture in Herder's work.

As important as the interdependence of the various parts of the social whole is the unplanned and noncontractual nature of social development.[8] Hume argues explicitly against the idea of an original, founding social contract in his *Essays*, and Mandeville, Smith, and Condorcet all stress the lack of accord between intentions and results, plans and later developments.[9] As Ferguson writes, "Nations stumble upon establishments which are indeed the result of human action but not of any human design."[10] Such a formulation makes clear the naturalistic anti-rationalism that characterizes most of the conjectural histories. Condorcet constitutes only a partial exception here: he does emphasize the advances made in thought and practice by rational thinkers who are forerunners of and eventually include scientists, innovators, and the technocrats of the future. Still, the ideas of these scientists and their ecclesiastical and royal opponents through history, until Condorcet's time, have been characterized by the ubiquity of unintended consequences, the unpredictable discrepancy between the intention and result of an action. For example, the introduction of gunpowder in Europe brought greater destructive capacity and multiplied the number of deaths in battle, but it also negated the military advantage the nobility derived from its exclusive possession and use of armor, swords, and horses.

Although it might not have been intended or expected to have this result, gunpowder helped bring to an end the era of aristocratic predominance.[11]

Finally, the narrative of development through stages, usually four—from hunting and gathering, to settled pastoralism, then farming, and finally commercial activity—which was widely acknowledged as the influential innovation of Smith and Ferguson, provided a framework for historical understanding that tacitly underlay or explicitly shaped much thought about social development for the next century and more.[12] Because it emphasized means of subsistence, for example, this framework was reconcilable with Marx's materialist, economistic understanding of history. The more general notion of three stages of social development—savage, barbarian, and civilized—was also codified and passed along by the conjectural histories, and its influence proved to be as widespread, if not even more general than that of four-stage theory; in fact, such a framework was almost ubiquitous and inescapable in social thought throughout the nineteenth century and into the twentieth. But the argument of this essay does not resolve into a tracing of the presence of four-stage or three-stage theory in the foundational texts of the social sciences or sociology. The stadial conception of history is a motif or a pattern, but it is only one element of the genre, not a genre itself. The genre of conjectural history can employ many specific narrative patterns, not all of which include three- or four-stage theory: speculative historical narratives by Mandeville, Rousseau, Millar, Herder, Kant, and others employ stages that vary from a small but unclear number to ten (in Condorcet) or more. The genre, however—the sum of its traits—is more capacious and more deeply influential than any of its single elements or common characteristics.

Certain typical traits allow us to distinguish between a Scottish and a French school of conjectural history. The French instances of the form generally focus less on graded, well-defined stages depending on changes in the means of subsistence, giving priority rather to mental states, and producing a history of the human mind more than a history of ways of organizing society.[13] In addition, although many of the French works accommodate utopian moments or impulses, they are also more likely than the Scottish examples to diagnose a falling off in social life that needs to be reversed in order for history to be brought back into accord with nature.[14] Here, Rousseau's *Discourse on Inequality* constitutes a prototypical example. By contrast, conjectural histories by the Scots tend to be more empirical, material, and stadial, with an emphasis on the unplanned nature of historical development and the doctrine of unintended consequences. As yet a third variety, the German speculative histories generally stress the organic nature of society and the growth from one period or stage to another.

Ferguson and Condorcet prove to be crucial precedents for the two major nineteenth-century progenitors of sociology, Comte and Spencer. Like many of the other writers of conjectural histories, Ferguson drew on travel narratives for his information about the customs, institutions, and morals of tribal peoples, and employed the comparative method in arguing that contemporary tribal societies provided an essential image of what the earlier societies in Europe must have resembled.[15] In fact, he repeatedly drew parallels between North American Indian tribes, the clans of Scottish Highlanders, and the phratries of the ancient Greeks whose depredations are recounted in the *Iliad*. As such a set of comparisons indicates, Ferguson was primarily interested in what he took to be the middle period or tribal stage of social life, with its characteristic values of loyalty, courage, energy, and action undertaken for the good of the group. He found deeply worrisome the decline in such virtues brought about by commercial society, which had provided such real advances as greater security, peace, and comfort than had been possible in earlier stages of society. Thus, his attitude toward the progress he depicts in civil society is ambivalent. He fears the corruption that may accompany too great a success in the civilizing process, and throughout his *Essay* emphasizes the continuing importance of struggle, competition, vigorous exertion, and military skills: "The most animating occasions of human life, are calls to danger and hardship, not invitations to safety and ease. . . . ; and the most respectable attributes of his [man's] nature, magnanimity, fortitude, and wisdom, carry a manifest reference to the difficulties with which he is destined to struggle."[16] A century later, Spencer similarly emphasized the crucial importance of struggle in producing improvement: "Without universal conflict there would have been no development of the active powers."[17] Although Spencer thus stresses the continuities between the struggle for existence among other animals and wars between human groups, he also anticipates that the skills and tools thus gained will in the future be put increasingly to other purposes, and that war will eventually become obsolete.

Condorcet pays more attention in his *Sketch* to the present era and to the final, future stage of social life than he does to the eight earlier periods. In each of the past stages, he discerns an advance in knowledge whose beneficial consequences are thwarted by an alliance of priests and kings who seek to retain their power by encouraging superstition and ignorance. As an example of such doubleness, Condorcet considers the period when the Arabs carried forward the light of science that they had inherited from the Greeks: "Les sciences y étaient libres, et les Arabes durent à cette liberté d'avoir pu ressusciter quelques étincelles du génie des Grecs; mais ils étaient soumis à un despotisme consacré par la religion. Aussi, cette lumière ne brilla-t-elle quelques moments que pour faire place aux plus épaisses ténèbres . . . L'on vit donc, pour la seconde fois, le génie abandonner les peuples qu'il avait éclairés; et c'est encore devant la tyrannie et la superstition qu'il est forcé de disparaître."[18] Thus, Condorcet establishes a historical narrative like the one Rousseau recounts in his *Discourse on Inequality*—a progress in decline, a persistence of unjust dominance. However, in the extraordinary tenth stage, Condorcet sees science in the future breaking through such stalemates and the coming of a scientific utopia administered by technocrats, in which young men and women are educated in conditions of equality, many infectious diseases are eradicated, and the average span of human life is extended dramatically. In this *Sketch*, he speaks as the inspired secular prophet of such a technological millenium. A generation later, Comte adopted a similar pose as the seer and high priest of a new religion based on scientific knowledge and planning.

Conjectural history helped prepare the ground for the social sciences in general, by means of the features and concerns shared by most or almost all works that participate in the genre. The turn away from providential to naturalistic explanations satisfies the one indispensable requirement for opening up the field of social action and institutions to study by placing it outside the constraints of a providence which short circuits logical thought and is often proclaimed by a religious authority. The other three features work together. If society functions as a whole, then investigating the operation of one part of the social field such as law, religion, or kinship will bring to light its interlinked and homologous relation to other parts, as well as its function in relation to the whole. (This formal possibility does not lead to a full-scale functionalism, partly because knowledge of the early societies remains so incomplete, partly because conjectural history is a narrative form, inherently diachronic rather than synchronic.) Moreover, the direction in which the functioning of the parts takes the whole society is not determined by decisions of political or religious leaders, intellectuals, or planners (again, Condorcet's future stage constitutes an exception), but by the customary behavior, the unplanned pursuit of interests by the obscure individuals who make up the population. Finally, however, the sum of these undirected choices takes the shape of a discernible pattern, a sequence of stages whose nature and order prove to be comparable for every society. The eighteenth-century conjectural histories therefore assert a universalizing progressive narrative, in which various societies have reached different stages at any one time. Of course, for almost all the conjectural historians (Herder and to a certain extent Rousseau and Condorcet being exceptions),

European societies stand at the highest point of this global and species-wide development. It remained for later thinkers to revise the ethnocentrism of the form and its universal, linear conception of social development, and this critique did not begin to be mounted in sociology as in most of the social sciences until the twentieth century.

With its historicist emphasis, progressive tendencies, and stadial conceptions, conjectural history contributed in particular to the thought of Comte and Spencer, the founders of the discipline of sociology. The relation between the earlier form and the later discipline does not follow a continuous line of descent, but can be characterized as genealogical in the sense that it reveals significant discontinuities, silences, and changes of direction. Many, perhaps most, thinkers in the last two centuries have argued that the French Revolution accounts at least in part for ruptures in forms of thought and discourse that produced the defining features of modern politics and thought. Georg Lukács attributed the historical novel to changes wrought by the Revolution, and Robert Wokler has recently traced to the Revolution the modern form of mass representative politics as rule by competing elites.[19] The sociological thought of philosophers such as Comte and Spencer registers the effect of the Revolution in two principal ways. For one thing, the consequences of the French Revolution, the way the dissolution of traditional feudal bonds and institutions led to a period of anarchy and bloodshed, strengthened the conviction of the organic nature of society, or the extent to which all groups and institutions in the social world are interconnected. In addition, and partly as a result of this increased sense of the precarious interrelatedness of all social functions, the nineteenth-century thinkers believe it is necessary to offer some substitute for religious faith to serve as a grounding for moral values and social cohesion. For both Comte and Spencer, the science of society itself, the sociological inquiry in which they are engaged, serves as a primary candidate for such a replacement for religion. Noting such divergences, however, should not prevent us from also exploring and assessing the commonalities between the conjectural historians of the eighteenth and the founding sociologists of the nineteenth century.

In Comte's case, the continuities arise from the delineation of a small number of universal intellectual stages which shape cultural and political institutions, a focus on advances in science and technology, and arguments for the correlation of intellectual with social conditions of life. Comte's writings, both early and late in his career, show that he was well acquainted with the conjectural historians. He repeatedly acknowledged their influence on his thinking, and he stressed in particular the extent to which he had been influenced by Condorcet, calling him his "précursor principal" and "père spirituel."[20] In assessing the contributions of his predecessors, he focused on the argument in Condorcet's *Sketch* that the history of human societies exhibits a progressive tendency as a result of the workings of a natural process:

> La conception générale du travail propre à élever la politique au rang des sciences d'observation a été découverte par Condorcet. Il a vu nettement, le premier, que la civilisation est assujettie à une marche progressive dont tous les pas sont rigoureusement enchaînés les uns aux autres suivant des lois naturelles.[21]

Both Condorcet and Comte viewed the history of (Western) societies as a series of stages of intellectual and technological or scientific accomplishment, although Comte understood there to be only three stages, where the earlier thinker had divided history into ten periods. Moreover, as Comte points out, Condorcet's divisions rather arbitrarily mark the beginnings of new stages by means of important events in science or technology, and thus fall short of establishing or corresponding to a logical framework.[22] The lack in Condorcet's account of a discernible shift in mode of thought from any one stage to the next gives evidence of the need for a more systematic classification of historical stages, the criteria for differentiating among them, and reasons for the progress they exhibit.

In Comte's account, all forms of knowledge and of society progress through the same stages of the theological, metaphysical, and positive, or the religious, philosophical, and scientific. The first two of these stages express forms of anthropomorphic thought, the earliest by ascribing will and power to all things, the second by allegorical personifications; the third, however, defines itself by accepting as knowledge the results of scientific observation and reasoning. On these grounds, Comte constructs a narrative of the progressive development of human sciences in which the most simple and abstract disciplines, mathematics and astronomy, reach a degree of positive perfection first, to be followed by physics, chemistry, and biology. Sociology will attain positive form last because it is the most complex and most dependent on particulars for the establishment of its truths. The law of the three stages and the sequence of the sciences constituted from the beginning the core of Comte's thought; the rest of his ideas took shape around these fundamental laws.

Condorcet's history of the stages of human thought also focused on the sciences, and although he does not make it an explicit methodological principle, his narrative also gives greatest prominence to the development of technological innovations and scientific insights from the more basic and simple to the more complex, in which the attainment of general applicability is based on command of more particulars. For example, in the Hellenistic period in the Fifth Stage, with Alexandria as the intellectual and cultural capital of the West, Condorcet discusses Archimedes' advances in geometry, mechanics, and hydrostatics, in calculating pi, determining the area of a sphere, and using parabolic mirrors; the foundational works of Hippocrates in medicine, and of Diophantus in algebra; and the advances of Hipparchus in astronomy.[23] Characteristically, in all these instances, Condorcet focuses on the accomplishments of a single figure of genius; in addition, in this early epoch, the distinctive advances consist of their establishment of first principles in many sciences, the simple but necessary axioms that define the field. As Comte later argued, these are the most basic insights in the most basic sciences, to be followed later by advances in these fields and the founding of the more complex sciences; in Condorcet, however, the notion of early advances in the simpler sciences remains at the level of an empirical observation rather than contributing a fully articulated, organizing principle for the history of the human mind.

For both Condorcet and Comte, these different stages of thought are correlated with stages of social organization, as well as with types of society and material conditions. According to Comte, a theological regime typically establishes an alliance between the ecclesiastical caste and an aggressive military, as priests give legitimacy to the warriors by whom they are in turn protected and obeyed. In a metaphysical stage, legists and lawyers carry out the ideals formulated by the philosophers, and the military shifts from an offensive to a defensive posture. Finally, in a positive era, the accurate knowledge of the world gained by scientists replaces belief and opinion, and the military form of organizing external affairs gives way to peaceful relations based on trade. For Comte, the history of the human mind is also a history of social stages. In his holistic understanding of society, each of the parts functions in accord with the others. Moreover, this view makes explicit use of analogies between societies and organisms and between the parts of each. In particular, Comte often argues that the life of the individual recapitulates the stages of life of the species to which he belongs, not only in biological development, but also in social, intellectual, and moral history. Individual development reveals the principal stages of social development, including most significantly the increasing subordination of passion and personal instincts to intelligence and the social faculties.[24]

In some areas, Comte differs clearly from Condorcet. For Condorcet, the appearance of priests constituted the first instance of duping and subordination of some men by others, whereas for Comte, the priestly class first separates man from material necessity. In addition, Condorcet believes that priests, having throughout history served as the agents of superstition and obscurantism, should have no place in the society of the future. By contrast, Comte believes that although Christianity has lost its moral authority and legitimacy, yet a new religion will be required to secure order and meaning in the future.[25]

Still, the views of both are striking for their orientation toward that future: Comte strongly defends Condorcet's concluding his conjectural history with an extended vision of developments in generations to come: "On a beaucoup reproché à Condorcet d'avoir osé terminer son ouvrage par un tableau de l'avenir. Cette conception hardie est, au contraire, la seule vue philosophique d'une haute importance introduite par Condorcet dans l'exécution de son travail."[26] Moreover, their perspectives converge in that Comte, like Condorcet, foresees the necessary and beneficent rise to power and authority of scientific technocrats, knowledgeable experts who will formulate and execute social policies, ministers in the science of social engineering and in the secular religion of humanity. Comte's works provide considerable and acknowledged evidence of his indebtedness to Condorcet and to the form in which he wrote in the *Sketch*.

Further evidence of Comte's continuing indebtedness to almost all of the conjectural historians can be found in his Positivist Calendar, which appeared as part of his new religion of humanity in the *Positivist Catechism* (1852).[27] In this calendar, composed of thirteen equal twenty-eight-day months, the names of heroes both of the mind and the spirit, both secular and religious, replace the names of the saints associated with days in the ecclesiastical calendar of the Christian churches. Comte retains the form of the ecclesiastical calendar, although he radically alters the content to produce in effect a serious parody of the form. The last week in the month named for Descartes, devoted to heroes of modern philosophy and history, for example, contains days devoted to more than half of the conjectural historians discussed here: Hume, Smith, Kant, and Condorcet are all commemorated every year; Ferguson earns a place as an alternate for leap year. The previous week includes a Vico day, with Herder as an alternate.

In addition to being well acquainted with these thinkers, Comte was also aware of the distinctive historical form they employed. Observing that Condorcet carried the investigations of Montesquieu further in the same direction, in order to determine the "développement successif de l'espèce humaine" ("successive developments of the human species"), Comte considers in the same category

> les efforts tentés en Angleterre dans le siècle dernier pour perfectionner la nature de l'histoire, en lui donnant le caractère explicatif ou scientifique, au lieu du caractère descriptif ou littéraire qu'elle avait eu jusqu'alors. En Allemagne, les travaux de Kant et de Herder sur la philosophie de l'histoire . . . manifestent, avec la même évidence, la tendance générale de notre siècle vers les doctrines positives en politique.[28]

Comte praises the conjectural histories of Herder and Kant for advancing historical thought, along with what must be the conjectural and philosophical histories of Hume, Ferguson, and Robertson (although he says these Scotsmen were working in England); all these, he asserts, serve as preparation for Comte's own positivist philosophy of history.

In fact, the *Course of Positive Philosophy* (1830–1842) can itself be considered as a revised and expanded conjectural history that provides an account of the forms of human thought from the earliest period to Comte's own time and even into the future. Like most of the eighteenth-century conjectural histories, the *Course* and the *System* divide all human history into a small number of stages: the theological, metaphysical, and positive succeed each other in Comte's universal narrative in the same way that savagery, barbarism, and civilization constitute a universal sequence in the earlier histories. In addition, Comte's argument for a natural progression of forms of thought closely parallels distinctive arguments of the conjectural historians working from psychological plausibility. For example, in the *Natural History of Religion*, Hume maintained that in the natural order of religious forms, animism and polytheism must have preceded monotheistic systems (chap. 1). Similarly, Ferguson traced the characteristic features of societies from the barbarian to the excessively civilized in his *Essay on the History of Civil Society*. Finally, like some, though not all, of the conjectural historians, Comte believes that the time of the effective preeminence of Christianity and other theistic religions is passing or has passed; and, unlike the earlier historians, he anticipates the need for a new religion as a source of moral authority.[29]

Spencer shared Comte's conviction that the effective authority of religion was waning, and that an alternate source of ethical authority could be based on a scientific study of society. In addition to this vision, resembling Condorcet's, of science replacing religion as social and political authority, Spencer stands in a discernible relation to the earlier form of conjectural history in other ways, even though he does not acknowledge the affiliation between his work and that of his predecessors. The method and argument in the *Principles of Sociology* (1876, 1893, 1896) in fact exhibit extensive homologies with the formal and conceptual structure of the conjectural histories. Much of the *Principles* is concerned with the early forms and development of the family, property, a military corps, and other social institutions. Moreover, in the *Principles*, Spencer, like the conjectural historians and like Comte, conceives of society as an organic whole, in fact as an organism, drawing attention to the coherence of the parts as they function together as a system. At its most general, after hundreds of pages focusing on specific illustrations of parallels between organs and social functions, between organisms and societies, this principle takes the form of asserting that "All kinds of creatures are alike in so far as each exhibits co-operation among its components for the benefit of the whole; and this trait, common to them, is a trait common also to societies."[30]

In addition, like most of the authors of conjectural histories, Spencer seeks to demonstrate that the unpredictable effects of unplanned and uncoordinated individual activity can be beneficial while regulation and planning may and almost always will produce results opposed to what was intended. For example, he cites Taine and Tocqueville as authorities establishing that in the years preceding the French Revolution, an excessive bureaucratic regulation of citizens' actions was making ordinary life "impracticable": the regulators of that day "contemplated only the effects of particular interferences on the actions of particular classes of men, and ignored the effects produced by a multiplicity of such interferences on the lives of men at large."[31] Finally, Spencer understood social history as a developmental process in which tightly knit, interrelated institutions, proving themselves fit, evolved through such unregulated activity toward greater complexity and greater interdependence, and away from the practices of war and empire.

Two stadial schemes inform Spencer's sociological thought. One of these is built on the contrast between military and industrial forms of social organization. This first contrast parallels Comte's distinction between the same terminal stages, although Comte adds a third, transitional stage (associated with a metaphysical form of thought), when the military organization shifts from an offensive to a defensive mode. The other set of stages in Spencer's case derives from the difference between a single and a compound (or doubly compound) society. A single society is a tribal, relatively homogeneous society, without permanent hierarchical divisions; a compound society is one that through conquest or internal divisions has incorporated different gradations, powers, even beliefs into its own structure (a doubly compound society has incorporated other societies several times). This criterion for stages of social development expands on the pioneering work of John Millar in his *Origin of the Distinction of Ranks*.

Both of these ways of describing stages of social organization—from military to industrial, and from simple to compound—depend on a progressive, evolutionary conception of history that Spencer finds to be at work also in inorganic natural processes.[32] Both exemplify what he considers to be the single, overriding principle of evolution throughout the universe: the movement from more simple and homogeneous to more complex, stable, and heterogeneous forms of matter and of life. For example, the earlier, simple stage of society is characterized by a small populace that is almost undifferentiated by occupation, role, and status; the later, compound societies show increasingly wide and numerous divisions of labor and distinctions of rank. In addition to biologists such as Bichat, who argued for increasing differentiation in organic forms, all those conjectural historians who observed and analyzed the importance of the division of labor and the growth of roles, occupations, and ranks in human society constituted important predecessors for Spencer's thinking in this regard—not only Millar, but also Smith in the *Wealth of Nations* and Ferguson in his *Essay on the History of Civil Society*. While the stages that Spencer employs do not conform exactly to those of the conjectural historians, he presumes the most widespread and characteristic division into periods established by the thinkers who worked in this genre: the distinction among savage, barbarian, and civilized periods of society.

Unlike Comte, who recognized Condorcet's importance as a thinker throughout his career, Spencer did not acknowledge his predecessors willingly. Still, it is reasonable to regard Ferguson and Smith as his most influential antecedents if one considers not only the importance of the division of labor and the three-stage history of society, but also the emphasis in these thinkers on the unforeseeable and beneficent results of actions undertaken in the pursuit of self-interest. Smith's notion of the invisible hand that turns selfish behavior to the general good is sufficiently well known. However, Ferguson explains even more emphatically the way non-economic behavior establishes results that could not have been predicted and indeed are not even recognized by those who have caused them:

> Mankind, in following the present sense of their minds, in striving to remove inconveniencies, or to gain apparent and contiguous advantages, arrive at ends which even their imagination could not anticipate, and pass on, like other animals, in the track of their nature, without perceiving its end . . . [T]he forms of society are derived from an obscure and distant origin; they arise, long before the date of

> philosophy, from the instincts, not from the speculations, of men.[33]

Similarly, Spencer argues in the *Study of Sociology* (1872) and the *Principles of Sociology* that the establishment of institutions, progress in thought, and improvements in the material conditions of life result not from planning and not because of but despite the intervention of governments and charities in the needs of a society. Such intervention constitutes the most wrong-headed and counterproductive kind of social action, he insists in "The Coming Slavery" and "The Sins of the Legislators" (both in *The Man and the State* [1884]):

> Legislators who in 1833 voted £20,000 a year to aid in building school-houses, never supposed that the step they then took would lead to forced contributions, local and general, now amounting to £6,000,000; they did not intend to establish the principle that A should be made responsible for educating B's offspring; they did not dream of a compulsion which would deprive poor widows of the help of their elder children.[34]

In these essays, he echoes not only Malthus's arguments against governmental efforts to relieve the poor, but also Ferguson's emphasis on the importance of struggle and the exertion of energies for the survival and advancement of social orders.[35]

Spencer also resembles the conjectural historians in his emphasis on the complicated interrelations among parts of a society as among parts of an organism. In fact, he carries this analogy to an extreme in the *Principles of Sociology*, where each chapter for several hundred pages traces a different way in which a principle of development in the organic world provides a parallel for a stage of social development. For example, he argues that just as societies divide first into two principal classes and then develop a third and mediating class that helps distribute material between them, so coelenterate animals after dividing into a body wall and an alimentary cavity develop a third part consisting of blood vessels and a pump that will distribute material between the parts of the organism: "In both individual and social organisms, after the outer and inner systems have been marked off from one another, there begins to arise a third system, lying between the two and facilitating their co-operation. Mutual dependence of the primarily-contrasted parts, implies intermediation."[36]

Most indicative, perhaps, of his relation to his Enlightenment predecessors, Spencer concentrates throughout the *Principles of Sociology* primarily on transitions between the earliest stage of social existence and the next stage of political, economic and ecclesiastical organization, between what he terms the tribal and the super-tribal conditions of social life—a shift on which the speculative historians also focused much of their attention. Moreover, he relies on the same sources and the same methods on which the eighteenth-century historians relied: he read numerous European narratives of travel as well as classical and contemporaneous ethnographic accounts of peoples, all of which offered evidence of life in the tribal stage. On the basis of such research conducted in the study or the library, he inferred or speculated concerning what must have occurred, what transitional, mediating states would have intervened in order to bring about the shift to a later, larger, more hierarchical and complex form of society.

Thus, for example, concerning the rise of a separate priesthood, he cites a wide sample of societies in their earliest stages and of tribal people that includes New Zealanders, people of Madagascar, Chinook and Bolivian Indians, Mayans and Inca, Javanese, Chinese, Japanese, Egyptians, Assyrians, Greeks, and ancient Scandinavians, among all of whom the patriarch "ceases to have the three-fold character of domestic, political, and ecclesiastical head," but remains ruler and priest. At this early stage, all felt the need to propitiate the ghost of the departed heads of families, so there was no distinction between the chief and head priest. However, as the chief's influence grows, other people, often younger brothers or other members of his family, are assigned different functions that had originally been united in one man: "With increase of a chief's territory, there comes an accumulation of business which necessitates the employment of assistants; whence follows the habit of frequently, and at length permanently, deputing one or other of his functions, such as general, judge, etc. Among the functions thus deputed, more or less frequently, is that of priest."[37] Again, Spencer provides a list of examples that includes the early Romans, the Mexicans, the Khonds, the Tahitians, the Mayans, the ancient Egyptians, the Dahomans, and the Inca. Finally, he notes that the same result may be produced not only by expansion of one tribe but by "the spread of a conquering tribe, and the establishment of its members as rulers over subordinate tribes," along with "local ministrations of the cult it brings with it."[38] As Spencer produces similar lists of sources and inferences concerning the development of military, ecclesiastical, commercial, and educational institutions, it becomes clear that he is using the same method as that employed by the earliest anthropological works of the 1860s such as J. B. McLennan's *Primitive Marriage* (1865) and Tylor's *Primitive Culture*, which were themselves strongly influenced by speculative history.[39]

In the above ways, we can see the sources, the narrative arc, the intellectual procedure and method, as well as the narrative form of conjectural history underlying and helping to shape Spencer's sociological writings.

Such nineteenth-century successors as Comte and Spencer adopted, adapted, and expanded not only motifs or strands of thought but narrative patterns and many of the distinctive features of the genre of conjectural history as practiced by Ferguson, Condorcet, Hume, Rousseau, Smith, Millar, Herder, and Kant. What is true for the nascent discipline of sociology also holds for other forms of social thought. Conjectural history played an important role in clearing the ground for new conceptions and understandings of social phenomena. It made available a method of constructing inferential arguments and narratives concerning forms of social life in times for which we have no documents and few if any remains. In offering a naturalistic, usually stadial account of society conceived as an organic whole, whose constituent parts operate in accordance with noncoercive orders generated by the pursuit of commerce, interests, and knowledge, this form of thought and genre of narrative opened the way to the definition and early constitution not only of sociology but also of other social scientific disciplines, including especially cultural anthropology and social psychology.

NOTES

I would like to thank Eric Gidal for organizing the panel of the 2006 meeting of ASECS at which an earlier version of this essay was presented, as well as the anonymous readers for SECC for their helpful suggestions for revision.

1. See in particular Gladys Bryson, *Man and Society: The Scottish Inquiry of the Eighteenth Century* (Princeton: Princeton University Press, 1945); Donald MacRae, "Adam Ferguson," in *Founding Fathers of Sociology*, ed. T. Raison (Harmondsworth: Penguin, 1969), 17–36; Alan Swingewood, "Origins of Sociology: The Case of the Scottish Enlightenment," *British Journal of Sociology* 21 (1970): 164–80, modified by Swingewood, *A Short History of Sociological Thought* (London: Macmillan, 1984); Lynn McDonald, *The Early Origins of the Social Sciences* (Montreal: McGill-Queen's University Press, 1993); and Christopher J. Berry, *Social Theory of the Scottish Enlightenment* (Edinburgh: Edinburgh University Press, 1997).

2. See William Lehmann, *Adam Ferguson and the Beginnings of Modern Sociology* (New York: Columbia University Press, 1930).

3. Dugald Stewart, "Account of the Life and Writings of Adam Smith, LL.D.," *Collected Works of Dugald Stewart*, ed. William Hamilton (Edinburgh: Constable, 1858), 10:1–98, 34.

4. For a discussion that analyzes the original state, the natural progression of society, and the final state reached in most conjectural histories, see H. M. Höpfl, "From Savage to Scotsman: Conjectural History in the Scottish Enlightenment," *Journal of British Studies* 17.2 (1978): 19–40.

5. Henry Home, Lord Kames, *Sketches of the History of Man*, 2nd ed., 4 vols. (Edinburgh: Creech, 1778), 2:109. For some examples of similar appeals to providence and the "finger of God" in the *Sketches*, see also 1:10, 22, 86, 91, 117; and 2:156, 203.

6. For the elaboration of this argument, see Istvan Hont, "The Language of Sociability and Commerce: Samuel Pufendorf and the Theoretical Foundations of the 'Four-Stages' Theory," *Jealousy of Trade: International Competition and the Nation-State in Historical Perspective* (Cambridge, MA: Harvard University Press, 2005), 159–84, esp. 175–76.

7. Concerning the earliest periods of society, "elle [la religion] ne nous défend pas de former des conjectures tirées de la seule nature de l'homme." Jean-Jacques Rousseau, *Discours sur l'origine et les fondements de l'inégalité parmi les hommes* (Paris: Flammarion, 1971), 159. "It [Religion] does not prohibit us from forming conjectures drawn solely from the nature of man."

8. On the significance of the unplanned production of social order in Scottish Enlightenment thought, see Ronald Hamowy, *The Scottish Enlightenment and the Theory of Spontaneous Order* (Carbondale: Southern Illinois University Press, 1987). On the importance of unplanned action and of avoiding regulation in Smith's understanding of the stages of economic development, see Istvan Hont, "Adam Smith and the Political Economy of the 'Unnatural and Retrograde' Order," *The Jealousy of Trade*, 354–88, esp. 373–75.

9. See David Hume, "Of the Original Contract," *Essays, Moral, Political, and Literary*, ed. Eugene F. Miller (Indianapolis: Liberty Press, 1987), 465–87.

10. Adam Ferguson, *An Essay on the History of Civil Society*, ed. Fania Oz-Salzberger (Cambridge: Cambridge University Press, 1995), 119.

11. Condorcet, *Sketch for a Historical Picture of the Progress of the Human Mind*, trans. June Barraclough (New York: Noonday, 1955), 112.

12. On the four-stage theory of social evolution, see Ronald L. Meek, *Social Science and the Ignoble Savage* (Cambridge: Cambridge University Press, 1976). Meek discusses the formulation of this framework of thought by the Scottish and the French philosophers of history of the late eighteenth century, and considers in particular the role of native Americans in this theory (they are the "not noble" savages referred to in the title).

13. For a thorough discussion of eighteenth-century French narratives of intellectual progress, see Jean Dagen, *L'Histoire de l'esprit humain dans la pensée française de Fontenelle à Condorcet* (Paris: Klincksieck, 1977).

14. For discussion of the qualifications of the idea of history as progressive in the French Enlightenment, especially the notions of decline and directionless

flux, see Henry Vyverberg, *Historical Pessimism in the French Enlightenment* (Cambridge, MA: Harvard University Press, 1958), 75–152.

15. On the importance of the comparative method in early anthropology, see George Stocking, *Race, Culture, and Evolution* (Chicago: University of Chicago Press, 1982), 26–27, and *Victorian Anthropology* (New York: Free Press, 1987), 154–56.

16. Ferguson, *Essay*, 47–48.

17. Herbert Spencer, *Principles of Sociology*, ed. Stanislav Andreski (Hamden, CT: Archon, 1969), 176.

18. Condorcet, *Esquisse d'un tableau historique des progrès de l'esprit humain*, ed. O. H. Prior (Paris: Boivin, 1933), 102. "With the Arabs the sciences were free, and to this freedom was due their success in reviving some sparks of the Greek genius; but they lived under a despotism sanctified by religion. So this light shone only for a few moments to give way to the blackest darkness . . . So we see for the second time the spirit of genius abandoning a people it had enlightened, and once again it is tyranny and superstition that drove it away." *Sketch*, 87.

19. Georg Lukács, *The Historical Novel*, trans. Hannah and Stanley Mitchell (Lincoln: University of Nebraska Press, 1962); Robert Wokler, "Repatriating Modernity's Alleged Debts to the Enlightenment: French Revolutionary Social Science and the Genesis of the Nation State," *The Social in Question: New Bearings in History and the Social Sciences*, ed. Patrick Joyce (New York: Routledge, 2002), 62–80. Wokler also examined the French Revolution as a watershed in social and political thought in "Saint-Simon and the Passage from Political to Social Science," *The Languages of Political Theory in Early-Modern Europe*, ed. Anthony Pagden (Cambridge: Cambridge University Press, 1987), 325–38.

20. Auguste Comte, *Système de politique positive, ou traité de sociologie*, 4 vols. (1851–1881: rpt. Osnabrück: Otto Zeller, 1967): 1:64, "principal precursor"; 4:300, "spiritual father."

21. Comte, *Système*, 4:109. "The general conception of the subject needed to raise politics to the level of the sciences of observation has been discovered by Condorcet. He was the first to see clearly that civilization is bound to follow a progressive course in which each step is strictly linked with the rest according to natural laws." Translations from this work are mine.

22. Comte, *Système*, 4:110.

23. Condorcet, *Esquisse*, 65–67; *Sketch*, 57–58.

24. *Auguste Comte: The Foundation of Sociology*, ed. Kenneth Thompson (London: Nelson, 1976), 154, 156, and 163.

25. Along with so many views that they held in common, Frank E. Manuel discusses this striking contrast between the attitudes of Comte and Condorcet toward religion in general, and Christianity in particular, in *Prophets of Paris* (Cambridge, MA: Harvard University Press, 1962), 282–83. Much of the material in the chapters on Condorcet and on Comte in this book also appears in Frank E. Manuel and Fritzie P. Manuel, *Utopian Thought in the Western World* (Cambridge, MA: Harvard University Press, 1979), 486–518 and 717–34.

26. Comte, *Système*, 4:118. "Condorcet has been reproached for daring to conclude his work with a picture of the future. This bold conception is, on the contrary, the only philosophical perspective of great importance that Condorcet introduced in carrying out his work."

27. See Auguste Comte, *Catéchisme Positiviste* (Paris: Garnier Frères, 1909), 338–39.

28. Comte, *Système*, 4:157, " . . . the efforts undertaken in England during the preceding century to perfect the writing of history, by giving it an explanatory or scientific character instead of the descriptive or literary one it had previously. In Germany, the works of Kant and Herder on the philosophy of history . . . display the general tendency of our century toward positive doctrines in politics."

29. In his analysis of Comte's thought, Frank Manuel stresses that Comte named himself the High Priest of Humanity and that his system came more and more to adopt Catholic forms with non-Christian content—such as saints' days, worship of a feminine principle, and excommunication of heretics. *Prophets of Paris*, 249–96.

30. Spencer, *Principles of Sociology*, 150.

31. Herbert Spencer, "The Great Political Superstition," in *The Man versus the State* (Cambridge: Cambridge University Press, 1994), 168.

32. By arguing for a continuity between the forces that have produced the stars and the earth and those that have shaped the history of life and especially human social life, Spencer's non-providential sociological vision bears a strong analogy with Herder's ultimately providential understanding of the growth of all things to realize their inner nature. See J. G. Herder, *Outlines of a Philosophy of History of Mankind*, trans. T. O. Churchill (London, 1800).

33. Ferguson, *Essay*, 119.

34. Herbert Spencer, "The Coming Slavery," in *Man versus the State*, 86.

35. In a significant convergence, both Comte and Spencer agree with Condorcet that increasing population will not derail the continued progress of humankind, and both dispute Malthus's contention that the majority of people will always have to live on the edge of starvation. See *Auguste Comte: The Foundation of Sociology*, ed. Thompson, 156–58, and Herbert Spencer, *On Social Evolution*, ed. J. D. Y. Peel (Chicago: University of Chicago Press, 1972), 50.

36. Spencer, *Principles of Sociology*, 54.

37. Spencer, *Principles of Sociology,* 580.

38. Spencer, *Principles of Sociology*, 585. The succeeding chapter, which traces the development of polytheism and monotheism through conquest and the return of polytheism after the appearance of theism, bears affinities both to Hume's *Natural History of Religion* and to Tylor's proto-anthropological *Primitive Culture*.

39. On Spencer's relation to ethnography and early anthropology, see Robert L. Carneiro, "Herbert Spencer as an Anthropologist," *Journal of Libertarian Studies*, 5 (1981): 153–210.

From the Forbidden to the Familiar: The Way of Natural Theology Leading up to and beyond the Long Eighteenth Century

STUART PETERFREUND

Overview

Natural theology is a meta-scientific discourse. As such, it seeks to reconcile and harmonize the truths discovered by that discourse which, in a given age, performs the function of scientifically explaining the natural world with the revealed religious truths of the Bible. The rhetorical foundation on which natural theology has always rested is the argument from design, which ascribes the perceived order of the natural, material world to God, the creator of that world, according to Genesis (1–2) and other pertinent biblical texts, such as the Book of Job (38–41). While the rhetorical basis of natural theology has remained constant, precisely what the source of the design in question is has not. Prior to a breakthrough that was made by Robert Boyle near the beginning of the long eighteenth century, the design in question was that of the creature: a personate, passionate God manifested himself in the ways of his animate, living creations.

But such design did not account for the operation of inanimate phenomena in such scientific discourses as those of chemistry and physics. In order both to save the phenomena and keep the faith, Boyle and others of the age, such as Isaac Newton, identified the design in question as that of the mechanism, which could be equally manifest in the anatomy of a creature, in the behavior of a gas under pressure, or in the regular motion of a clockwork universe. A somewhat distant and dispassionate artificer, Boyle's God manifested himself in the ways of his mechanisms. For Boyle, the world and all the creatures in it are like the great clock of the Strasbourg cathedral.

But when the focus of scientific inquiry shifted back in the late eighteenth century from the study of the mechanism to the study of the creatures, with the goal of moving from a contemplation of anatomy and physiology to an understanding of how life itself is possible and how it occurs, the design of the mechanism lacked the necessary explanatory power, and the design of the creatures was seen for the fanciful variant of the bestiary tradition out of which it arose. For a time the argument from design became both fanciful and strained as scientists who were also religious apologists struggled to devise a designer-God with whom a burgeoning catalogue of scientific lore could be reconciled. Ironically enough, Charles Darwin—who in his middle and later years was, to say the least, estranged from the practices of the Anglican Christianity that Boyle had embraced—offered a solution, applying the demographic analysis of Thomas Malthus to devise the concept of natural selection and relocating the site of design from the mechanism to the system. To this very day, the argument from design, as mobilized by advocates for intelligent design, finds its locus in the design of the system.

In the essay that follows, I shall lay out each of the three phases of the argument from design in order to show how each of the loci was used to mount the argument from design and to focus in on the moment of transition from one locus to the next.

The Design of the Creature

By the time that modern science became the focus of concerted intellectual interest and inquiry in England in the last third of the seventeenth century, natural theology was already a concept familiar to English thinkers. As Barbara J. Shapiro notes, "beginning in the mid-1650s, John Wilkins and Seth Ward at Oxford, the Cambridge Platonists, and a number of others developed a rational or natural theology that repudiated the anti-intellectualism which characterized so many of the enthusiasts." As it evolved, according to Shapiro, natural theology steered the middle course between such enthusiasm, on the one hand, and atheism on the other.[1]

But the natural theologians of the mid-seventeenth century were hardly the first in England to be familiar with or espouse the concept, and an understanding of some of the thinking that preceded the mid-seventeenth century may help to explain why the discourse of natural theology developed in the way it did. Francis Bacon, writing in *The Advancement of Learning* (1605), defines the term as follows:

> Natural Theology is also rightly called Divine Philosophy. It is defined as that knowledge, or rudiment of knowledge, concerning GOD, which may be obtained by the light of nature and the contemplation of his creatures; and it may truly be termed divine in respect of the object, and natural in respect of the light. The bounds of this knowledge, truly drawn, are that it suffices to refute and convince Atheism, and to give information as to the law of nature; but not to establish religion.[2]

Proposing as the goal of natural theology the attainment of "knowledge" that results from the "contemplation of [God's] creatures" is tantamount to proposing natural theology as a propadeutic to divine revelation itself. To the knowledge resulting from such contemplation, Bacon, writing in *Valerius Terminus* (1603), ascribes the potential to undo the nescience brought about by the fall itself:

> And therefore it is not the pleasure of curiosity, nor the quiet of resolution, nor the raising of the spirit, nor victory of wit, nor inablement for business, that are the true ends of knowledge; some of these being more worthy than other, though all inferior and degenerate; but it is a restitution and reinvesting (in great part) of man to the sovereignty and power (for whensoever he shall be able to call the creatures by their true names he shall again command them) which he had in his first state of creation. And to speak plainly and clearly, it is a discovery of all operations and possibilities of operations from immortality (if it were possible) to the meanest mechanical practice. (Bacon, *Works*, 3:222).[3]

The attainment of "the true ends of knowledge"—the contemplation and calling "the creatures by their true names"—is a state of affairs epitomized by Adam in Genesis 2:19-20. But Bacon's decision to characterize these operations as *natural theology* has a precedent in need of some unpacking. It seems likely that Bacon's source for the phrase *natural theology*, in spirit if not verbatim, is Raymond of Sabunda, the author of the text now known as the *Theologia Naturalis* (ca. 1431).[4] Bacon came to Raymond—or at least to the concept of natural theology as the discourse resulting from the studious contemplation of the animals—by way of Michel de Montaigne, Raymond's translator (*Théologie Naturelle* [1569]) and biographer (*Apology for Raymond Sebond* [1568,]), as well as the author whose *Essais* (1580; 1588) were an acknowledged and important early literary influence on Bacon's essays and his thought.

Raymond's original title, *Liber creaturarum seu naturae seu liber de homine propter quem sunt creaturae aliae*, announces the decision to focus on the animals—all the animals. And the title, in proposing the two complementary categories of discourse—one of which is "books"—would seem to justify that decision on the basis of what would subsequently become the Protestant understanding that, given the existence of "the Book of Nature and the Book of Scripture . . . there was an obligation to study and understand both. . . ."[5] As Bacon views the process, contemplating and calling "the creatures by their true names" is possible in large part because knowledge pertaining to those creatures and knowledge pertaining to oneself are both forms of natural knowledge that presuppose the existence of a transcendently ordained design, and suggest that, understood correctly, the correspondences to be observed between the creatures and their human observer are not so much analogies as intimations of the existence of an anagogy. This is a position that Raymond is at pains to establish. In *Théologie Naturelle*, he concludes his discussion of humanity and the four ranks or orders of creatures by observing,

> we must remember that by the comparison of the general fit which exists between man and lower things, and of the fit of the lower things among themselves, we have risen to the understanding of a nature that is above ours, supreme and infinite; we have discovered its qualities and its grandeur and have found in it being, life, sensation, and understanding quite other than that of our scale of nature.[6]

Notwithstanding his conclusions, Raymond's method has strong affinities with that of the older bestiary tradition, as that emerged from late classical thought—above all, from Pliny the Elder's *Natural History* (77 CE). In his *Apology*, Montaigne, paraphrasing Raymond, states that "we often shed tears at the loss of animals which we love: they do the same when they lose us." Montaigne then cites by way of confirmation lines from book 11 of the *Aeneid*: "Post bellator equus, positis insignibus, Aethon / It lachrymans, guttisque humectat grandibus ora."[7] As Pliny observes, "several stories are told of horses that would let their master ride them, who defended their rider in battle, or who grieved at the death of their master."[8]

Raymond claims that there is a fittedness to be observed among the creatures themselves, and between the creatures and their human observer. If humanity's place between the creatures and God means that its position relative to God is the same as that of the creatures relative to humanity, then it is plausible to postulate that humanity's relationship to "a nature that is above ours, supreme and infinite," similarly entails a degree of fittedness, albeit anagogical rather than analogical. Aethon's tears put a human face on his existence, thereby suggesting that the workings of a God who created both the animals and humanity—the latter arguably in his image—involve a first-hand acquaintance not only with how to confer, but also with how to display, affect. God's creatures, as Raymond understands them, suggest that the agent responsible for weeping warhorses and a weeping humanity is itself, in some "supreme and infinite" manner, able to weep.

For his part, Bacon is careful to set limits on the uses to which knowledge resulting from "the contemplation of [God's] creatures" can be put. These limits bespeak a fundamental doctrinal disagreement between Bacon, on the one hand, and Raymond and Montaigne, on the other. Knowledge of God that is "obtained by the light of nature and the contemplation of his creatures," serves, according to Bacon, "to refute and convince Atheism, and give information as to the law of nature; but not to establish religion. For as all works show forth the power and skill of the workman, and not his image; so it is with the works of God, which show the omnipotency and wisdom, but do not portray the image of the maker" (Bacon, *Works*, 4:341).

Here, Bacon follows Calvinist doctrine. In the *Institutes* (1536), Calvin holds that the workings of nature that manifest divine providence are "lodged in the act."[9] The act itself can be mundane and general—for example, the effect of wind on ocean waves (*Institutes*, 1.16.7 [1: 206]). Or the act can be miraculous and specific—for example, the last-minute substitution by God of a ram for Isaac as his father, Abraham, prepares to offer up a sacrifice (1.16.4 [1: 202]). But neither act may be said to reveal God's image, whether literally or essentially. As Calvin observes, "the order, reason, end, and necessity of those things which happen for the most part lie hidden in God's purpose" (1.16.9 [1: 208]). For Calvin, as for Bacon after him, providence operates in the world by means of a *via negativa*.[10] The former cites with approval Romans 11:33, a crucial verse in Paul's exposition of election, to contrast God's revealed will with "another hidden will, which may be compared to a deep abyss; concerning which Paul also says: 'O depth of the riches and wisdom and knowledge of God! How unsearchable are his judgments, and how inscrutable his ways!'" (*Institutes*, 1.17.2 [1: 212-3]). That occulted portion of providential design having to do directly with humanity's contemplation of the creatures and its own creaturehood works far more powerfully than the portion made manifest.[11]

Had it been restricted to "the contemplation of [God's] creatures," natural theology would never have become a major meta-scientific discourse of the long eighteenth century.[12] Yet it is worth noting that, notwithstanding Calvin's injunctions against peering too deeply into nature to seek its design—an offense tantamount, it would seem, to seeking evidence of one's election—natural theology was just such a discourse by the last third of the seventeenth century. With unintended irony, natural theologians (and Boyle Lecturers) such as John Ray and William Derham use the same verse that Calvin had used to enjoin against peering too deeply into the design of nature to celebrate the explanations of design resulting from such peering.

For example, Ray's explanation, in *The Wisdom of God Manifested in the Works of Creation* (1689; 1717), of how "the Manner of the Rain's Descent" is superior to "a continual Stream like a River . . . [which] would gall the Ground, wash away Plants by the Roots, overthrow Houses, and greatly incommode, if not suffocate Animals," concludes, "we might in this Respect also cry out with the Apostle, *O the Depth of the Riches both of the Wisdom and Knowledge of God*!"[13] Ray's successor as Boyle Lecturer, William Derham, reads Paul against himself, as it were, arguing that "all *God's Works*" are "contrived with the utmost Sagacity, and ordered with plain wise Design, and ministering to admirable Ends. For which reason St. Paul might well affirm of those *poimata* [i.e., creatures] of God, That the *invisible Things of God, even his Eternal Power and Godhead, are understood by them*. And indeed they are most easily. . . ."[14]

In *The New Atlantis* (1614–17), Bacon, steadfast in maintaining his Calvinist commitment, but ever eager to see the effects of the scientific revolution for which he advocates, imagines what it might be like to fathom what Calvin terms "another hidden will, which may be compared to a deep abyss." As related by one of the "Fathers" of "Solomon's House," which is sometimes also known as "the College of the Six Day's [sic] Works" (Bacon, *Works*, 3:146), the research that these wise men engage in is conducted in deep abysses of a sort—"large and deep caves of several depths" (3:156). And the findings of this research, announced in language that is a virtual echo of the passage from *Valerius Terminus* cited above, include ancient wisdom (*prisca sapientia*): "the knowledge of Causes, and secret motions of things; and the enlarging of the bounds of Human

Empire, to the effecting of all things possible" (3:156).[15] However vividly he may have imagined this project, Bacon could not move beyond the imagining.

The Design of the Mechanism

But in his observations that "all works show forth the power and skill of the workman, and not his image," and that "the works of God . . . show the omnipotency and wisdom, but do not portray the image of the maker" (Bacon, *Works*, 4:341), Bacon left open an alternative line of argument for someone like Robert Boyle, a scientist of decidedly Baconian leanings, as well as the natural theologian whose bequest funded the lecture series that provided the occasion for texts such as Ray's *Wisdom of God Manifested* and Derham's *Physico-Theology*.[16] Bacon's "workman" God is Boyle's God as well—the master-builder of this world who, according to Boyle's *Usefulness of Natural Philosophy* (1663), was "pleased to construct this vast fabrick."[17]

But there is an important distinction to be observed between Bacon and Boyle on the question of what work or "works" should be understood as fitting to serve as the synecdoche for the physical world. Bacon's "creatures" are not the same thing as Boyle's "fabrick." The distinction is worth elaborating. Bacon's natural theology is based on the project of recovering, in as much detail as possible, the design of the creature. That creature, which embodies its design, exists as the earthly effect of a divine cause: God, who is a perfect and complete being.[18] God brings cause to bear by giving command—*yehi* ["Let there be], and the effect is the creature, which is God's signature, as it were, and which, as such, is legible to Adam. Adam in his turn names the creature by reading that signature, and by so doing knows, in several senses, God's true character.[19]

Boyle's natural theology does not focus on the design of the creature per se—at least not in the same millenarily motivated way that Bacon's natural theology does. While Boyle allows that knowledge of the creatures is not at odds with theology, it is no substitute as a "Book," or systematized body of knowledge, for theology. As he states in *The Excellency of Theology, as Compar'd with Natural Philosophy* (1674), "a man need not be acquainted with, or unfit to relish, the lessons taught us in the Book of the Creatures, to think them less excellent than those, that may be learned in the Book of the Scriptures . . . the preference of this last Book is very consistent with an high esteem and an assiduous study of the first" (Boyle, *Works*, 4:7).[20]

But at very nearly the same time that he was privileging "the Book of the Scriptures" over "the Book of the Creatures," Boyle, writing in *A Disquisition about the Final Causes of Natural Things* (1677?), was making what Timothy Shanahan calls "'animal-metaphysical' arguments" in support of the premise that "some of God's ends in nature are knowable."[21] Specifically, Boyle argues that "there is no part of nature known to us, wherein the consideration of final causes may so justly take place, as in the structure of the bodies of animals." For an example, Boyle proposes "the vertebrate eye," which "is so little fitted to any other use in the body, and is so exquisitely adapted for the use of seeing, and that use is so necessary to the welfare of the animal, that it may well be doubted, whether any considering man can really think, that it was not destinated to that use" (Boyle, *Works*, 5:424-5).[22]

Boyle's argument celebrates "the power and skill of the workman" responsible for the creatures (although Boyle does not speculate on "his image"). Moreover, Boyle's identification of the eye as "destinated" would appear to reintroduce the matter of God's character, not in the guise of handwritten names, but in the guise of handiwork—the very artifice that is reported either as "and it was so" or as "and God saw that it was good" (Gen. 1:7, 1:11ff.). But the focus is not on the design of the creature, but on the design and use of the eye *as a mechanism* by means of which to learn something about "the power and skill of the workman," whose works reveal that power and skill, "but do not portray the image of the maker."

Another glance back to Bacon at this point proves instructive: In his posthumous *Sylva Sylvarum* (1627) Bacon posits a series of "experiments in consort touching the eyes and sight." In the first of these, experiment 867, Bacon makes clear his belief that the eyes work not on the basis of a mechanical principle, but on the basis of a spiritual principle. "The eyes do move one and the same way; for when one eye moveth to the nostril, the other moveth from the nostril. The cause is motion of consent, which in the spirits and parts spiritual is strong" (Bacon, *Works*, 2:628).

Although they continue to invoke the primacy of Bacon as scientific visionary and natural theologian alike, subsequent discussions by natural theologians of living creatures, including human beings, focus on the design of the mechanism rather than the design of the creature. In surveying the creatures taken as a whole, Ray concludes that their number and diversity display "the same Superiority of Knowlede [sic]" that an "Artificer" displays "by contriving Engines of the same Kind, or for the same Purposes, after different Fashions, as the moving of Clocks or other Engines by Springs instead of Weights."[23]

To return to Boyle's example of "the vertebrate eye": Ray also represents it as a mechanism. "Now to this Use and Purpose of informing us what is Abroad round us in this aspectable World, we shall find this Structure and Mechanism of the Eye, and every Part thereof, so well fitted and adapted, as not the least curiosity can be added."[24] Derham, for his part, surveys "the *Parts* and *Mechanism* of this admirable Organ the Eye," concluding that "we cannot but stand amazed, when we view its admirable Fabrick, and consider the prodigious exactness, and the exquisite Skill employed in every part ministering to this noble and necessary sense."[25]

Ultimately, Boyle's position, and the position of the natural theologians who followed him, is that the entire natural world is a mechanism, and that the creatures, materials, and natural processes—aggregated mechanisms comprising the natural world—exist in relation to its totality as does a microcosm in relation to a macrocosm.[26] The relationship of microcosmic to macrocosmic mechanism is nowhere more clearly figured than in Boyle's *Free Inquiry into the Vulgarly Received Notion of Nature* (1686). There, in arguments intended to refute Scholastic notions derived from Aristotle regarding God's periodic intervention in the natural world, which would reduce all of the creatures to "puppets," Boyle proposes an elaborate figuring of the natural world as a macrocosmic clockwork, the microcosmic analogue of which is the great clock of the Strasbourg cathedral. Of the Scholastics, Boyle says,

> And methinks the difference betwixt their opinion and God's agency in the world, and that which I would propose, may be somewhat adumbrated by saying, that they seem to imagine the world to be after the nature of a puppet, whose contrivance indeed may be very artificial, but yet is such, that almost every particular motion of the artificer is fain (by drawing one wire or string, sometimes another) to guide and oftentimes over-rule that actions of the engine; whereas, according to us, it is like a rarer clock, such as may be that at Strasburgh [sic], where all things are so skillfully contrived, that the engine being once set in motion, all things proceed, according to the artificer's first design, and the motions of the little statues, that at such hours perform these or those things, do not require, like those of puppets, the peculiar interposing of the artificer, or any intelligent agent employed by him, but perform their functions upon particular occasions, by virtue of the general and primitive contrivance of the whole engine.[27]

If not in the case of the argument from the design of the creature, then most certainly in the argument from the design of the mechanism, there emerges the anticipation of the "black box," as Bruno Latour understands the term, which he borrows from cybernetics. The "black box" saves the phenomena of input and output, but at the same time it occults the specific details of its operation and moots discussion of final causes. Moreover, the "black box" promotes "automatism," a condition in which "a large number of elements is made to act as one," thereby promoting what Thomas S. Kuhn terms "normal science," operating under the aegis of a stable paradigm.[28]

For the rest of the seventeenth and much of the rest of the eighteenth century, the argument from design operated on the premise that understanding the design of the mechanism—and everything was presumed either to be a mechanism or a part or piece of a larger mechanism—meant understanding something about the designer. For example, Ray argues, "we may fetch an Argument of the Wisdom and Providence of God from the convenient Situation and Disposition of the Parts and Members of our Bodies.They are seated most conveniently for Use, for Ornament, and for Mutual assistance."[29]

What Ray then sets out to do is to demonstrate how the design of the human being comports with its mandate, having been created in God's "own image," to "be fruitful, and multiply, and replenish the earth, and subdue it, and have dominion over the fish of the sea, and over the fowl of the air, and over every living thing that moveth upon the earth" (Gen. 1:27–8). Humanity's "*erect Posture* . . . is a Privilege and Advantage given to Man, above other Animals." Making full use of the microcosm-macrocosm correspondence, Ray figures the senses, with their place in the human head, "as Sentinels in a Watch-Tower, to receive and convey to the Soul the Impressions of External Objects." Those sensory organs are encased in "a Skull so hard, thick, and tough, that it is almost as easy to split a Helmet of Iron as to make a Fracture in it. This covered with Skin and Hair, which serve to keep it warm, being naturally a very cold Part, and also to quench and dissipate the Force of any Stroke that shall be dealt it, and retund the Edge of any Weapon." Bilateral symmetry is a design feature bespeaking redundancy of function and spare parts. We have two of most things, "so, if by any cross or unhappy Accident one should be disabled or rendered useless, the other might serve us tolerable well; whereas, had a Man but one Hand, or one Eye, &c., if that were gone, all were gone, and we left in an evil Case."[30]

Derham's arguments are virtually identical to Ray's, and if anything, they foreground the biblical intertext even more strongly than Ray's. Of human posture, Derham observes, "the Thing that presents itself to our View, is the *Erect Posture* of Man's Body: which is far the most, if not the only, commodious Posture, for a Rational Creature, for him that hath Dominion over the other Creatures." Concerning the skull, Derham follows Ray closely, asking (rhetorically), "where could those faithful Watchmen the Eye, the Ear, the Tongue be so commodiously placed, as in the upper part of the Building?" While Derham does not discuss the skull in quite as much military detail as Ray does, Derham does remark of the vital organs, including the brain, "how well are they barricaded either with strong Bones, or deep Lodgments in the flesh, or some such the wisest, and fittest Method, most agreeable to the Office and Action of the Part?" And for Derham as for Ray, bilateral symmetry means spare parts: "what an incomparable Provision hath the infinite Contriver of Man's body made for the Loss of, or any Defect in some of the Parts we can least spare, by doubling them?"[31]

The Design of the System

As useful as invoking the argument from the design of the mechanism was in forwarding the natural theology of Ray and Derham, the argument contained within itself the seeds of its own destruction, because it lacked any sense of the entelechy by means of which divine design is translated into something—a phenomenon, process, and above all, a creature—that develops and lives in real time, but only for a finite period. Just as the universe of Boyle and Newton contained no provision for the concept of energy, the argument from the design of the mechanism contained no provision for a source of that mechanism's energy or a means of regulating such energy to the end of orderly, consistent, and uniform development.[32]

Toward the end of the eighteenth century, advances in anatomy and physiology had diverted science from the single-minded contemplation of the mechanism and brought it back to a contemplation of the creature as a mechanism that took form and lived because of some indwelling principle. To be sure, Richard Saumarez and Charles Bell marveled at the mechanism, even as they dissected and studied it ever so closely. But something intangible—call it élan vital, Lebenskraft, or energy—both organized living matter and made it live.

Saumarez, a reproductive physiologist and precursor of modern genetics, makes what he calls *energy* connate with God. In *The Principles of Physical and Physiological Science* (1812), Saumarez argues that "it is the DEITY OMNIPOTENT, by whose infinite power the universe in general, is governed and directed, who is the first cause, and the first mover; —so it is with the power of life which constitutes the first cause, and the first mover of every living system, in particular, by which it is modeled and formed.[33]

Bell, a skillful surgeon and an anatomist and physiologist of the nervous system, equates vital energy with respiration. But it should be remembered that the source of respiration—human respiration, at any rate—is *ruach*—"the breath of life" (Gen. 2:7) that God imparts and the human soul itself. After the fall, this energy can take two variant forms, apparently. Bell spends several pages in *The Hand: its Mechanism and Vital Endowments as evincing Design* (1833), discussing right-handedness verus left-handedness (and footedness as well). Those who are right-handed (and footed) tend in general to be strong, well-coordinated, hard working, and do well in life. Those who are left-handed (and footed) tend in general to be weak, poorly coordinated, lazy, and do not do well in life. Righties (L. *dexter*) are dextrous; lefties (L. *sinister*), downright sinister.[34]

The moment that marked the final eclipse of what Neal C. Gillespie calls natural theology's "identity position" and the return of the bestiary tradition was the publication, in 1844, of Robert Chambers' *Vestiges of the Natural History of Creation.* After a more-or-less skillful synopsizing of much of contemporary science, including things such as the nebular hypothesis and the developing fields of electricity and chemistry, Chambers in his conclusion tries to argue that this wealth of discovery must point to the existence of a personate Creator-God: back to Raymond. In Chambers' account, "the horse is startled by marvellous objects, as a man is. The dog and many others shew tenacious memory. The dog also proves himself possessed of imagination in the act of dreaming. Horses, finding themselves in want of a shoe, have of their own accord gone to a farrier's shop where they were shod before. Cats, closed up in rooms, will endeavour to obtain their liberation by pulling a latch or ringing a bell"[35]

Discredited at this point for the sincere believer who wanted his/her religious beliefs to comport with her/his scientific knowledge, Gillespie's "identity position" left a believer only the alternative "idealist position"—the one laid out by William Whewell in *On Astronomy and General Physics* (1833), the third of the Bridgewater Treatises, and subsequently in his *History of the Inductive Sciences* (1857). [36] But beyond Whewell's position that there must be something godlike to account for this curious, complex, and diverse universe, there is another argument from design that is, or at least has the capacity to be, religiously neutral and does not assume the operation at some level of a personate creator-God. This third form of the argument from design focuses on the design of the system, which depends on a combination of mathematical laws and the properties of the energy, matter, animals, or other entities that exist within the system ordained by those laws. The regular and specifiable phenomena that occur within such a system—for example, evolution—are the result of how successful any given species is at finding food and reproducing itself in an environment that is subject to change as the result of other systems and/or laws governing the lives of species and their interactions. That is the position that Darwin, no friend to organized religion, assumes in *The Origin of Species* (1859).

Origin concludes, as I shall, with Darwin's "entangled bank," which is the microcosmic type of precisely such a system. The biodiverse flora and fauna of this imagined site have been produced by laws acting all around us. These laws, taken in the large sense, being Growth with Reproduction; Inheritance which is almost implied by reproduction; Variability from the direct and indirect action of the external conditions of life, and from use and disuse; a Ratio of Increase so high as to lead to a Struggle for Life; and as a consequence of Natural Selection entailing Divergence of Character and the Extinction of less-improved forms.

While the imagined site may be grand, it is not special, just as no act of animate creation is special. Darwin reprises Genesis 2:7, the soul-making verse, with an interesting difference: "the breath of life" is not breathed into Adam, the ur-scientist, alone among the creatures. Rather, life is held to have been "breathed into a few forms or into one," and a system operating on the basis of "laws acting all around us."

There is grandeur in this view of life, with its several powers, having been originally breathed into a few forms or into one; and that, whilst the planet has gone cycling on according to the fixed law of gravity, from so simple a beginning endless forms most beautiful and most wonderful have been, and are being, evolved.[37]

With the Darwinian synthesis, the argument from design takes on a quality that neither of the previous dispensations of the argument possessed. Fervency and plausibility give way to elegance and instrumentality. By decoupling the argument from its theological commitments, Darwin makes it at least a plausible means of explaining complex scientific phenomena. And much of the ink expended since had been focused on a question that could not have been asked by a Bacon or a Boyle: does the existence of a design perforce imply or necessitate the existence of a designer?

NOTES

1. Barbara J. Shapiro, *Probability and Certainty in Seventeenth-Century England* (Princeton: Princeton University Press, 1983), 83.

2. *The Works of Francis Bacon*, ed. James Spedding, Robert Leslie Ellis, and Douglas Denon Heath, 7 vols. (London: Longman, 1857–9), 4:341. Subsequent references to Bacon, *Works*, will appear in the text of the essay parenthetically by volume and page.

3. See Charles Webster, *The Great Instauration: Science, Medicine and Reform: 1626–1660* (New York: Holmes & Meier, 1975), 22–23. Webster observes that "investigations conducted into secondary causes, and with utilitarian ends in mind, would incur no risk of transgression, but instead glorify God, and restore man's dominion over nature." Despite Bacon's own caveats, however, Webster correctly characterizes his approach as "fundamentally historical and eschatological. Man's dominion over nature was sacrificed at the Fall; but the Bible gave many instances of the restoration of knowledge under God's grace."

4. See Hugo Friedrich, *Montaigne*, 2nd ed. (Bern and Munich: A. Francke, 1967), 94–96. The title of the first printed edition (Lyon, 1484), was *Liber creaturum seu naturae seu liber de homine propter quem sunt creaturae aliae*. By 1496, the Martin Flach edition, printed in Strasbourg, bore the short title *Theologia naturalis*, followed by *Liber creaturum*.

5. *The Book of Creatures or of Nature or the Book about Man on Whose Account Other Creatures Exist*. See Shapiro, *Probability and Certainty*, 271.

6. Raymond of Sabunda, *La théologie naturelle de Raymond Sebon*, tr. Michel de Montaigne, 2 vols. (Paris: Louis Conard, 1932–5), 1:88; my translation.

7. Michel de Montaigne, *An Apology for Raymond Sebond*, ed. and trans. M. A. Screech (Harmondsworth: Penguin, 1987), 43. Screech renders the Latin as follows: "Then comes Aethon, the war-horse, stripped of its insignia, weeping and bathing his master's wounds in mighty tears."

8. Pliny, *Natural History*, 8:64, as cited at http://bestiary.ca/beasts/beast212.htm

9. John Calvin, *Institutes of the Christian Religion*, tr. F. L. Battles, ed. J. T. McNeill, 2 vols. (Philadelphia: Westminster Press, 1960), 1.16.4 (1:202). Subsequent references to *Institutes* will appear in the text of the essay parenthetically by book, section, subsection, volume, and page.

10. See John C. Briggs, *Francis Bacon and the Rhetoric of Nature* (Cambridge, MA: Harvard University Press, 1989), 46. Briggs cites "Paul's pronouncement in Hebrews 11:3 on the world's nature as a sign" ["Through faith we understand that the worlds were framed by the word of God, so that things which are seen were not made of things which do appear"], and on "the impossibility of imaging forth rather than encoding the divine purposes," as being crucial to "Calvin's . . . key to understanding Genesis." Commenting on that understanding, as expressed in the *Commentary upon the First Book of Moses, Called Genesis* (1554; tr. 1578), Briggs observes that for Calvin, "God is

present in his Creation in the sense the he does not leave himself 'without witnesse.' But the world is really what does *not* appear."

11. See Briggs, *Rhetoric of Nature*, 46, 50.

12. See my essay "Imagination at a Distance: The Baconian Double-Bind, Natural Theology, and the Way of Scientific Explanation in the Seventeenth and Eighteenth Centuries," *The Eighteenth Century: Theory and Interpretation* 41:2 (2000), 110–40.

13. John Ray, *The Wisdom of God Manifested in the Works of Creation*, 7th ed. (1717; New York: Arno Press), 89–90.

14. William Derham, *Physico-Theology, or a Demonstration of the Being and Attributes of God, from the Works of Creation*, 4th ed. (1716; New York: Arno Press, 1977), 1–2.

15. Newton was also fascinated by the *prisca sapientia*. See Gale E. Christianson, *In the Presence of the Creator: Isaac Newton & His Times* (New York: Collier Macmillan, 1984), 255.

16. See J. R. Jacob, *Robert Boyle and the English Revolution* (New York: Burt Franklin, 1977), 32–33, and Rose-Mary Sargent, *The Diffident Naturalist: Robert Boyle and the Philosophy of Experiment* (Chicago: University of Chicago Press, 1995), 35–41.

17. *The Works of the Honourable Robert Boyle*, ed. Thomas Birch, 6 vols. (1772; Hildesheim: Georg Olms, 1965–6), 2:33. Subsequent references to Boyle, *Works*, will appear in the text of the essay (parenthetically) by volume and page. Boyle's characterization of the world as "this vast fabrick" ostensibly figures the world as architecture, but *fabrick* can be a figure for a mechanism as well. In *Physico-Theology*, Derham, "surveying the *Parts* and *Mechanism* of this admirable Organ the Eye," concludes that "we cannot but stand amazed, when we view its admirable Fabrick, and consider the prodigious exactness, and the exquisite Skill employed in every part ministering to this noble and necessary sense (96)."

18. Asked his name by Moses after he has made himself known by means of the burning bush, "God said unto Moses, I AM THAT I AM: and he said, Thus shalt thou say unto the children of Israel, I AM hath sent me unto you" (Exod. 3:14). The Hebrew form of that name, *hayah v'hayah*, is declined from the same root as *yehi*, and both are implicated in the name *Jehovah*.

19. For a discussion of how later writers such as George Dalgarno and John Wilkins sought to recuperate the "real character" of language before the Tower of Babel (Gen. 11:1–9), if not the language of Adam himself, see Robert Markley, *Fallen Languages: Crises of Representation in Newtonian England, 1660–1740* (Ithaca: Cornell University Press, 1993), 63–94.

20. Boyle's arguments in this passage tend to bear out Barbara Kaplan's suggestion that Boyle's move to Oxford in 1656 may be viewed at least in part as signaling his decision to distance himself from London's scientific radicals and expressing his solidarity with the moderates who had preceded him to Oxford. *"Divulging of Useful Truths in Physick": The Medical Agenda of Robert Boyle* (Baltimore: Johns Hopkins University Press, 1993), 41–42, 184n.

Kaplan bases her argument on James R. and Margaret C. Jacob, "The Anglican Origins of Modern Science: The Metaphysical Foundations of the Whig Constitution," *Isis* 71 (1980), 251–67, esp. 253–54.

21. For the conjectural compositional history of Boyle's *Disquisition*, see Thomas Birch, *The History of the Royal Society*, 4 vols. (London: A. Millar, 1756–57), 4: 553, who states that it was written at the request of Henry Oldenburg, first Secretary of the Royal Society, and was completed before his death in 1677, although it went unpublished until 1688. See also Timothy Shanahan, "Teleological Reasoning in Boyle's *Disquisition about Final Causes*," in *Robert Boyle Reconsidered*, ed. Michael Hunter (Cambridge: Cambridge University Press, 1994), 177–92, esp. 183.

22. Shanahan, "Teleological Reasoning," in Hunter, *Robert Boyle Reconsidered*, 183.

23. Ray, *The Wisdom of God Manifested*, 25. The reference to springs as opposed to weights may be an oblique reference to Robert Hooke, Boyle's assistant, and an inventor and engineer interested in springs and spring-driven devices. Boyle's work with gases focused, among other things, on "the spring of air."

24. Ray, *The Wisdom of God Manifested*, 249.

25. Derham, *Physico-Theology*, 96.

26. See Sargent, *The Diffident Naturalist*, 71–72, 91; Boyle, *Works*, 2:57. Although Boyle rejected a number Paracelsus's chemical notions, such as that of salt, sulfur and mercury as the *tria prima*—the three universal chemical constituents—he concurred with the Paracelsian position that studying nature is walking "*in the ways of God.*" Moreover, Boyle may well have encountered the notion of the microcosm-macrocosm correspondence—specifically, the correspondence of the human being as microcosm to the natural world as macrocosm—in Paracelsus. See *Paracelsus: Essential Readings*, ed. and tr. Nicholas Goodrick-Clarke (London: Crucible, 1990), 84–85. In his *Opus Parmirum*, Paracelsus argues for the correspondence in the following terms:

> For the Great World has all the human proportions, divisions, parts, members just as man has; and man receives these in food and medicine. The parts are separated one from another for the sake of the whole and its form. In science their general body is the *physicum corpus*. So man's body receives the body of the world, as a son his father's blood; for these are one blood and one body, separated only by the soul, but in science without separation.

27. Boyle, Works, 5:251-52. Not to make too much of Boyle's choice of the Strasbourg Cathedral clock analogy, it is worth noting that Boyle's laboratory assistant Robert Hooke was the designer and artificer of spring-loaded clocks like the one discussed by Boyle, as opposed to the pendular alternative championed, not surprisingly, by Leibniz in *L'Horologie* (1658).

28. Bruno Latour, *Science in Action* (Cambridge, MA: Harvard University Press, 1988), 2, 131; Thomas S. Kuhn, *The Structure of Scientific Revolutions*,

3rd ed. (1962; Chicago: University of Chicago Press, 1996), 23-34, 43-51. Shanahan, cited in notes 21 and 22 above, reads Boyle's *Disquisition about Final Causes* as answering some of the questions both begged and deflected by the argument from the design of the mechanism.

29. Ray, *The Wisdom of God Manifested*, 229.

30. Ray, *The Wisdom of God Manifested*, 221, 229, 232-33, 234.

31. Derham, *Physico-Theology*, 284, 298, 302.

32. See my essay "The Re-emergence of Energy in the Discourse of Literature and Science," *Annals of Scholarship* 4:1 (1986): 22–53.

33. Richard Saumarez, *The Principles of Physical and Physiological Science; Comprehending the Ends for Which Animated Beings Were Created; and an Examination of the Unnatural and Artificial Means of Philosophy Which Now Prevail* (London: R. Edwards for T. Egerton, 1812), 44. See also my essay "An Early Response to Shelley's The Necessity of Atheism." Keats-Shelley Journal 36 (1987): 26–31.

34. Charles Bell, *The Hand: its Mechanism and Vital Endowments as evincing Design* (London: W. Pickering, 1833), 14, 91–5. Bell's was the fourth of eight the Bridgewater Treatises, published as the result of an £8,000 bequest by The Right Honourable and Reverend Francis Henry, Earl of Bridgewater for a series of texts to continue to argue for the reasonableness of the Christian religion along the lines laid down by William Paley in *Natural Theology*.

35. Robert Chambers, *Vestiges of the Natural History of Creation*. Introd. Gavin de Beer. (1844; rpt. New York: Humanities Press, 1969), 336. See also Neal C. Gillespie, "Divine Design and the Industrial Revolution: William Paley's Abortive Reform of Natural Theology." *Isis* 81 (1990): 214–29, esp. 222.

36. Gillespie, "Divine Design and the Industrial Revolution," 222.

37. Charles Darwin, *Origin of Species*, in *Darwin*, ed. Philip Appleman, 3rd ed. (New York: W. W. Norton, 2001), 174. See also Neal C. Gillespie, *Charles Darwin and the Problem of Creation* (Chicago: University of Chicago Press, 1979).

The Barrows of History

TONY C. BROWN

"Standing before the Miamisburg mound," the painter Barnett Newman asks "what difference if the shape is on a table, a pedestal, or lies immense on a desert?"[1] Though he puts the question rhetorically, Newman nevertheless goes on to mark a profound difference between such earthworks ("perhaps the greatest art monuments in the world") and other kinds of artworks and artifacts. A mound, he says, is "nothing that can be shown in a museum"; it is "a work of art that cannot even be seen, so it is something that must be experienced there on the spot."[2] Site specific and, offering little to the view, indifferent to institutional display, mounds refuse museological archiving and exhibiting practices. Certainly mounds can be destroyed (most have been) but they cannot, as the economy of the archive demands, be destroyed and preserved at once. A mound of earth cannot be cut from its original context (the act of destruction) and resituated within the new context of the museum archive (the act of preservation), available for study or exhibition: its covering of grass and trees would fall away; it would come apart, lose its shape; it would no longer cut into the wide Midwestern sky.[3]

One might say that the Miamisburg Mound is itself an archive, that it forms a potential gathering place for various objects, like the bones of the deceased, which would be the archive's content. Yct—and this is crucial—

the mound as such, the mound *as a mound*, exists only by denying access to whatever it contains. It hides its contents from view such that one cannot tell, looking towards a mound, whether it contains anything more than mere earth. As Ephraim G. Squier and Edwin H. Davis put it in their foundational work, *Ancient Monuments of the Mississippi Valley* (1848), what a mound holds and so what it holds out for a certain knowledge is only "disclosed by the mattock and the spade."[4] Otherwise a mound gives little to notice, especially the classically conical mound like that at Miamisburg. Whereas one can at least organize effigy mounds within a taxonomy of animal types (alligators, bears, birds, "serpents"), what those mounds exhibit—bends and lines, specific and varied characteristics—the conical mound does not (see figs. 1–3). That mound's form appears at best simply characteristic of what *it is*. A largely blank surface of earth, presenting few if any isolatable features that one could describe, the mound differs from the surrounding landscape only by a certain angle of incline.

The mounds' minimal difference from the landscape may help to explain why the full range of known sixteenth- and seventeenth-century European comment on the earthworks amounts to a passing reference in the chronicles of Hernando de Soto's expedition (1539–1543). In June 1541 the expedition came upon "some very high mounds [*cerros*], made by hand"; but as with the expedition's discovery of the Mississippi River (which "did not," Mark Twain points out, "excite that amount of curiosity . . . [to] thus move other adventurers to go at once and explore"), its happening upon mounds did not ignite European interest in seeking them out.[5] Not until 1750 do we find perhaps the first mention in English of a mound, itself characterized by the earthwork's failure to strike the observer, Thomas Walker, either as awe-inspiring or as an object for further consideration.[6] Even when Europeans lived in areas dotted by earthen mounds (as did French traders, for example, in the Nashville area), before the 1770s they gave mounds little consideration.[7] As Squier and Davis note, "The fact of the existence, within the valley of the Mississippi river and its tributaries, of many ancient monuments of human labor and skill, seems to have escaped the notice of the adventurers who first made known to the world the extent and fertility of that vast region."[8] One might say, then—given that early Europeans appear to have traveled through land laced with mounds without seeing them (or at least without recording having seen anything like them)—that Newman's claim that a mound "cannot even be seen" proves to be of great historical insight.[9]

But late in the eighteenth-century Euro-Americans start to realize that for the waves of settlers now heading into the Ohio Valley the earth might not be all that is before them. Not only were there the bands of Indians still

Figure 1. Indian Mound, Mound Cemetery. Pike County, Ohio, circa 1940–49. Courtesy of the Ohio Historical Society.

surviving disease and displacement, there were these things in and of the earth itself. While I do not suggest that an age of insight now surpasses one of blindness (most obviously, mounds remain hard to see to this day, just as they remain largely unacknowledged) we find late in the eighteenth century a particularly acute moment of initial, if at best partial, recognition.[10] The questions that nineteenth-century writers would obsessively ask of the earthworks—what are they? and where did they come from?—belies the initial and striking difficulty Europeans had in coming to terms with the shock of their *being there*. And in turn we today have found it difficult coming to terms with that late eighteenth-century shock.

The various nineteenth-century accounts of the earthworks have been subject to much scholarly attention, as have the earthworks in and of themselves. We have a large library of existent scholarship on both topics.[11] What remains mostly ignored is the particular pressure that the mounds placed upon late Enlightenment thinking, and it is that pressure that I will focus on in this essay. I want to suggest that more than merely describing tumuli and other earthworks, like walls and fortifications, late eighteenth- and early nineteenth-century writers struggle to establish the grounds to

Figure 2. Serpent Mound. Adams County, Ohio, circa 1960-1980. Courtesy of the Ohio Historical Society.

acknowledge and to think the earthworks. And that struggle plays out most vividly, and with the most far-reaching implications, in attempts to understand the conical mounds of the Ohio Valley. For unlike the fortifications—and even, we can add, the platform mounds common to the southern Mississippi Valley—the conical mounds seemed lacking in a clear purpose and in those straight and perpendicular lines understood to suggest human invention. When considering early European engagements with the earthworks of the so-called American Bottom, then, the relevant question becomes: How does a certain deviation in terrain become recognizable as a mound? And further, what takes place when it does?

Recognizing a Mound

While the geography of European engagement in North America cannot explain the lack of interest in the earthworks prior to the 1770s, late eighteenth-century settlement patterns do play a role in facilitating the attention initially afforded the mounds. Previously, the spheres of direct

Figure 3. Indian Mound. Rainy River (circa 1914), by Carl Gustave Linde. Courtesy of the Minnesota Historical Society.

and sustained European action in North America were restricted to the Atlantic coast and Hudson Bay (Britain), Florida and Texas (Spain), and the Great Lakes, including the St. Lawrence and Mississippi Rivers (France), augmented by travels into other areas by traders, missionaries, and explorers. While some Europeans had entered the Ohio Valley (British traders begin passing beyond the Alleghenies in the 1740s), prior to the 1770s the area remained largely unexamined, while at least one early map of North America suggested the area did not exist: in an engraving entitled "Carte d'un nouveaux monde" from Louis Hennepin's *Description de la Louisiane, nouvellement découverte au sud-ouest de la Nouvelle France* (1683), Lake Erie lies west of Virginia, immediately north of Florida (fig. 4).[12] But after the new United States claimed the territory from Québec, the Ohio Valley became a place of ever-extensive Euro-American settlement, in a movement that put large numbers of Europeans in close proximity to numerous earthworks, primarily ancient fortifications and conical mounds.

In some cases seeing a mound and knowing it to be such became unavoidable. Thomas Ashe, for example, who traveled through Cincinnati

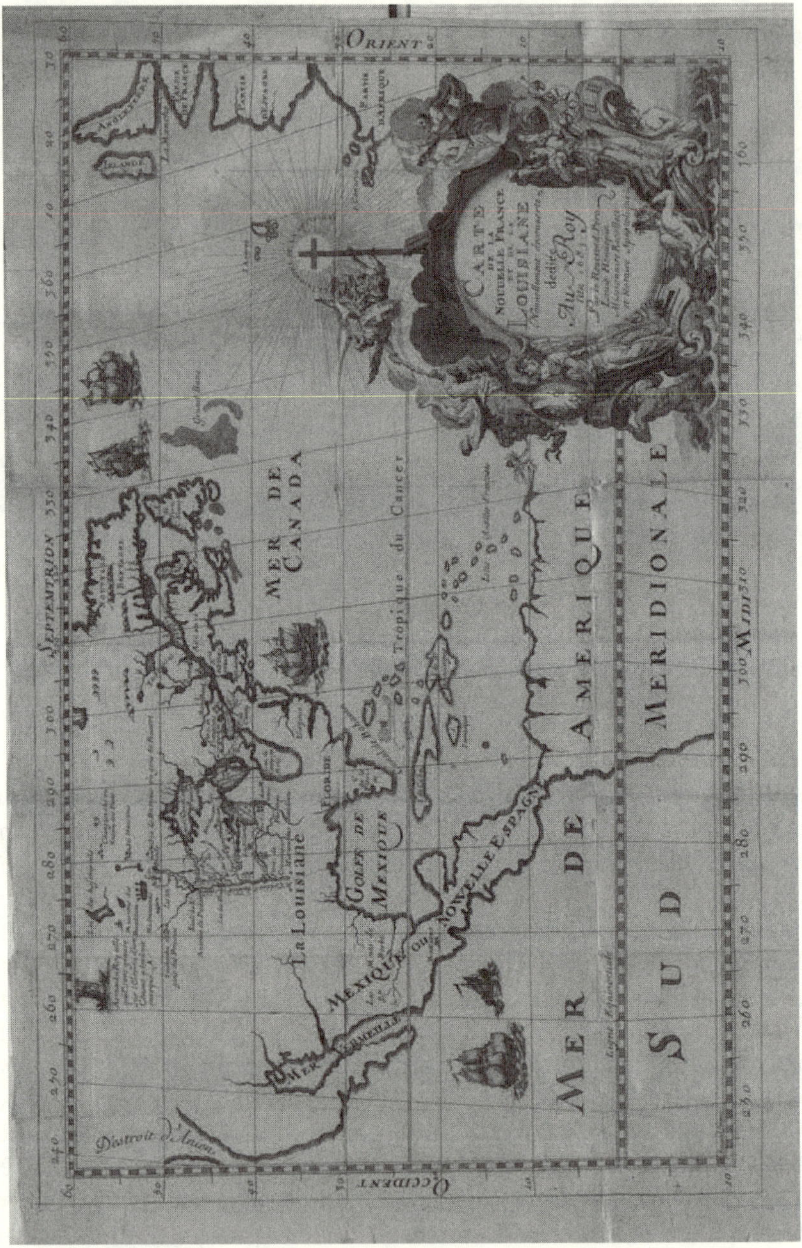

Figure 4. Map of New France and Louisiana, from Louis Hennepin's *Description de la Louisiane* (Paris, 1683). From the collection of the James Ford Bell Library, University of Minnesota, Minneapolis, MN, USA.

in 1806, described the presence there of a "barrow or funeral pile . . . seated in the centre of the upper and lower town on the edge of the upper bank": "The principal street leading from the water is cut through the barrow, and exposes its strata and remains to every person passing by. Children often amuse themselves in undermining the banks, till large quantities fall down in which they search for, and often find arrow points, beads, and many other curiosities."[13] But closer proximity to the earthworks did not itself entail closer scrutiny or much greater recognition: problems persist not only in perceiving the existence of particular mounds but in acknowledging the very possibility that such monuments could exist.

Concerning the earthworks' possibility, their existence did not sit well with the image of North America and its inhabitants common to the dominant strains of Enlightenment political philosophy. As is well known, for Hobbes, Locke and Montesquieu alike, America was waste land, populated by itinerant savages alone.[14] Of the three, Montesquieu proves notable for considering evidence contrary to his conclusions. And that evidence concerns a group of Indians to which his source, the Jesuit Père Mathurin le Petit, attributed the production of monumental earthworks.[15] If we can believe such accounts as le Petit's, says Montesquieu, the Natchez of Louisiana formed a centralized, even despotic society, yet they lacked, like other North American Indians, the use of money that would bind them together within a single exchange economy, and, by implication, the means of extensive cultivation that would ordinarily enable such social organization.[16] The absence of a complex social organization means, for Montesquieu as for others, an attendant absence of monumental architecture. For without a division of labor how could the necessary and large laboring population be supported?

Montesquieu, aiming to reconcile le Petit's account with his own, suggests that if the Natchez were bound together the binding agent must have been superstition. Otherwise it would prove impossible to explain why members of the group submitted freely to despotism, as each must have done in the absence of economic forces tying them either to the land or to one another. As the prejudices of superstition "sont supérieurs à tous les autres préjugés" it remains the only agent that could have held the Natchez together, binding them, if not to a place, then to a despot-priest who lived in a certain place and who must be paid a certain tribute.[17] This suggests (in Montesquieu's own terms) that despite the absence of the means (cultivation) and the markers (money) of large-scale exchangeable or transferable surplus, the Natchez could have exhibited certain characteristics of state-based existence and thus have established organized labor. In other words, insofar as their immaterial attachment could underwrite a division of labor it could have rendered them able to produce monumental earthworks—what Chateaubriand later called the "pyramides des tombeaux indiens."[18] Still, such socially organized, large-scale production conflicted so strongly with the image of Indian mobility that the possibility of a North American Indian state-based society remained an object of great skepticism for Montesquieu. Hence it is notable that, despite what Montesquieu's source says, he himself does not register the possibility that the Natchez produced the extensive monuments le Petit records, an undertaking that would perhaps have guaranteed the Natchez's statehood.

Europeans experienced closely related difficulties coming to terms with the existence of particular mounds. The mounds did not seem to show themselves, to give themselves to comprehension, making the problem of recognition persist even when the presence of a mound lay beyond doubt—a difficulty, then, that cannot be explained away as a mere lack of information. Thomas Jefferson, for example, in his *Notes on the State of Virginia* (1787), does not seem to know quite how to acknowledge the mounds, and when he does, he does so reluctantly. Anthony F. C. Wallace has argued that Jefferson's reticence is especially notable given that the widely-read Jefferson would likely have come across recently published work on aboriginal architecture.[19] Certainly Jefferson appears to have known of native-built fortifications, and in the *Notes* he mentions, without elaborating, that mounds of "differing sizes" can "be found all over this country."[20] Nonetheless Jefferson famously claims, writing in the tradition of Montesquieu *et al.*, "to know of no such thing as an Indian monument: for I would not honour with that name arrow points, stone hatchets, stone pipes, and half-shapen images. Of labour on the large scale, I think there is no remain as respectable as would be a common ditch for the draining of lands."[21] "[U]nless," he adds, "it be the Barrows"—earthen burial mounds, like the one on his estate whose excavation he goes on to describe.[22] It is by excavating and so destroying the mound that Jefferson finds something to describe: apprehending a mound *as* a mound appears to involve the more uncertain act of recognizing that *there is* something rather than the expected *terra nullius*.

Adopting Neil Hertz's concept of "the end of the line," I would suggest that for early European observers a mound appears almost at "a point of nonreflective opacity" where one can barely tell if the earth reflects only itself or the action of human labor.[23] For Hertz that opacity lies at the end of a line of sight where one perceives "the residual tension of minimal difference, of black against black."[24] With the mounds the "minimal difference" concerns the presence or absence of difference itself: has human labor altered the landscape and so introduced a certain difference, or does human labor remain absent from a therefore undifferentiated scene? In short, a mound in "the end of the line" mode makes opaque the difference between difference and indifference. Crucially, that opacity has the potential to invade one's perception of any substantial earthen deviation.

We can recognize such an opacity at work in William Bartram's claim, in his *Travels through North & South Carolina, Georgia , East & West Florida* (1791), to have seen various magnificent mounds like the following:

> Not far distant from the terrace or eminence, overlooking the low grounds of the river, many very magnificent monuments of the power and industry of the ancient inhabitants of these lands are visible. I observed a stupendous conical pyramid, or artificial mount of earth, vast tetragon terraces, and a large sunken area, of cubical form, encompassed with banks of earth; and certain traces of a larger Indian town, the work of a powerful nation, whose period of grandeur perhaps long preceded the discovery of this continent.[25]

Archaeologists have never found these monuments. It seems that what Bartram took as works of ancient "power and industry" were in this case objects of natural formation. "The only landmark that seems to fit Bartram's description," writes Robert Silverberg, "is a large wooded hillock of natural origin; a nearby 'sunken area' also appears to be a purely natural feature."[26] With Bartram we see the mounds' potential to operate like E. T. A. Hoffman's Olimpia, whose external appearance proved so natural that when she is revealed as an automaton "an absurd mistrust of human figures began to prevail."[27] The mounds' formal proximity to natural formations invades the perception of any mound-like appearance. By neither clearly establishing their difference from the environment nor clearly reflecting the action of human labor, the mounds do not appear to announce their being through the negation necessary for identity to be established ("this is no longer nature but art, no longer earth but monument").

Knowing a Mound

What makes Hertz's concept so valuable for us is that its explanatory power remains in effect when Europeans become certain that they are dealing with a work of art and not of nature. For even when late eighteenth-century Europeans freely acknowledge a mound's existence, they do not necessarily reduce the end-of-the-line opacity. Rather the tendency is to displace it, as observers try to see reflected in the earthworks the mounds' builders. "[T]he mounds and their contents," write Squier and Davis, "serve to reflect light more particularly upon [the builders'] customs and the condition of the arts among them. Within these mounds we must look for the only authentic remains of their builders."[28] Yet we find in account after account the claim that the earthworks' origins and purpose remain stunningly opaque: writing nearly fifty years before Squier and Davis, Thaddeus Harris says that when it comes to the mounds, "All serves to surprise and to embarrass the mind"; and writing fifty years after Squier and Davis, Lindesay Brine notes that, "The great earthworks in Ohio are the subject of much antiquarian interest and conjecture. Several surveys of them have been made for the purpose of ascertaining their purpose and the probable period of their construction, but nothing definite has yet been determined."[29] So if observers had expected the earthworks to give up the nature of their artificers, what tends to happen instead, as the likes of Harris and Brine suggest, is a shifting of Hertz's "point of nonreflective opacity" from the earthworks' shape to their origins and functions.

Though European observers fail to attain the certain knowledge they seek, they do succeed in opening up a wide field of conjecture. Particularly, Europeans begin to imagine at the end-of-the-line, where mound and mound-builder would reflect one another, an unknown, primitive American race. Distinguished from *les nations sauvages* surviving them, the ancient American civilization or semi-civilization was variously thought to descend from one of the Lost Tribes of Israel, from a twelfth-century Welsh migration, from an unknown group that crossed into North America via a land-bridge from Asia, or from other potential sources. Now, insofar as American antiquarian and archaeological endeavors of the time engaged in intellectual nation-building, we might say that with the mounds they were seeking to solve a certain ordinal problem: if in the beginning the American Republic formed a cardinal set of thirteen states, its severance from England left the United States wanting a causal priority of its own; in lacking apparently organic national-cultural origins, it seemed a second without a first and therefore founded arbitrarily and somewhat irrationally. The mounds appeared to offer a way out of that bind. On the one hand, they suggested, in their monumental aspect, a tangible historical depth, one belonging to the lands now known as the United States and one that for some proved comparable with what Europe could claim. And on the other hand, they served to open a potential line of descent for the nation, one that was not only separate from, but of greater antiquity than, the Indians'.

But to attach the earthworks to the national interest, and so detach them from the surviving Indian groups, one would need to establish who built the earthworks. That information was less than forthcoming: the mounds did not reflect clearly on their own origins. As the nineteenth century opened, then, attempts to make lucid the mounds' origins extensively exercised the Euro-American imagination—for given the dearth of evidence it was by and large only the imagination that remained to supply what direct observation could not.

William Wordsworth addresses imagination's role in facing an obscure past, in what is perhaps the only major contemporary attempt to address mounds (though not American mounds) within the context of an extended exploration of the imagination as an aesthetic faculty. As Wordsworth writes in his account of Salisbury Plain's "monumental hillocks",

> 'twas my chance
> To have before me on the downy plain
> Lines, circles, mounts, a mystery of shapes
> Such as in many quarters yet survive,
> With intricate profusion figuring o'er
> The untilled ground (the work, as some divine,
> Of infant science, imitative forms
> By which the Druids covertly expressed
> Their knowledge of the heavens, and imaged forth
> The constellations), I was gently charmed,
> Albeit with an antiquarian's dream,
> And saw the bearded teachers, with white wands
> Uplifted, pointing to the starry sky,
> Alternately, and plain below, while breath
> Of music seemed to guide them, and the waste
> Was cheared with stillness and a pleasant sound.[30]

The action which Wordsworth performs in viewing mysterious shapes including mounds—populating the scene with figures imaginatively drawn—is what those wanting to describe the mound builders must perform, whether the writer's intent be scientific or artistic. But whereas Wordsworth could turn to a long conjectural tradition positing an ancient druidic culture in the area of Stonehenge, those imagining the mound builders could not.[31]

Local Indians' silence concerning the mounds' origins helped mark the earthworks as ancient ruins.[32] No longer objects of either use or memory, the mounds appeared as remains of an age long since past. (Beyond any question of whether local Indians deliberately withheld information, we should note several reasons why local groups might have had little to say about the mounds. Some Indian groups continued to build and/or use mounds into the seventeenth and, in the case of the Natchez, eighteenth century, but suddenly ceased to exist in numbers that could support their previous activities. Reasons for the cessation of such activity include a changing climate, Indian warfare and movement, and the decimating force of European diseases which traveled well in advance of Europeans themselves.[33]) But the Indians' silence also adds to the general uncertainty pertaining to the earthworks. The "antiquarian's dream" is reduced either to a grasping after any possible content at all, or, as Sarah J. Hale suggests in her "Genius of Oblivion: A Tale" (1823), to a groundless flight of an impotent fancy. Describing the mounds as objects beyond both fancy and fable, Hale embraces the earthworks as ruins lost to human understanding of any kind:

> But nothing, with romantic zest,
> Created such deep interest,
> As when the Western wilds they draw,
> Describe those ancient Forts they saw,
> And those huge Mounds where, buried, lie
> Secrets of dark antiquity,
> So deep that fancy checks her flight,
> Consigning to Oblivion's night
> Those wonders of the olden dead,
> That speak, beneath our silent tread,
> Of Nations perished—Kingdoms fled!
> Yes, fled—and Fable's wildest wing,
> Untired before, can search or bring
> No date, memento, whence to trace
> Their founder, origin or race;
> Not even in Fiction's annals nam'd;
> They flourished—fell—unsung, unfam'd.[34]

By suggesting that mounds confound the powers of fancy Hale makes the dialectical point that it remains only the imagination that, even if in the service of scientific intent, can begin to fill in what is missing. To which we can add that whatever theory one does advance, it will require that one argue for an origin of a certain type.

The claim that the mound builders descend from one of the Lost Tribes, for example, installs a primitive American race whose existence can be squared with the biblical account of world history. It is, in other words, an argument in support of a certain Judeo-Christian world-view, one that many early accounts of the earthworks were at pains to uphold.[35] In doing so, such accounts recall earlier efforts like John Webb's *An Historical Essay Endeavoring a Probability that the Language of the Empire of China is the Primitive Language* (1669). There, Webb asks how a civilization like China could exist, largely unknown in Europe until recently and unmentioned in the Bible. In answer to his own question, Webb suggests that Noah settled China after the flood, and that—Webb's main contention—some of Noah's descendants remained there, managing to maintain the primitive language spoken in Eden. In a similar way many late eighteenth-century writers felt pressed to ask how a civilization like that of the mounds' builders could have come to exist in North America, given the Bible's silence on this race of people. Accordingly these writers, like Webb, would appear less concerned to historicize the mounds than to determine their place within the Bible's pre-existing framework.

Yet a noticeable gap separates Webb's China from the builders of the mounds. That China presents an existent, complex civilization is beyond doubt for Webb, as is the fact that the Chinese possess written records covering five thousands years. Things are less clear with the mound builders. Though they engaged in monumental architecture and so would seem to constitute a civilization, their apparent lack of written records puts that status in question—as does, of course, their use of packed earth rather than bricks or masonry, which also separates them from the "Mexicans" and "Peruvians," to whom Webb refers.[36] So whereas Webb had conceived China as the ideal version of any social order (which for Webb necessarily means a state-based order), when late eighteenth-century Europeans confront the mounds, they end up approaching the earthworks as products of a culture markedly different from their own. That the mounds' makers be considered such seemed to be demanded by the questions that the mounds themselves prompted. Understanding the earthworks comes to prove less an issue of finding the truth itself in a single point of origin beyond all contradiction (Webb's *primitive* language) than of establishing a true account of them, including how particular works were built, and—crucially—in what context.[37]

We can usefully examine here Caleb Atwater's important account, "A Description of the Antiquities Discovered in the State of Ohio" (1820), which Warren K. Moorehead, writing in 1901, claims inaugurated North American archaeology.[38] Atwater, like Webb, believes the Bible to be "the most authentick, the most ancient history of man."[39] But unlike Webb, Atwater posits the existence of discrete national (today we would say *cultural*) entities that possess certain characteristics which differentiate them both spatially and temporally from other nations. That is to say, Atwater does not look to locate a single primitive group lodged outside of all temporal corruption. Rather, a nation is a nation for him because it is something formed temporally and differentially. Describing the spatial axis, he notes how the historical Egyptians' "pyramids and temples, medals and monuments, show us a comparatively civilized people," building such great public works at a time when "their neighbours were rude barbarians."[40]

For Atwater the Egyptian case suggests that we should not expect all indigenous inhabitants of North America to be either civil or savage, nor should we expect the same group to have always and only constituted a civilization. Civilized or semi-civilized groups producing monumental architecture may well have existed alongside other groups whose way of life bore scant resemblance to a civilized existence, just as that same civilized group may have been, at other moments in its history, entirely savage.

Atwater adds a further level of complexity to his historical outlook by maintaining that the mounds were not likely built by the same group. "Our Antiquities belong," he writes, "not only to different eras, in point of time, but to several nations."[41] This means that a given earthwork potentially belongs to any number of ancient nations, a situation that demands of archaeologists a highly contextualizing methodology. For potentially every earthwork that they consider could be different in its origins than any other known earthwork. Of course, that difference is to be revealed by finding objects in the earthworks, in whose reflection one might trace their makers. But then, following the demands of his methodology, Atwater extends to each object his premises, insisting that a given object may have various functions: "those articles belonging to the same era and the same people, were intended by their authors to be applied to many different uses."[42] At bottom, then, Atwater's broadly historicist methodology requires that one have access to specific human-produced objects that can be understood to have several national purposes. Understanding those purposes will in turn enable one to build an account of the object's users, suggesting features of their way of life, modes of reproduction, and so forth.

But the historicist approach advanced by Atwater faced a significant problem: how to comprehend the mounds historically when they appear to remove themselves from an historical understanding? Or rather, how to meet the demands of *l'histoire* and render in a narrative form these things that do not easily give over to narration?[43] For added to the mounds' minimal difference from the surrounding environment is their perceived lack of difference over time. As Squier and Davis note, mounds do not appear subject to the losses of time: "When covered with forests, and their surfaces interlaced with the roots of trees and bushes, or when protected by turf, the humble mound bids defiance to the elements which throw down the temple and crumble the marble into dust."[44] The mounds' singularity, their recalcitrance vis-à-vis the spatial and temporal axes, meant for Atwater and those who followed him that they could gain access to potentially functional and thus representative objects only by opening mounds up for archaeological examination.

Atwater's attention to a mound's own context rather than the context supplied by the biblical narrative might be considered an advance in knowledge generally (it certainly resembles our own practices today, in this "our era of historicisms").[45] It might also suggest an increase in regard for the earthworks themselves in their respective particularities. But above all it means that the archaeologist needs to cut up an earthwork, either sinking a shaft into it to remove a cross-section of earth, or conducting a full excavation or removal of the mound. In short, for historicists to find what they need to produce an historicist account of a mound, they must cut into it, altering or destroying the earthwork.

The simple destruction of a mound will not, of course, serve historicists' aims. Moreover, they will need to locate a certain sense of historical agency in the mound and its context, the apparent obscurity of which works to foreground their own act of temporal alteration, which they introduce with the slice of the cutting, altering the mound in time in a bid to turn it into an object that exhibits a temporal reference. How, then, can historicists find the source or agency of history in the object rather than in their own act of cutting, and do so in a way that procures order from an action of destruction? It is arguably to obviate the force of such problems that early archaeologists adopted the "stratigraphic principle" developed by geologists.[46] That principle enabled a degree of conceptual framing hitherto unavailable. In 1848, Squier and Davis sum up the principle's virtue: "It is in this view, that the fact of stratification is seen to be important . . . it will fix beyond all dispute, the origins of many singular relics."[47] Historicists engaged in archaeological practice could now perceive the unfolding yet structurally isolated layers of time by way of the likewise temporal—and apparently natural and so indisputable—process of sedimentation. In other words, they borrow from nature a principle of stability otherwise unavailable in the products of non-natural activities, including their own actions.

The great strength of the stratigraphic principle proved to be its ability to allow a degree of plotting. Its fixing "beyond all dispute, the origins of many singular relics" enables the reframing of the *singular relic* as a representative object. Upon retrieving a series of representative objects one can begin to frame a mound as an historical production. Further, if whoever made the objects made the earthwork, then one can examine the different types of objects discovered at different layers to determine the context or contexts of the mound's use and construction. The representative objects, indexed stratigraphically, begin to facilitate a certain telling. That is to say, excavation makes a form of narrative possible—even if in cutting-up the mound one destroys the referent of what one wants to preserve in the telling (see fig. 5). By cutting up a mound and binding one's findings in

Figure 5. Carriage Factory Mound during excavation. Ross County, Ohio, 1897. Courtesy of the Ohio Historical Society.

a narrative form, one can thus frame a mound *as historical*: as, therefore, laden with history and so with determinate content. If, as Gordon M. Sayre notes, the mounds prove amenable to various narratives, we can add the point that they only appear directly amenable at all to European thought once they are rendered as objects that can be narrated.[48]

Facing the Mounds

Throughout this essay I have remained silent on what the mounds might mean for Native American groups. In doing so I have risked replicating what we might call the late Enlightenment's silencing of Native voices. Certainly the various earthworks that remain are proving significant today in the wider context of American Indian efforts to regain stolen material objects, and to claim recognition for long-ignored or disparaged sacred sites.[49] But what stands out in the late Enlightenment accounts which have been my focus is the common claim of Indian silence concerning the mounds. And I would suggest that the perceived silence actually shapes the European understanding of the earthworks in crucial ways, above all augmenting the mounds' own indifference to comprehension. The resulting situation—the augmenting of European incomprehension by Indian silence—might mean that any effort to recover lost indigenous voices in the late eighteenth- and early nineteenth-century debates on the mounds requires (at least in part if not in whole) that we attend to the force that a perceived silence can exert.[50] In other words, what might be the significance, vis-à-vis the debate on the mounds, of someone or something standing at a marked remove from the demands of a historical understanding?

To consider this question more closely we need to return to the issue of how early Europeans tried to establish an historical understanding of the mounds. As we saw, in making a mound over as an object of narration, Atwater and other early archaeologists produced an object that served as a cipher for historical functions of which it in turn appeared as the product. That approach entails initially isolating two planes, one for the mound and one for historical context, with a successful historical account being one that brings about the two planes' *rapprochement*, combined to form a single indissoluble plane. But this synthesis in turn obscures a crucial component of the historicizing operation. By framing a mound as an object embedded in an historical context one makes it stand for something else no longer present or operating (forms of social organization, certain social functions, and so forth). The archaeologist, that is, obliterates the mound not once but twice, first cutting it up and second recasting it as an object telling of what it is not—that is, as allegorical. Here we find an attempt to recover a lost voice of sorts, an attempt to make the earthworks speak, albeit to *speak otherwise*.

Of course the aim of nineteenth-century historicism was to turn the allegoric into the symbolic, aligning the symbol with what it symbolizes—or the object with the context. But insofar as the mound *as a mound* continues to fall outside an adequate historicization, to refuse speech or its archaeological equivalent, it hinders the initial separation of planes (putative object and context) necessary for the subsequent symbolization through *rapprochement*. The mound's immanence, its being unto itself, renders it recalcitrant to the necessary separation, right up to and even beyond its own destruction. Which is why I want to suggest, in conclusion, that for late Enlightenment Europeans the mounds remain as things that force a certain open-ended allegorical operation. *This* is the unrelenting source of pressure the mounds exert on European thinking.

By "open-ended allegorical operation" I do not mean that a mound itself becomes a signifier forever in pursuit of a signified. I mean that the opening in question enters into the allegorical sign in such way that the mound's status as a signifier comes into doubt. We might say that it remains, in the strongest sense of the word, a *thing*: that is, the mound holds off the attempt to reduce it to an object that reflects an absent concept whose recovery would complete the allegory.[51] Certainly the allegorical sign presupposes a disjunctive temporal dimension (it tells of something else necessarily anterior to it) from within a temporal movement (it tells of this something else anterior to it precisely by *telling* of something else, narrating and so presenting a certain temporal dimension). But as archaeologists begin to make dissected mounds out as objects of narration, the need to translate a mound into such terms by way of its destruction proves symptomatic of how time is also what mounds trouble. How can there be a signified to come when the putative signifier edges out of time? Before being cut into (or *analyzed*, recalling that word's etymological derivation) a mound does not even exhibit, as does a more or less decayed Egyptian pyramid, the sequence of its construction—the placing of one stone upon another. In themselves, mounds can be said to obey *duration* but not *succession*; they endure but they do not succeed along a line of differing historical contexts.

Perhaps better than anyone Newman recognized the mound's open challenge to time, even as he saw that the Miamisburg Mound's reference was to time and not to space. What struck Newman was the way the mound did not give over to a sense of succession, to being, in his terms, one object among others within a built landscape. Insistently and indifferently, the mound remains.[52] Newman takes this to mean that the earthwork stands forth as if a sublime pulsation in time: "Suddenly one realizes that the sensation is not one of space or [of] an object in space. It has nothing to do with space and its manipulations. The sensation is the sensation of time—and all other multiple feelings vanish like the outside landscape."[53] Like Robinson Crusoe's footprint, the mound obliterates one's sense of everything else ("all other multiple feelings vanish like the outside landscape"). The only remaining sensation is that of the instant ("*here*"), of the time-outside-of-time, the time that does not take its place within the before and after of consciousness derived from Descartes and Locke.[54] One might say that it is this which the historicist appears unable to face up to, destroying the mound so as to return it to history and therefore to the disciplinary frameworks of archaeology and historiography.

NOTES

A 2006 Faculty Summer Fellowship/McKnight Summer Fellowship from the Graduate School, University of Minnesota-Twin Cities, supported me in the writing of this essay.

1. Barnett Newman, "Ohio, 1949," in *Selected Writings and Interviews*, ed. John P. O'Neill (New York: Knopf, 1990), 174.

2. Newman, "Ohio, 1949," 174. The Miamisburg Mound, located in southwest Ohio, measures nearly seventy feet in height, and more than eight hundred feet in circumference at its base.

3. On the archive's double orientation towards destruction and preservation, see Jacques Derrida, *Mal d'archive: une impression freudienne* (Paris: Galilée, 1995).

4. Ephraim G. Squier and Edwin H. Davis, *Ancient Monuments of the Mississippi Valley*, ed. David J. Meltzer (Washington, D. C.: Smithsonian Institution Press, 1998), 139. For a sustained account of Squier and Davis's contribution to American archaeology and to the understanding of the mounds, see Terry A. Barnhart, *Ephraim George Squier and the Development of American Anthropology* (Lincoln: University of Nebraska Press, 2005).

5. Luys Hernández de Biedma, "Relation of the Island of Florida," trans. and ed. John E. Worth, in *The De Soto Chronicles: The Expedition of Hernando De Soto to North America in 1539–1543*, 2 vols., ed. Lawrence A. Clayton, Vernon J. Knight and Edward C. Moore (Tuscaloosa: University of Alabama Press, 1993), 1:239. Mark Twain, *Life on the Mississippi*, in *Mississippi Writings* (New York: Library of America, 1982), 231. As Twain continues: "Apparently nobody happened to want such a river, nobody needed it, nobody was curious about it; so, for a century and a half the Mississippi remained out of the market and undisturbed" (232).

6. In his posthumously published *Journal of an Exploration in the Spring of the Year 1750*, Thomas Walker writes: "Below the mouth of this Creek, and above the mouth are the remains of Several Indian Cabbins [*sic.*] and amongst them a round Hill made by Art about 20 feet high and 60 over the Top. we [*sic.*] went up the River, and Camped on the Bank." Thomas Walker, *Journal of an Exploration in the Spring of the Year 1750* (Boston, 1888), 49. Robert Silverberg locates a slightly earlier reference, from Cadwallader Colden's *The history of the Five Indian nations of Canada, which are dependent on the province of New-York in America, and are the barrier between the English and French in that part of the world* (London, 1747), which I cite in full: "Their funeral Rites seem to be formed up on a Notion of some Kind of Existence after Death: They make a large round Hole, in which the Body can be placed upright, or upon its Haunches, which after the Body is placed in it, is covered with Timber, to support the Earth which they lay over, and thereby keep the Body free from being pressed; they then raise the Earth in a round Hill over it" (16). See Robert Silverberg, *Mound Builders of Ancient America: The Archaeology of a Myth*

(Athens, OH: Ohio University Press, 1986), 28. I would suggest there remains an important difference between Colden's and Walker's respective mentions of "a round Hill" which places Walker's reference more firmly in the tradition of subsequent mound observation. Colden attends to a localized burial practice governed by largely pragmatic concerns (how to bury a certain person in the most appropriate way), describing a process whose outcome proves not entirely different to what Catharine Maria Sedgwick once called "the little mounds of earth" to be seen in a New England cemetery (Sedgwick, *Hope Leslie, or, Early Times in the Massachusetts*, ed. Carolyn L. Karcher [New York: Penguin Books, 1998], 177). Walker, in contrast, observes an existing and prodigious earthwork "made by Art," whose existence was unexpected and whose purpose and origin remain unapparent.

7. Roger G. Kennedy, *Hidden Cities: The Discovery and Loss of Ancient North American Civilization* (New York: Free Press, 1994), 3. The French presence in the Mississippi Valley took the form mostly of traders whose education at home was minimal, and whose institutional support in Louisiana was famously thin. They wrote little of their experiences and traded by attaching themselves to local native trading networks, seldom venturing far from their own base. For an overview of the French in North America, see Alan Taylor, *American Colonies: The Settling of North America* (New York: Viking, 2001), 363–95; and specifically on the French in the Mississippi Valley, see Louise Phelps Kellogg, "France and the Mississippi Valley: A Resume," *TheMississippi Valley Historical Review* 18 (1931): 3–22. On how the particular way the French inhabited North America affected their ethnographic output, see William Y. Adams, *The Philosophical Roots of Anthropology* (Stanford: CSLI Publications, 1998), 202–03, 205, 213.

8. Squier and Davis, *Ancient Monuments of the Mississippi Valley*, xxxi.

9. I use *European* to indicate something or someone of European origin or descent. When wanting to underscore the American aspect of something or someone of European origin or descent, I use *Euro-American.*

10. For an account of the continuing difficulty or failure to acknowledge mounds, see Laurie Hovell McMillin, *Buried Indians: Digging up the Past in a Midwestern Town* (Madison: University of Wisconsin Press, 2006).

11. See, in particular, Silverberg, *Mound Builders*; Kennedy, *Hidden Cities*; Gordon Sayre, "The Mound Builders and the Imagination of American Antiquity in Jefferson, Bartram, and Chateaubriand," *Early American Literature* 33.3 (1998): 225–49; and Steven Conn, *History's Shadow: Native Americans and Historical Consciousness in the Nineteenth Century* (Chicago: University of Chicago Press, 2004), 116–53. For an overview of archaeological research into the mounds, see George R. Milner, *The Moundbuilders: Ancient Peoples of Eastern North America* (London: Thames & Hudson, 2004).

12. On the lack of ethnographic interest in the Ohio Valley for much of the eighteenth-century, see Michèle Duchet, *Anthropologie et histoire au siècle des lumières* (Paris: Albin Michel , 1995), 41.

13. Ashe continues: "I made a regular search myself, and found the barrow constructed precisely after the manner of that I described to you near the banks of the Muskingum. The dead repose in double horizontal tiers; between each tier are regular layers of sand, flat surfaced stones, gravel and earth. I counted seven tiers, and might have discovered more, but was compelled to desist from the annoyance of the multitude gathered about me." Thomas Ashe, *Travels in America, performed in 1806, for the purpose of exploring the rivers Alleghany, Monongahela, Ohio, and Mississippi, and ascertaining the produce and condition of their banks and vicinity* (Newburyport, MA, 1808), 207–08.

14. Thomas Hobbes, *Leviathan*, ed. Richard Tuck (Cambridge: Cambridge University Press, 1991), 89–90; John Locke, *Two Treatises of Government*, ed. Peter Laslett (Cambridge: Cambridge University Press, 1988), 285–302; and Montesquieu, *De l'esprit des lois*, in *Œuvres complètes*, ed. Roger Caillois (Paris: Gallimard, 1951), 531–41.

15. Montesquieu cites as his source on the Natchez a letter written by Mathurin le Petit from New Orleans, on July 12, 1730, and published in *Lettres édifiantes et curieuses, écrites des missions étrangères par quelques missionnaires de la compagnie de Jésus* (Paris, 1731), 106–113.

16. Montesquieu, *De l'esprit des lois*, 536–41. Here Montesquieu seems to depart from his source, for le Petit explicitly notes how some of the Natchez "sont employez à la agriculture. " However, even in le Petit's account that cultivation is performed *for* the despot as one of several such tribute-type activities, including hunting, fishing, and domestic service. The Natchez appear not as an agriculturally-based society, but as a society that includes cultivation as one activity among others. See *Lettres édifiantes et curieuses*, 112–13.

17. Montesquieu, *De l'esprit des lois*, 541.

18. François-René de Chateaubriand, *Atala*, in *Atala, René, Les aventure du dernier abencerage*, ed. Pierre Moreau (Paris: Gallimard, 1971), 40. Chateaubriand based his understanding of the Natchez on Charlevoix's account of them. Charlevoix describes the Natchez settlement as one approaches it from the river: "Plusieurs Monticules s'élèvent au-dessus de cette Colline, & quand on les a passés, on aperçoit de toutes parts de grandes Prairies, séparées par de petits Bouquets de bois, qui font un très bel effet." Upon the first, natural hill (*Colline*) the Natchez have erected (*s'élèvent*) hillocks or mounds (*Monticules*). Pierre-François-Xavier de Charlevoix, *Histoire et description générale de la Nouvelle France, avec le Journal historique d'un voyage fait par ordre du roi dans l'Amérique Septentrionale* (Paris, 1744), 3:414.

19. Anthony F. C. Wallace, *Jefferson and the Indians: The Tragic Fate of the First Americans* (Cambridge, MA.: Harvard University Press, 1999), 131–43. See also the discussion of Jefferson in Kennedy, *Hidden Cities*, 125–51.

20. Thomas Jefferson, *Notes on the State of Virginia*, ed. William Harwood Peden (New York: Norton, 1972), 97. On Jefferson's knowledge of earthen fortifications, see Wallace, *Jefferson and the Indians*, 136; and Kennedy, *Hidden Cities*, 135.

21. Jefferson, *Notes on the State of Virginia*, 97.

22. Jefferson, *Notes on the State of Virginia*, 97–98. Jefferson describes the burial mound he excavates: "It was of spheroidical form, of about 40 feet diameter at the base, and had been of about twelve feet altitude, though now reduced by the plough to seven and a half, having been under cultivation about a dozen years" (98).

23. Neil Hertz, *The End of the Line: Essays on Psychoanalysis and the Sublime* (New York: Columbia University Press, 1985), 219, 221.

24. Hertz, *End of the Line*, 218. My use of Hertz's concept differs slightly in emphasis from Hertz's account. He finds that the opacity located at the end of the line of sight—there where one is looking—tends to double the relation between viewer and viewed. I, however, will restrict my focus to the obscurity of what is viewed.

25. William Bartram, *The Travels of William Bartram* (New York: Dover, 1955), 56–57; see Sayre, "Mound Builders," 239.

26. Silverberg, *Mound Builders*, cited in Sayre, "Mound Builders," 239.

27. E. T. A. Hoffmann, "The Sand-Man," in *The Best Tales of Hoffmann*, ed. Everett Franklin Bleiler (New York: Dover, 1967), 211.

28. Squier and Davis, *Ancient Monuments of the Mississippi Valley*, 139.

29. Thaddeus Mason Harris, *The journal of a tour into the territory northwest of the Alleghany Mountains; made in the spring of the year 1803* (Boston, 1805), 148; Lindesay Brine, *Travels amongst American Indians: Their Ancient Earthworks and Temples* (London, 1894), 55.

30. William Wordsworth, *The Prelude, 1799, 1805, 1850: Authoritative Texts, Context and Reception, Recent Critical Essays*, ed. Jonathan Wordsworth, M. H. Abrams and Stephen Charles Gill (New York: Norton, 1979), bk. 12, lines 338–53. I use the 1805 *Prelude* throughout. Note that in the 1850 version, Wordsworth changes "mounts" to "mounds" (Wordsworth, *Prelude*, bk. 13, line 338).

31. Indeed Wordsworth's Druids form the third of three ancient native cultures with which his reveries populate "the plain of Sarum." Wordsworth, *Prelude*, bk. 12, line 314. Wordsworth was familiar with accounts of Stonehenge and its environs, such as William Stukeley's *Stonehenge: A Temple Restor'd to the British Druids* (London, 1740).

32. European accounts commonly claim the Indians' silence on the mounds. Writing in 1772, David Taitt suggests that present-day Indians can give no "Account of the Reasons of their being made." David Taitt, "Journal of David Taitt's Travels," cited in Donald A. Ringe, *The Pictorial Mode: Space and Time in the Art of Bryant, Irving and Cooper* (Lexington: University Press of Kentucky, 1971), 134. While the January 1775 issue of the *Royal American Magazine* includes an anonymously published essay on earthworks in "Shawanese country," where the writer maintains that "Who the constructors of it were, the Indians who live in neighbourhood to it, have no tradition upon which we many depend. . . . The present Indian inhabitants were not the builders, and they can give no satisfactory account of who were." "A Plan of a Fort and Intrenchment in the Shawanese Country," *Royal American Magazine* 2.1 (1775): 29. We should note that some earlier French accounts do provide descriptions

of mounds in use, specifically in the case of the Natchez, who were, before the French largely annihilated them in 1731, perhaps the last practicing Mississippian culture encountered by Europeans. See Colin G. Calloway, *One Vast Winter Count: The Native American West before Lewis and Clark* (Lincoln: University of Nebraska Press, 2003), 103–04.

33. On climate change and disease, see Calloway, *One Vast Winter Count*, 98–108. Richard White notes how the "huge area between the Ohio River and the Northern shores of the Great Lakes [had been] emptied of inhabitants by the Iroquois," who had carried on an extended war with the Algonquian-speaking groups of the Ohio Valley in the first half of the eighteenth century. Richard White, *The Middle Ground: Indians, Empires, and Republics in the Great Lakes Region, 1650–1815* (Cambridge: Cambridge University Press, 1991), 11.

34. Sarah J. Hale, "The Genius of Oblivion: A Tale," in *The Genius of Oblivion* (Concord, MA, 1823), 24–25.

35. On this point, see Conn, *History's Shadow*, 118, 123–24.

36. In this way, encountering the mounds bears scant resemblance to the early Spanish encounter with the cities of Mexico. Certainly the likes of Hernán Cortés and Bernal Díaz express wonder when considering these cities; see Hernán Cortés, *Letters from Mexico*, ed. and trans. Anthony Pagden (New Haven: Yale University Press, 1986), 67–68, 83–85; Bernal Díaz del Castillo, *The Discovery and Conquest of Mexico, 1517–1521*, ed. Genaro García, trans. A.P. Maudslay (New York: Da Capo Press, 1996), 190–92. But both Cortés and Díaz note how they were often told of the cities by the various Amerindian groups they met on their way to Montezuma's great city on the lake. And if Díaz compares the latter to "the enchantments they tell of in the legend of Amadis" (190), it is a city that cannot be missed. Moreover, it is a living, operative city, with permanent architecture ("great towers and cues and buildings rising from the water, and all built of masonry" [Diaz, 190]); a large central market ("where each and every day upward of thirty thousand people come to buy and sell" [Cortés, 67]); and a regulating government which leads Cortés to liken Mexico to "Venice or Genoa or Pisa" (68).

37. On the seventeenth-century understanding of *origin* as a point prior to contradiction, see Alvin Snider, *Origin and Authority in Seventeenth-Century England: Bacon, Milton, Butler* (Toronto: University of Toronto Press, 1994).

38. While Atwater's act of cutting into a mound was not original (Jefferson had done so fifty years before him), what Atwater did differently, following the methodological framework he adopted, was to perform and write up his excavation with an entirely new level of detail. With that detail, Warren K. Moorehead (who conducted the major excavations of Cahokia in the 1920s) suggests that Atwater first "directed men's eyes towards a strange pre-Colombian culture." Moorehead, "A Century of American Archaeology," cited in Conn, *History's Shadow*, 119–20. See also Warren K. Moorehead, *The Cahokia Mounds*, ed. John Edward Kelly (Tuscaloosa: University of Alabama Press, 2000).

39. Caleb Atwater, "Description of the Antiquities Discovered in the State of Ohio and Other Western States," *Archaeologia Americana* 1 (1820): 195.

40. Atwater, "Description of the Antiquities," 199.

41. Atwater, "Description of the Antiquities," 111.

42. Atwater, "Description of the Antiquities," 111.

43. On the demands of *l'histoire*, see Jacques Rancière, *The Names of History: On the Poetics of Knowledge*, trans. Hassan Melehy (Minneapolis: University of Minnesota Press, 1994).

44. Squier and Davis, *Ancient Monuments of the Mississippi Valley*, 139.

45. On "our era of historicisms," see Jonathan Culler, *The Literary in Theory* (Stanford: Stanford University Press, 2007), 9.

46. Moorehead, "Century of American Archaeology," cited in Conn, *History's Shadow*, 119–20.

47. Squier and Davis, *Ancient Monuments*, cited in Conn, *History's Shadow*, 126.

48. Sayre, "Mound Builders," 226.

49. On mounds as scared sites, see Peter Nabokov, *Where the Lightning Strikes: The Lives of American Indian Sacred Places* (New York: Viking, 2006), 35–51. See also Tamara L. Bray, ed., *The Future of the Past: Archaeologists, Native Americans, and Repatriation* (New York: Garland, 2001); Michael F. Brown, *Who Owns Native Culture?* (Cambridge, MA: Harvard University Press, 2003); Rosemary J. Coombe, *The Cultural Life of Intellectual Properties: Authorship, Appropriation, and the Law* (Durham: Duke University Press, 1998); and Barbara Alice Mann, *Native Americans, Archaeologists and the Mounds* (New York: Peter Lang, 2003). As burial sites, many mounds recently gained certain protections under Federal law, through the Native American Graves Protection and Repatriation Act of 1990 and its subsequent amendments.

50. One would of course be tempted—knowing as we do that the processes of exclusion, forgetting, and erasure mark so much of the knowledge produced of Native Americans—to consider the belief in Indian ignorance as way of silencing their past. But this obscures the fact that the problem with the mounds was not one of establishing European hegemony over other historical narratives but of being able to produce an historical understanding of them at all. This does not mean that Euro-American attempts to historicize the mounds took place without much racism and much disavowal: if anything, it signifies that Europeans found it difficult even to produce convincing historical accounts of the mounds through the well-worn avenues of racism and disavowal. For a sustained meditation on closely-related issues, see Michel-Rolph Trouillot, *Silencing the Past: Power and the Production of History* (Boston, MA: Beacon Press, 1995), and especially his discussion of the Haitian Revolution as "unthinkable" (70–107).

51. Bill Brown, "Thing Theory," *Critical Inquiry* 28 (2001): 5–6.

52. Newman, "Ohio, 1949," 174–75.

53. Newman, "Ohio, 1949," 175.

54. See Jean-François Lyotard, "The Sublime and the Avant-Garde," in *The Inhuman: Reflections on Time* (Stanford: Stanford University Press, 1991), 90; see also Jean-François Lyotard, "Newman: The Instant," in *The Inhuman* , 78–88. Compare with Keith H. Basso, "Wisdom Sits in Places: Notes on a Western Apache Landscape," in *Senses of Place*, ed. Steven Feld and Keith H. Basso (Santa Fe: School of American Research Press, 1996), 53–90.

Sex Education in the Enlightened Nation

SHANE AGIN

Any study of sex education in the eighteenth century necessarily runs into a nominative and conceptual difficulty: what, after all, does one mean by the expression "sex education," when applied to an era that undeniably would not have recognized it? From this question grows another which constitutes in fact the central focus of this study: how might a sex education program for young women, conceived on a general scale, that is, beyond the intimate space of the confessional or the boudoir, characterize, or be characteristic of, an enlightened nation? The question is fundamental not only to our knowledge of the eighteenth century, but also to our knowledge of the birth and development of a reasoned discourse on sex. And, as such, the question of a sex education program goes directly to the heart of nothing less than our understanding of the Enlightenment as a mentality and as a social project.

Michel Foucault, in the first tome of *Histoire de la sexualité*, *La Volonté de savoir*, famously observes that modern Western civilization has never developed an *ars erotica*, in which the truth of sex could be derived from the practice of pleasure. Instead, he continues, Western civilization was the only one to have a *scientia sexualis* in which the truth of sex could be revealed by the *aveu* or confession, a practice instituted by the Church and continued through Freud.[1] In *Schooling Sex: Libertine Literature and*

Erotic Education in Italy, France, and England, 1534–1685, James Grantham Turner disputes Foucault's claim as well as the critical short-sightedness of many *dix-huitièmistes* who seem, according to him, to have the misguided notion that libertinage and libertine literature were purely an invention of the eighteenth century. Not only is there a vast tradition of libertine literature predating the eighteenth, he rightly notes, but it is this same vast tradition which constitutes the *ars erotica* ignored by Foucault.[2] The goal of this study is to offer an alternative perspective on the question in which sexual knowledge is neither a function of confession nor of libertinage, a perspective in which both the Church and the libertine are excluded, a perspective in which alternative models of *scientia sexualis* and *ars erotica* coexist within a singular conception of sex education. Sex education programs might seem a topic more appropriate to recent times and places, but, as I hope to show, the idea was in fact seriously pondered by least one eighteenth-century philosopher, who in both his personal life and his philosophical and literary works, attempted to redefine the ways in which people of his time approached the issue of sex.

The early 1770s saw an important confluence of events in the life of Denis Diderot. In the autumn of 1772, his only child, Angélique, was to be married, and shortly after the wedding, Diderot was to begin a long journey to the court of St. Petersburg to thank in person his great patron, Catherine II. For Diderot, the two events were deeply connected. It had been, after all, Catherine's generosity that had allowed him to marry off his daughter with a somewhat sizable dowry. Had his sense of gratitude to Catherine not been so great, it is unlikely that Diderot, never one for traveling in the first place, would have left behind his beloved daughter, married and now with child, to make the tedious trip to St. Petersburg. Angélique's pregnancy weighed heavily on Diderot's mind as he made his way to Russia. The dangers of childbirth and the difficulties of protecting infants from disease were particularly well known to Diderot, who, with his wife, had already lost in infancy three children of their own before the somewhat unexpected birth of Angélique in 1753. Fortunately, his fears were put to rest, when he learned, on his arrival at St. Petersburg, that Angélique had given birth to a boy and that both she and the child were doing well.

In many respects, Diderot's daughter had benefited from both a national effort to reduce the number of infant mortalities and an individual effort on the part of her philosopher father to raise an enlightened daughter. Driven by an erroneous fear of population decline, France, towards the end of Louis XIV's reign, began a systematic campaign to increase the number of births and, of equal importance, reduce the number of deaths in childbirth.[3] The fear of depopulation, promulgated by Montesquieu in the *Lettres persanes* and shared by many other philosophers of the day including Voltaire and Diderot himself, gained widespread currency during the eighteenth century, serving as a basis for critiques of the Church and its insistence on celibacy for the clergy and continence for the lay. This critique is made nowhere more forcefully than in Diderot's own *Encyclopédie* article "Célibat" (1752), which has been justly described by Jacqueline Hecht as an "Enlightenment reference document on the matter."[4]

After giving a perfunctory history of celibacy in various ancient and modern cultures, Diderot then exposes what he views to be its problematic sociological and philosophical bases. Celibacy, for him, denies the social nature of man. Someone practicing celibacy violates a natural law, unless, he adds, "il n'en ait été dispensé par quelqu'autorité supérieure à celle de la nature, afin qu'il soit bien clair qu'il ne s'agit nullement ici du célibat consacré par la religion; mais de celui que l'imprudence, la misanthropie, la légerté, le libertinage, forment tous les jours; de celui où les deux sexes se corrompant par les sentiments naturels mêmes, ou étouffant en eux ces sentiments sans aucune nécessité, fuient une union qui doit les rendre meilleurs, pour vivre, soit dans un éloignement stérile, soit dans des unions qui les rendent toujours pires."[5] However, the exemption that Diderot allows for religious celibacy is of course predicated on the existence of "an authority greater than nature" that he had been in the process of extricating from his own metaphysical system since the *Essai sur le mérite, ou la vertu*, his peculiar 1745 re-writing of Shaftesbury's *An Inquiry Concerning Virtue, or Merit*.[6]

In this work, he criticizes any religion that would deny man's nature as a sign of virtue, "comme s'il fallait cesser d'être homme pour se montrer *religieux*."[7] In the absence of God, or at least in the absence of a distinction between God and nature, celibacy had no justification. Moreover, we see that, in the set of situations referred to above, for Diderot, celibacy does not simply mean sexual abstinence. Rather, it encompasses a wide range of other behaviors and attitudes that one might call *socially* abstinent. Among those listed, we find imprudence, misanthropy, thoughtlessness, and even libertinage. While it might seem paradoxical to consider libertinage as a form of "celibacy," Diderot's point is clear: for him, any type of behavior that extracts the individual from, or does not contribute directly to, the social body, is deemed celibate. According to this view, celibacy is thus both a natural and a social form of sterility, artificially suppressing the natural urge to reproduce, rendering human relations unproductive, and clearing the way for various forms of physical and social decadence to take root in the individual. By channeling his sexual desire into practices which do not directly lead to procreation and the production of more citizens, the libertine practices, according to Diderot, a form of social celibacy. Not only did celibacy therefore contradict human nature, it also ran counter to the overall interests of society, whose wealth the *philosophe*, as an avowed populationist, measured by the number of its inhabitants.[8]

And within eighteenth-century French society, no other establishments so overtly symbolized celibacy as the monastery and the convent.[9] The fear of France's shrinking population combined with an increasing mistrust of monastic life in general—a mistrust fueled by social isolation, secrecy, and several well-publicized scandals involving the debauchery of some clergy and challenges to the legality of the forced vocation—brought convents and monasteries under greater scrutiny in eighteenth-century France. It was this very same scrutiny which interestingly led to two interrelated developments: first, increased debate on the roles of convents and monasteries, especially in relation to education; and second, the privileging of convents and monasteries as settings within the pornographic literature of the time.[10]

In "Célibat," Diderot, perhaps for fear of censorship, does not directly address the more scabrous issue of debauchery in the monasteries. Instead, focusing his analysis on the relationship between monastic celibacy and society, he writes:

> Il nous resterait pour compléter cet article, à parler du célibat monastique: mais nous nous contenterons d'observer avec le célebre M. Melon, 1°, qu'il y aurait un avantage infini pour la société & pour les particuliers, que le prince usât strictement du pouvoir qu'il a de faire observer la loi qui défendrait l'état avant l'âge de vingt-cinq ans; ou, pour me servir de l'idée & de l'expression de M. Melon, qui ne permettrait pas d'aliéner sa liberté avant l'âge où l'on peut aliéner son bien.[11]

If both national and individual wealth are indeed functions of the number of people in a country and in a family, as the populationists of the time contended, then it is in the interests of the State to safeguard the liberty of each individual to be a productive, in the sense of *reproductive*, member of society. The State should then work to make the abnegation of procreative liberty as difficult as possible. For the *philosophe*, in the battle over souls, the interests of the State should thus outweigh those of the Church.

Choosing not to broach the subject in "Célibat," Diderot saved his most exactingly detailed depiction of the physiological and moral disorders associated with monastic life for his famous novel, *La Religieuse*, which was composed throughout the early 1760s but remained unpublished during the author's lifetime, and in which a forced novice, Suzanne Simonin, recounts her various encounters with the lesbian, sadistic, and mad nuns found inside the walls of French convents. Diderot was particularly aware of the potential moral and physiological dangers of life inside the convent. On this issue, it is important to recall that his own sister Angélique, after whom his daughter was named, had died insane in a convent—a death for which he held the Church responsible.

There is little doubt that his sister's death influenced in subtle but important ways the education that his daughter received. Angélique was instructed privately, far away from the convent, in a home shared by a philosopher father and a devout mother. This upbringing in which reason and faith live, albeit somewhat tumultuously at times, under the same roof was designed to instill in her a reverence for knowledge and a respect for piety. This was surely Diderot's intention: he wanted his daughter to be intelligent but able to conform to the rules of a society dominated by the Church; he wanted her to be enlightened, but free of the difficulties that had plagued him in his various battles with religious authorities.[12]

These competing and commingling currents of enlightenment and piety, reason and faith were most apparent in the days leading up to Angélique's wedding to François Caroillon de Vandeul, a young man from Diderot's hometown of Langres. Like any good *père de famille*, Diderot viewed his daughter's marriage as one of his principal responsibilities. However, beyond the typical religious preparations and financial negotiations involved in an eighteenth-century wedding, Diderot was also concerned with preparing his daughter for her future life as a mother and a wife. To this end, we find him announcing in a letter to his friend Friedrich Melchior Grimm, dated March 1771, roughly one year before Angélique's wedding, that his daughter's planned trip to the countryside has had to be postponed so that she might take a lesson in anatomy from Mlle Biheron, France's preeminent sculptor of anatomical wax models.[13]

Diderot does not immediately elaborate on the nature of this lesson, but in a letter to his priest brother, written shortly after the wedding, he gives some indication of their content. When the *abbé* Diderot had refused to attend the wedding on the grounds that the daughter of such a contemptible philosopher must be, by association, as immoral as her father, the elder brother replied:

> Monsieur l'abbé, ce qu'on apprend au couvent, elle le sait mieux que celles qui y ont passé leur jeunesse, mieux que vous peut-être, et elle n'est pas sur le reste une pécore comme elles. Il y a bientôt deux mois qu'elle est mariée, et elle a conservé et j'espère qu'elle gardera toute sa vie, la simplicité, la douceur, la modestie d'une jeune fille. La modestie, la

> pudeur; entendez-vous, monsieur? et savez-vous à quoi elle doit ce privilège si rare que les gens du monde remarquent en elle? A trois cours d'anatomie qu'elle avait faits chez une demoiselle Biheron aussi recommandable par son talent que par sa sagesse, avant que de passer dans le lit nuptial.[14]

As this passage illustrates, Diderot traces his daughter's simplicity, sweetness, modesty, and *pudeur*, a word with overt sexual connotations that does not translate easily into English, not to her religious education (which has nonetheless been assured by her mother), but to the anatomy lessons (which, in the letter, have passed from one to three) that she took from Mlle Biheron before slipping into the "nuptial bed." It is at this point that the true nature and content of Mlle Diderot's euphemistically labeled "anatomy lessons" becomes clearer: they were lessons in what might somewhat anachronistically be called sex education.[15]

Mlle Biheron's anatomy lessons thus represent both a continuation and a radical change in attitudes surrounding women's education in eighteenth-century France. On the one hand, with her exactingly detailed anatomical models of the female body, she clearly belongs to the tradition of midwives and *matrones*, most famously exemplified by the king's midwife, Mme du Coudray, who, as a part of the nationwide movement to reduce infant mortality, travelled around the French countryside with her famous "machine," training women in the skill of delivering babies; on the other, with her exactingly detailed models of male anatomy and her incorporation of the issue of sex and sexual relations into her anatomical demonstrations, she breaks with the tradition of midwifery by treating women not only as mothers but also as wives, that is, as sexual beings.[16]

The issues of women's social roles and female sexuality had become an increasing concern for Diderot in the days leading up to Angélique's wedding. In 1772, the year of the marriage, he published in the *Correspondance littéraire*, the journal edited by Grimm, a review-essay of Antoine-Léonard Thomas's *Essai sur le caractère, les mœurs et l'esprit des femmes dans les différents siècles* (*Essay on the Character, the Mores and the Spirit of Women in Different Centuries*). Dissatisfied with Thomas's work, which he considered to be a too cerebral analysis of women, he offers instead what he calls a more "sentimental" examination of the subject. Titled "Sur les femmes" ("On Women"), his brief article bears the undeniable mark of his preoccupation with his daughter's transition from Mlle Diderot to Mme de Vandeul. In it, the issue of sex is immediately and daringly foregrounded.

Partly because of their physiological constitution, partly because of the frivolity and idleness of their station in life, women, he writes, nurture their passions, allowing them to become an obsession or "un point fixe" ("a fixed point"). This fixed point then "s'étend sans mesure; et pour devenir folle, il ne manquerait à la femme passionnée que l'entière solitude qu'elle recherche."[17] This image of the solitary madwoman clearly evokes the nun and, on a more personal level, the tragic circumstances surrounding the death of Diderot's sister. The Church (and implicitly French society at large) encourages young women in this physically and psychologically unhealthy pursuit by offering them the isolated space they seek. The convent, for Diderot, is thus the ideal setting for a descent into madness.

The image of the isolated madwoman is then immediately contrasted with that of the unhappy wife, for whom sexual relations are a duty to be suffered with an air of Christian resignation. On this latter figure, Diderot writes: "La soumission à un maître qui lui déplaît est pour elle un supplice. J'ai vu une femme honnête frissonner d'horreur à l'approche de son époux; je l'ai vue se plonger dans le bain, et ne se croire jamais assez lavée de la souillure du devoir."[18] The intimacy of this vivid portrayal leads one to wonder if, once again, Diderot's knowledge did not come from first-hand experience, if the image of the wife repulsed by sex was not, in fact, a depiction of his own wife, Antoinette, with whom he had entertained difficult rapports since the early days of the marriage. Whether or not Diderot was consciously referring to his sister and wife in "Sur les femmes" is uncertain. What is certain is his desire to steer Angélique clear of the figures of the solitary madwoman and the unhappy wife.

As we see, the *philosophe*'s analysis of the dangers faced by women in eighteenth-century French society is grounded in the belief that physiological constitution and social environment concur in determining actual behavior.[19] Within this understanding, sex, as a both biological and social activity, occupies a privileged position in philosophical discourse—it is the place where nature most dramatically confronts nurture. As for the physiological component of sex, Diderot, influenced by the theory of the humors still prevalent in much eighteenth-century medical discourse, believed strongly in the dangers that seminal retention posed to men and, perhaps even more acutely, to women.[20] According to him, the accumulation of seminal fluid in the body can potentially result in madness. From this belief grows the *philosophe*'s radical and oft-cited proposition that it may prove beneficial "to lend nature a hand on occasion."[21] In *La Suite de l'Entretien*, a peculiar text written as something of a coda to his *Le Rêve de d'Alembert* (written around 1769, but not published during his lifetime), this advice, which Diderot somewhat mischievously puts in the mouth of his fictive portrait of the renowned eighteenth-century doctor Théophile de Bordeu, elicits the following discussion:

> Mlle de l'Espinasse. Voilà une doctrine qui n'est pas bonne à prêcher aux enfants.
> Bordeu. Ni aux autres. Cependant me permettrez-vous une supposition? Vous avez une fille sage, trop sage, innocente, trop innocente; elle est dans l'âge où le tempérament se développe. Sa tête s'embarrasse, la nature ne la secourt point; vous m'appelez. Je m'aperçois tout à coup que tous les symptômes qui vous effraient naissent de la surabondance et de la rétention du fluide séminal; je vous avertis qu'elle est menacée d'une folie qu'il est facile de prévenir et qui quelquefois est impossible à guérir; je vous en indique le remède. Que ferez-vous?
>
> Mlle de l'Espinasse. A vous parler vrai, je crois . . . mais ce cas n' arrive point . . .
>
> Bordeu. Détrompez-vous; il n'est pas rare, et il serait fréquent, si la licence de nos mœurs n'y obviait . . . Quoi qu'il en soit, ce serait fouler aux pieds toute décence, attirer sur soi les soupçons les plus odieux, et commettre un crime de lèse-société que de divulguer ces principes. Vous rêvez.[22]

The idea of a crime of *lèse-société* goes to the heart of the problem of sex in eighteenth-century France, as Diderot saw it. For him, the discrepancy between physical functioning and social education on matters related to sex creates an untenable situation in which individuals, especially women (the example that Bordeu gives of the good daughter is far from arbitrary), are forced to choose between their health and their standing, their mental and corporeal wellbeing and their reputation. Put simply, biological development and social development are in conflict with one another. Being sexually active at the age of sexual maturity, in accordance with nature, leads to social degeneracy (once again, especially for women). Refraining from sexual activity, in accordance with the dominant social mores, leads to physical and psychological degeneracy.

The social institutions of the period made the situation of young women even worse. The most common way of dealing with sexual desire at a time in which people, primarily for economic reasons, were marrying at later ages, was to place young women in convents, which as we have seen, was far from being a practical solution, according to the *philosophe*.[23] Becoming sexually active before marriage, while potentially beneficial to a young woman's health, ran the obvious risk of bringing dishonor to the family, making her virtually impossible to marry.

Given these scenarios, masturbation seemed to Diderot and others a good option—it preserved physical health and yet, as a solitary act, it did not compromise the individual socially. When Mlle de l'Espinasse asks Bordeu if he has ever had occasion to suggest such a treatment to the mothers of suffering girls, the doctor responds that he indeed has. And to her query about the course of action that these mothers decided to take, he replies: "Toutes, sans exception, le bon parti, le parti sensé . . . Je n'ôterais pas mon chapeau dans la rue à l'homme suspecté de pratiquer ma doctrine; il me suffirait qu'on l'appelât un infâme. Mais nous causons sans témoins et sans conséquence.[24]

Bordeu has indeed advised his "doctrine" of masturbation. However, he has done so only in the specific case of young women whose illness stems directly from the retention of seminal fluid, and he has done so only in private settings. Men, it would appear, need no such prompting; and to promulgate such beliefs openly in eighteenth-century French society would be, as Bordeu had previously remarked, to risk accusations of impropriety, even debauchery. The discussion of masturbation, and more specifically the discussion of female masturbation found in *La Suite de l'Entretien*, illustrates Diderot's awareness of the differences between male and female sexuality and of the role played by society in relegating discussions of female sexuality to purely private spheres.

The physiology of sex thus exerts tremendous influence on social relations. Returning to the example of the honest wife's revulsion to sex, Diderot, in "Sur les femmes," remarks, "Cette sorte de répugnance nous [meaning men] est presque inconnue. Notre organe est plus indulgent. Plusieurs femmes mourront sans avoir éprouvé l'extrême de la volupté. Cette sensation, que je regarderai volontiers comme une épilepsie passagère, est rare pour elles, et ne manque jamais d'arriver quand nous l'appelons. Le souverain bonheur les fuit entre les bras de l'homme qu'elles adorent. Nous le trouvons à côté d'une femme complaisante qui nous déplaît."[25] Consequently, it is this physiological difference in sexual response that determines, at least in part, relations between husbands and wives. If men and women were able to experience sexual pleasure in similarly efficient ways, then the institution of marriage would be radically altered, ostensibly for the better in Diderot's eyes. Orgasm would be the uniting principle of the marital relationship; sex would no longer be viewed by wives as a repugnant "duty" to be suffered; and the nuptial bed would become the site of what Diderot, in a nod to his own secular naturalism, calls the *sovereign happiness*.

Unfortunately, as he states, the sovereign happiness remains all but unknown to women, and the differences in male and female anatomy and male and female sexual response continue to exert a negative influence on relations between the sexes. Moreover, in a male-dominated society, as Diderot goes on to note, little if anything is done to change the situation. Their educations neglected, young women are kept in a state of sexual ignorance, misleadingly presented and praised as moral innocence. This, in turn, results in many of the problems faced by young women who are physiologically mature but socially unprepared. According to Diderot, the passage into sexual maturity is the key moment in a woman's life when true education has to be assured "[. . .] car c'est à cet instant critique qu'une jeune fille devient ce qu'elle restera toute sa vie, pénétrante ou stupide, triste ou gaie, sérieuse ou légère, bonne ou méchante, l'espérance de sa mère trompée ou réalisée."[26] In other words, it is at this moment that the young woman becomes an actual *moral* being, capable of virtue or vice. If left ignorant, she risks falling into an unsatisfying marriage, or worse, falling victim to libertine predators. Perpetuating sexual ignorance in young women thus constitutes a grave social problem for Diderot.

The key to ensuring the exercise of virtue is thus to educate young women to recognize vice; however, as Diderot adds, "La seule chose qu'on leur ait apprise, c'est à bien porter la feuille de figuier qu'elles ont reçue de leur première aïeule. Tout ce qu'on leur a dit et répété dix-huit à dix-neuf ans de suite se réduit à ceci: Ma fille, prenez garde à votre feuille de figuier; votre feuille de figuier va bien, votre feuille de figuier va mal."[27] Clearly Diderot felt that women should be educated beyond the placement of their metaphorical fig leaves; that is, beyond a general abhorrence and shame associated with the body and beyond a superficial knowledge of original sin, which as Jean Bloch has demonstrated, was actively inculcated in them by the various educational orders of the Church.[28] They needed to understand both the *biological* and the *social* nature of their relations with men in order to prevent illness and avoid the traps laid by a galant society.

Diderot implicitly held the example of his own daughter's "enlightened" upbringing as an alternative to the prevalent means of female instruction discussed in "Sur les femmes." Contrary to the vast majority of young women, whose innocence was purely a function of their ignorance, Angélique owed her innocence, as Diderot declared in the letter to his brother cited above, to her education. The "anatomy lessons" offered by Mlle Biheron to Mlle Diderot thus exist as a remarkable example of Enlightenment praxis. In them, we see the passage from a general theory to a specific application. They are Enlightenment made manifest. This being said, the euphemism by which he refers to them and the secrecy with which he surrounds them in his correspondence serve to demonstrate the danger that these lessons represented in eighteenth-century French society. Like Bordeu's "doctrine" for treating certain disorders, Mlle Biheron's "anatomy lessons" were a private affair. If word got out that Diderot had taken measures to ensure his daughter's sexual education, he (and she) would have been subject to accusations of moral impropriety.

The problem of openly discussing sex was, for Diderot, deeply rooted in the general ambiguity and hypocrisy surrounding sexual relations in eighteenth-century French society itself. It was a society built around a concept of pleasure that consisted in the simultaneous nurturing and compromising of virtue, a society caught between the poles of abstinent purity and libertine pleasure. To change French attitudes about sex, nothing less than a complete revolution was needed, one in which the physical and social elements of sexual relations were no longer in conflict with one another and the institutions which served to reinforce this antagonism no longer held sway. It was, however, difficult even to imagine such a radically different France. Caught between the sexually repressive dogma of the Church and the prurient intellectualism of libertinism, eighteenth-century French society allowed little room for the proponents of enlightenment to broach the subject of sex.

Interestingly, at the same time that Diderot was reflecting on these very issues of sex and society, a drastically different model of national attitudes about sex quite literally landed on his desk. In 1771 Louis-Antoine de Bougainville published the much-anticipated account of his travels, titled *Voyage autour du monde* (*Journey Around the World*). Interest in Bougainville's trip had been growing since his return to France in 1769. In his company was a young man from the isle of Tahiti named Aotourou, whose diverse sexual beliefs and customs had been sensationally reported in the journals of the time. If readers made their way through Bougainville's minute corrections of maps and tedious discussions of winds and currents, it was in all likelihood to get to the explorer's descriptions of the exotic lands and peoples that he had encountered along the way, and in particular to get to his descriptions of Tahiti and the peculiar sexual mores found there.

Soon after its publication, Diderot began to write a review of the work, and although the review was never published, it formed the basis for a subsequent, more substantial text, whose full title read *Supplément au voyage de Bougainville ou Dialogue entre A. et B. sur l'inconvénient d'attacher des idées morales à certaines actions physiques qui n'en comportent pas* (*Supplement to the Journey of Bougainville* or *Dialogue between A. and B. on the Problematic Consequences of Attaching Moral Ideas to Certain Physical Actions Which Do Not Contain Them*). While the main title communicates the work's formal status as a continuation of

Bougainville's original, the somewhat cryptic subtitle suggests the work's primary focus: it is an exposition of the difficulties caused by attaching moral ideas to certain physical acts. And as to the nature of these moral ideas and these physical acts, it quickly becomes clear that, in the *Supplement*, Diderot sets himself the task of examining the problem of attaching the ideas of good and bad to the very basic physical act of sex. What Bougainville's depiction of Tahiti offered the *philosophe* was thus an alternative model of sexual attitudes and comportments that contrasted sharply with those found in France, a country in which sex seemed irrevocably imbued with morality and immorality.

In his *Voyage autour du monde*, Bougainville presents Tahiti as a place of free sexual commerce in which desire (seen albeit from a decidedly male perspective) never goes unfulfilled. In Tahiti, the men and older women offer the younger women to the Frenchmen as either a good to be traded or as a sign of hospitality. Bougainville describes the Tahitian's peculiar way of receiving guests in the following terms:

> Chaque jour nos gens se promenaient dans le pays sans armes, seuls ou par petites bandes. On les invitait à entrer dans les maisons, on leur y donnait à manger; mais ce n'est pas à une collation légère que se borne ici la civilité des maîtres de maisons; ils leur offraient des jeunes filles; la case se remplissait à l'instant d'une foule curieuse d'hommes et de femmes qui faisaient un cercle autour de l'hôte et de la jeune victime du devoir hospitalier; la terre se jonchait de feuillage et de fleurs, et des musiciens chantaient aux accords de la flûte un hymne de jouissance. Vénus est ici la déesse de l'hospitalité, son culte n'y admet point de mystères, et chaque jouissance est une fête pour la nation.[29]

The culture that Bougainville depicts here clearly differs from the one he left behind in France in which sexual relations were subject to a myriad of complex social and religious codes. From a world marked by the moral repression of the clergy and the stylized decadence of libertines, he had arrived at a place that he describes at different moments as both a "Garden of Eden" and a "new Cytherea." Unburdened of the stigma attached to it in France (a stigma which, according to Diderot, lay at the root of both repressive and libertine viewpoints), sex on Tahiti seemed to Bougainville open, uninhibited, and innocent; and sexual pleasure seemed to him to be the greatest virtue around which their familial, political and religious institutions were constructed. This being said, what is missing from Bougainville's account is an analysis of the belief system that subtended

Tahitian sexual mores. In his depiction of Tahiti as something of a sexual utopia, he never seeks to understand exactly why sexual pleasure would be a cause for national celebration.

Hence, Diderot's *Supplément*. In his addendum to Bougainville's *Voyage autour du monde*, the *philosophe* poses this very question in order to arrive at the conclusion which constitutes the work's subtitle. He seeks to know the reasons behind Tahiti's apparent glorification of sexual pleasure; that is to say, what lay behind the development of this nation's radically different ideas and approach to sexual relations. For him, the answer lay not in the love of sensual pleasure for sensual pleasure's sake, but in the potential of sensual pleasure to result in the birth of children. It is thus procreation, not sexual recreation, that is the cause for national celebration in Tahiti. Wealth is measured in children; or, as one native explains to the somewhat hapless Jesuit priest accompanying Bougainville's expedition in Diderot's version:

> Sache, mon ami, qu'ici la naissance d'un enfant est toujours un bonheur, et sa mort un sujet de regrets et de larmes. Un enfant est un bien précieux, parce qu'il doit devenir un homme; aussi [. . .] Un enfant qui naît, occasionne la joie domestique et publique: c'est un accroissement de fortune pour la cabane et de force pour la nation: ce sont des bras et des mains de plus dans Tahiti; nous voyons en lui un agriculteur, un pêcheur, un chasseur, un soldat, un époux, un père.[30]

In Diderot's version of Tahiti, we have thus moved from a hedonistic paradise of free sexual exchange to a populationist paradise in which children (as opposed to women and the sexual favors they offer) are the ultimate sign of wealth. We have moved from "jouissance" to "naissance," from pleasure to birth, as the ultimate source of celebration for the nation. Consequently, within this populationist-structured society, it is Bougainville and his men, and not the young Tahitian women, who are in reality the "victims of hospitable duty," for they receive nothing but fleeting pleasure in their sexual commerce with the natives while the Tahitians reap the truly valuable commodity of new sets of arms for the home and nation. When the almoner wonders about the fate of "conjugal tenderness and paternal love" in such a society, the Tahitian responds, "Nous y avons suppléé par un autre, qui est tout autrement général, énergique et durable, l'intérêt."[31]

In the *Supplément*, which once again like *La Religieuse* and *Le Rêve de d'Alembert* was not published during the author's lifetime, Diderot depicted Tahiti as neither a utopian land nor a model for France to emulate.[32] For Diderot, the devoted *père de famille*, it was clearly not a question of replacing paternal love with blind economic interest in French society. Nor was it simply a question of adopting a purely utilitarian view of sex. Rather, as the full title of the work suggests, he was attempting to imagine a nation in which sex and sexual relations were conceptualized in a radically different way than in France, outside the moral ideas of good and evil, right and wrong. Bougainville's Tahiti thus provided the *philosophe* with a controlled environment in which he could perform something of a mental experiment in social organization. However, in exposing the "problematic consequences of attaching moral ideas to certain physical actions"—consequences that resulted in the artificially repressive, anti-natural dogma of the Church and the libertine alike—he was also trying, in the *Supplément au voyage de Bougainville*, to create a space for the discourse of reason in which a reappraisal and reformation of the sexual beliefs and practices held in France might take place outside Church dogma and libertine hedonism.[33]

It was this same general dissatisfaction with the discourse surrounding sexual mores in France that ultimately had compelled Diderot to arrange for Angélique's anatomy lessons with Mlle Biheron. So great was the *philosophe*'s approval of this form of sexual education that when Mlle Biheron's traveled to England to give a demonstration of her anatomical models at the Royal Society, he recommended her services to his friend, the politician John Wilkes, whose own daughter was approaching the age of marriage:

> Je vous prie de l'acueillir et de lui rendre tous les bons offices qui dépendent de vous. Ma fille a fait avec facilité et sans dégoût un cours d'anatomie chez elle. Si vous m'en croyez, vous engagerez Mademoiselle Wilkes à prendre quelques-unes de ses leçons. Quoique ce ne soit point l'objet du voyage de Mademoiselle Biheron, comme elle joint à ses connaissances un grand caractère de bienfaisance, je ne doute point qu'elle ne se fît un plaisir de vous obliger dans votre enfant.[34]

The letter to Wilkes is important, for it marks the first indication that Diderot was beginning to view such "anatomy lessons" as a more generalized program for the education of women that adhered to the project of enlightenment.

With Angélique married, Diderot began the journey to Russia. On his arrival in St. Petersburg in October of 1773, Diderot was granted the rare privilege of daily personal audiences with the Empress, in which he was asked to give brief lectures on a variety of subjects ranging from the history of law and police enforcement in France to the history of his own *Encyclopédie.* The intellectual overlap that developed between preparations for Angélique's marriage and what he believed to be his role as advisor to the Empress manifests itself in many of the topics he chose to discuss in his lectures, among which we find: Essay 16: On the Institute for Young Women; Essay 17: On the Same Subject; Essay 25: Public Schools; Essay 27: On Private Education—The Problem at the Base of this Type of Education—Competition for Placement as the Remedy to this Flaw; Essay 30: On the Education of Abandoned Children; and finally, Essay 35: Anatomy Lessons in the Institute for Young Women. The subjects indicate a striking preoccupation with education and educational institutions, particularly, the education of young women. Eventually, Diderot grouped these memoranda together under the title *Mélanges philosophiques, historiques, etc.* (*Philosophical, Historical, Etc. Miscellany*).

Fewer than two weeks after his arrival in Russia, Catherine personally took the philosopher on a tour of the Smolny Monastyr, which had been converted into a school for noble girls. Diderot was struck by the institute, which presented itself as a viable and, for him, welcome alternative to the religious institutions that continued to monopolize public instruction for young women in France. An educational institute free from the control of the Church compelled him to reflect on a curriculum that would adhere to the Enlightenment ideal of the dissemination of knowledge for the improvement of society. In Essays 16 and 17 on the Institute for Young Women, Diderot contrasts his daughter's education with that provided at Smolny, even going so far as to concede to the Empress that her school does a better job of preparing young women for life as "honest and useful citizens of the nation" than he and his wife were able to do with Angélique. He does, however, offer one suggestion to Catherine in terms of the Smolny Monastyr's curriculum: "Le seul point, plus ou moins important selon le coup d'œil sous lequel on le considérera, le seul point, dis-je, qu'on ait omis, c'est un petit cours d'anatomie sur des pièces en cire et injectées qui aient la vérité de la nature, sans en offrir le dégoût."[35] Diderot then goes on to reveal that he had arranged for Angélique to take such an anatomy lesson and had been pleased with the results.

Abandoning the vague rhetoric that had marked his earlier letters on the anatomy lessons, the *philosophe* explains to the empress openly and in great detail the practical use of such lessons. According to him, they served to cut his daughter's curiosity about sex at the root; and with her curiosity satiated, she did not seek to discover for herself the truth about sex from a less virtuous source. Her imagination was thus lulled and her morals remained all the more pure. These lessons taught her the concepts of *pudeur* and *bienséance*, as well as the perils and potential outcomes of the approach of men. They prepared her for her conjugal duties as a wife and they instructed her on the process of childbirth. And finally, all of this knowledge served the very basic function of helping to preserve her health and wellbeing.

After laying out the practical reasons for such study, Diderot then explains to the Empress the conditions in which the lessons were given:

> Mais, me direz-vous, où a-t-elle pu prendre ces connaissances anatomiques, sans conséquence? Chez une demoiselle, très habile et très honnête, où j'ai fait mes cours d'anatomie, moi, mes amis, vingt filles de bonne maison, et cent femmes de la société, science qu'elle a rendue assez commune parmi nous. Des pères y ont mené leur fils et leur filles séparément. On formait une compagnie et l'on prenait les leçons en commun.[36]

Here, the *philosophe* reveals for the first time the full extent of the public of Mlle Biheron's anatomy lessons. No longer presented as a single anomalous event organized by a philosopher father for his soon-to-be-wed daughter, the anatomy lessons are conceptualized and presented as an "enlightened" project for a larger public composed of both men and women. Whether or not Mlle Biheron's anatomy lessons were actually attended by such a large public in France remains unverified. It could well be that, in his pitch for the institutionalization of such a sex education program in the Smolny School, Diderot was embellishing its scope and acceptance. What remains undeniable, however, is his desire to see such a program enacted on a larger scale.

Like an underground movement committed to social reformation, the public Diderot envisions for such anatomy lessons would seek to contribute to the betterment of society by ensuring the physical and psychological well-being of its sons as well as its daughters. Still naively clinging to his image of Catherine as an enlightened ruler, he hoped that she would take this educational reform movement above ground, integrating it into the curriculum of the School for Noble Girls housed in the Smolny Monastyr. In this way, the *philosophe* anticipated that Russia would succeed where France had failed. It would approach his ideal of the enlightened nation committed to the improvement of the lives of its citizens through the liberation of the discourse surounding sexual relations and mores from libertine and clergy alike.

NOTES

1. Michel Foucault, *Histoire de la sexualité I. La volonté de savoir* (Paris: Gallimard, 1976). See in particular pages 76–78.

2. James Grantham Turner, *Schooling Sex: Libertine Literature and Erotic Education in Italy, France, and England, 1534–1685* (Oxford: Oxford University Press, 2003).

3. For a comprehensive study of the natalist movement in eighteenth-century France, see Carol Blum's *Strength in Numbers: Population, Reproduction, and Power in Eighteenth-Century France* (Baltimore: Johns Hopkins University Press, 2002).

4. Jacqueline Hecht, "From 'Be Fruitful and Multiply' to Family Planning: The Enlightenment Transition," *Eighteenth-Century Studies* 32.4 (1999): 546.

5. ". . . one has been released from this duty by some authority greater than nature, so that it may be very clear that here it's in no way a question of celibacy consecrated by religion, but of that formed each day by imprudence, misanthropy, thoughtlessness, and libertinage; of that where the two sexes, corrupting one another through their own natural sentiments or unnecessarily suppressing in themselves these same sentiments, flee a union which should make them better in order to live either in sterile isolation or in unions which render them even worse." See Denis Diderot, "Célibat" in *L'Encylopédie, ou Dictionnaire raisonné des sciences des arts et des métiers* (Paris: Chez Briasson, David, Le Breton, Durand, 1751), 2:804. This and all subsequent translations are mine.

6. It is thus not without some irony that Diderot refers his readers in the line immediately preceding his supposed religious exemption for celibacy to his *Essai sur le mérite, ou la vertu*, a work in which he attempts to demonstrate that virtue can exist independently of religion. See Denis Diderot, *Œuvres complètes*, eds. Jean Assézat and Maurice Tourneux, 20 vols. (Paris: Garnier Frères, 1875), 1:3–122.

7. ". . . as if it were necessary to stop being a man in order to show oneself religious." *Œuvres complètes*, 1:10. Bordeu. Vous l'allez voir. Mademoiselle, pourriez-vous m'apprendre quel profit ou quel plaisir la chasteté et la continence rigoureuse rendent soit à l'individu qui les pratique, soit à la société. Mlle de l'Espinasse. Ma foi, aucun. Bordeu. You're going to see it. Mademoiselle, could you explain to me what advantage or what pleasure chastity and rigorous temperance bring either to the individual who practices them or to society. Mlle de l'Espinasse: My goodness, none. *Œuvres complètes*, 2:184.

8. Diderot's critique of celibacy and the social institutions that promote it found its most radical expression in his later *La Suite de l'Entretien* (1769). Bordeu. Vous l'allez voir. Mademoiselle, pourriez-vous m'apprendre quel profit ou quel plaisir la chasteté et la continence rigoureuse rendent soit à l'individu qui les pratique, soit à la société. Mlle de l'Espinasse. Ma foi, aucun. Bordeu. You're going to see it. Mademoiselle, could you explain to me what advantage or what pleasure chastity and rigorous temperance bring either to the individual

who practices them or to society. Mlle de l'Espinasse: My goodness, none. *Œuvres complètes*, 2:184.

9. In spite of his claim to excuse those whose celibacy is sanctified by religion, in "Célibat" Diderot reserves his most direct critique of the practice for "Christian society." According to him, it is in the interest of society that Catholic clergy, like their Protestant counterparts, should be allowed to marry and have families.

10. See chapter 5, "School of Virtue, School of Vice," of Mita Choudhury's *Convents and Nuns in Eighteenth-Century French Politics and Culture* (Ithaca: Cornell University Press, 2004), 129–54.

11. In order to complete this article, we have only to speak of monastic celibacy, but we will have to content ourselves by observing, with the famous M. Melon, that "there would be an infinite advantage for society and individuals if the prince strictly used his power to have enforced the law that forbids this state before 25 years of age; or, to borrow the idea and expression of M. Melon, the law that forbids relinquishing one's liberty before the age at which one can relinquish one's possessions." See "Célibat" 2:806.

12. On the struggle between Monsieur and Madame Diderot in the education of Angélique, see Eva Jacobs, "Diderot and the Education of Girls," in *Woman and Society in Eighteenth-Century France: Essays in Honour of John Stephenson Spink*, ed. Eva Jacobs, et al. (London: Athlone Press, 1979), 83–95.

13. For more on the life and work of Mlle Biheron, see Georges Boulinier, "Une femme anatomiste au siècle des Lumières: Marie Marguerite Biheron (1719–1795)," *Histoire des sciences médicales* 35.4 (2001): 411–23.

14. Monsieur l'abbé, what one learns in the convent, she knows better than those who have passed their youths there, better than perhaps even you, and on other matters, she's not a bumpkin like they are. Almost two months have passed since her marriage, and she has retained and I hope that she'll keep her entire life, the simplicity, the sweetness and the modesty of a young girl. The modesty, *la pudeur*, do you understand, monsieur? And do you know to what she owes this rare privilege that people remark in her? To three anatomy lessons that she took with Mlle Biheron, a woman who's as commendable for her talent as for her wisdom, before passing into the nuptial bed. See letter dated 13 November 1772 in Diderot, *Correspondance*, 16 vols. (Paris: Editions de minuit, 1955), 12:164.

15. On the particularity of Mlle Biheron's anatomy lessons, see my "'Comment se font les enfans?' Sex Education and the Preservation of Innocence in Eighteenth-Century France," *MLN* 117 (2002): 722–36.

16. In an inventory of Mlle Biheron's cabinet d'anatomie, we find listed "une verge soigneusement confectionnée en cire" ["a penis carefully constructed in wax"]. See Boulinier, "Une femme anatomiste au siècle des Lumières," 413. For a thorough presentation of Madame du Courdray's life and work, see Nina Rattner Gelbart's *The King's Midwife: A History of Madame du Courdray* (Los Angeles: University of California Press, 1998).

17. "This fixed point extends without limit; and to become mad all that is missing for an impassioned woman is the complete solitude that she seeks." *Œuvres complètes*, 2:252.

18. "Submission to a master whom she does not like is, for her, a form of torture. I have seen an honest woman shudder in horror at the approach of her husband; I have seen her dive into the bath and never believe herself completely cleansed from the stain of duty." *Œuvres complètes*, 2:252.

19. Diderot's belief in the reciprocal roles and influence of biology and society on the development of women tends to undermine Elisabeth Badinter's rather reductive depiction of the *philosophe*'s thoughts on the subject. Attempting to paint Diderot as a strict biological determinist, she writes: "La thèse de Diderot est lumineuse de clarté: la femme est un être de passions et d'émotions commandée par son utérus. Tout le restes' en déduit." ["Diderot's thesis is brilliantly clear: Women are passionate and emotional beings, dictated by their uterus. Everything else derives from that."]. See the preface to *Qu'est-ce qu'une femme?*, ed. Elisabeth Badinter (Paris: P.O.L éditeur), 34–35.

20. The production and retention of seminal fluid in both males and females was a commonly shared belief among many philosophers of the time. See for example Buffon's discussion of the subject in volume 2, chapter 10 of the *Histoire naturelle*, titled "De la formation du fœtus," in Georges Louis Leclerc, comte de Buffon, *Œuvres complètes*, 6 vols. (Paris: Chez Furne et compagnie, 1838), 3:122–36.

21. "La nature ne souffre rien d'inutile; et comment serais-je coupable de l'aider, lorsqu'elle appelle mon secours par les symptômes les moins équivoques? Ne la provoquons jamais, mais prêtons-lui la main dans l'occasion." ["Nature allows for nothing of no use; and how would I be guilty of helping her when she calls on my aid by the most obvious symptoms? Let's never provoke her, but lend her a hand when necessary."] *Œuvres complètes*, 2:185.

22. Mlle de l'Espinasse: There's a doctrine that shouldn't be taught to children. Bordeu: Nor to others. However, will you allow me one supposition? You have a good daughter, too good, innocent, too innocent. She's at the age where temperament begins to develop. Her head becomes troubled; nature provides no relief. You call me. I immediately observe that all the symptoms which are frightening you are born from the overabundance and the retention of seminal fluid. I warn you that she's threatened by a madness that's easy to prevent and that's sometimes impossible to cure. I tell you the remedy. What will you do? Mlle de l'Espinasse: To tell you the truth, I believe . . . but this situation doesn't arise . . . Bordeu: Think again. It's not rare, and it would be more frequent if the licentiousness of our morals didn't already take care of it. Whatever it may be, to reveal these principles would be to trample all decency, to attract the most odious suspicions, and to commit a crime of *lèse-société*. You're dreaming. *Œuvres complètes*, 2:185–86.

23. On the postponement of marriage, see Hecht, "From 'Be Fruitful and Multiply' to Family Planning," 537.

24. "All, without exception, took the good course of action, the sensible course of action. I would not tip my hat to a man in the street suspected of practicing my doctrine. It would suffice me to know that he was called a vile man. But we are chatting without witnesses and without consequence." *Œuvres complètes*, 2:186.

25. "This type of repugnance is almost unknown to us. Our organ is more indulgent. Many women will die without ever having felt the heights of voluptuous pleasure. This sensation, which I consider as a passing epilepsy, is rare for them, yet never fails to arrive when we call it. The sovereign happiness escapes them even in the arms of the man they adore. We instead find it next to a complaisant woman for whom we don't even care." *Œuvres complètes*, 2:252.

26. "for it is at this instant that a young girl becomes what she will remain the rest of her life, astute or stupid, sad or gay, serious or light, good or wicked, the hopes of her mother dashed or realized." *Œuvres complètes*, 2:257.

27. "The only thing they are taught is to wear correctly the fig leaf they have received from their first ancestor. All that is said and repeated to them for eighteen to nineteen consecutive years can be reduced to this: My daughter, pay attention to your fig leaf; your fig leaf looks all right or your fig leaf doesn't look all right." *Œuvres complètes*, 2: 261.

28. See Jean Bloch, "Nature corrompue et santé corporelle: Sexualité et éducation en France au XVIIIe siècle," in *Sexualité, mariage et famille au XVIIIe siècle*, eds. Olga B. Cragg and Rosena Davison (Québec: Presses de l'Université Laval, 1998), 321–33.

29. "Each day our men would walk around unarmed, either alone or in small groups. They would be invited to enter into the homes of the Tahitians where they would be fed, but the civility of the masters of the households wasn't limited to small meals; they would also offer young girls. The hut would immediately fill with a curious crowd of men and women who would make a circle around the guest and the young victim of hospitable duty; flowers would be strewn over the ground and musicians, accompanied by flutes, would sing a hymn to sexual pleasure. Venus is here the goddess of hospitality; her cult doesn't admit any mysteries, and each act of sexual pleasure is a celebration for the nation." See Louis-Antoine de Bougainville, *Voyage autour du monde par la frégate du Roi* La Boudeuse *et la flûte* L'Etoile, ed. Jacques Proust (Paris: Gallimard, 1982), 235.

30. "Know, my friend, that here the birth of a child is always a happy occasion and his death a subject of regret and tears. A child is a valuable good, because he must become a man . . . a child who is born brings about domestic and public joy: it's an increase in the fortune of the hut and of the nation: these are additional arms and hands in Tahiti; we see in him a farmer, a fisherman, a hunter, a soldier, a husband, and a father." *Œuvres complètes*, 2:227–28.

31. "We have replaced them with another, otherwise general, energetic and lasting feeling, that of interest." *Œuvres complètes*, 2:236.

32. In a provocative reading of the *Supplément au voyage de Bougainville*, which focuses primarily on the economic system depicted in the text, Wilda

Anderson has suggested that it is, in fact, an anti-utopian work. According to this interpretation, Tahiti would thus be, for Diderot, a "philosophical trap to be avoided," because it necessarily leads to "alienation from the dynamically material world and hence to cultural atrophy and oblivion." While Anderson's reading is clearly intended to push the envelope, I feel that she is correct to question conventional interpretations of the *Supplément* which would attempt to present Diderot's re-writing of Tahiti as the author's own model for "natural" sexual relations within a "normative" social environment. See chapter four, "Dismantling a Utopian Economics," in Wilda C. Anderson, *Diderot's Dream* (Baltimore: Johns Hopkins University Press, 1990), 127–67.

33. As much is expressed by the character "B" of the dialogue found within the *Supplément.* When asked by his interlocutor what course of action should be taken in France in regards to sex, he responds, "Nous parlerons contre les lois insensées jusqu'à ce qu'on les réforme ; et, en attendant, nous nous y soumettrons." ["We'll speak out against senseless laws until they are reformed; and while waiting, we'll submit ourselves to them."] Then, recalling the Jesuit priest who enjoyed the company of a young Tahitian woman, he concludes, "Imitons le bon aumônier, moine en France, sauvage dans Tahiti." ["Let's imitate the good chaplain: monk in France, savage in Tahiti."] *Œuvres complètes*, 2:249.

34. "I pray you to welcome her and to give her all the good services that depend on you. My daughter took with ease and without disgust an anatomy course from her. If you trust me, you'll engage Mademoiselle Wilkes to take some of her lessons. Although this is not the purpose of Mademoiselle Biheron's trip, since her knowledge is joined to her great, charitable character, I have no doubt that she would enjoy obliging you with your child." Letter dated 19 October 1771, Diderot, *Correspondance* ed. Georges Roth, 16 vols. (Paris: Editions de minuit, 1955–70), 11:211.

35. "The only point, more or less important according to the perspective from which one considers it; the one point, I mean, that has been omitted is a little course on anatomy incorporating wax models that are lifelike without being distasteful." See Diderot, *Mémoires pour Cathérine II*, ed. Paul Vernière (Paris: Garnier, 1966), 86.

36. "But, you'll say, where was she able to acquire this anatomical knowledge without repercussions? With a very honest and skillfull *demoiselle*, where I took my courses on anatomy—a science which she made common for me, my friends, twenty girls from good homes, and one hundred women from society. Fathers took their sons and daughters there separately. We formed a company and took the lessons together." See Diderot, *Mémoires pour Cathérine II*, 87.

Snapshots of Family Intimacy in the French Eighteenth Century: The Case of Paul et Virginie

SUZANNE R. PUCCI

For Roland Barthes, "Le premier homme qui a vu la première photo . . . a dû croire que c'était une peinture: même cadre, même perspective. La Photographie a été, est encore tourmentée par le fantôme de la Peinture" . . . ["The first man who saw the first photograph must have thought it was a painting: same framing, same perspective. Photography has been, and is still, tormented by the ghost of Painting."[1]] This essay explores the tableau in terms of its role as a "phantom" or "ghost" that effectively shadows the family photo as a previous and significant early paradigm of domestic intimacy.[2] I suggest that family photos constitute an ulterior development of eighteenth-century representations. My essay is attempting, in other words, to trace this genealogy of the family picture.

Increasingly, "intimacy" has become in the last fifteen years the object of literary, historical, social, and psychological analysis, though recently the term has often been confined primarily to describing western romantic sentiments in terms of relations within and increasingly outside of conventional marriage. Such is the case in Anthony Giddens's *Transformation of Intimacy,* Zygmunt Bauman's *Liquid Love: The Frailty of Human Bonds,* and Lauren Berlant's edited collection entitled *Intimacy.*[3] In effect, sociologist Stephanie Coontz recently contrasts a concept of intimacy with marital relations in her latest book, *Marriage, a History,* subtitled *From Obedience to Intimacy, or How Love Conquered Marriage*.[4] "Intimacy" in these texts and contexts is a term and a concept that has been appropriated most recently to define what lies specifically outside the domestic as well as marital spheres.

Yet the relation of intimacy to the domestic sphere does have resonance today even if the exact term is not always used. There is a current attempt in sociological studies to understand whether the *lack* of family closeness, of intimacy, that many feel stems, as Coontz says, from a "nostalgia trap" for "The Way We Never Were," or whether such a thing as domestic intimacy has in a real sense been lost and that "The Way We Really Are Now" involves coming to grips with families that are indeed changing.[5] My study employs the term "domestic intimacy" in order to raise the issue of close family sentiment which those historians, particularly of *mentalités,* have studied as emerging in the eighteenth century.[6] Thus, my interest in the subject of domestic intimacy derives from a question I pose at a time in contemporary society when intimacy has come into focus as a problematic notion both in terms of conjugal and couple relations as well as in terms of a mythical and/or changing landscape of the family.

An often neglected aspect of what now binds or what in the past bound family members together is the way this closeness or lack thereof was and is perceived; that is, how it has been represented at particular moments and through which media. I do not look here to historical or sociological evidence to understand attitudes in the late eighteenth century toward the question of family bonds. Rather, this essay turns to the textual and/or pictorial strategies that uncover the inclinations and (dis)avowed desires and tendencies as they inhabit and organize representations of domestic intimacy.

In his text *Emile*, Jean-Jacques Rousseau mentions, seemingly in passing, what became in effect a powerful cultural convention: "Il n'y a point de *'tableau'* plus charmant que celui de la famille" (my emphasis).[7] "Picture" here could refer to painting or engraving, as well as to a concept of tableau, but of course certainly not to the photograph of the late nineteenth and twentieth centuries. Yet Rousseau articulated what did emerge in the nineteenth-century photograph and what remains operative today as well: the family as a domestic unit is "charming" perhaps because it is conceptualized and often conceived as a cohesive picture.

Rousseau goes on in the beginning of book 1 of *Emile* to elaborate on the dangers and pitfalls that can disrupt such a charming picture.[8] What disfigures ["défigure"] the picture of the family is precisely the dispersion of its members: if the children are "*eloignés*" or *"dispersés"* in convents, colleges, etc., they no longer dwell in the home; as Rousseau says, they are *"ailleurs,"* "elsewhere." They thus dwell outside the common space of "the paternal home" and outside the picture as well. Even at such times as they might gather for a family ceremony, when they will be *"rassemblés,"* they would remain distant, *"étrangers"* ["strangers"] to each other. The sense of family union is generated from notions of the collective living space. The spatial elements of the tableau are paralleled by the enclosures of the paternal home. From the moment family members do not inhabit the same space, they become distant strangers to each other. And once they have left the home they are no longer part of the picture. The unity of both family and its collective image is threatened. To put it another way, the spatial organization that defines tableau also constitutes a principal defining criterion of the thriving "charming" family. The family picture is thus not just a convenient metaphor for representing domestic intimacy; here, it is also an analogue that introduces and thematizes a spatial model.

Whether a nostalgic idea of the past, an ideal never actually realized, or a truly lost history, domestic intimacy claims a salient place in western conventions of the family in the eighteenth century as well as in contemporary culture through a vital link to pictorial representation. Rousseau is certainly not alone in identifying new family sentiment within the frame of a spatial entity such as the tableau. Diderot's use of "tableau" was crucial to his aesthetic and social theory of bourgeois drama, as Peter Szondi first pointed out in his distinction between Diderot's notion of "Tableau versus coup de théâtre." [9] Indeed, examples of this privileged figure of "tableau" abound in Diderot's critical writing about theater as well as in his plays. The *philosophe* is struck, for instance, by the picture of maternal love in a particular scene of Racine's tragedy *Iphigénie*. Diderot singles out the domestic role in contrast to the public or political role of Iphigenia's mother, and this focus takes shape in his discussion precisely within the semantic and visual frames of "tableau":

> Si la mère d'Iphigénie se montrait un moment reine D'Argos et femme du général des Grecs, elle ne me paraîtrait que la dernière des créatures. La véritable dignité, celle qui me frappe, qui me renverse, c'est le *tableau de l'amour maternel* dans toute sa vérité.[10]

The sentiment of domestic love that Diderot identifies here with tableau becomes the central preoccupation of this new genre of domestic tragedy. I have discussed Diderot's dramatic theories and theatrical practice in his plays *Le fils naturel* and *Le Père de famille*, which were both constructed on the model of the tableau: these plays featured description of stage props clearly demarcating the enclosures of domestic interiors; characters both physically and discursively framed within family blood relations; thematic boundaries distinguishing between strangers, even intruders, and family members; and frames sharply delimiting the stage from an audience positioned external to it.[11] Diderot's and Rousseau's configuration of family in and as tableau participates in and helps institute a western tradition that dictates the experience of family attachment as deeply rooted in the enclosures and frames of pictures and ultimately in the snapshots that in our own century document but also still give shape to domestic intimacy.

In effect, those whose objective as historians is to document the family tend themselves to use the picture and its frames or enclosures to delineate domestic intimacy in its substantive difference from earlier models. Thus, Lawrence Stone refers to the "more sealed off and private family type that was to develop in the seventeenth and eighteenth centuries;" indeed, Stone speaks of the "walling off of the nuclear family."[12] It is no coincidence that the historian Raffaella Sarti introduces her book on the early modern European family in terms of a painting:

> If this book is a painting, then what does it depict? And what does the frame exclude? The title provides the answer: *Europe at Home: Family and Material Culture 1500–1800*. Its spatial and chronological boundaries are those of Europe in the early modern era.[13]

Sarti describes her history of the family in terms of temporal boundaries that parallel architectural and spatial boundaries of the home and that constitute as well the conceptual enclosures of home.

Most importantly, Philippe Ariès emphasizes the introduction of a new kind of interaction between family members in terms of a distinctly spatial model reminiscent of the enclosure of tableau:

> Dans le monde des sentiments et des valeurs, la famille ne comptait pas [auparavant] autant que le lignage. Or [ce lignage] apparaît très différent du *sentiment de famille*, tel qu'on l'a vu se dégager de l'iconographie des 16ième–17ième siècles. . . . [Le lignage] s'étend aux liens du sang sans égard aux valeurs nées de *la cohabitation et de l'intimité. Le lignage n'est jamais réuni dans un espace commun, autour d'une même cour. Au contraire, le sentiment de famille est lié à la maison, au gouvernement de la maison, à la vie dans la maison.* [14]

"Maison" in French refers of course both to the house, its architectural and physical properties as a domicile, as well as to the sense and sentiment of home. The relation between architectural and emotional enclosures becomes explicit here as Ariès' remark reveals a new focus, in my view, reflects a major cultural shift reorienting the representation of family experience from a previously dominant *diachronic* model of lineage to a *synchronic*, thus indeed spatial, model of domestic intimacy.

The historical line of descendants passing from one generation to the next offers a concept of family that is diachronic, that is, developed and continued through time, while the synchronic presents a distinctly spatial model formulated in and as the place of house and home. As Ariès remarks, "a common space, a single courtyard" is where the "line," or lineage, is gathered into one common collective entity. The opposition between genealogical relations linking family members across generations, even distant centuries, and the contrasting interaction of individuals relating in a simultaneous contemporary moment within a particular intimate domestic space introduces a useful and suggestive paradigm, one that explains, at least in part, Ariès's own emphasis on representation and iconography throughout his book. From the family conceived in the chronological blood filiations of genealogy according to the model of lineage, a major shift takes effect to a *spatial model* of the domestic: to the *domestic* articulated as a *spatial* entity. I propose this shift to spatial enclosure and simultaneous interaction within that space as an explicit paradigm for those "charming pictures of the family" that retain a certain continuity throughout early modern society and that carry over into our own current preoccupation with photographs, with snapshots of the family.

For Richard Sennett, during this early modern period the "home" became the secular version of spiritual refuge, or what he terms the "geography of enclosure." A new "geography of safety" was established in a "shift from sanctuaries in urban centers such as the protective spaces surrounding the cathedral to the enclosures of the domestic interior." [15] The move to a new intimacy of the domestic interior takes place through the multiple enclosures that mark off and separate those excluded from those who dwell within the bounded spatial and simultaneously constructed sentimental formation and formulation of home. Ariès relies in his book on spatial representation, on family pictures to document, to *explain* the shift to the new social and cultural phenomenon of domestic intimacy; my own perspective locates these prevalent spatial representations as constitutive themselves of the phenomenon of domestic intimacy.

These "charming tableaux" elaborate spatial and visual properties that were produced in often exclusively verbal as well as in theatrical and in actual pictorial representations, such as in the growing number of genre paintings exemplified by Greuze's depictions of domestic dramas and interiors. Yet the measure of the tableau as an exceptionally operative paradigm of domestic intimacy can be illustrated just as well, if not tested perhaps best of all, in fiction. Although conceived at this time mainly as linear and chronological, narrative is in effect enlisted toward new, contrasting ends, specifically in the text of Bernardin de Saint-Pierre's novel *Paul et Virginie*. Published in 1788, 1789, 1800, and throughout the nineteenth and twentieth centuries, it became a best seller of huge proportions, published in more than 500 editions through 1960.[16] One reason it might have garnered such interest is this novel's subversion of its generic form by deploying a shift to spatial as opposed to linear and temporal paradigms. And the determining cause for this shift is directly traceable to the dominant concern in this text with representing domestic intimacy.

Initially, the novel appeared as part of Bernardin de Saint-Pierre's larger work, *Etudes de la nature,* studies on the flora and fauna as well as on the society and culture of the island he visited, Mauritius (then called the Ile de France). Its success was such that it soon had become translated in many European languages; thus, in the last thirteen years of the century it was published in thirty-six French editions and twenty translations.[17] *Paul et Virginie* overdetermines the "geography of enclosure" in this tale of exotic distances whose principal subject turns out, surprisingly, to be domestic intimacy. In effect, the novel short-circuits a linear development of the plot by depicting from the very outset its tragic end. Along with its geographical distance from France, from Europe, comes a temporal distance which, we will see, also entails a spatial displacement from the story's events. These are strategies which employ narrative in the service of fashioning a picture. In the novel's first sentence, we are transported to a far away place and to a distant time: "Sur le côté oriental de la montagne qui s'élève derrière le Port-Louis de l'Ile de France, on voit dans un terrain jadis cultivé, les ruines de deux petites cabanes."[18] These cabins are the vestige of lives now over; they become a focus for the story which has already ended before it has begun. As European readers, we are not just far from this land geographically; we also have been positioned outside the temporal limits of events that have already taken place. The reader is situated as spectator, as viewer of "ruins" whose history we are about to uncover as in a kind of archeological excavation. Far from being placed *in media res* of the characters' dilemmas or actions, the reader beholds the site of the island and the story from the distant quiet and stasis of its aftermath, its tomb.

Most significant in this *incipit* to *Paul et Virginie* is the detailed picture of the natural setting that necessitates a spectator's, a listener's as opposed to a reader's, perspective:

> A l'entrée de ce bassin, . . . les échos de la montagne répètent sans cesse le bruit des vents qui agitent les forêts voisines, et le fracas des vagues qui brisent au loin sur les récifs; mais au pied même des cabanes on n'entend plus aucun bruit, et on ne voit autour de soi que de grands rochers escarpés comme des murailles.[19]

The crashing of waves and whipping of the wind that form the backdrop and offer a visual and audible panorama create a profound silence by forming a protective barrier around the cabins. And this silence that surrounds the viewers/readers disconnecting us from the past of any noise or life of the former inhabitants has a distinctly visual counterpart in the "huge rocks [escarpés] that surround one like walls." The effect of such textual indices is to frame through distancing and separating the world that once resided within that domain from the rest of the island, from Europe and France, and from the reader/viewer. As also becomes clear, this representation functions in its physical, visual, and (non) audible depictions to cut off the time of the story from the time of the narration itself. The novel enlists silence and ruins for a purpose that coincides with its subversion of narrative structure.

Narrative voice plays a crucial role in this strategy of estrangement and framing. Though first-person discourse does emerge after the opening lines in the figure of a traveler attracted by this site in his trips around the island, the initial description takes place in the third-person-objective "*on*" ["*one*"]. Nothing personalizes the estrangement and separation that permeate the novel's opening picture ("On n'entend plus aucun bruit, on ne voit autour de soi. . . . ") Following the introductory paragraph, a shift to first-person narration seemingly brings the text into line with conventional eighteenth-century fictional discourse. Yet the first-person "I," so customary from Montesquieu to Rousseau and throughout the popular eighteenth-century epistolary genre, functions here to attenuate the importance and effect of first-person narration, in which, as Montesquieu said about telling one's own story, "D'ailleurs, ces sortes de romans réussissent parce que l'on rend compte soi-même de sa situation actuelle; ce qui fait plus sentir les passions que tous les récits qu'on en pourrait faire."[20]

In effect, the first-person narrator—this anonymous stranger on the island—meets and immediately defers to the narrative of a second first-person narrator, an old man, a *vieillard*, who knew and loved the cabin dwellers and witnessed all past events of the story leading to this scene of desolation. This solitary witness only at moments is actually incorporated into the story; he represents himself consistently as belonging to the *outside* of the story, to its frames. Thus, the first-person here is the one who is actually the furthest from the story. For what he will recount will be for the most part not his own; his voice is placed at various removes from the events and situation of the main characters. Thus, we are relayed from a pictorial scene and a disembodied perspective of "one who sees" ["on voit"] or "hears" ["on n'entend plus"], to an anonymous traveler beholding the tableau of sea and landscape which enclose the cabins, to a narrator who does not belong to the family whose story he will tell but who, mainly as spectator himself, witnessed the lives of those whose absence, whose distance is so pronounced, so acutely and carefully measured and whose lives are seemingly so inaccessible.

Yet it is precisely these manifold separations, distances, and estrangements produced at the outset—geographical, spatial, temporal, narrative—that constitute the crucial frames that enclose and illustrate within them a tableau of domestic intimacy. Like the initial descriptions of the exotic silent and solitary place of the two cabins, other pictures are introduced throughout that insist on the complementary attributes of distance and proximity as crucial signifiers of domestic intimacy. The narrative systematically dissolves all the initially imposed distances and boundaries.

The story tells of two women, one of modest birth called throughout the novel only Marguérite and one of aristocratic lineage, Mme de la Tour, both of whom from a necessity born of scandal have fled into exile far from French society and their own blood relations. Mme de la Tour fled with her beloved husband from the family who had spurned her choice of a less than aristocratic *gentilhomme*. On the other end of the social spectrum, Marguérite, from a simple Breton family, had been abandoned by an aristocratic lover despite her pregnancy. In both cases, the scandal stems from social conventions based on lineage and birthright that interfere with, indeed preclude conjugal and familial love or accord. The tension in French society between such dominant social conventions and the growing importance of domestic life and sentiments is separated into contrasting geographic sites and worlds. The exotic Mauritius in this way becomes the site of a new kind of domestic world.

The exile of these women is articulated from the outset in spaces that signify at the same time both estrangement and all-encompassing enclosures. Leaving Europe behind and a husband who soon died trying to provide for them, Mme de la Tour seeks "un petit coin de terre" where she and her one possession, a woman slave from Madagascar, might cultivate enough to live on.[21] Mme de la Tour seeks out a place even more remote and removed from the already scarce population of the island. Thus, she leaves the city of Port-Louis and moves from the "île presque déserte" to an even more remote site where she hopes to find an "asile caché" and where she can "s'y retirer comme dans un nid".[22] Her desire to "se réfugier," to "take refuge, to withdraw," is complemented by the appearance of Marguérite already settled at the deserted site and by their progressively concerted joint attempt to raise their children. Terms abound that signify enclosure: "enclos," "retraites charmantes," "retraites paisibles."[23] The description of these women, their children born on the island (Paul and Virginie), and their faithful servants who establish intimacy also among themselves with their marriage, draws numerous protective enclosures around the domain of their cabins, their land, and their reciprocal emotional attachments.

In contrast to the lineage of blood relations which both at the beginning and at the end of the novel reaches from France as far as Mauritius to differentiate between social and economic classes and privileges, causing disruption and ultimately disintegration of the family entity, the two households share everything. They become one unit in which can be discerned no differentiation, no spatial, temporal, or emotional distance. Marguérite and Mme de la Tour are united by the same needs and almost identical misfortunes, calling each other "les doux noms d'amie, de compagne, de sœur; elles n'avaient qu'une volonté, qu'un intérêt, qu'une table. Tout entre elles était en commun."[24] In cabins which are contiguous, each woman owning a slave married to the slave of the other, their parcels of land like their homes are not just touching, they are cultivated each for the other; they dissolve into one.[25]

The narrator recounts the dissolution not just of territorial and property boundaries but of all barriers. In constant focus, this new domestic intimacy is carried over from mothers onto the relations between them and their children, and between Paul and Virginie. Like brother and sister, they are fed at the same breast, each woman nursing her own and the child of the other mother: "Elles prenaient plaisir à les mettre ensemble dans le même bain, et à les coucher dans le même berceau. Souvent elles les changeaient de lait."[26] More and less than siblings, these two children, like twins, like lovers, occupy the same cradle, the same bed, the same small enclosure of the bath, the same daily and hourly space: "La nuit même ne pouvait les séparer; elle les surprenait souvent couchés dans le même berceau, joue contre joue, poitrine contre poitrine, les mains passées mutuellement autour de leurs cous, et endormis dans les bras l'un de l'autre."[27]

Incest in a sense is not a threat since the children are not blood related; yet their physical and emotional closeness is informed by the appellations of brother and sister early on: "Lorsqu'ils surent parler, les premiers noms qu'ils apprirent à se donner furent ceux de frère et de sœur."[28] These terms are only partially metaphorical. The intimate proximity of their everyday lives lacks only genetic ties and is reinforced by the insistence everywhere on the absence of distance or separating boundaries. Sibling incest here is both avoided and consistently intimated. Their latent romantic attachment is prevented from developing into a fully sexual rapport only by the death of Virginie in the latter part of the novel, but their relation serves the purpose of signaling an affirmative, desirable, if unresolved ambiguous link among romantic love, conjugal relations and domestic intimacy.[29]

The concrete proximity within the quotidian creates the love that binds individuals to each other in contrast to the ties of blood relations alone which remain in this novel abstract and distant geographically as well as sentimentally. Here as elsewhere in the eighteenth century the model of close family sentiment and attachment is articulated, as we saw above in the passage from Rousseau, in pictures of enduring continuous physical, emotional, temporal, and spatial proximity. As Virginie says, "Tout ce qui a été élevé ensemble s'aime."[30]

Thus, lineage and blood relations are persistently trumped by, and rerouted through, those ties that become intimate in the experience and shared sentiment of living in close domestic proximity. Multiple terms work to minimize any space, physical and/or sentimental, separating the members of this utopian clan and in particular Paul and Virginie. Lack of distance and separation in terms such as "attachement" abound: "Rien en effet n'était comparable à l'attachement qu'ils se témoignaient déjà."[31] As the old man observed the two children one day taking refuge from the rain: "Ces deux têtes charmantes renfermées sous ce jupon bouffant me rappelèrent les enfants de Léda enclos dans la même coquille."[32]

So overdetermined is the emphasis on intimacy in this domestic vision that everything distant takes on negative value, particularly anything coming from Europe. Thus, Mme de la Tour à propos of a nasty letter from her aunt in Paris: "Le malheur ne m'est venu que de loin; le bonheur est autour de moi."[33] Within these delineated spaces, even the children's education underscores a rejection of distant past and far away events in favor of local, present intimacy repeated endlessly in the replication of everyday ritual:

> Ils ne s'inquiétaient pas de ce qui s'était passé dans des temps reculés et loin d'eux, leur curiosité ne s'étendait pas au-delà de cette montagne. Ils croyaient que le monde finissait où finissait leur île; et ils n'imaginaient rien d'aimable où ils n'étaient pas.[34]

Indeed, the temporal dimension of Paul and Virginie's childhood is basically transformed into a repetition of their daily life pattern in which each day and activity resembles or is identical to the next: "Chaque jour était pour ces familles un jour de bonheur et de paix."[35] The experience of close sibling and parental relations where there are no differences coincides with this insistence throughout the first part of the story on similarity and resemblance between daily recurring activities. One of the rare uses of the narrator's first-person "I" comes as the old man recounts the meals he shared with them: "Combien de fois, à l'ombre de ces rochers, ai-je partagé vos repas champêtres. . . ?"[36] Even the seasons resemble each other from year to year as they form the background for activities that in their recurrence suspend movement and time:

> Dans la saison pluvieuse ils passaient le jour tous ensemble dans la case, maîtres et serviteurs, occupés à faire des nattes d'herbes et des paniers de bambou. On voyait rangés dans le plus grand ordre aux parois de la muraille des râteaux, des haches, des bêches; et auprès de ces instruments de l'agriculture les productions qui en étaient les fruits, des sacs de riz, des gerbes de blé, et des régimes de bananes. . . .[37]

The rain outside helps focus this picture of intimate family life within the confines of their modest cabin as in a genre scene, while the description of the tools positioned along the walls with the fruits of their labor arranges these objects almost as would a still life painting. Whether it be the storms of the season or the stories told to the children of robbers and shipwrecks, the often hostile outside world repeatedly frames this little familial utopian society within the safety of its own company and walls: "La nuit venue, ils soupaient à la lueur d'une lampe; ensuite Mme de la Tour ou Marguérite racontait quelques histoires de voyageurs égarés la nuit dans les bois de l'Europe infestés de voleurs, ou le naufrage de quelque vaisseau jeté par la tempête sur les rochers d'une île déserte."[38]

Stories of lost travelers, European thieves and violent shipwrecks surround the family like a cocoon, separating fictions of lost souls, adventure and danger from the eventless everyday of home until a real ship erupts into the plot, wrecking the tranquility as well as the unity of the family, and breaking up the family picture. Before this catastrophic event, which begins with Virginie's taking the ship to France and meeting her aunt in Paris to claim her birthright and rightful place within the family lineage—before the shipwreck that ruins all hope of Virginie's reaching again the sacred boundaries of home—the plot languishes. The insistent present and local symmetry of everyday domestic repetition and stasis have allowed, in effect, no interruption, little action, no event.[39] The family tableau remains intact as a fixed unity unto itself due in great part to the narrative which, particularly in this first section of the novel, functions to undermine its own generic linear tendencies.

The first-person narrative of the *vieillard*, as discussed earlier, functions most often in the capacity of a first-person but disappears into the voice of a spectator or witness—a witness to family unity, a necessary spectator to their story, to their family pictures. Earlier in the century, such an external first-person voice is often found in the preface to novels such as Marivaux's *La Vie de Marianne*. This "I" of the Preface refers to one who found Marianne's "authentic" manuscript and delivered it to an editor; or, in the case of Montesquieu's *Lettres persanes*, the preface presents the first-person voice of a neighbor who lived for years next to the two Persians and who introduces their letters through his role as mere mediating translator. The *vieillard* of *Paul et Virginie* is a neighbor as well who in the second part of the story plays a larger though not really personal role. He recounts, witnesses, and will even share in the family sorrow, attempting, without success, to help Paul overcome the loss of Virginie with the wisdom of a hermit. So the first-person "I" of earlier eighteenth-century novels, possibly an editor or translator outside the story, here takes up that external first-person perspective within the story itself. And whereas Montesquieu's Persians, Marivaux's Marianne, and Rousseau's characters in *La Nouvelle Heloïse* tell their story in first-person epistolary or memoir discourse, the first-person narrator's role in Bernardin de Saint-Pierre's novel is clearly relegated to an exclusively external perspective where it is undermined by other priorities.

An assertion of the "I" point of view would be disruptive, would make too much of an exception in a narrative attempting to create a tableau of domestic unity. First-person discourse is thus limited to conversations among the four major characters, conversations with each other. We can listen in on these conversations in the novel as the members of this family recount their sentiments and thoughts to one another. But this kind of interrelation takes place most frequently in third person-narration. In effect, the mention of Virginie in this novel occurs most often in a context in which Paul is invoked and vice versa. Mention of either one of the children or of the mothers always immediately contextualizes that person in relation to at least one of the three others and often to all four. Such interrelations of one person with another take place without necessarily using the labels of "mother," "daughter," "son," etc., but function throughout just like the familial labels that by definition always invoke more than one family member. "Mother," for instance, is a relational term since it signifies more than a woman in a particular role. The term "mother" always of necessity implies the child; "brother" necessarily invokes a sibling, etc. The first part of the novel that sets up this family community weaves a domestic intimacy out of just such continued criss-crossing references. To tell a story as "I" has become too lonely, too disconnected from the domestic picture.

This is precisely the dilemma of Mistress Henley in the novel *Lettres de Mistress Henley publiées par une amie*, written at the end of the century in 1784 at about the same time as *Paul et Virginie*.[40] In Isabelle de Charrière's celebrated novel, a woman recounts her personal story in first-person letters written to a friend. The subject of these letters and of her emotional turmoil involves the very question of whether she can, whether she wants to, integrate herself as wife and mother into the family into which she has recently married. The narrator recounts her life story and present difficulties to a friend— it could have been to her diary, to the reader, but to no one with whom she lives her life. Mistress Henley is most unhappy as this outlying "I" who cannot find her own individual place within the family. Letters provide her a place where she can give vent to her personal sentiments and thus where she defines an individual if isolated identity. This text is indeed an excellent example in epistolary fiction of the ability of the letter writer to "render an account of one's own present situation" (Montesquieu, *Lettres persanes*, "Préface," 43). And clearly in this novel, letters have themselves become the only place for her to achieve such self-expression and definition.

Written laments to a friend about her unhappiness focus on the ways she has been expected to assimilate into the household of her husband, his daughter from a previous and now deceased wife, and his servants. The desire to become part of this family is from the outset mitigated by frustration at not being able to lay claim to a domestic role that allows her an identity of her own. And with these failures of successful integration comes a contrasting desire not to fit into the family structure that would incorporate her entirely or, it seems, not at all. Her letters constitute an outpost where such conflicting sentiments can be articulated, where the desire to be appreciated is accompanied by resistance to her husband and the family group which would assimilate and appropriate her.

Mistress Henley tells throughout her letters of countless episodes in which her reserved, highly rational and rather dismissive though kind husband neither understands nor appreciates her sentiments, her character, her ideas. These conflicting aims of assimilating into versus existing outside the family structure continue throughout five of the six letters. Yet in the novel's last letter, Mistress Henley announces the end of this special kind of correspondence. "Après celle-ci [letter] je n'en veux plus écrire du même genre."[41] The epistolary "I" remains separate and separately defined, which is, of course, the very problem. For the continuation of this personalized subject perspective in writing acts as an impediment to the assimilation of Mistress Henley into domestic life. Seen from the exigencies of the family picture, Mistress Henley understands the necessity precisely of renouncing her first-person perspective in favor of joining for better and for worse the greater domestic entity.

The shift to a more integrated family role is prepared, indeed, already performed, in the sentence that describes what will now transpire: "Un billet vous apprendra de loin en loin que *votre amie* vit encore jusqu'à ce qu'elle ne vive plus" (my emphasis).[42] This is Mistress Henley's announcement that she will from now on assimilate, fade, into the family unit. In the reference to herself now as "votre amie" ["your friend"], she has already become a third-person, "amie." And though we never do get a family picture, the integration of Mistress Henley into the domestic scene takes place definitively through this repudiation of a first-person writing "I." This first-person narrative is being subsumed under a new kind of relationship to the domestic community.

Mistress Henley intends to fit into her name, her surname, her husband's family name, which is tellingly the only proper name used throughout. On such a note of renunciation, the novel ends. "Dans un an, dans deux ans, vous apprendrez, je l'espère, que je suis raisonnable et heureuse, ou que je ne suis plus."[43] Either she survives as part of the picture she will now join, or she will no longer exist. This allusion to her possible real death includes a somewhat happier alternative; yet in either case, whether she dies a literal death or whether the death is that of her individuated perspective, Mistress Henley ceases to exist as the "I" of her letters.

The nineteenth century tended to move away from use of first-person perspective. For various reasons, a shift takes place to a third-person narrative voice in most novels, from Georges Sand to Balzac, Stendhal, Flaubert, Hugo, Zola, etc. One possible reason for this shift becomes apparent at the end of the eighteenth century in such a seminal novel as that of Bernardin de Saint Pierre in which the first-person point of view is relegated through a displacement to the margins as a spectator of the domestic picture; or in a related scenario, as in the case of Mistress Henley, the story involves precisely the drama of renouncing a first-person perspective in favor of a domestic unit. In both these eighteenth-century novels, a first-person narrator assumes a transitional role, one in the process of shifting into a third-person narrator.

The emphasis everywhere apparent in the text of *Paul et Virginie* on pictures of domestic intimacy is thus projected onto narrative perspective and descriptive strategies of spatial as well as temporal distancing and proximity. From the first pages of the novel, descriptions of nature play a considerable role in this formation of family pictures. As mentioned earlier, the exotic Indian ocean and the mountains, wind, and forests of the Ile de France form natural barriers that enclose these intimate households. But trees, clearings, even bird nests participate in lending shape to spaces that inform and replicate the maternal and sibling enclosures of intimacy. Nature in this novel is introduced as wild and virgin in pointed contrast to European formalized cultivation at the same time that nature operates as the domesticated and domesticating frames of the family picture.[44] We are told, for instance, that Paul upon reaching adolescence learned to cultivate their land, transforming their "vaste enclos" into an "amphithéâtre de verdure," but without straying from nature's order: "Mais en assujettissant ces végétaux à son plan, il ne s'était pas écarté de celui de la nature. . . ."[45] What is this nature that is identical to its domesticated and artful cultivation?

Such domestication is visible, moreover, in the names with which this community endows each site in nature where they shared some regular activity. In their "vast enclosure," or "bassin," "Rien n'était plus agréable que les noms donnés à la plupart des retraites charmantes de ce labyrinthe."[46] A particular rock, or clearing, "un cercle d'orangers, de bananiers et de jameroses plantés autour d'une pelouse, au milieu duquel Virginie et Paul allaient quelquefois danser se nommait LA CONCORDE."[47] The most prized site is endowed with a name: "Mais de tout ce que renfermait cette enceinte rien n'était plus agréable que ce qu'on appelait LE REPOS DE VIRGINIE."[48] And within these special enclosures—clearing, circle, lawn—situated already within the larger enclosure of the island, two fruits, coconuts, gifts to Paul and Virginie, were planted and soon grew into trees, trees which like the persons of this intimate world, "Déjà [ils] entrelaçaient leurs palmes. . . ."[49] The ultimate proximity and intimacy between the mothers, between mothers and their children and their servants, between brother and sister is framed again by the tableaux of nature that accompany this text both in the multiple verbal descriptions as well as in the proliferation of illustrations, of actual pictures that frame the family from the very early editions of this novel.

It is thus not surprising that just about every edition of *Paul et Virginie* has been accompanied by pictorial illustrations.[50] Says Jean Adhémar of these illustrations: "Les illustrateurs, donc attirés comme le public par cet exotisme et ces vives couleurs, ont bien souvent su rendre le ton du roman; leurs images, plus encore que le texte, ont nourri les imaginations au XIXième siècle. . . ."[51] Whether these illustrations capture the tone of the novel better than the text itself is a moot question. As can be seen in the illustrations included here, these graphic depictions constitute an additional domestic frame in that they reinforce and duplicate the already pictorial moments of domestic intimacy frozen in time in the narrative. Within these pictures, the profusion of nature's flora functions consistently to frame the picture of intimacy. With the exception of its first appearance as part of the third edition of Bernardin Saint-Pierre's *Etudes de la Nature* in 1788, the novel has included engravings, which often like the luxurious Curmer edition of 1838 were carefully supervised by the author himself.[52]

Genre scenes, images of common domestic life, are dominant in these illustrations.[53] These scenes tend to show the children Paul and Virginie enfolded in each other's arms in the enclosures of cradle, bath, and the arms of their mothers; in most all these illustrations, the children are also held within the frames of a highly stylized and exotic flora and fauna. These floral borders that edge the illustrations seem to hold these families within their embrace. The principal characteristic of this pictorial nature is the climbing, the intertwining of branches, flowers, and vines that not only frame the scene but also grow into the picture where they function visually to interlace, to entwine, one person or group, one cabin, with another. This is a nature both domestic and wild in its intertwining that at moments breaks into the frame and invades the pictures.

Thus the island, while often the scene of utopian experiment in the eighteenth century as in the *Ile des esclaves* of Marivaux or much earlier in the model *Utopia* of Thomas Moore, plays a different and in a way more significant role in Bernardin de Saint-Pierre's novel. The spatial enclosure of the island that provides protection and distance from the conventions of European society, while similar to other utopias, has a particular resonance within this text. The island replicates itself and is replicated ad infinitum throughout the novel in its capacity of spatial, physical, and sentimental closure and enclosure that shapes the text into its myriad pictures of domestic intimacy.

In this *mise en abîme,* this imbrication of frames and enclosures that holds the world still, any event that erupts into such pictures is bound to be catastrophic. The violent storm and ship that breaks upon the rocky shores of the island bring a tragic end to this family. Yet the choice of a shipwreck defines not just the climactic event of the story; it defines the nature of event itself as being catastrophic to the intimacy, to the stability and immobility of these domestic pictures. The ship comes from afar, from Europe, and constitutes the liaison with the world that this other world is protecting against. As the ship crashes into the island reef, it crashes into that world, disrupting it forever.

The death of each one of the family members after the shipwreck taking the life of Virginie is consecrated in the tombs that are often represented in illustrations accompanying the text:

> On a mis auprès de Virginie, aux pieds des mêmes roseaux, son ami Paul, et autour d'eux leurs tendres mères et leurs fidèles serviteurs. On n'a point élevé de marbres sur leurs humbles tertres, ni gravé d'inscriptions à leurs vertus; mais leur mémoire est restée ineffaçable dans le cœur de ceux qu'ils ont obligés.[54]

The term "tertre" with reference to a funereal site denotes "une élévation de terre recouvrant une sépulture."[55] In other words, no gravestone was erected according to the text to identify the family members. Yet in the illustrations for several editions, including that of 1806 and the Curmer edition of 1838, we see rectangular if blank stones leaning against the mounds of earth that hold the family sepultures. The tomb stones that frame nothing but their own stasis, their own stillness, are lying within a sheltering forest glade and framed as well as attached to each other by the vines and tropical abundance that proliferate in all the illustrations. The stasis of death resembles the repetition of their daily domestic intimacy in life created in pictures of this calm, immobile society in which nothing happens. The tombs that are represented in text and in illustration occupy the same position as previously these family members occupied in life, residing each one next to the other, and now without any event able to interrupt, to intrude on, this ultimate enclosure.

Death is familiar to the photograph. It is, as Barthes says, a witness to "ce qui a été," to the "what has been."[56] Indeed, photography brings back, represents each time one looks, what is now no longer: "cette chose un peu terrible qu'il y a dans toute photographie: le retour du mort."[57] In *Paul et Virginie,* the reader looks at each tableau, each family picture that repeats what is missing—a domestic intimacy that is already no more—and yet in terms of a social and historical referent, an intimacy which perhaps has not yet been. The tableaux both written and pictorial in this novel give evidence of an intimacy situated in an exotic world that evokes and introduces a new private domestic sphere. Before the age of photography, yet already *foreshadowing* this very modern age, before the "explosion of the private into the public" the reality of domestic intimacy depends on the bounded shape of tableaux that must of necessity be framed by the outsider, the viewer, the reading public.[58] (fig.1-5)

Figure 1. Mme de la Tour shown pregnant with Virginie and becoming close friends with Marguérite and her newborn, Paul. Looking on is Mme de la Tour's slave Marie, from Bernardin de Saint-Pierre, *Paul et Virginie*, Léon Curmer, 1838.

Figure 2. The childhood of Paul and Virginie, pictured here with their mothers and their servants Marie and Domingue, from Bernardin de Saint-Pierre, *Paul et Virginie*, Léon Curmer, 1838.

26 PAUL

avaient donné le jour. Déjà leurs mères parlaient de leur mariage, sur leurs berceaux; et cette perspective de félicité conjugale, dont elles charmaient leurs propres peines, finissait bien souvent par les faire pleurer : l'une se rappelant que ses maux étaient venus d'avoir négligé l'hymen, et l'autre d'en avoir subi les lois; l'une de s'être élevée au-dessus de sa condition, et l'autre d'en être descendue : mais elles se consolaient, en pensant qu'un jour leurs enfants, plus heureux, jouiraient à la fois, loin des cruels préjugés de l'Europe, des plaisirs de l'amour et du bonheur de l'égalité.

Figure 3. Marguérite and Mme de la Tour bathing their children together, from Bernardin de Saint-Pierre, *Paul et Virginie*, Léon Curmer, 1838.

ET VIRGINIE. 27

Rien, en effet, n'était comparable à l'attachement qu'ils se témoignaient déjà. Si Paul venait à se plaindre, on lui montrait Virginie; à sa vue, il souriait et s'apaisait. Si Virginie souffrait, on en était averti par les cris de Paul; mais cette aimable fille dissimulait aussitôt son mal, pour qu'il ne souffrît pas de sa douleur. Je n'arrivais point de fois ici, que je ne les visse tous deux tout nus, suivant la coutume du pays, pouvant à peine marcher, se tenant ensemble par les mains et sous les bras,

Figure 4. The close attachment between Paul and Virginie, from Bernardin de Saint-Pierre, *Paul et Virginie*, Léon Curmer, 1838.

Figure 5. Paul and Virginie lost together one day in the forest, from Bernardin de Saint-Pierre, *Paul et Virginie*, Léon Curmer, 1838.

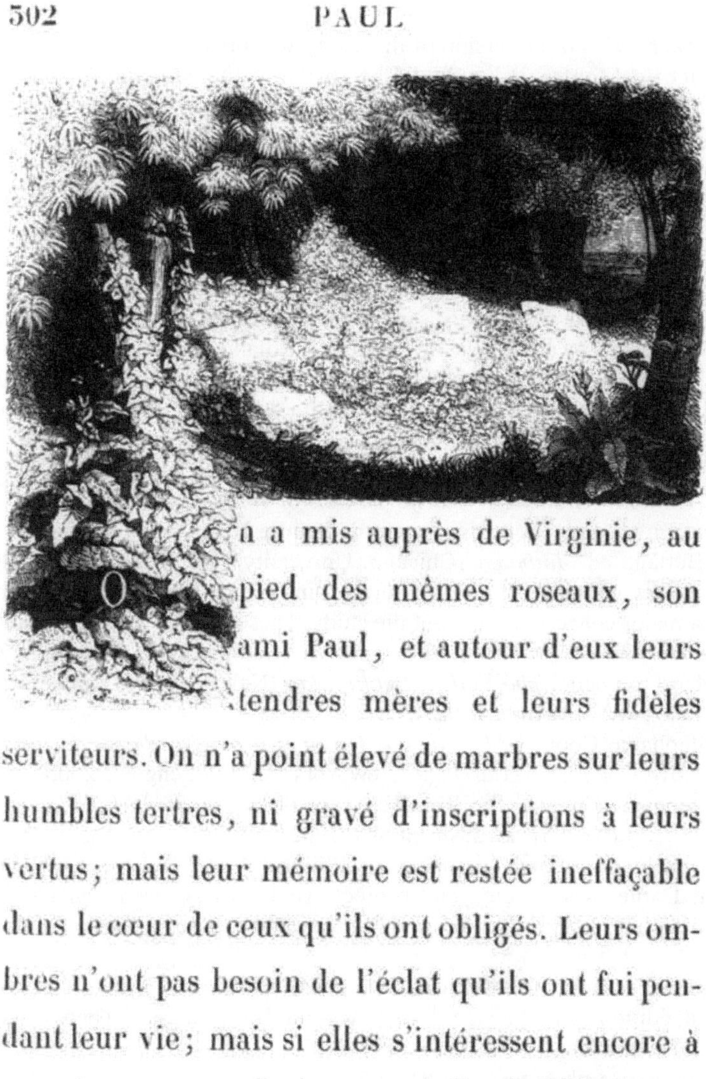

502 PAUL

On a mis auprès de Virginie, au pied des mêmes roseaux, son ami Paul, et autour d'eux leurs tendres mères et leurs fidèles serviteurs. On n'a point élevé de marbres sur leurs humbles tertres, ni gravé d'inscriptions à leurs vertus; mais leur mémoire est restée ineffaçable dans le cœur de ceux qu'ils ont obligés. Leurs ombres n'ont pas besoin de l'éclat qu'ils ont fui pendant leur vie; mais si elles s'intéressent encore à ce qui se passe sur la terre, sans doute elles aiment à errer sous les toits de chaume qu'habite la vertu laborieuse; à consoler la pauvreté mécontente de

Figure 6. The tombs of Paul and Virginie surrounded by those of their mothers and their servants, from Bernardin de Saint-Pierre, *Paul et Virginie*, Léon Curmer, 1838.

NOTES

An earlier and shorter version of this essay was presented at the 2006 *ASECS* conference in Montreal. I would like to thank the *Maison Suger*: *Centre international de recherche, d'acceuil et de coopération pour chercheurs étrangers de haut niveau de la Fondation Maison des Sciences Humaines,* where my residence during two months in 2006 allowed me to complete the writing and necessary research in Paris at the Bibliothèque nationale de France.

1. Roland Barthes, *La Chambe Claire*, Cahiers du Cinéma (Paris: Gallimard, 1980), 54–55. "The first man who saw the first photograph must have thought it was a painting: same framing, same perspective. Photography has been, and is still, tormented by the ghost of Painting." Roland Barthes, *Camera Lucida*, trans. Richard Howard (New York: Hill and Wang, 1981), 30.

2. This essay derives from my larger book-length project to be entitled *Domestic Intimacy: Snapshots of the Family in Eighteenth-Century France.*

3. I refer to such studies as those which address "intimacy" in their title such as Anthony Giddens's *Transformation of Intimacy: Sexuality, Love and Eroticism in Modern Societies* (Stanford: Stanford University Press, 1992), or Lauren Berlant, ed. *Intimacy* (Chicago: University of Chicago Press, 2000), as well as books which while not featuring "intimacy" in the title nevertheless make it a major concern throughout the study. These include Zygmunt Bauman's *Liquid Love: On the Frailty of Human Bonds* (Cambridge: Polity Press, 2003), and Richard Sennett's *The Fall of Public Man* (New York and London: Alfred Knopf, 1977; W.W. Norton, 1992).

4. Stephanie Coontz, *Marriage, a History: From Obedience to Intimacy* , or *How Love Conquered Marriage* (New York: Viking Penguin, 2005).

5. Stephanie Coontz, *The Way We Never Were: American Families and the Nostalgia Trap* (New York: Basic Books, 1992).

6. This includes such historians as Phillipe Ariès, Georges Duby, Roger Chartier, Daniel Roche, etc., and projects such as *Histoire de la vie privée*, sous la direction de Philippe Ariès et Georges Duby, 5 vols. (Paris: Seuil, 1985, 1999).

7. Jean-Jacques Rousseau, *Emile*, eds. Bernard Gagnebin et Marcel Raymond, édition de La Pléiade (Paris: Gallimard, 1969), 262. "There is no more charming picture than that of the family. . . ."

8. The entire passage reads as follows:

> Il n'y a point de tableau plus charmant que celui de la famille, mais un seul trait manqué défigure tous les autres. Si la mère a trop peu de santé pour être nourrice, le père aura trop d'affaires pour être précepteur. Les enfans, éloignés, dispersés dans des pensions, dans des couvens, dans des collèges, porteront ailleurs l'amour de la maison paternelle, ou pour mieux dire, ils y rapporteront l'habitude de n'être attachés à rien. Les frères et les soeurs se connoitront à peine. Quand tous seront

> rassemblés en cérémonie, ils pourront être fort polis entre eux; ils se traitteront en étrangers. Sitôt qu'il n' y a plus d'intimité entre les parens, sitôt que la société de la famille ne fait plus la douceur de la vie, il faut bien recourir aux mauvaises mœurs pour y suppléer. Où est l'homme assés stupide pour ne pas voir la chaîne de tout cela. (262)

[There is no more charming tableau than that of the family, but only one missed feature disfigures all the rest. If the mother has too poor a health to nurse, the father will be too busy to be their tutor. The children, far away, dispersed in pensions, convents, schools, will always bring elsewhere the love of the paternal home, or to say it better, they will develop the habit of being attached to nothing. Brothers and sisters will scarcely know each other. When assembled all together for special events, they might be very polite to each other; they will treat each other as strangers. As soon as there is no longer any intimacy between the parents, as soon as the society of the family no longer constitutes the pleasures of life, there is necessary recourse to bad habits as compensation. Where is the man stupid enough not to see the chain linking all that] (my translation).

9. Peter Szondi, "Tableau and Coup de Théâtre : On the Social Psychology of Diderot's Bourgeois Tragedy," *New Literary History* 11.2 (1980): 323–43.

10. Denis Diderot, *Œuvres esthétiques*, ed. Paul Vernière (Paris: Garnier, 1965), 91, my emphasis and my translation:

> If the mother of Iphigenia behaved for one moment as the Queen of Argos and wife of the Greek commanding general, she would seem to me the least worthy of creatures. True dignity, that which strikes me, which astounds me, is *the tableau of maternal love* in all its truth.

For Jay Caplan, "The tableau in Diderot is a sort of fetishistic snapshot in which the transitoriness of the real world is magically transformed into an ideal fixity" *Framed Narratives: Diderot's Genealogy of the Beholder* [Minneapolis: University of Minnesota Press, 1985], 18). As I am developing it here, the *tableau* is linked most specifically to the fixity of the ideal family.

11. "Snapshots of the Family: Picture Perfect," *Esthetics of Intimacy/ Esthétiques de l'intime,* L'Esprit Créateur, eds. Elizabeth Arnould-Bloomfield and Suzanne R. Pucci , 44.1 (2004): 68–82.

12. Lawrence Stone, *Family, Sex and Marriage in England, 1500–1800* (London: Penguin, 1977 [1979, 1982]), 69; 149.

13. Raffaella Sarti, *Europe at Home: Family and Material Culture, 1500–1800*, trans. Allan Cameron (New Haven: Yale University Press, 2002), 3; *Vita de Casa, Abitare, mangiare, vestire nell'Europa* (Rome, Italy: Laterza & Figli, 1999).

14. Philippe Ariès, *L'Enfant et la vie familiale sous l'Ancien Régime* (Paris: Plon, 1960), 239; *Centuries of Childhood: A Social History of Family Life*, trans. Robert Baldick (New York: Random House, 1962), 356 (my emphasis):

> In the world of sentiments and values, the family didn't count previously as much as lineage. . . . Now, [lineage] is very different from the concept of family such as we have seen it develop in the iconography of the 16th and 17th centuries. [Lineage] extended to the ties of blood without regard to the emotions engendered by cohabitation and intimacy. The line was never gathered together within a common space, around a single courtyard. In contrast, the sentiment of family is tied to the house, to the government of the house, to life in the house.

(This last important sentence of the quote was left out in Baldick's English translation of the French text. The translation and emphases are mine.)

15. Richard Sennett, *The Conscience of the Eye: The Design and Social Life of Cities* (New York: Knopf, 1990; Norton, 1992), 21.

16. Jacques-Henri-Bernardin de Saint-Pierre, *Paul et Virginie* in *Etudes de la Nature,* (Paris: P.F. Didot le jeune, 1788), 4:1–227, BN (Res. P. R. 641). The popularity of this text was enormous. As Robert Mauzi relates: "*Paul et Virginie* fut après *La Nouvelle Héloïse* et *Les Liaisons dangereuses*, le dernier triomphe de la littérature romanesque du XVIIIième siècle" (*Paul et Virginie,* Bernardin de Saint-Pierre, éd. établie par Robert Mauzi [Paris: Garnier-Flammarion, 1966; Flammarion, 1992], 9). [*Paul & Virgine* was after the *Nouvelle Héloïse* and *Les Liaisons dangereuses* the last triumph of novelistic literature of the eighteenth century.] The number of editions of this novel from the time of its initial publication is quite astounding. And the accompanying prints that were published almost from the beginning (and that I will discuss) continued to proliferate in most editions as well as to appear independently without the text of the novel. See Paul Toinet (*Paul et Virginie: Répertoire bibliographique et iconographique* [Paris: G.-P. Maisonneuve et Larose, 1963]), who enumerates the more than 500 editions of the novel in 170 years from the time of its appearance until 1963; his book also traces the diverse sets of prints that appeared separately from the novel.

17. At first, the novel *Paul et Virginie* took the form of volume 4 of *Etudes de la nature*, published in 1788. The first time this novel appeared separately was in 1789. Speaking of the novel's astounding success, P. Toinet proclaims:

> Car, ce succès, il fut d'emblée foudroyant et universel: si l'édition originale, enrobée dans les *Etudes de la Nature* est de 1788, la première édition séparée hors de France—peu importe qu'elle ait été une contrefaçon—est de la même année; si la première édition séparée en France est de 1789, elle est de la même année en Angleterre, de 1791 en Italie, de 1794 en Allemagne, de 1798 en Espagne. Les treize années du XVIIIième siècle finissant voient apparaître 56 éditions dont 36 du texte français et 20 de traductions; encore ne faut-il pas oublier les adaptations théâtrales et les gravures ou suites de gravures séparées. (*Paul et Virginie: Répertoire bibliographique et iconographique,* 2)

[For, this success was from the start amazing and universal: if the original edition, enclosed in *Studies of Nature* is from 1788, the first separate edition outside of France—no matter that it had been pirated—is from the same year; if the first separate edition in France dates from 1789, it dates from the same year in England, from 1791 in Italy, from 1794 in Germany, from 1798 in Spain. The last thirteen years of the eighteenth century saw 56 editions 36 of which in French and twenty translations; moreover, the theatrical adaptations and the engravings or separate sets of engravings should not be forgotten.]

18. "On the eastern side of the mountain which rises behind Port-Louis of the Ile de France, one can see on a piece of once cultivated land the ruins of two small cabins." (*Paul et Virginie,* préface, commentaires, notes par Jacques Van Den Heuvel [Paris: Le Livre de pôche, 1984], 155). All quotations from the novel will be taken from the above illustrated edition which derives from Bernardin de Saint-Pierre, *Paul et Virginie* (Paris: L. Curmer, 1838, 1938. BN [Y2 758, Y2 186, etc.]). All English translations of *Paul et Virginie* are my own.

19. *Paul et Virginie,* 155–57. "At the entrance to this basin. . . ., echoes from the mountain incessantly repeat the sound of winds that stir the neighboring forests, and the fracas of waves that break far away on the reefs; but at the foot itself of the cabins one can no longer hear any noise at all; one can only see the surrounding huge rocks steep as walls."

20. Montesquieu, *Lettres persanes,* texte présenté et commentaires par Laurent Versini (Paris: Imprimerie Nationale, 1986), 43. "D'ailleurs, ces sortes de romans réussissent ordinairement, parce que l'on rend compte soi-même de sa situation actuelle; ce qui fait plus sentir les passions que tous les récits qu'on en pourrait faire." ["Besides, these kinds of novels usually succeed because one renders an account oneself of one's present situation; which makes one feel more passions than all the stories one can tell about them" (my translation).]

21. *Paul et Virginie,* 160, "a little piece of land."

22. *Paul et Virginie,* 160, "almost deserted island"; "hidden sanctuary"; "withdraw there as in a nest"; "to take refuge there."

23. *Paul et Virginie,* 193, "enclosures"; 194, "charming retreats"; 199, "peaceful retreats."

24. *Paul et Virginie,* 167, 169, "the sweet names of friend, of companion, of sister; they had only one will, one interest, one table. Everything between them was in common."

25. *Paul et Virginie,* 166. Throughout the novel, we hear of the faithful slaves Marie (belonging to Mme de la Tour) and Domingue (belonging to Marguérite) who marry and whose union consolidates and extends the formation of intimacy among parents and their children to those who live with them (166). Though they are introduced as slaves, the two mothers are shown to love and depend on them as well as to dress with a simplicity like that of slaves (167). In other places, such as the description of the disposition of their tombs where they lie next to their mistresses who lie close to their children Paul and Virginie, the term "slave" is exchanged for "fidèles serviteurs" ["faithful servants"].

26. *Paul et Virginie,* 169, "They took pleasure in washing them in the same bath and in putting them to sleep in the same cradle. Often they switched and nursed the other's child."

27. *Paul et Virginie,* 170, "Even night couldn't separate them; it surprised them often sleeping in the same cradle, cheek against cheek, breast against breast, their hands mutually clasped around each other's neck, asleep in each other's arms."

28. *Paul et Virginie*, 170, "When they learned how to talk, the first names they learned to call each other were those of brother and sister."

29. Reference to their eventual marriage and "félicité conjugale" ["conjugal felicity"] is made by the two mothers from the children's infancy (169). See my essay, "The Nature of Sibling Incest and Domestic Intimacy in Diderot's *Le Fils naturel*," *Eighteenth-Century Studies* 30. 3 (1997): 271–87, in which I discuss the many eighteenth-century representations of near sibling incest as a formulation of a new kind of close family attachment. One hypothesis for its repetition is that intimate emotional experience was identified primarily until then as romantic love. As a result, this new familial close sentiment is articulated through those already known conventions of amorous sentiment. Sibling intimacy/incest functions as in the rhetorical figure of catachresis. This is a figure, like the *leg* of a table, a term borrowed to signify what doesn't (yet) have its own name. This essay along with my article mentioned above, "Snapshots of the Family: Picture Perfect," shows a similar process of framing in both theater and narrative. As my book-length study on domestic intimacy will reveal, the tableau with its frames and focus on simultaneous grouping/delimiting of family within the same space functions in painting, theater, and as shown throughout my article here, in narratives of the later eighteenth century.

30. *Paul et Virginie,* 216, "All who have been raised together love each other."

31. *Paul et Virgine,* 170, "Nothing in effect was comparable to the attachment they already showed each other."

32. *Paul et Virginie*, 171, "Those two charming heads enfolded in these bouffant skirts reminded me of the children of Leda enclosed in the same shell."

33. *Paul et Virginie*, 177–78, "Misfortune has come to me only from afar; happiness is right next to me."

34. *Paul et Virginie*, 171, "They were unconcerned by what happened in distant times and far away from them; their curiosity didn't extend beyond this mountain. They believed that the world finished with their island; they imagined that nothing could be agreeable there where they weren't."

35. *Paul et Viginie,* 191, "Every day was for these families a day of happiness and peace."

36. *Paul et Virgine,* 201, "How many times in the shadow of these rocks did I share your rustic meals . . . ?"

37. *Paul et Virginie,* 201, "In the rainy season, they spent the day all together in the cabin, masters and servants, occupied in making braids of herbs and baskets of bamboo. One could see arranged in the greatest order on the wall

rakes, hatchets, hoes; and next to these instruments of agriculture the fruits of their labors, sacks of rice, sheaves of wheat, bunches of bananas."

38. *Paul et Virginie,* 201, "Come night, they supped by the light of a lamp; then Mme de la Tour or Marguérite recounted some stories of travelers lost in the night in the woods of Europe infested with robbers, or the shipwreck of some ship thrown by the storm against the rocks of a deserted island."

39. See Robert Mauzi (*Paul et Virginie,* ed. R. Mauzi [Paris: Garnier-Flammarion 1992], Préface, 20) who comments on the lack of event in the first part of the novel:

> "Toute une première partie du récit est consacrée à l'évocation du monde détruit, monde immobile où le temps ne coule pas, où il ne se passe rien. Les anecdotes, les épisodes n'introduisent aucune action." ["The whole first part of the narrative is devoted to evoking a world destroyed, immobile where time doesn't pass, where nothing happens."]

40. Isabelle de Charrière, *Lettres de Mistress Henley publiées par son amie,* ed. Joan Hinde Stewart and Philip Stewart (New York: MLA Publications, 1993). Translation of this text will be from the English edition: *Letters of Mistress Henley published by her friend,* trans. Philip Stewart and Jean Vaché (New York: MLA, 1993).

41. *Lettres de Mistress Henley,* 38, "After this one, I do not wish to write any more [letters] in this style," 36.

42. *Lettres de Mistress Henley,* 38, "A note will inform you from time to time that *your friend* still lives until she no longer does," 36 (my emphasis).

43. *Lettres de Mistress Henley,* 45, "In a year, in two years, you will learn, I trust, that I am reasonable and contented, or that I am no longer," 42.

44. See Jean-Michel Racault's excellent essay ("Système de la toponymie et organization de l'espace Romanesque dans *Paul et Virginie,*" *SVEC* 242 [1986]: 377–415), which centers on a study of names of places, particularly proper names given by the characters throughout the novel. Racault points out the named open and closed spaces that dominate and that create spatial distances on the one hand and close intimate spaces on the other (387); he doesn't, however, relate the production of both these kinds of spaces to the intimacy of family pictures.

45. *Paul et Virginie,* 193, "vast enclosure"; "amphitheater of vegetation"; "But in subjecting this vegetation to his plan, he hadn't strayed from that of nature."

46. *Paul et Virginie,* 194, "Nothing was more agreeable than the names given to most of the charming retreats in this labyrinth."

47. *Paul et Virginie,* 196, "A circle of orange and banana trees and wild roses planted around a lawn, in the middle of which Virginia and Paul went sometimes to dance was named HARMONY" (author's emphasis).

48. *Paul et Virginie,* 196–97, "But of everything this enclosure encircled, nothing was more agreeable than what was called VIRGINIE'S HAVEN" (author's emphasis).

49. *Paul et Virginie,* 197, "Already [they] intertwined their fronds."

50. Toinet, *Paul et Virginie: Répertoire*, 3.

51. Toinet, *Paul et Virginie: Répertoire*, 134, "The illustrators, thus attracted as was the public by this exoticism and bright color, often knew how to render the tone of the novel; their images, even more than the text, nourished the imagination of the nineteenth century" (my translation). The edition of 1789, which is the first edition of *Paul et Virginie* standing alone, is also the first illustrated edition done by Moreau le Jeune and J. Vernet. The first suite of illustrations separate from the book were done by Shall in 1791 (Toinet, 135–36).

52. Bernardin de Saint-Pierre, *Paul et Virginie (*Paris: L. Curmer, 1838, 1938), BN(Y2 758, Y2 186, etc.). A "Table des noms des dessinateurs et des gravures" lists 315 drawings and engravings in this edition. All illustrations at the end of this essay are taken from the 1838 Curmer edition.

53. See Richard Rand, "Love, Domesticity, and the Evolution of Genre Painting in Eighteenth-Century France," in *Intimate Encounters: Love and Domesticity in Eighteenth-Century France,* ed. Richard Rand (Hanover, NH: Hood Museum of Art, Dartmouth College; Princeton: Princeton University Press, 1997), 4. "The increasingly narrow meaning of the term was in large measure a response to the new seriousness with which scenes of everyday life were regarded in the second half of the century." According to Rand, the growing importance of the term "scenes of life" distinguished genre from landscape and still life. "In 1791, Quatremère de Quincy would define genre painting as a 'scene of common or domestic life.'"

54. *Paul et Virginie,* 309, "Next to Virginie, at the foot of the same reeds, her friend Paul was placed, and around them their tender mothers and their faithful servants. No marble was raised on their humble graves, neither were inscriptions on their virtue engraved there; but their memory has remained indelible in the hearts of those they helped."

55. *Le Petit Robert,* "elevation of earth covering a grave" (my translation).

56. Barthes, *La Chambre Claire,* 97; *Camera Lucida* ["what has been"] trans. Howard, 85.

57. Barthes, *La Chambre Claire,* 9; *Camera Lucida* ["this rather terrible thing in all photography: the return of the dead"] trans. Howard, 23.

58. Barthes, *Camera Lucida* trans. Howard, 98.

Images of Barbaric Spain in Eighteenth-Century British Travel Writing

ANA HONTANILLA

Europe has traditionally been studied as a political, economic and cultural unity that historically developed in connection with the ideas of Christianity, civilization, and empire. After the New World was "discovered," Europe's imperial and civilizing mission was no longer contained within its western boundaries but also occurred within an expanded sense of geography. This is to say that the status of civilized and civilizing Europe was not defined solely from within its geographical limits but also in contrast to its colonial world. Much of the work of describing the discovery, interpreting the exploration, and articulating the connection of the newly-found territories to the motherland in Europe was done through the writings of explorers, ambassadors, soldiers, adventurers, and missionaries. The recovery and analysis of these various kinds of travelers' narratives about foreign and exotic places where they went and lived have brought a new perspective to our understanding of the historical development of the imperialized world.[1]

Throughout the fifteenth and sixteenth centuries, Spanish explorers and conquistadors in America predominantly produced the colonial discourse. During the eighteenth and nineteenth centuries, the imperial discourse was for the most part a British and French production, not only in America but in Africa, Asia, and even Europe as well. In the process of examining the rise of British and French imperialism during the eighteenth century, it is crucial to acknowledge these nations' reaction to the 'Other' beyond their shores. But it is also of prime importance to investigate how they constructed the European 'other.' As Katherine Turner has argued, post-colonial studies that assume an undifferentiated European imperial center during the eighteenth and nineteenth centuries presuppose homogeneity among European nations, which in practice did not exist.[2] Enlightened notions of civilization and culture served to delineate the division between civil society and barbarism, between Europe and the rest of the world. However, the Enlightenment served to demarcate new ideological borders that not only operated in the overseas colonial world but also within the boundaries of Europe itself. Therefore, the initially uniform picture of imperial Europe or the assumption that modern Europeans defined themselves as a single people breaks down in the context of describing the literature of inter-European tourism, most visibly, perhaps, in British travel writing concerning Spain.

In the following essay, I limit my exploration of British travel writing to accounts regarding Spain during the eighteenth century. I study how these narratives produced and disseminated a perception of Spain as an uncivilized and barbaric country, ruling it out as a member of "Enlightened Europe." Spaniards' religious practices were generally tied in with ancient paganism and therefore the population was commonly perceived by foreign visitors as pagan and primitive. In addition, the Spanish Inquisition provided the travelers with a dangerous, threatening ethos that promptly resolved any doubts of whether or not Spain was an enlightened civilized country. The seemingly outdated commercial and political institutions of Spain also contributed, in the minds of British explorers, to the formation of a nearly enslaved population in need of liberation from the tyranny of governmental tax control and its subsequent state of poverty. The local inhabitants too closely resembled the Indian or African *savages* and exhibited a state of personal and cultural corruption, as well as an economic dependence only potentially alleviated by adopting British institutions.

A postcolonial analysis of British inter-European travel accounts shows how differential forms of religious, political, scientific, economic, and social progress in eighteenth-century Spain highlighted discrepancies in the stage of the same civilizing path that all European societies should attain.[3] As the idea of civilization emphasized the movement towards political, economic, and scientific progress, demanding an accumulation of spiritual, technical, economic, and political values in the evolution of a nation, not all countries, and particularly not the Iberian countries, matched up with eighteenth-century British standards of commercial and political reforms. Therefore, the location of Spain as a civilized country became extremely problematic.

By referring to Spain's dramatic change of status from imperial power to a culturally-regressive and economically-dependent land, I do not intend to insinuate that these eighteenth-century British travel narratives contemplate Spain in the same way as travel literature later constructs India, Africa, or South America. A key distinction upon which I base my study of the representation of eighteenth-century Spain is the difference between the notions of imperialism and colonialism. Colonialism refers to a specific dynamic of strictly political systems of rule by one group over another when the dominant one claims the right to exercise exclusive sovereignty over the second and to shape its destiny. Imperialism, by contrast, is a much broader term that may emphasize various aspects of international relationships. Imperialism could refer to the power or purposefulness of colonial rulers. It may also refer to less obvious and direct kinds of control or domination by one people or country over others. Pertinent to this study is the less formal sort of domination through cultural or economic imperialism, which has always been closely related with economic underdevelopment and is currently associated with the notion of globalization.

David Spurr has suggested that the imperial-colonial discourse is neither a restricted collection of texts nor a monolithic operative system. Instead, the imperial discourse is a series of discursive strategies, each tailored to precise historical conditions, yet having in common certain elements. Spurr draws his examples of analysis primarily from British, French, and American fiction and non-fiction writings regarding India, Africa, and Latin America. A few of the rhetorical devices he studies in Western imperial discourse are the persistent surveillance from a hierarchically superior eye; the right of appropriation and exploitation of native wealth; demonstrations of moral superiority, which involves a continual debasement of local customs; and the perception of the 'Other' as the site for cruelty, torture, and death.[4]

Treading on the unstable ground of the discourse of imperialism, my discussion identifies the gestures and signs of this discourse in eighteenth-century British travel accounts. My study aims to explore how British travel writings *produced* the image of a decadent and backward Spanish Empire for British readers at a particular moment of Britain's expansionist trajectory. I study how signifying practices of the travel narrative encoded and legitimated aspirations of economic and commercial expansion while elaborating England's differentiated conceptions of its own imperial mission in relation to the falling empire that Spain was imagined to represent. In the pages that follow, a close reading of British travel narratives reveals how

Spain, while being excluded from modern notions of civilization and Enlightenment, was also perceived as a market for British commercial and economic advantage, fostering an image of dependency closely linked with economic and political decline. I show how Spain was transformed, from a harmful imperial model into a real or imaginary site for cultural degradation and economic exploitation.

* * *

From 1660 to 1780, the history of traveling in Europe was marked by the emergence of a new model for traveling, that of the Grand Tour. The purpose of the Grand Tour was to complete the education of young men of the ruling classes by exposing them to the treasured artifacts and ennobling society of the Continent. It typically occurred after formal studies at Oxford or Cambridge University and lasted from one to five years. The Tour was a social ritual intended to prepare these young men to assume the leadership positions already assigned to them at home. The first outcome intended was an understanding of the classical tradition. As England's overseas empire expanded, well-to-do Englishmen observed parallels between their nation and the Roman Empire. In 1776, Samuel Johnson indicated that "A man who has not been in Italy, is always conscious of an inferiority. . . . The grand object of travelling is to see the shores of the Mediterranean. On those shores were the four great Empires of the world; the Assyrian, the Persian, the Grecian, and the Roman—All our religion, almost all our law, almost all our arts, almost all that sets us above savages, has come to us from the shores of the Mediterranean."[5] England, therefore, looked back to the different Mediterranean empires as a measure of its own. Italy clearly represented a way to learn the roots of civic republicanism and was the locus to find corresponding similarities between imperial Rome and the new British expansionism. Spain, by contrast, was the still living, if failing, rival empire that embodied principles England had once conflictingly emulated and since the Reformation continuously sought to displace.[6] Another objective of the Grand Tour was for travelers to mingle with the social and political elite of the different countries visited. The unified form of identification for those in equal positions across courts created a link between the higher classes in Britain with their counterparts on the Continent, imposing upon the Grand Tourist a sense that he ought to share the common responsibility for the welfare of Europe as a whole.[7]

However, as Jeremy Black correctly notes, Spain was not often visited on the Grand Tour. According to Black, the reasons were Spain's inaccessibility and the inconveniences and discomfort that were part of travel in the country at the beginning of the eighteenth century.[8] John Lynch also points out that, during the eighteenth century, the rivalries between the two countries were still alive as Spain continued to occupy the role of England's political rival and also its most dreaded religious enemy. In this way "informal war or real war [. . .] rather than peace was the normal condition of Anglo-Spanish relations."[9] Therefore, travelers from England undertook the journey to Spain with a completely different reasoning. Visitors to Spain were not young aristocratic tourists completing their education and becoming acquainted with their enlightened Continental counterparts. Instead, travelers in Spain were merchants, appointed officials joining diplomats in times of peace, and soldiers posted in strategic locations in times of war. They typically entered Spain via Lisbon, Perpignan, or Gibraltar and tried to enjoy their experience in Spain the best they could, since no peer would take an assignment in the country because of its undesirability. As late as 1783, an anonymous Polite Traveler corroborated the unpopularity of Spain for the foreign tourist in the following way:

> Nothing but necessity can induce a man to travel in Spain: he must be an idiot, if he make the tour of this country from mere curiosity, unless he has a design to publish memoirs of the extravagancies of human nature. In that case, he cannot do better, for he will every where find pride, baseness, poverty, ignorance, bigotry, superstition, and ridiculous ceremonies. This is a faithful abstract of the character of the Spaniards.[10]

Spain did not offer any of the amenities a polite traveler would expect in a civilized country other than extravagant material that will guarantee the writing of fascinating and unique memoirs. The Polite Traveler summarized the preconceptions of what a barbaric society should be like and inexorably found features in Spain to fit this model. Among the soldiers, merchants, and diplomats stationed in Spain, many were widely traveled and knowledgeable. Some of them were interested in adventure, and through their readings of travel narratives they had probably familiarized themselves with the habits of peoples who were considered uncivilized by British standards. Therefore, an excellent way for these soldiers and diplomats to take advantage of their placement in Spain was to record the peculiarities of this mysterious country that ultimately helped them to enter the competitive publishing world.

One of those designated officers forced to stay in Spain was John Armstrong, an engineer who in the beginning of 1738 was stationed in the Balearic Island of Minorca, located in the Mediterranean Sea. There he wrote, most probably between 1740 and 1742, *The History of the Island of Minorca*. The first edition of the book was published in 1752 and a second edition in 1782 under the new title *Letters from Minorca*. Armstrong's *History of Minorca* includes seventeen letters and a map, and is addressed to Richard Offarrel, the Colonel and Brigadier General in command of the administration of the island during the years of his placement. In his account, Armstrong attempted to describe the situation of the island; its dimensions; the government, taxes and number of inhabitants; trade and manufactures; and the customs and manners of the Minorquins. He indicated that he became proficient in Spanish in order to learn, "from the best Authorities" and from "any authentick Materials" that came into his possession, the civil history, constitution, produce, antiquities, cities, buildings, and life style of the country.[11] His design was to offer a topographical description of Minorca with the minerals found there, to present a natural history of the island by collecting and classifying fossils, and to inquire after the animal and vegetal kingdoms. Armstrong indicated that he embraced his work not as a naturalist or as a botanist, but instead as an economist who wished to learn the use the natives made of their natural resources. Indeed, Armstrong's attitude with regard to civil life in Minorca is based on his perception of the government's economic policy, production system, and foreign exchange. As he explains: "I have ever thought it a useful and entertaining Study, to enquire into the Trade and Manufactures of a Country, and to note down whatever was excellent or defective in either; from hence a valuable Lesson is learned, of imitating the one, or avoiding the other."[12]

However, soon after he started his inquiries in Minorca, Armstrong promptly discovered with astonishment and concern that there was neither industry nor foreign trade on the island, and that the poor locals "trifled away their Time in childish Amusements, and neglected almost every Advantage of their Climate and Situation, and were contented to import a thousand Necessaries, and twice the Number of Superfluities, from foreign Countries, for which they paid ready Money."[13] Twenty years later, Christopher Hervey, brother of William Hervey, British Ambassador to Spain from 1758 to 1761, similarly declared that "all the necessaries of life are very dear in Spain, which must be the case of a country that abounds in gold, and nothing else. . . . Gold alone can never make a nation plentiful, on the contrary, that very gold must go to other kingdoms to buy what the indolence of the inhabitants denies them in their native country."[14]

Armstrong observed that people in Minorca continued with their old constitution, and as a consequence, they paid a multitude of taxes and impositions to the government. The inhabitants also had large sums extorted from them for the support of their clergy, "as they are excessively burthensome and oppressive." Hence the population of all districts ran into great debts, which were continually increasing. But the poverty of the island was by no means compensated by the wealth and affluence of individuals, as he indicated was the case of Genoa. On the contrary, individuals from every class were loaded with numerous taxes that fell heavily on their industry, and therefore "all traffick with them, [is] as our merchants do with the Savages, exchanging Beads, Pictures, and Baubles, for every Thing of Value they have in the World."[15] Armstrong, then, easily concluded that native Minorquins wasted their lives away in indolence under the oppression of the Church and government with no regard for the opportunities and natural resources offered by the island.

Armstrong's words regarding the exchange system of Spain with Great Britain brings to mind seventeenth-and eighteenth-century trade lists of British ships trading with Africa in which there appeared, along with salt, brandy, cloth, and iron, items such as rings, false pearls, bugles (small glass beads), looking-glasses, little bells, false crystals, shells, bright rags, glass buttons, small brass trumpets, amulets, and arm rings.[16] Going further back in time, Armstrong observations were significantly similar to Christopher Columbus' remarks regarding the reactions of the Caribbean natives when the Spaniards negotiated with them. As Tzvetan Todorov explains in *The Conquest of America*, for Christopher Columbus the natives did not understand the value of things since "all they have they give for any trifle we offer them, so that they take in exchange pieces of crockery and fragments of glass goblets. . . . Even bits of broken cask-hoops they took in exchange for whatever they had, like beasts."[17] Ironically, in Armstrong's account, the Spaniards appeared as the naïve *savage*, ignorant of the value of their own wealth and giving it away for trifles of little worth. Furthermore, Armstrong proudly explained that the English presence on the island was already having an impact on the natives' taste and customs. Many of the inhabitants naturally desired to imitate the British and consequently learned how to multiply their needs and wants to the point of falling "into a Way of Luxury and Extravagance, perfectly new to them."[18] The position of the Englishmen in the island is therefore translated into terms of superiority, with the native Minorquins dwelling in an inferior evolutionary state of the economic progress and England feeding into their ignorance and commercial dependency.

In *Culture and Society*, Raymond Williams studied how in the eighteenth century the idea of culture initially arose as a response to emergent commercialism and to the new political and social developments of the time. Culture emphasized the role of intellectual and moral thought as a court of appeals to be set over the processes of practical judgments. It offered itself as an impartial view that regarded economic wellbeing or material happiness as the touchstone of moral evaluation.[19] Against this intellectual and moral utilitarian background, even if Spain had been and still was considered an imperial power, the country was clearly perceived and judged as the antithesis of the enlightened commercial society. In a world where commerce made man gentle and trade eventually would make war archaic, Spain was declared to be in an earlier stage of cultural development. The Spanish Monarchy was seemingly committed to old-fashioned notions of tax control, which in Armstrong's view had caused the Spaniards to fall into a decadent indolence and had prevented them from dedicating themselves to civilizing commercial ventures. Notwithstanding that the Spaniards exhibited a number of habits that Armstrong regarded to be at the opposite pole of civilization, there was no consequent need to instruct them in the ways of commercial civil society. On the contrary, Spain's economic dependence on England was a point of great satisfaction for John Armstrong.

Despite of Armstrong's triumphant observations, the Reverend Edward Clarke, chaplain to Ambassadors Benjamin Keene and George William Hervey from 1758 to 1761 in Madrid, worried that the balance of commercial exchange between Spain and Great Britain during the decade of the 1760s was declining. This descent was due to, among other factors, the increasingly tough French and Dutch competition over Spanish markets.[20] In his *Letters Concerning the Spanish Nation,* Clarke recalled with nostalgia the reign of the last Habsburg Charles II, a time when Spanish commercial exchange was unquestionably under England's control and the country took off "at least two thirds of all the produce of SPAIN, which made our manufactures an easy purchase to the Spaniards, who nevertheless paid us a very considerable balance in bullion."[21] Unfortunately, since the accession of the French House of Bourbon to the Spanish monarchy, France shared a "great part of the gold and silver of the Spanish West-Indies, in return for her silk, her linen, and other manufactures introduced into Spain."[22] For Clarke, Spain was the locus of fierce international competition for access to Spanish and Spanish American consumers. The struggle for influence in the Spanish Empire and for control over its traffic signaled one of the major themes of the eighteenth-century's antagonistic Anglo-French relations since the War of Spanish Succession (1702–1713).[23]

Clarke recognized that in spite of fierce French competition, England's trade with Spain was still considerably extensive. This commercial exchange mainly consisted of English manufactures for raw materials from the

Peninsula and the Spanish-American colonies. Since the seventeenth century, peninsular and colonial consumer demand was satisfied by the importation of foreign goods, a situation that led to a steady increase in Spain's foreign debt. During the eighteenth century, the intellectual elite in the service of King Charles III recognized that the increase in consumption of foreign goods was detrimental to the already declining national industries and that the increasing international debt also caused a large financial loss for the Spanish state.[24] In Clarke's view, this situation was maintained due to the regressive Spanish domestic industry, generally behind not only because of state's regulations and the natives' indolence but also because of the "oppressive spirit of that superstition which reigns there, under the mask of religion."[25]

Regarding the Spaniards' religious practices, most travel accounts offered puzzled representations of popular customs and rituals of the Spanish Catholic Church. At the beginning of the century, in his *Trip to Spain*, an anonymous officer of the British Royal Navy observed that "it is their Custom to [...] recommend themselves to the Relicks they carry about them, by which they hope to Prosper."[26] He also indicated that "at the Corner of every Street, and, indeed, in almost every Stable, there's a Statue of our Blessed Virgin, with a pair of Beads in her hand, Dressed after the Country Fashion, with a Wax-Candle or Lamp burning before her; for these people are most Abominably Superstitious, or rather Abominably Religious."[27] French travel writer Marie-Catherine d'Aulnoy (1650–1705), whose work became popular in English translation, suggested that indeed Spaniards "pay an excessive Devotion to the Blessed Virgin, and put an extraordinary confidence in her; there's hardly any Man that does not wear a *Scapular*, or some embroidered *Image*, that hath toucht some of those that are held to be *miraculous*."[28] John Armstrong declared that "there is no Degree of Superstition into which these People have not been led," since after all the religious practices of the Spaniards do not differ a great deal from those of the Moors.[29] He continued explaining that Spaniards "pay large contributions towards praying the Souls out of Purgatory; and many Times a devout Person gives a Hog, a Sheep, and even a Fowl, to be sold by Auction, and the Money applied to this pious Use."[30] On holidays, the religious establishment entertained the populace with spectacles and comedies "making all the publick Diversions subservient to their Interests."[31] Therefore, the Priests and Friars lived well in Minorca; they ate and drank wine freely from the best harvests of the island, indulged themselves in conversation with the opposite sex, and had free access to all private houses.[32]

In his *Travels through Spain and Portugal*, Major William Dalrymple, stationed at a garrison at Gibraltar in 1774, observed that "Religious bigotry and superstition still prevail here." To prove his statement, he ironically explained the fetishistic procedure followed by the court doctors to cure the prince's illness in the following way: "The Prince of Asturias' son being extremely ill, and given over by the physicians, the bones of a saint were sent for from Alcala, and brought in procession to the palace, to work his cure; but unfortunately, the saint was not in humour to perform the miracle, and the poor infant died."[33] Major Dalymple also commented on simple gestures or signs and indicated that "not a woman gets into a coach to go a hundred yards, nor a postillion on his horse, without crossing themselves; even the tops of tavern bills, and the directions of letters, are marked with crosses."[34] Alexander Jardine, another English officer who was stationed and had traveled in Spain, also indicated in his *Letters from Barbary, France, Spain, and Portugal* that "nothing but the rapacity of the Catholic church, and the great influence of their clergy over the minds of this superstitious people, could make the tithes and religious contributions so productive as they are found to be in Spain."[35]

Edward Clarke proposed a detailed explanation regarding the origin of the religious practices observed in Spain. In his view, the Spanish Church remained pure, uncorrupted, and *unpapist* until the eighth century. Before that time, there was no image-worship, no prayers addressed to saints or angels, no purgatory, no sacraments, no transubstantiation, no auricular confession, and no adoration of the host. However, from the eighth century onward, perhaps due to the influence of the Muslim traditions after the invasion of the Peninsula in 711, "paganism artfully, and by almost imperceptible insinuations, gradually stole in, wearing that mask or vizor, which we now call Popery. Whatever triumphs Christianity may formerly have gained over the Gentile worship; Paganism, in all catholic countries, is now entirely revenged; she triumphed in her turn from the moment she established herself in the form of Popery."[36] Therefore the absurdity of Catholic practices was beyond measure, ridiculous; and more specifically, in all Roman Catholic, apostolic, *papist*, temples everything was pagan. In this sense, Clarke noted a number of striking resemblances between Catholic practices and paganism. For instance, he highlighted the similarities between the use of the ancient *Thura* and the modern incense; the *aspergillum lavacrum* and the holy water; the ancient *votiva tabulae* and the modern votive limbs; the Spanish *Flagelantes* and the old self-lashing priests of Jove; the mass for the dead and the parentation of the heathens; and little pictures or images of the Virgin Mary and the talismans of the ancients.[37]

The religious and profane aspects of the luxurious Roman Catholic ceremonies were the reasons that led seventeenth-century Protestant European travelers to connect the objects of Catholic worship with those of the African fetish adoration, as Pieter de Marees commented in his *Description and Historical Account of the Gold Kingdom of Guinea*, published in 1602.[38] Later, in 1705 Dutch merchant Willem Bosman in *A New Accurate Description of the Coast of Guinea* suggested that if "it was possible to convert the Negroes to the Christian religion, the Roman Catholics would succeed better than we should, because they already agree in several particulars, especially in their ridiculous ceremonies."[39] Bosman provided the concept of the fetish that intellectuals of the eighteenth century used in the elaboration of enlightened theories about primitive religions. In 1757, French philosopher Charles de Brosses coined the word "fetishism" and in his work introduced the term to the French intellectual community.[40]

Eighteenth-century British travelers in Spain echoed Dutch merchants' perceptions and associations between Catholic and African religious rituals. The Protestant British enlightened mind, in contrast to Catholic beliefs, was felt to have risen above superstitions and ancient fetish worshiping and it could not regard with indulgence a branch of Christianity imagined to be still mesmerized by the magical powers of crosses, images, and amulets. As enlightened observers, these travelers in Spain were rational male Europeans passing across the English Channel and not only going to a distant place but also regressing back in time to an archaic zone populated by dervishes and fetish worshipers. These traditions derived from an Institution that for centuries Europeans had unquestionably considered not only the direct heir of Christendom, but also the foundation of early Europe's imperial mission. In these travel narratives, however, Catholic beliefs came to be regarded as pagan practices. The debasement of Catholicism, as it became associated with the habits of distant peoples who were considered to be primitive by European standards, by association made Spain fit into the model of the barbarian at an early stage of cultural development. This degradation of Catholicism excluded Spain from enlightened notions of Christianity, while it confirmed the cultural distance of Protestant societies and established their moral superiority.

But even more than Catholics' pagan practices, the Spanish Inquisition continually provided material for condemnation of a special nature. The Holy Tribunal embodied the monstrous, the inexplicable, and the obscure part of human nature and primal societies. It offered the vaguely threatening and dangerous drama of the most morbid, primitive, cruel instincts. Travelers in Spain were probably well-versed in the treatises concerned with the history of the Inquisition, such as the Reverend M.A. Baker's *The*

History of the Inquisition, as It Subsists in the Kingdoms of Spain, Portugal, Sc.[41] In all these works, the Inquisition was represented as "the most bloody, as well as the most terrible Court, that ever was invented [and] Wherever it exerts its Authority, Men forget to search the Scriptures, or to gain a rational Belief in CHRIST."[42] In addition to the historical accounts, a number of more of less fictionalized personal narratives of Englishmen who adventured in Spain and had to endure the cruel prosecution of the Inquisition were also available.

In 1724, Isaac Martin published his *Tryal and Sufferings* in which he relates his experience with the Holy Tribunal during the years he lived and worked as a merchant in Malaga on the southern coast of Spain. Martin blamed a local Irishman who turned him into the Inquisition under the accusation of publicly speaking against the Catholic religion.[43] In 1756 and later in 1770, John Marchant also published his *Bloody Tribunal: or, an Antidote Against Popery*, a review of the "horrid Cruelties of the Inquisition." The book contained a description of "the most dreadful and exquisite Tortures" inflicted upon several people who have "unhappily fallen into the Hands of those Tyrants." The book was designed for the use and instruction of all Protestant families to secure them against the attacks of the papacy that were threatening Protestant liberties and religion.[44] *The Loyal Marthyrs: or the Bloody Inquisitor*, published in 1775, was an eight-page poem that narrates the story of a newly-married British couple who agreed to travel into foreign countries for their honeymoon. As soon as they entered Spain, both of them were seized by surprise, separated, examined, and charged with crimes they had never committed, tortured, convicted and condemned to be burnt alive by order of the Inquisition.[45] *The History of the Inquisition* published anonymously in Dublin 1798, besides providing an explanation of the historical evolution of the institution also included a short sentimental narrative by a French girl. The girl related how, when she was fifteen years of age, she was taken away from her family under false accusations of having committed a crime against religion. While under the Inquisition's custody, Maria found out that she had been set up to follow the luck of countless girls before her: she was forced to become the mistress of the General Inquisitor Don Francisco Torrejón if she wanted to remain alive.[46]

According to these stories Spaniards and on occasion foreigners residing in Spain appeared unprotected by the restraining constructs of a more advanced, free, tolerant, and enlightened constitution. The contrast with other European Nations seemed stark and absolute. In France and Germany, philosophers since the sixteenth century had advanced numerous arguments denouncing tyranny, prosecution, suppression of truth, the Inquisition, judicial torture, shedding of blood in the name of infallibility, and divine rights. In the seventeenth century, John Locke in England and Baruch Spinoza in the Netherlands elaborated the two principal traditions of religious toleration theories.[47] In Spain, however, no toleration theory had been developed and the Inquisition remained, for enlightened Europeans, as the most atrocious continuation of fanaticism. In his *Letters* Clarke understood that "there is an undoubted resemblance between a Spanish Inquisitor, and a Dioclesian, a Caled, or a Mustapha. . . . Such a tribunal, shocking as it is to humanity, has nothing but false political ends to plead in its excuse: And where nature and religion must be sacrificed, such a policy is only worthy of a Machiavel, a Ximenes, or an Emperor of Japan."[48] Although in practice the religious and political tolerance in northern Europe was far more complicated than the elaboration of theories and possible idealizations may suggest, upon the persistence of the Holy Tribunal, Clarke cannot help but say that "the tender mercies of the inquisition are cruel; and if this be the justice of a Christian country, let me be thrown among barbarians."[49]

Clarke also complained that the medieval Spanish blind zeal in matters of religion had destroyed many remains of classical antiquity and that in the eighteenth century this old fanaticism still continued under the direction of monks and inquisitors. Books were prohibited, torn, or burnt if they contained anything against the Catholic faith: "As they formerly thought the Bible would appear to more advantage, when the pagan poets were destroyed; so they are still of opinion, that popery will always appear best, when evidence of its imposture is suppressed."[50] But at least Clarke noticed some changes in the Spaniards' religious extremism. He merrily celebrated that in the last twelve years (since 1748?) no *Auto de fe* had taken place in Madrid. Nevertheless, he proceeded to minutely relate the circumstances of the last one performed at the Plaza Mayor in Madrid. A Jew, his wife, and their thirteen-year old daughter were all condemned to be burned alive. While the father and the mother were burning, the young girl was released by the inquisitors with the purpose of converting her by the power of their rhetoric, and the threat of immediately undergoing the same death as her parents. The child, however, rejected her cruel converters, and vaulted back in the fire, giving a shining example of the force of young piety, and heroic fortitude equal to that of the most unshaken martyr.[51]

The Inquisition and the *Autos de fe* perfectly justified expressions of outrage, in the view of the British travelers, while they also provided a macabre diversion. These chronicles expanded on the diabolical cruelties of the Spanish Inquisition with narratives significantly enlivened by exaggeration and unchecked fantasies. The continuation of the operations of the Inquisition, to the horror of other Europeans, lent renewed vigor to the old stereotype of the backwardness and cruelty of the Spanish character.

Spain and its still-effective Inquisition satisfied the traditional demand for someone to play the role of the uncivilized other within nearby countries. Hence the fascination with religious fanaticism, bloodthirsty inquisitors, and unjustified atrocities inflicted upon innocent victims. The persistence of barbarity within the boundaries of Europe became the object of interest and attraction, as it perhaps offered a cathartic image of enlightened Britain's own past. Madness, barbarism, cruelty, and torture: all seemed closer to the surface in Spain, offering a constant source of grief. But British travelers experienced this dark tragedy safely by virtue of the aesthetic mediation of their narratives, whose cathartic power increased with cultural distance.[52]

The Spanish people, then, were governed by barbaric institutions, similar to those of uncivilized contemporary and ancient societies, a situation that urgently required cultural, social, economic, and political redemption. Following this line of thought, John Armstrong discussed not only the economic assimilation of Minorca, which had been inevitably in place for a number of years already, but also a possible political integration of the island to the crown of Great Britain. On this matter, he regretted that in 1713 the Minorquins did not accept the opportunity to be integrated into the benevolent British system:

> And though these Islands have been at different times delivered up to the Pillage of some of the most consuming Tyrants that ever disgraced human Nature by seeming to be of the Species, the Minorquins fatally missed a favourable Opportunity of becoming Partakers of all the various Benefits of the mildest Constitution of Government upon Earth. For at the Time that the Treaty of Utrecht yielded their Country to Great-Britain, if they had made Application that they might for the future be governed according to our Laws, I make no doubt but their Request would have been readily complied with.[53]

Although in need of the new liberal British system that would procure for them freedom and affluence, the people of Minorca simply appeared stuck within the old dynamic of feudalism. In Armstrong's writing, there is no sense that different cultures evolve in a different way regarding their social and political order; rather, he set forth a single standard of economic and political organization to which all nations must aspire. For Armstrong, there was no better constitution of government than that of Great Britain, and common sense dictated its acceptance as such, regardless of different peoples' historical traditions or political evolution.

Likewise, Edward Clarke reinforced the powerful cultural myth of British political liberty when he stated the following:

> Let an Englishman go where he will, to Spain or Portugal, to France or Italy; let him travel over the whole globe, he will find no constitution comparable to that of GREAT BRITAIN. Here is no political engine, no bastile, no inquisition, to stifle in a moment every symptom of a free spirit rising either in church or state; no familiar, no alguazil to carry off each dangerous genius in arts or science, to those dark and bloody cells.[54]

Many other contemporary travel writers would undeniably have agreed with Clarke's remark that what he gained by writing about his experience during his post in Spain was to provide the reader with "a fresh proof of the happiness, which he enjoys in being born a Briton; of living in a country, where he possesses freedom of sentiment and of action, liberty of conscience, and security of property, under the most temperate climate, and the most duly poised government in the whole world."[55]

As the ideology of British commercial imperialism became progressively hegemonic, Spain and the notion of the Spanish Empire rapidly evolved as the paradigm of an archaic tyranny that had progressively yielded into an unrestricted expansionist power. In the sixteenth century the Spanish monarchy could be portrayed as the self-assured champion and exporter of Christian values, the secular arm of the papacy, and the sole guardian of political stability within Europe.[56] In the eighteenth century, however, the perception of the Spanish State and government shifted from that of universal Christian monarchy to oriental and barbarian despot.[57] Montesquieu summarized the role of Spain in the New World in the following terms: "To preserve America, [Spain] did what even despotic power itself does not attempt; she destroyed the inhabitants. To preserve her colony, she was obliged to keep it dependent even for its subsistence."[58] Armstrong, for his part, explained that under the tyrannical Spanish rule in Minorca "[People] have lived long under a hard Government, and have Spirits broke to Servitude, and Bodies inured to Labour. They are effectually subdued to a blind Obedience to those that are set over them, and seem cheerful and contended under Poverty and Oppression."[59] To Armstrong, the subjects of the Spanish monarchy have groaned under all forms of tyranny around the globe, and have been reduced to a state of slavery that has forever suffocated their ambitions for independence and domesticated their sprits into permanent submission. Spanish societies are therefore distant from the enlightened political model since "their ancient Freedom has been long lost, and the very Spirit of Liberty seems at present to have no Existence among them, and their Courage is vanished with it; as if an enslaved People were of Opinion, they had nothing left that was worth fighting for."[60]

The general anti-Spanish sentiment of the sixteenth and seventeenth centuries found new expression in the eighteenth century. Although it still preserved the factor of religious fanaticism of the Spaniards already present in the *black legend*, it added new political and commercial elements of judgment. The portrayal of Spain was empirically qualified by the country's demonstrated incapacity to partake in the values of the new hegemonic liberal humanism. As a consequence, Spain and its people were universally excluded from the idea of civilized Europe on grounds of commercial and political backwardness. In the eighteenth century, the civility of human societies was established by the nature of their economic and political organization. This categorization provided a hierarchy of political configurations in Europe while plotting these "evolving" institutions in the temporal dimension along a single line of development.

However, this notion that societies could be hierarchically classified according to their degree of political and economic advancement coincided with (and paradoxically, supported) the opinion that inherent ethical differences existed among peoples, and created intrinsic differences in character. Armstrong attributed the failure to pursue the advantageous prospect of joining the British crown to the decadence of the Spanish character, as if the inhabitants of the island became incapable of comprehending the value of political stability and freedom. Regarding the native temperament, Armstrong granted that the Minorquins demonstrated courage while they were engaged in continual wars with the Moors. Nevertheless, since the end of hostilities in 1492, he observed that, "what *Tacitus* says of the antient *Gauls*, *Gallos in Bellis floruisse, accepimus, mox segnities cum otio intravit, amissa vitute, pariter ac libertate,* may with equal Justice be applied to them: For as a long War trains an unwarlike Nation to Military Exploits, so a profound Peace, with a total Difuse of Arms, in Process of Time naturally dejects the Spirits of a People, and renders them supine and dastardly," to the point of sinking them "into shameful Degeneracy and Indolence."[61] Furthermore, Minorquins "seldom practice those Diversions and Exercises in which the more warlike People of Europe delight."[62] Besides establishing an obviously parallel between imperial Romans and the British on the one hand, and the ancient Gauls and the Minorquins on the other, what is striking in his opinions is his perception of the absolute dissoluteness and corrupt nature of the native Spaniards.

Minorquins are "naturally contentious" and "suspicious of one another"; they "have a watchful jealous eye"; the little they learn in schools "is soon lost again"; "sciences are . . . unknown" to them; and they "seldom make [social] entertainments."[63] Moreover, Spaniards are not great visitors, preferring the life of domestic quiet and retirement. Fortunately, Armstrong observed, this privacy is suitable to the economy they have to comply with for it is more agreeable to their passive disposition and natural taciturnity; and finally it enables the men to keep their wives under constant observation. Henry Swinburne went as far as to delineate the specific traits of the Spanish character:

> The listless indolence equally dear to the uncivilized savage, and to the degenerate slave of despotism, is no where more indulged than in Spain; thousands of men in all parts of the realm are seen to pass their whole day, wrapped up in a cloak, standing in rows against a wall, or dosing under a tree. In total want of every excitement to action, the springs of their intellectual faculties forget to play; their views grow confined within the wretched sphere of mere existence. . . . The *poor* Spaniard does not work, unless urged by irresistible want, because he perceives no advantage accrue from industry. As his food and raiment are purchased at a small expence, he spends no more time in labour, than is absolutely necessary for procuring the scanty provision his abstemiousness requires.[64]

According to David Spurr, in colonial discourse every personal weakness has its political counterpart. Uncivilized society, according to this logic, corresponds to the uncivilized mind and body. The qualities assigned to the individual savage such as dishonesty, suspicion, superstition, indolence, and lack of self-discipline are reflected more generally in societies characterized by corruption, tribalism, and the inability to govern themselves. In the same way, social or economic problems, undeveloped industry or trade, and unemployment come to be associated with individual filth and laziness.[65] The poverty of Spain, therefore, can be also traced to the indolence, cowardice, cruelty, and deceitfulness of the Spanish character, marking the individual as both cause and emblem of a more general degradation.

Perhaps due to this personal and general ruin, the Minorquins "neglected to take this salutary step" of becoming British at the beginning of the occupation. As a consequence of their native passivity, twenty years into British administration Armstrong judged it to be more convenient for the islanders to continue to be governed by their old laws without the slightest modification.[66] He adduced this because "their mean Natures are apt to be too much exalted by Prosperity and Power, which give them a Glimpse of greater Happiness than they are able to compass, and then they grow factious and malecontent."[67] Likewise, Christopher Hervey believed that Britain ought by no means to attempt to open the eyes of the Spaniards since their blindness was of too much service to England, not to wish them to continue in it. The balance of commerce, notwithstanding long wars, infinitely favored England, leading Hervey to conclude "I dare say they receive twice as many goods from us as we from them."[68] In the same way, Colonel Dalrymple believed that the Englishmen should let the Spaniards enjoy their apathy while Britons "live happily, and triumph in the felicity of being formed a native of that country, where literature and commerce is encouraged and improved by liberty."[69] Therefore, political intervention and ideological indoctrination depended on Britain's invested interests in the land or perhaps its widespread fears of resuscitating its dreaded centuries-old competitor.

* * *

On November 22, 1975, two days after the death of General Francisco Franco, the new head of State King Juan Carlos I addressed the nation for the first time in his new political role:

> The idea of Europe would be incomplete without a reference to the presence of the Spaniard and without a consideration of the activity of many of my predecessors. Europe should reckon with Spain, and we Spaniards are Europeans. It is present necessity that both sides understand this to be so and draw the consequences that derive therefrom.[70]

As Paul Preston has noted, it may seem surprising that the monarch of Spain had to emphasize the Continental character of a country whose geographical situation alone appears to qualify it unquestionably as part of Europe. However, most Europeans have often placed Spain beyond the pale of central European civilization due to the persistence of its backwards social, economic, and religious behavior; the vestiges of Moorish culture; and particular aspects of the country's landscape.

In Spain, since the second half of the eighteenth century, the argument over the advantage of adapting national institutions to those of the rest of Europe versus the benefits of progressive isolation has been the center of national political controversy. In the nineteenth century a number of prominent figures still emphasized the singularity of Spain's historical experience and geographical positioning from the rest of Europe. In the *Episodios Nacionales*, Benito Pérez Galdós, one of the most prominent literary figures of nineteenth-century Spain, projected the image of the country as "a *sui generis* political entity uncontaminated by Europe."[71] The historian Américo Castro also maintained that "the Spaniards live alongside Europe, but ultimately they were alien to it."[72] By contrast, for prominent nineteenth-century lawyer, writer, and politician Joaquín Costa, Europeanization provided the key to open the future of Spain, and José Ortega y Gasset contended that if Spain mainly consisted of an unresolved problem Europe was the answer to this dilemma.[73] The twentieth century, as Preston notes, saw the legendary exploitation by General Franco of the isolationist nationalist sentiment to protect his own position whenever international censure threatened to converge with domestic opposition to challenge his regime.[74]

Neither the start nor finish of what has been a long historical process, the eighteenth-century representations of Spain examined above document one particularly interesting moment in the evolution of Spain's centuries-old alienation from Europe. British travel writings regarding Spain exhibit a number of rhetorical characteristic that emphasized Spain's degradation and alienation against England's superiority. These travelers' privileged point of view offered them aesthetic pleasure as well as authority, conveying a sense of mastery over the unknown and over what was perceived as strange. The examination of Spain's territory, of economic resources, social life, and religious practices constructed through a cultural distance favored demonstrations of Britain's moral superiority and the expression of its right to appropriate and exploit the natives' wealth. Travel writers' continual debasement of local customs, and their perception of the "Other" as a site for cruelty, torture, and death, presented sufficiently morbid material to entertain their readers and also offered a justification for British righteousness, exploitation, and economic dominance. All of these perceptions further confirmed –and validated– Spain's supposed inferiority and isolation in regard to the rest of Europe.

NOTES

This article grew out of a presentation at the International Seminar on the Eighteenth Century ISECS "The Idea of Europe in the Eighteenth Century" in Genoa, Italy, October 2005. I would like to thank my colleagues and friends Jeff Curran, Stephanie O'Hara, Carmen Sotomayor, and Maria Paz Moreno for their help with the English version of this paper. Thanks to Will Derusha and Margaret Ewalt for providing invaluable help in earlier drafts. I thank Linda Zionkowski and the anonymous reviewers of *SECC* for their excellent comments and suggestions for revisions.

1. In the English-speaking academic world, the close reading championed especially by the new historicism and the practice of discourse analysis was aimed not at the individual productions of a single canonical author but at the production of a collective corpus of travel texts. This innovative approach has created a new body of knowledge about imperial-colonial discourse and its variations. *Orientalism* is the first major work of contemporary criticism to take travel writings as part of its analysis. Edward Said examines British travel literature as a body of work that produced what he terms 'Orientalism;' a concept that since 1978 has offered particular insight into the operations of colonial discourses and therefore of Western imperial domination of the 'East.' See Edward Said, *Orientalism* (New York: Pantheon Books, 1978) and Peter Hulme and Tim Young, eds., *The Cambridge Companion to Travel Writing* (Cambridge: Cambridge University Press, 2002), 8. Following Said's line of inquiry, Mary Louise Pratt's *Imperial Eyes* has become a model of how and for what purposes to analyze accounts of foreign or exotic places written by men from the Western or "developed world" who enjoy some kind of authority of speech. *Imperial Eyes* has provided an adaptable model for analyzing how "travel books by Europeans about non-European parts of the world went (and go) about creating the domestic subject of Euroimperialism." Pratt also emphasizes that scholars of European travel books regarding Europe have pointed out that many of the conventions and writing strategies associated in her book with imperial expansionism characterize travel writing about Europe as well. She suggests, then, that related dynamics of power and appropriation are likely to be found in European travel writing about Europe. Mary Louise Pratt, *Imperial Eyes: Travel Writing and Transculturation* (London: Routledge, 1992), 4, 10.

2. Turner also observes that while much of the period's literature of travel and exploration of exotic lands is self-consciously couched in the language of Enlightenment empiricism, that of European travel narratives gives way to less exclusive registers, both reflecting and encouraging the activities of increasing numbers of middle-class travelers in Europe. British travel writers converted their narratives of the European countries they visited not only into an accumulation of natural or ethnographical observations with occasional philosophical, political, and economic reflections, but also textualized the gender and class privileges they embodied. Katherine Turner, *British Travel Writers in*

Europe, 1750–1800: Authorship, Gender, and National Identity (Aldershot: Ashgate, 2001), 21.

3. Norbert Elias, *The Civilizing Process*, trans. Edmund Jephcott, 2 vols. (New York: Urizen, 1978), 1:5.

4. David Spurr, *The Rhetoric of Empire: Colonial Discourse in Journalism, Travel Writing, and Imperial Administration* (Durham: Duke University Press, 1993), 1–12.

5. James Boswell, *The Life of Samuel Johnson*, ed. George Birkback Hill, rev. L. F. Powell, 6 vols. (Oxford: Clarendon Press, 1934–50), 3:36.

6. Elizabethan expansionism adopted the Spaniards' logic for exploration and conquest, and made its initial claim to legitimacy in the name of the duty to convert the pagans to the faith. See Anthony Pagden, *Lords of All the World: Ideologies of Empire in Spain, Britain and France c.1500–c.1800* (New Haven: Yale University Press, 1995), 36–37. Exploring a different angle of early British expansionism, Nicolas Canny studies how at the mid-sixteenth century, the Irish—a people with whom the English had always had some familiarity— came to be regarded as uncivilized, thereby providing a justification for indiscriminate slaying and expropriation. See Nicholas Canny, "The Ideology of English Colonization: From Ireland to America," in *Theories of Empire, 1450–1800,* ed. David Armitage, vol. 20 of *An Expanding World: The European Impact on World History* (Hampshire: Aldershot, 1998), 20:179–202.

7. James Buzard, "The Grand Tour and After (1660–1840)," in *The Cambridge Companion to Travel Writing,* ed. Peter Hulme and Tim Young (Cambridge: Cambridge University Press, 2002): 37–52, 41.

8. Jeremy Black, *The British Abroad: The Grand Tour in the Eighteenth Century* (New York: St. Martin's Press, 1992), 76–77; and *The British and the Grand Tour* (London: Croom Helm, 1985), 17, 22.

9. John Lynch, *Bourbon Spain, 1700–1808* (Oxford: Basil Blackwell, 1989), 131–32.

10. *The Polite Traveler: Being a Modern View of Part of Italy, Spain, Portugal and Africa* (London, 1783), 92.

11. John Armstrong, *Letters from Minorca; Describing the Constitution, Government, Produce, Antiquities, and Natural History, of that Island* (Dublin, 1782), v, vi.

12. Armstrong, *Letters*, vii.

13. Armstrong, *Letters*, vii.

14. Christopher Hervey, *Letters from Portugal, Spain, Italy and Germany, in the Years 1759, 1760 and 1761*, 3 vols. (London, 1785), 1:259.

15. Armstrong, *Letters*, 99–100.

16. Mary Kingsley, *West African Studies* (London: Macmillan, 1899), 612–25; and David Simpson, *Fetishism and Imagination: Dickens, Melville, Conrad* (Baltimore: Johns Hopkins University Press, 1982), 29.

17. Quoted in Tzvetan Todorov, *The Conquest of America*, trans. Richard Howard (New York: Harper and Row, 1984), 38.

18. Armstrong, *Letters*, 122.

19. See Raymond Williams, *Culture and Society: 1780–1950* (New York: Columbia University Press, 1983), xviii–xix.

20. Edward Clarke performed his duty in Madrid for nearly two years, until 1762 when Spain entered the Seven Years' War, forcing Hervey and the members of his delegation to abandon the city. This event interrupted Clarke's original design to elaborate a much larger and more expansive work about Spain, which only added problems to the difficulties he had previously encountered such as the extremely reserved character of Spaniards as well as the "cautions they use, and the suspicions they entertain with regard to hereticks." Edward Clarke, *Letters Concerning the Spanish Nation: Written at Madrid during the Years 1760 and 1761* (London, 1763), ii. In 1765 and 1770 the German and French editions were respectively published.

21. Clarke, *Letters*, 252.

22. Clarke, *Letters*, 252.

23. Jeremy Black, *Natural and Necessary Enemies: Anglo-French Relations in the Eighteenth Century* (Athens, GA: University of Georgia Press, 1987), 2.

24. See José Cadalso, *Cartas marruecas* (Madrid: Cátedra, 1995), 185–86; Juan Sempere y Guarinos, *Historia del lujo y de las leyes suntuarias de España* [*History of Luxury and Sumptuary Laws of Spain*], 2 vols. (Madrid, 1788), 2:85; Manuel Romero del Álamo, *Efectos perniciosos del lujo: las cartas de D. Manuel Romero del Álamo al* Memorial Literario de Madrid (1789) [*Pernicious Effects of Luxury: Letters by D. Manuel Romero del Álamo al* Memorial Literario de Madrid] (1789) (Oviedo: Publicaciones Universidad de Oviedo, 1985), 18; Jerónimo de Uztáriz, quoted in Marcelo Bitar Letayf, *Los economistas españoles y sus ideas sobre el comercio en las Indias* [*Spanish Economists and Their Ideas Regarding the West Indies Commerce*] (Mexico: Instituto Mexicano de Comercio Exterior, 1975), 105–15; Melchor de Macanaz quoted in Bitar, *Los economistas españoles*, 159. Contemporary historians who have studied the economic dependency of eighteenth-century Spanish and Spanish American markets upon international imports are José Ignacio Fortea Pérez, "The Textile Industry in the Economy of Cordoba at the End of the Seventeenth and the Start of the Eighteenth Centuries: a Frustrated Recovery," *The Castilian Crisis of the Seventeenth Century*, eds. I.A.A. Thompson and Bartolomé Yun Casakilla (Cambridge: Cambridge University Press, 1994), 136–67; Jean Olivia McLachlan, *Trade and Peace with Old Spain, 1667–1750* (Cambridge: Cambridge University Press, 1940); Joaquim Nadal Farreras, *Comercio exterior y subdesarrollo: España y Gran Bretaña de 1777–1914: política económica y relaciones comerciales* [*Foreign Commerce and Underdevelopment: Spain and Great Britain from 1777–1914: Political Economy and Commercial Relations*] (Madrid: Instituto de Estudios Fiscales, 1978).

25. Clarke, *Letters*, 263.

26. *A Trip to Spain: or, a True Description of the Comical Humours, Ridiculous Customs, and Foolish Laws, of that Lazy Improvident People the Spaniards* (London, 1705), 9.

27. Officer, *A Trip to Spain*, 12.

28. Marie-Catherine d' Aulnoy, *The Ingenious and Diverting Letters of the Lady's Travels into Spain. Being the Truest and Best Remarks Extant on that Court and Country* (London, 1706), 264. To differentiate his narrative from previous accounts, Edward Clarke pointed out in his preface to *Letters Concerning the Spanish Nation* that *The Lady's Travels into Spain* was obsolete by the middle of the eighteenth century and no longer offered a just description of life in Spain. He also indicated that *The Lady's Travels into Spain* had actually been pirated from a French book originally titled *Les Délices d'Espagne*. Clarke, *Letters*, iv.

29. Armstrong, *Letters*, 202, 212.

30. Armstrong, *Letters*, 202.

31. Armstrong, *Letters*, 202.

32. Armstrong, *Letters*, 201.

33. William Dalrymple, *Travels Through Spain and Portugal, in 1774; with a Short Expedition Against Algiers, in 1775* (London, 1777), 49.

34. Dalrymple, *Travels*, 49.

35. Alexander Jardine, *Letters from Barbary, France, Spain, Portugal. By an English Officer,* 2 vols. (London, 1788), 2:58. Jardine was educated in the Royal Military Academy of Woolwich and published his *Letters from Barbary, France, Spain, and Portugal* in 1788; a second edition appeared in 1790.

36. Clarke, *Letters*, 11.

37. Clarke, *Letters*, 12–15.

38. Pieter de Marees, *Description and Historical Account of the Gold Kingdom of Guinea*, trans. Albert van Dantzing and Adam Jones (Oxford: Oxford University Press, 1987), 36.

39. Willem Bosman, *A New Accurate Description of the Coast of Guinea* (New York: Barnes & Noble, 1967), 154.

40. See Charles de Brosses, *Du culte des dieux fétiches ou parallèle de l'ancienne religion de l'Egypte avec la religion actuelle de la Negritie* (París: Fayard, 1989).

41. M.A. Baker, *The History of the Inquisition, as It Subsists in the Kingdoms of Spain, Portugal, & c.* (London, 1734). An extensive number of books was published in Great Britain about the Inquisition, the majority of them during the first half of the eighteenth century. A non-exhaustive list includes the English translation of Philippus van Limborch, *The History of the Inquisition*, trans. Samuel Chandler, 2 vols. (London, 1731); Bernard Picart, *The Ceremonies and Religious Customs of the Various Nations of the Known World*, 7 vols. (London, 1733–39); Anonymous, *A General History of the Proceedings and Cruelties, of the Court of Inquisition; in Spain, Portugal* (London,1737); Anonymous, *A Short View; or History of the Inquisition of the Kingdoms of Spain, Portugal, &c. To this Day* (London, 1739).

42. Baker, *The History of the Inquisition*, vi–vii.

43. See Isaac Martin, *The Tryal and Sufferings of Mr. Isaac Martin, Who Was Put into the Inquisition in Spain, for the Sake of the Protestant Religion.*

Written by Himself, and Dedicated to His Most Sacred Majesty King George, by Whose Gracious Interposition He Was Releas'd (London, 1724).

44. John Marchant, *The Bloody Tribunal: or, an Antidote Against Popery. Being a Review of the Horrid Cruelties of the Inquisition, as Practised in Spain, Portugal, Italy, and the East and West-Indies* (London, 1756), 1.

45. Anonymous, *The Loyal Martyrs: or, the Bloody Inquisitor. Being a Just Account of the Inhuman Barbarities Used in the Inquisition of Spain* (Worcester, 1775?).

46. *History of the Inquisition, as it Existed in the Kingdoms of Spain, Portugal and in Both the Indies* (Dublin, 1789), 62–78.

47. See Jonathan Israel, "Spinoza, Locke and the Enlightenment Battle for Toleration," in *Toleration in Enlightenment Europe,* ed. Ole Peter Grell and Roy Porter (Cambridge: Cambridge University Press, 2000), 102–13.

48. Clarke, *Letters*, 16.

49. Clarke, *Letters*, 34.

50. Clarke, *Letters*, 14.

51. Clarke, *Letters*, 37.

52. Spurr, *The Rhetoric of Empire*, 47.

53. Armstrong, *Letters*, 99.

54. Clarke, *Letters*, vii.

55. Clarke, *Letters*, vi.

56. See Franz Bosbach, "The European Debate on Universal Monarchy," in *Theories of Empire, 1450–1800,* 20: 81–98.

57. See Anthony Padgen, *Spanish Imperialism and the Political Imagination* (New Haven: Yale University Press, 1990), 13–36, and *Lords of All the World: Ideologies of Empire in Spain, Britain and France c.1500–c.1800* (New Haven: Yale University Press, 1995). Padgen studies how two of the most prominent Neapolitan political and economic theorists of the eighteenth century, Paolo Mattia Doria and Antonio Genovesi, began to present Spain in the light of a tyrannical ruler.

58. Charles de Secondat, baron de Montesquieu, *The Spirit of Laws*, 2 vols. (London, 1777), 1:130.

59. Armstrong, *Letters*, 198.

60. Armstrong, *Letters*, 197.

61. Armstrong, *Letters*, 197.

62. Armstrong, *Letters*, 204.

63. Armstrong, *Letters*, 198–201.

64. Henry Swinburne, *Travels Through Spain, in the Years 1775 and 1776* (London, 1779), 369–70.

65. Spurr, *The Rhetoric of Empire*, 76.

66. Armstrong, *Letters*, 97.

67. Armstrong, *Letters*, 198.

68. Hervey, *Letters*, 259–60.

69. Dalrymple, *Travels*, 77.

70. Quoted in Paul Preston and Denis Smyth, *Spain, the EEC and NATO* (London and Boston: Routledge and Kegan Paul, 1984), 24.

71. Quoted in Raymond Carr, *Spain, 1808–1975* (Oxford: Clarendon Press, 1982), 105.

72. Américo Castro, *The Spaniards: An Introduction to Their History* (Berkeley: University California Press, 1971), 563.

73. Joaquín Costa, *Reconstitución y europeización de España y otros escritos* (Madrid: Instituto Estudios Administración Local, 1981), xxvii.

74. Preston, *Spain,* 27.

The Good, the Bad, and the Sentimental Savage: Native Americans in Representative Novels from the Spanish Enlightenment

MARK R. MALIN

Alluding to the critical interest in the theme of the Noble Savage, Ter Ellingson includes the following epigraph in *The Myth of the Noble Savage*: "Advice from a World Wide Web search engine, after finding more than 1,000 references to the 'Noble Savage': *Refine your search*."[1] Apparently, the topic has not lost its allure despite Hayden White's contention that "the theme of the Noble Savage may be one of the few historical topics about which there is nothing new to say."[2] While White maintained that there was little scholarly disagreement on the subject, the literary representation of natives continues to draw critical attention as the wide body of literature attests. Little, however, has been written about the depictions of natives in Spanish enlightenment prose fiction, either translations or original novels.[3] Colonial accounts of actual encounters with New World inhabitants are major constituents of the canon, yet literary accounts from Spanish writers from the Enlightenment are less well known.

Early Spanish explorers documented their encounters with natives in the literature of the Colonial era, some of which were more anthropologically accurate than others. Despite this colonial tradition, criticism of eighteenth-century texts in Spain in which the representation of natives was a major theme has not enjoyed the currency that it has in France and other nations. In his informative and compelling historical study of the relationship between

Spaniards and natives, David Weber, cites a personal communication with Joaquín Alvarez Barrientos, who assures Weber that the good Indian as literary protagonist in Spain "no tuvo tanto eco ni utilidad como en otras culturas."[4] Weber goes on to explain this in part by stating that "Catholic Spain had rejected the deism that allowed some European intellectuals to believe in the natural virtue of pagans."[5] While this is a very plausible explanation for a dearth of novels that reject Catholicism, it does not account for the conspicuous absence of the theme of the so-called Noble Savage in Hispanist criticism.

The fact that the theme of the Noble Savage has not enjoyed greater currency does not necessarily mean that it does not bear further consideration. It may just mean that the search for texts may require patience and perseverance. At one point, it was thought that Spain's Enlightenment literati had ignored the epistolary novel, but Ana Rueda's *Cartas sin lacrar* and other studies clearly prove otherwise. In fact, studies such as Alvarez Barrientos' *La novela del siglo XVIII* (and Reginald Brown's work before that) have disproved conclusively the all too common assertion writers in eighteenth-century Spain did not cultivate the novel.[6] It is true that the representation of natives was not as common a theme in Spanish literature as it was in French texts. However, natives do appear in some late eighteenth-century prose fiction in Spain, and this essay will explore three such works.[7] One is a translation of a novel whose major theme is the portrayal of natives; the second is another translation in which the portrayal of natives is but a subplot or episode of the novel; and the third is an original Spanish novel.

The question of the legitimacy of emphasizing translations is a valid one. While I do not agree with Juan Ignacio Ferreras that eighteenth-century Spanish literature is "poor," it is certain that the translation of novels was a significant activity during the time.[8] Both Alvarez Barrientos and Joaquín Marco write that the moral didacticism of a novel, translated or original, and its influence on Spain's youth were considered more important than whether a work was original or not, so there was little distinction between translating and writing something new.[9] However, in many cases, as Alvarez Barrientos notes, the translations could actually be considered original works in that the translators had to make omissions, adaptations, and changes when they rendered the foreign texts into Spanish to make them suitable for Spanish political or moral aesthetics.[10] Because novels were popular in England and France, and because in many cases their didacticism was considered appropriate by governmental and ecclesiastic censors, translating them was a significant form of literary production in Spain at the end of the eighteenth century and the beginning of the nineteenth.

Gaspar Zavala y Zamora's translation of a French novel of disputed authorship entitled *Odérahi, histoire américaine: contenant une peinture fidelle des moeurs des habitans de l'intérieur de l'Amérique Septentrionale*, translated into Spanish as *Oderay, usos, trages, ritos, costumbres y leyes de los habitantes de la América Septentrional* (1804, based on the French edition of 1801) responds to the public's penchant for exoticism and a morality in line with Spanish customs. At one point *Oderay*'s authorship had been attributed to Chateaubriand, but subsequent scholarship suggests that the author may have been Baron Ambroise Palisot de Beauvois, a renowned naturalist, though doubts persist. [11] This text is central to my analysis because its ideology most closely parallels the representation of the Rousseauian model of the so-called Noble Savage. In addition, the theme of representation is the major focus of the novel, whereas in the other texts the theme is a subordinate one. Next, the intriguingly entitled *Amelia, o los desgraciados efectos de la extremada sensibilidad. Anécdota inglesa* (177?), translated by the anonymous D.J.F.S., is one of many texts during the period that highlighted the theme of a young woman's choice of a husband.[12] *Amelia* presents an interesting case in that natives are portrayed as sentimental beings capable of savagery. But the primary thrust in representing natives is the portrayal of the complex relationship among them, the rebelling colonists, and the mother country, a relationship crucial to Spain in an era during which independence of its own colonies was a significant concern. Finally, Antonio Valladares y Sotomayor's monumental nine-volume work which is a collection of anecdotes held together by its epistolary structure, but the author describes it as a novel in the title: *La Leandra, novela que comprehende muchas* (1797).[13] Volumes 2 and 3 contain Eduardo's account of his adventures after being shipwrecked on an island inhabited by cannibalistic natives. In all cases of the representation of natives, authors portrayed them in a variety of ways depending on the ideology they wished to promote. Noble portrayals could suggest a criticism of supposedly enlightened Europe, while characterizing natives as savages could justify continued repression. In *La Leandra*, Valladares uses natives to promote a conservative Catholic propaganda, thus breaking from customary European representations of natives whose primitivism suggested a noble innocence.

Oderay tells the story of a Frenchman who is adopted by a tribe of Indians called the Nadovessinos in the Great Lakes region of what is now the United States. As the novel begins, he is writing a letter to his beloved Eugenia back in France, and to her he recounts his capture. At first, he writes, a tribe of natives that he describes as a "tropa de indios bárbaros" had taken him and his partners captive.[14] After beating him and his companions, the natives leave the Frenchman for dead. But he survives and travels on, only then to fall prey to the Nadovessinos who also begin to torture him. Ultimately he is spared when Oderay, an Indian princess, sees him as the return of her deceased brother.[15] Oderay rescues him and she and her father take him into their own home, for they see in him the spiritual reincarnation of their lost beloved one. The rest of the novel tells of his life with the tribe, their customs, and his relationship with Oderay.

For most of the novel, the natives, and especially Oderay herself, appear as essentially righteous and upstanding. They would not, however, meet the criteria that Ter Ellingson uses to describe what he calls the "myth of the Noble Savage" because they are not unconditionally noble. Ellingson notes that most writers actually did not describe the nobility of "Noble Savages" as "an ontologically essential rather than a trait-ascriptive nobility."[16] Rather, he claims, the so-called nobility of natives is much more relative, and they are, therefore, not truly "noble." In *Oderay* the author's attitude towards natives is ambivalent in that he praises some customs while he criticizes others, as we will subsequently see.[17] The presence of this ambivalence suggests that even when a portrayal leaned towards the positive, the attitude towards natives was not an absolute. As Hayden White suggests, the very notion of the Noble Savage also "brings to the fore . . . the notion of the ignoble savage" so that both binomials figured prominently in European portrayals of natives. According to White, for example, "Diderot and Rousseau both used the Noble Savage idea to attack the European social system of privilege, inherited power and political oppression. The ignoble savage idea is used to justify the slave trade."[18] He suggests that the Rousseauian concept of the Noble Savage was conceived after the outcome of the struggle for supremacy between natives and colonizers was already settled; therefore, natives as virtuous beings, untainted by society, served to promote liberty and other characteristics considered essential in a truly enlightened European society.[19]

Oderay follows the Rousseauian model to a great degree: there are repeated examples of the author's (and by extension the translator's) admiration for the philosophical system and way of life of the Nadovessinos. Certainly one goal of *Oderay* is to suggest that this lifestyle is a model for imitation by European "civilized" society in which the concepts of parental control, nobility as a trait inherited by bloodline, despotism, and clergy privilege still held sway. The goal is not to gain better conditions for natives, or to promote better relations between settlers and natives, but rather to promote a more just society in Europe, and especially in Spain, through the translation of the work.

The choice to translate a text like *Oderay* may also have had as much to do with its sentimentality as it did to the theme of the Noble Savage. The sentimental novel, both original and in translation, along with the sentimental drama were very much in vogue in Spanish literature in the late eighteenth and early nineteenth centuries. In part, this reflected an interest in the philosophy that underpinned the genre. While a detailed analysis of the relationship between the sentimentalism of these works and the rationalist philosophy that informed them is beyond the scope of this essay, it is important to note the influence during the Spanish Enlightenment of the ideas of moralists such as Shaftesbury, Locke, Hume, Smith, and perhaps most notably Rousseau.[20] Sentimental works appealed to readers not only for their plots, but because the expression of sentiment was intended to inspire sympathy and move readers to action.

The description of natives' lifestyles and customs in *Oderay* may not be anthropologically accurate, but their rectitude and virtue are allegorical of the commonplaces of Enlightenment philosophy that underlay the novel of sensibility.[21] The natives in fact seem like stock sentimental characters as they shed copious tears and openly demonstrate their feelings and compassion. Zavala y Zamora indicates his own admiration for their beliefs by adding approbatory commentaries in footnotes. In addition to the characters' sensibility, another commonplace of the sentimental novel is the expression of the need to control one's emotions, *Oderay* purports to show that Europeans could learn to control their own passions by emulating the natives. In one instance, overcome by emotion, Oderay restrains herself by running to a mountaintop to look down upon nature and fill herself with the idea of the Supreme Being. Afterwards, she returns to Onteree "con más fortaleza."[22] Zavala y Zamora praises her control in a footnote commenting that "¡Oh, si imitaran nuestras europeas este virtuoso esfuerzo sobre sus pasiones!"[23] Beyond their sentimentalism and self-control, the natives are also generous and hospitable. Once the tribe has accepted that Onteree will be with them, they respond by making him part of the community and offering all they have to him, thus demonstrating how they eschew the concept of "mine and thine," a trait that modern theorists of the so-called Noble Savage deem universally praiseworthy.[24]

The author also emphasizes that the natives in *Oderay* allow their children to choose their own marriage partners rather than subjecting them to parental tyranny by forcing them into marriages of convenience. When Onteree tells Oderay of his love for Eugenia, she is shocked when he reveals that his parents had another bride selected for him. Oderay asks him: "¿Tu padre, dices que no consintió que Eugenia fuese tu esposa? ¿Luego en tu país no es el hombre libre para casarse con la mujer que ama? ¿Luego puede allí un padre dejar abrasar de amores a su hija?"[25] By praising the natives' virtues as parents, the author and the translator criticize the European custom of choosing partners based on social position or wealth rather than love. Similarly, the Indians' familial relationships are sentimental instead of authoritarian. As Oderay says, in her community "los hijos . . . se divierten al lado de sus padres y jamás oyen de su boca palabra alguna dura que hiera su corazón."[26] Given this precedent, Oderay cannot understand the relationship between Onteree and his family, and she even refers to Onteree's relationship to his parents as one of servitude rather than affection. Onteree lends textual authority to the superiority of natives' customs by recounting that while he suffered during the first week or so of his captivity, unaccustomed as he was to what he calls the "salvajes costumbres" ("savage customs"), "no tardé en hallarlas mil veces preferibles a las de los europeos."[27] He praises the freedom the Nadovessinos enjoy, their belief in working for the common good, their love of country, and their lack of greed, among other attributes.

While such praises predominate in *Oderay*, not all natives are uniformly noble, nor for that matter are the Nadovessinos unilaterally above reproach. The narrator relates customs and beliefs that were foreign or antithetically opposed to Christian/European concepts. Some notable examples include how the natives hang cadavers in trees instead of burying them, their tolerance of bigamist practices, and warriors' expectations of anonymous sexual favors to reward bravery on the battlefield. Furthermore, the fact remains that while the narrator was protected and adopted by the Nadovessinos, he and his companions had been brutally tortured, and some were even killed at the onset. Some versions of the Noble Savage suppose that violence was unknown in native cultures until they had contact with Europeans. Yet Steven Leblanc refutes such popular mythologized views of natives, citing ample anthropological evidence showing that natives had been involved in bloody warfare and ecological destruction long before contact with outsiders.[28] And all of the Indian tribes described in *Oderay* are capable of violence. The first tribe that captured the Europeans, for instance, tortured the narrator, while the Chipeveses, an enemy tribe of the Nadovessinos, kidnap and brutalize Oderay.[29] When the Nadovessinos blindly quench their thirst for vengeance over what happened to Oderay, Onteree tries to get them to temper their actions as the text criticizes their unreasonable, bloodthirsty retaliation. The Nadovessinos have many admirable characteristics, but they are prone to violence that goes beyond a defense of their sovereignty and self-interests.

The goal of *Oderay* was not so much to paint faithful representations of natives, but to represent them as savages who, despite their primitivism and proclivity to violence, seem to lead a more enlightened lifestyle than the Europeans. Despite not being above reproach, the natives in *Oderay* follow Enlightenment philosophical precepts and share a number of desirable traits. The natives are selfless, democratic, respectful of their progeny, sensitive, and sympathetic: values that empiricists like Shaftesbury, Smith, Locke, Hume, Condillac and Rousseau, among others, promoted in their writings. They do not have private property, they eschew the terms of "mine and thine," and they disdain absolutism.[30] Nor does the violence of the natives in *Oderay* stray from the Rousseauian model. Rousseau's native was not necessarily a peaceful being because the tribes he depicts in his discourses were no longer in a natural state. Rousseau, in fact, believed that law and education were necessary in any society to ensure that civilization would not plunge once again into a state of permanent violence, and he shows this by demonstrating the violence of natives.[31] That the native in *Oderay* is a mix of admirable and execrable traits allows the author to advocate for the emulation of some characteristics while still asserting the need for social constraints and personal restraint. That is, while the portrayal of natives in *Oderay* does not fall entirely within Ter Ellingson's criteria for nobility, the balance of positive and negative traits serves an ideological end in suggesting that Europeans could learn from Native American societies.

But there may be more to the portrayal of customs that violated Europeans norms. Hayden White maintains that there is critical agreement on how the portrayal of natives served Enlightenment ideological ends, but he also maintains that new light may be shed on the theme of the Noble Savage by stressing the "fetishistic nature" of it.[32] In his examination of early accounts of natives, he notes anomalies in their portrayal: a distinction was drawn "between a *normal* humanity (gentle, intelligent, decorous, and white) and an *abnormal* one (obstinate, gay, free and red)." The opposition allowed natives to be treated "as need, conscience or desire required."[33] As White notes, commentators who described behavior violating European taboos against "nakedness, lawlessness, sexual promiscuity and cannibalism" may have projected "repressed desires onto the lives of the natives," even if they viewed such desires with horror and disgust.[34]

This paradox in the portrayal of natives helps explain their ambiguous depiction in *Oderay*. The title of the novel makes it explicitly clear that the book intends to tell the story of the sentimental relationship between Oderay and Onteree as it portrays the natives' customs. Both author and translator admire much about the Nadovessinos but indicate shock when describing customs such as the rite in which warriors would visit a woman's tent to receive sexual favors for their daring exploits in defense of the homeland. The fact that Oderay rejects all such attempts shows her moral superiority, but the description of the custom allows illicit desire to be projected on the cultural traits of the "Other." A similar interpretation could be made of Oderay's willingness to share Onteree with his French bride in a state of bigamy. These practices and others such as the treatment of the dead violate European norms and taboos, yet the portrayal of such customs could allow readers vicariously to enjoy the acts while at the same time deploring them.

Oderay underscores the notion that the natives could benefit from the civilizing effects of European influences in their belicose nature and in some of their customs. As Weber makes clear in *Bárbaros*, there were still pitched battles between Spaniards and natives in some parts of Spanish America, and there was still considerable debate on the best way to deal with the "native question."[35] As *Oderay* implies, the concept or allegory of the Noble Savage undercuts the European concept of nobility. Yet while the projection of taboos onto the natives and the negative portrayal of enemy tribes of the Nadovessinos allow the novel to serve as an allegory of freedom, they also prevent it from condemning Spain for continued persecution of natives by portraying natives' untoward attributes.

But the reason for translating this particular novel was probably not limited to a desire to promote continued Spanish hegemony in the New World or to criticize European customs. Political considerations of a different sort might have held sway as well: the theology of the Indians in the novel is close enough to a Catholic deism that Spanish censors would be able to find it acceptable with Zavala y Zamora only having to make minor revisions and excisions in the text. Guillermo Carnero observes that in order to make the religious content more palatable, Zavala y Zamora selectively translated those scenes in which comparative theology is discussed.[36] While Rousseau was openly critical of Church orthodoxy in his writings, Zavala y Zamora translated a text that stops short of such polemics. Ridiculing the Church and questioning the clergy's prerogative would have incurred governmental or religious censorship in Spain. *Oderay* advocates for progressive Enlightenment values without vilifying European customs and religious authority, and some European customs and mores are in fact praised by their contrast with native vices. Europeans can be credited with trying to teach the natives to temper their actions, while the novel still urges enlightened citizens to learn fundamentally progressive ideas by emulating the nobility of the "savages."

The role of natives to inspire imitation in *Amelia* is much more limited in that their nobility serves only to exhort parents to allow their children free reign in choosing their mates. Rodney Rodriguez points out that the subtitle of the novel, *o los desgraciados efectos de la extremada sensibilidad*, suggests that the narrative promotes with the need to control one's emotions.[37] He maintains, however, that in reality the novel's main thrust is to warn parents of what can happen when they fail to understand the "sentimientos sinceros de las hijas."[38] Set during the American Revolutionary War, *Amelia* tells the story of a young English girl who, though she tries to deny it at first, falls in love with a soldier named Carlos Dolsey. When her maid recognizes the depth of the sentiment, and tells Amelia that she is in love, Amelia insists that she will control her passions and cede to her parents' wishes for her. She resolutely exclaims "¡O! Yo venceré, yo desharé este sentimiento."[39] Ultimately, though, she cannot deny her true feelings, and when her parents inform her that they have chosen another man for her, she becomes desperate. Similar to one plot line in *Oderay*, then, this conflict between true love and parental obedience sets the backdrop as Dolsey goes off to serve his king in the fight against the American colonists' bid for independence.

Tortured by her twin allegiances of love for Dolsey and her duty to her parents, Amelia disguises herself as a man in order to go to America to visit him, and blames her exalted passions for her taking these desperate measures. Once in America, she finds Dolsey injured on a battlefield, shot not by an insurgent colonist, but by "la flecha de un salvaje."[40] Later Amelia falls ill, because to save Carlos she had sucked the wound made by what turns out to have been a poisoned arrow. The narrator describes that "se descubrió que la herida de Carlos que había chupado Amelia, estaba emponzoñada: ésta es una de las acciones atroces de la barbarie de los salvajes de América."[41] Because of savage barbarism, their only hope for her survival is to find another "savage" who knows medicinal plants. So, aided by a translator and guide, Zami, they set off to find one such native they had heard of named Mozema.

Once they find the medicine man, we learn that he had lost his son, a victim of the colonizing British. Mozema accuses Zami of betrayal as he curses his son's assassins. At first, Mozema refuses to help Amelia, but when finally he does agree, it is because his sentimental side allows him to see her as a surrogate daughter. Carlos begs Mozema: "resuscitadme a una esposa querida . . . sí, me pareces sensible."[42] Sentimental literature was a predominant force in eighteenth-century literature, and Spain was no exception. And while terms such as sensible and sentimental cannot be precisely defined, sympathy was considered a cornerstone of humanity.[43]

By emphasizing Mozema's sentimentality and his capacity for empathetic identification with others, *Amelia* also brings to the fore his humanistic character rather than relegating him to the ontological status of barbaric savage. Along with appealing to his humanity, Dolsey also convinces him that the real blame for the war falls on the leaders rather than the soldiers who purportedly had killed his son.[44] Mozema travels to visit Amelia in Philadelphia only to realize that he cannot cure her because the arrow, and therefore the poison, came not from an Indian after all, but from an enemy of the Indians. He explains that it was not an Indian, but rather "la mano de estos pérfidos [europeos] es quien ha despedido la flecha emponzoñada que te arrebata a tu mujer."[45]

Being responsible for the death of Mozema's son, the British appear the ultimate villains in the novel. However, Dolsey convinces Mozema that the natives' enemy is not the British soldier, but, rather the government behind the soldier. The British government as an entity usurps individual freedoms and threatens the autonomy of Native Americans. But it turns out that the real threat to the natives is not the British or even the British government, but instead the rebelling colonists. This becomes clear when it is revealed that it was actually the colonists who both killed Mozema's son, and injured Dolsey. The colonists then are responsible for Amelia's ultimate demise and Carlos's as well, since he dies of grief ("dolor") knowing that nothing can save his beloved Amelia. Natives in this short novel are barbarous but also possess salvational sensibility, while colonists are ultimately shown to be the the common enemy.

Amelia portrays the natives as savages capable of sentimentalism and sensibility who recognize the need to love and support their children unconditionally. Yet their compassion is nonetheless a product of the civilizing effects of the British who encourage them to express their sympathy. Hayden White has argued that there were two opposed and contradictory "ways of conceiving the relationship between Europeans and the natives." One way took natives to be *continuous* with Europeans, and this conception of natives "underlay the policy of conversion." Conversely, natives were also seen as "existing *contiguously* to the Europeans," as either superior or inferior, and it was this relationship that "underlay ... the policies of war and extermination."[46] In *Amelia* both the continuous and the contiguous relationships exist. The novel then could serve a dual propagandistic purpose, stirring up sentiment against rebelling colonists and still unpacified natives, while allowing natives still to serve as an allegory of freedom.

This novel's apparent popularity in Spain during the late Enlightenment probably arose more from its moral message of letting children choose their own destiny than from its portrayal of natives. It supports children in their demands for autonomy as it warns of the effects of unrestrained passions, but these typical Enlightenment themes are not the only ones in the novel. It also conjures the allegory of the Sentimental Savage living in close contact with nature (recalling the theme of the return to a Golden Age) as it subtly undermines the anti-Hispanic *leyenda negra* by intimating that natives, despite their sentimentality, may not be far from barbarianism, and therefore in need of civilization and perhaps proselytization or conversion. In fact, the conversion of natives continued to be the cornerstone of Spanish policy in its American colonies.[47] The representation of natives in *Amelia* reflects European prejudices and stereotypes. It also defends colonizers in their struggle against their colonies' independence at a time when Spain was losing its own colonies in the early 1800s.

Yet we should not discount the fact that from a literary perspective, the figure of the savage was very much in vogue during the period. Michelle Buchanan suggests that the representation of natives in eighteenth-century fiction is more a literary topos than an accurate portrayal of Native American customs and realities. Buchanan even questions whether "le bon sauvage" is indeed an important link in the chain of philosophical and psychological elements which so decisively change the substance of French literature during the eighteenth century, or whether he is one of the many stock characters."[48] But even if this is true, the native still serves a crucial ideological function to illustrate the disastrous consequences that ensue when parents control their children too closely. The myth of the Noble Savage did play a role in the development of Enlightenment philosophy, but there is not just one common model of the character, nor is the philosophy or ideology the native embodies universal. In *Oderay*, the natives are primarily benevolent, while in *Amelia* they are decidedly more ambivalent. In *La Leandra*, the natives, or at least those natives who have not converted to Catholicism, lack any redeeming characteristics whatsoever.

Antonio Valladares y Sotomayor's *La Leandra* is a nine-volume unfinished epistolary novel whose narrative complexity Ana Rueda describes in *Cartas sin lacrar*.[49] Separated by geographical distance, two friends, Aniceta and Leandra, maintain their friendship with an epistolary bridge as they tell each other of their lives during their separation. In recounting their experiences, they insert narratives that others have told, and the inclusion of these embedded tales adds to the novel's complexity. In one such tale, Leandra's suitor, Eduardo, tells of his ill-fated trip to visit his family's holdings in Jamaica in volumes 2 and 3 of the novel. On his way to America, he stops in London to take on supplies, and there he meets Camilo. The two become friends and set sail together, but when they run into tempestuous weather they become shipwrecked on a strait between two islands, one of which is inhabited by cannibalistic savages. The unfavorable portrayal of natives in *La Leandra* presents an interesting comparison with *Oderay* and *Amelia*. The few natives who escape reprobation in Valladares' narrative are those who have been exposed to both Catholic dogma and Castilian language.

After taking Eduardo and Camilo prisoners, ravenous and blood-thirsty natives prepare them for sacrifice and consumption. However, with his head on the chopping block, Eduardo is saved when a warrior reluctantly follows the orders of the princess Tupalteca to free him. The warrior only acquiesces to her will because his ultimate goal is to seek Tupalteca's hand in marriage. Later we learn that the princess has been educated by a Spanish native, Afra, who had arrived on the island as a teenager. Afra lived with Tupalteca because the latter's father was the *cacique* of the island, and Tupalteca's humanity is attributable directly to the Catholicism and Castilian that Afra taught her. Logically then, the other Indians' continued barbarism stems from their not having been exposed to the same benevolent influences.

This episode is testimony of Valladares' Catholic orthodoxy, as he shows that the only cultured and physically attractive islanders are either Spaniards or baptized natives.[50] In fact, when Eduardo describes Tupalteca, his description recalls that of a European woman rather than a native islander. The first time he saw her was while he was in a room awaiting his fate after having been spared execution, and he narrates her arrival:

> Dentro de corto rato se presentó en [la pieza] acompañada de otras dos, una india, cuyo semblante infundía veneración. Su blanco color, distinto de todas las demás, que era amulatado, tez fina, ojos grandes y negros, correspondiendo igualmente a formar una mujer hermosa todas las demás partes de su rostro y cuerpo.[51]

These looks that distinguish her from the others are directly attributable to both her nobility and her having had contact with Spanish religion and language. While Rousseau and others used the allegory of the Noble Savage to reject "nobility's claim to privilege," in Valladares' novel the savage is barbarous and nobility's claim to privileged status is upheld. Valladares subverts the Rousseauian model of the Noble Savage as a vehicle for his more conservative ideology.

As Ter Ellingson notes, one trend in the portrayal of natives was a form of competition to see who could describe the discovery of the most savage, inhuman, and barbarous people to date.[52] Eduardo's tale seems to fit this classification. Tipomacín, who, like Tupalteca, has been educated in Castilian and baptized a Catholic, provides a typically one-sided negative portrayal of the barbarity of his fellow natives and their religion. He states that once he learned Catholic ways, he and the other baptized natives came to realize "lo inhumana y horrible que nos parecía la [religión] que nuestros compatriotas profesaban, sobre la cual ya nos había hecho conocer María sus ridículas ceremonias, bárbaros ritos y crueles preceptos, todo doctado por el enemigo común, sostenido por los supersticiosos sacerdotes y creído por el ignorante y bárbaro pueblo."[53]

While for Rousseau, and subsequent writers who used his model the Noble Savage was allegorical of a return to an unspoiled life, untarnished by European concepts of government, nobility, and personal possession, Valladares refutes the utopian portrayal of natives so common in European Enlightenment narratives. Native life in *La Leandra*, by contrast, is one of darkness, cannibalism, and savagery, far from the model of allegorical idealism. Valladares does not, however, eschew Enlightenment precepts, but rather maintains that the European model is the true ideal of progressive society. To make the contrast between civilization and barbarism complete, Leandra has a dream that she reveals and inserts into her recounting of Eduardo's tale.

This dream, as Ana Rueda accurately describes it, is that of an Enlightenment utopia.[54] But the dream also explains the significance of the inclusion of Eduardo's tale in weaving the ideological message of the novel. In her dream, Leandra and her extended family, like Eduardo, are on a boat, and they too become shipwrecked between two islands. They fear being captured by cannibals when they see canoes rowing towards them. However, the fate that awaits them is the opposite of the one that befell Eduardo. Rather than being abducted and devoured by cannibals, they are instead transported to an island whose government, customs, agriculture, and economy exemplify the European Enlightenment ideal. This island enjoys wealth, employment, industry, agricultural abundance, and charity. The dream is an antidote to those narratives that suggest that the real utopia is a return to a pre-civilization Golden Age.[55] Instead, utopia in *La Leandra* is tied more closely to the realization of an ideal Catholic piety. Catholicism's ability to civilize is also made explicit in the earlier scene on the island. The dream warns readers in Spain that their religious customs have become weak and lackadaisical, and therefore they risk sliding toward barbarism. Allegorically, Spain is shipwrecked between the two islands. The country can sway towards savagery and end up like the island that

Eduardo and Camilo had landed upon, or it can lean towards the utopia that Leandra had found.

In her dream, Leandra and her family stay with the governor who invites them to attend mass. The residents of this island, he informs them, walk in to church with their eyes straight ahead and fixed on the altar and the celebrating priest. They dare not look at who else is or is not in attendance, and care nothing for social appearances; going to mass means partaking in the sacrament, not, he says, as it is in Spain, an activity involving seeing and being seen. The governor chastises their indecency when they show up dressed for mass as they would have done in Spain, dressed in *basquiña* y *mantilla*,[56] and he asks where they are going. When his wife replies that they are going to mass, he answers,

> Señoras, ... en las Iglesias de esta Isla, no se admiten esas composturas tan descompuestas. Si os vieran mis buenos isleños descubiertas la mitad de las cabezas, tan rizados los cabellos, con tantas flores en ellos, tantos lasos para sujetar los sentidos, penachos, cintas, con otros cachivaches que no sé sus nombres, y esos, que según os oí anoche, los llamáis cachirulos, y yo los nombraría carruchos para enganchar las más remisas voluntades: si os vieran, digo, con esas caidas o grandes rizos, que sirven de cubierta al pecho, las gargantas desnudas, parte de los hombros, y algo más, se horrorizarían de modo que pudieran temerse funestas consecuencias. Y a la verdad, esa moda ¿os parece que es propia y decente para presentarse en la casa de Dios, y donde está tan real y verdaderamente como en el cielo?[57]

Delighted to hear of the *enlightened* church behavior expected on the island, Leandrita rushes off to change, exclaiming "¡Ay Dios, mamá mía ... voy corriendo a ponerme en los términos que ha dicho el señor Gobernador, para ir a misa a la Iglesia; que verdaderamente debe ser con la mayor modestia en el vestido, y la más grande ternura en el corazón."[58] The warning is that unless Spaniards adopt some measures of civility in their religious customs and practices, they run the risk of sliding down the teeter totter toward the side of the flesh-eating, human-sacrificing barbarians on the other side of the strait. At the center of enlightened values—indeed, civilization itself—lies proper church etiquette. Whereas in the Rousseauian model Church hierarchy limits freedom, traditional Catholicism is the centerpiece of Valladares' Enlightenment model.

The representation of natives in *La Leandra* resembles that of some early conquistadors who described their barbarism as a way of justifying the treatment of Native Americans in the colonial era. The inhabitants of the island in the novel are bloodthirsty barbarians, without hint of civilizing traits. When Eduardo was rescued, he lost track of Camilo, and when he asks María, as Tupalteca prefers to be called, about his probable fate, she describes her countrymen's customs: "Supongamos, que ha sido tu amigo sangriento despojo de la crueldad de algún indio, que en medio de la sedición, entró en el templo, le condujo a su casa, y está barbaramente regocijando a su vientre con la carne de su semejante; que es lo que presumo."[59] Because of the natives' cruelty, Eduardo can justify killing if it is necessary to do so in order to elaborate a successful escape plan. After all, as María points out, "morir confesando la Ley de Dios y matando a sus enemigos creo firmemente que será alcanzar la vida eterna."[60]

Yet while the natives in *La Leandra* are barbarous, the novel makes it clear that conversion to Catholicism can save them. Instead of being an allegory of freedom to criticize European customs, native barbarism in the novel shows the benefits of European civilization and the power of Catholicism. Eduardo's tale, which takes up most of the second half of volume 2 and continues on into volume 3 of the novel, repudiates those who have blasphemed Spain and its imperialist project by their propagation of the so-called *leyenda negra*. More than anything, however, the purpose of the episode of Eduardo y Camilo is to defend Catholicism, and attack other religious forms, both Protestantism and native superstitions.[61]

The Noble Savage was an allegorical figure and how authors portrayed the relationship between natives and Europeans depended on their motives. If the desire were to advocate for conversion, writers emphasized the continuity between natives and Europeans, and if the desire were to advocate for their extermination then they were shown to be contiguous to Europeans.[62] In *Oderay* continuity is emphasized; *Amelia* offers a mix of continuity and contiguity; and in *La Leandra* the native is contiguous to the Europeans. Of the three novels in this study, *Oderay* comes the closest to presenting a Romanticized portrayal of the native as an ideal pre-civilization noble being. The author describes rites, customs, songs, and traditions of natives, but the principal goal seems to be to create a narrative that emphasizes Enlightenment ideals with the native serving as an allegory for these values. *La Leandra* offers a more straightforward case of propaganda, a one-sided description of native barbarism designed to defend colonization and conversion, and even, when necessary, the extermination of natives themselves. In the case of *Amelia*, the narrative defends the claim that natives needed the civilizing influence of Europeans, a claim that allowed the hegemonic culture to exercise its dominance. It also shows that the human trait of sensibility crosses ethnographic boundaries. The portrayal of natives follows stereotypical models that reflect European prejudices, and the novel to some degree defends colonization and rejects the colonies' independence by exonerating the British of all wrongdoing. But it also uses the figure of a native who loves his children and defends their autonomy as a literary trope for criticizing European parents' unhealthy control over their children.

In all three novels, the natives' function as characters who propagate the texts' ideology outweighs their function as accurate portrayals of a cultural "Other" aimed at increasing understanding between Europeans and New World inhabitants. Most importantly, as good, bad, sentimental, and Other, the figure of the native addresses the distinct challenges facing Spain. Zavala y Zamora advocates for a more egalitarian and enlightened nation while the translator of *Amelia* supports the mother country as it argues for filial autonomy. Valladares, however, maintains the status quo of the *antiguo régimen*. Since the establishment of the Bourbon monarchy in Spain in 1700, but especially with the reforms of Carlos III (1759–1788) and into the nineteenth century, the term "las dos Españas," or "the two Spains," had been used to describe the polarizing division between reformers and traditionalists in the country. The novels examined here, from the Enlightenment ideology of *Oderay* to the conservative orthodoxy of *La Leandra*, express graphically this ever-more-divisive split in Spanish society and politics.

NOTES

I would like to thank the Office of the Dean of the College of Randolph-Macon College as well as the Committee on Faculty Development for providing the funds to travel to Montreal where I presented a preliminary version of this paper at the 2006 ASECS Conference. I would also like to thank the readers of this essay for their valuable comments and suggestions. Initial research into this theme took place during a sabbatical leave: Randolph-Macon College graciously provided valuable time and a Rashkind grant that funded my work.

1. Ter Ellingson, *The Myth of the Noble Savage* (Berkeley and Los Angeles: University of California Press, 2001), np.
2. Hayden White, *Tropics of Discourse* (Baltimore: Johns Hopkins University Press, 1978), 183.

3. Carmelo Virgillo discusses the representation of natives in Latin America fiction; see "Primitivism in Latin American Fiction," in *The Ibero-American Enlightenment*, ed. A. Owen Aldridge (Urbana: University of Illinois Press, 1971), 243–55. Juan Ignacio Ferreras offers a bibliographic article about the native in nineteenth-century Spanish fiction: see "El tema americano en la novela española del XIX. Orígenes y desarrollo," *Cuadernos hispanoamericanos* 279 (1973): 546–83. To my knowledge, the theme of the native in eighteenth-century Spanish fiction remains largely untouched.

4. "did not have the repercussions or the utility as it did in other cultures." David Weber, *Bárbaros: Spaniards and Their Savages in the Age of Enlightenment* (New Haven: Yale University Press, 2005), 290 n. 118. All translations are mine.

5. Weber, *Bárbaros*, 42.

6. Joaquín Alvarez Barrientos, *La novela del siglo XVIII* (Madrid: Ediciones Jucar, 1981); Reginald F. Brown, *La novela española, 1700–1850* (Madrid: Ministerio de Educación Nacional, 1953); and Ana Rueda, *Cartas sin lacrar: La novela epistolar y la España Ilustrada, 1789–1840* (Madrid: Iberoamericana, 2001).

7. While this study focuses on the native in novels, dramas translated and performed in Spain with native protagonists is a theme that would bear further examination. In fact, two of the writers whom I feature in this study were prolific translators of dramas, and Zavala y Zamora translated at least one other novel about natives, *Camiré, novela americana.*

8. Ferreras, "El tema americano," 553.

9. Joaquín Marco, "Notas a una estética de la novela española (1795–1842)," *Boletín de la Real Academia Española* 46 (1966): 116. For more on translations of novels in the eighteenth century, see Alvarez Barrientos, *La novela del siglo XVIII*, 198–213.

10. Barrientos, *La novela del siglo XVIII*, 207–08.

11. The novel had originally been attributed to Chateaubriand, but scholars agree that the real author of the French text was probably Ambroise-Marie Palisot de Beauvois. For details see Joaquín Alvarez Barrientos, "Novela," in *Historia literaria de España en el siglo XVIII*, ed. Francisco Aguilar Piñal (Madrid: Editorial Trotta, 1996), 273. For his part, Guillermo Carnero states that the novel "no es una imitación ni una adaptación de *Paul et Virginie* (como habiá sugerido Ignacio Ferreras), sino la traducción directa y casi literal del anónimo *Odérahi*, que estudió y editó Gilbert Chinard a partir de la edición de Paris de 1801" ["is not an imitation nor an adaptation of *Paul et Virginie* (as Ignacio Ferreras had suggested), but rather a direct and almost literal translation of the anonymous *Odérahi* that Gilbert Chinard studied and edited using the Paris edition of 1801"]. See his introduction to the Spanish translation of Zavala y Zamora, *Oderay, usos, trages, ritos, costumbres y leyes de los habitantes de la América Septentrional*, in *Obras narrativas I*, ed. e intro. Guillermo Carnero (Barcelona: Universidad de Alicante, 1992), 49. Carnero states that Paul Hazard in 1923 had suggested that the author may have been

the botanist Ambroise-Marie Palisot de Beauvois (Carnero, *Obras*, 49). Maurice Chazin, however, warns against making an absolute judgment in the absence of concrete facts; see Maurice Chazin, "Chateaubriand 'Le Chantre D'Odérahi,'" *Modern Language Notes* 47.4 (1932): 238. A number of websites provide information about Palisot de Beauvois's important botanical work as well as his descriptions of American insects (http://www-museum.unl.edu/research/entomology/workers/APalisot.htm), but none of the sites consulted mentions this literary work.

12. Alvarez Barrientos points out the curiously high number of translations that dealt with this theme; see *La novela del siglo XVIII*, 207. The edition of the novel I cite is the 1818 edition published by Estevan in Valencia located in the Brown University Library, but as Rodney Rodriguez notes, editions of the novel also appeared in 1813 and 1815. See Rodney Rodriguez, "El discurso narrativo moral y su recepción en la España de Fernando VII," *Actas del X Congreso de la Asociación de Hispanistas*, eds. Antonio Vilanova, Josep Bricall, and Elias Rivers (Barcelona: Promociones y Publicaciones Universitarias, 1992), 1434. In addition to these editions that Rodriguez cites is an 1827 edition published again in Valencia and this time by Mompié, a copy of which can be found in Oberlin College Library's Special Collections. The novel was published in a collection with *Federico y Maclovia*. In fact, the edition in the library at Brown University comes with an illustration from *Federico y Maclovia*, which reveals something about how novels were printed and bound during the early years of the nineteenth century. It was customary at the time for subscribers to purchase the text and the illustrations separately and have them bound by a book binder. I surmise that the illustration accompanying *Federico y Maclovia* was purchased as part of the collection, but was bound with *Amelia* when this latter novel was bound separately. I thank Ed Vermue, curator of Special Collections of the Oberlin College Library, for this information. The Biblioteca Valenciana has multiple copies of both the 1815 and the 1827 editions of *Amelia*, which suggest the novel's popularity, especially since copies exist in several libraries in the U.S. as well. In the 1827 edition, there appears an index of titles published by Mompié, including a translation of Chateaubriand's novel dealing with the literary topos of the Noble Savage, *Atalá o los amores de dos salvages en el desierto*.

13. Antonio Valladares y Sotomayor, *La Leandra: novela original que comprehende muchas* (tomos 2 y 3) (*La Leandra: Original Novel that Includes Many*, [volumes 2 and 3]) (Madrid: Oficina de Antonio Ulloa, 1797).

14. "a troop of barbarous Indians;" Zavala y Zamora, *Oderay*, 139.

15. Interestingly enough, the image that was printed with the text is not of an Indian at all, but rather a Christian image of the good pastor; Zavala y Zamora, *Oderay*, 146.

16. Ellingson, *Myth of the Noble Savage*, 46.

17. Carnero maintains that *Oderay* "sigue fundamentalmente el despliegue del mito del buen salvaje, básicamente asignado a la muchacha india. . . . Sus rasgos aquí son la lealtad, el pacifismo, la falta de ambición y de afán de riqueza,

la hospitalidad, la solidaridad y el desprendimiento; la autenticidad y la espontaniedad sentimental y amorosa." [Oderay] "fundamentally follows the mold of the myth of the Noble Savage, basically assigned to the Indian girl. . . . Her traits are loyalty, pacifism; sentimental and amorous authenticity and spontaneity." He also claims that "ese mito es un subterfugio crítico desde el que poner mejor de manifiesto la corrupción de la sociedad que se considera civilizada; "that myth is a critical subterfuge from which to more directly point out the corruption of a society that considers itself civilized." Zavala y Zamora, *Oderay*, 45.

18. White, *Tropics of Discourse*, 191.

19. White, *Tropics of Discourse*, 192.

20. A number of critics have explored the influence of moralist philosophy in Spanish Enlightenment thought and in eighteenth-century Spanish drama, including Russell Sebold, *El rapto de la mente: Poética y poesía dieciochescas* (Barcelona: Anthropos, 1989); David Gies, "Sensibilidad y Sensualismo en la poesía dieciochesca," in *Ideas en sus paisajes: Homenaje al Profesor Russell P. Sebold*, eds. Guillermo Carnero, Ignacio Javier López, and Enrique Rubio (Alicante: Universidad de Alicante, 1999), 215–24; Yvonne Fuentes, "British Aesthetics and the Picturesque in Spain: Jovellanos's Affinity with England," *Hispania* 87.2 (2004): 210–19; María Jesús García Garrosa, *La retórica de las lágrimas: La comedia sentimental española, 1751–1802* (Valladolid: Secretariado de Publicaciones, Universidad de Valladolid, Caja Salamanca, 1990); Joan Lynn Pataky-Kosove, *The "Comedia Lacrimosa" and Spanish Romantic Drama (1773–1865)* (London: Tamesis Books, 1977).

21. Writing about the sentimentalism of *Oderay* in his introduction to his edition of the novel, Guillermo Carnero notes that the most notable characteristic of the text is its synthesis of sentimentalism and exoticism.

22. "with more fortitude." Zavala y Zamora, *Oderay*, 207.

23. "If only our European women would imitate this virtuous control over their emotions." Zavala y Zamora, *Oderay*, 207.

24. Ellingson, *Myth of the Noble Savage*, 25.

25. "Your father, you say, did not give consent for Eugenia to be your wife? Then in your country a man is not free to marry the woman he loves? So, a father can allow his daughter to be burned up by love?" Zavala y Zamora, *Oderay*, 158.

26. "the children have fun alongside their parents and never does one hear from parents a hard word that would break their spirit." Zavala y Zamora, *Oderay*, 159.

27. "It did not take long for me to find them [the customs] a thousand times preferable to European customs." Zavala y Zamora, *Oderay*, 167.

28. Steven A Leblanc, *Constant Battles: The Myth of the Peaceful, Noble Savage* (New York: St. Martin's Press, 2003), xi.

29. Zavala y Zamora, *Oderay*, 186.

30. Stelio Cro, *The Noble Savage: Allegory of Freedom* (Waterloo, Ontario: Wilfrid Laurier University Press, 1990), 129, 135. Cro maintains that Rousseau

perpetrated a myth of the Noble Savage to show their world as a utopia free from the tyranny of churches or kings; for Rousseau the Noble Savage is not an anthropological reality, but rather an embodiment of his intuitions on the value of freedom and the means to ensure its survival.

31. Cro, *The Noble Savage*, 147.

32. White, *Tropics of Discourse*, 183.

33. White, *Tropics of Discourse*, 187–88.

34. White, *Tropics of Discourse*, 187.

35. While Weber's entire book focuses on the relationship between Spain and natives in the New World, see in particular chapters 3 and 4. Weber, *Bárbaros*, 91–178.

36. Carnero writes that "Zavala ha manipulado prudentemente la respuesta de Oderay (pp. 93–94) a la pregunta de Onteree sobre su idea del Ser Supremo, eliminando comparaciones físicas entre el hombre y la Divinidad que remiten a un antropomorfismo demasiado primitivo. Un poco después (pp. 101–102), en el fragmento que empieza 'Quando quería hablarla de la religión cristiana . . . ,' ha hecho desaparecer alusiones irreverentes a la confesión, la teofagia eucarística y la religión cristiana en general, y también a la leyenda negra antiespañola relativa a la conquista de América." "Zavala has prudently manipulated Oderay's response to Onteree's question about the idea of the Supreme Being, eliminating physical comparisons between man and Divinity that go back to an excessively primitive anthropomorphism. A little later (pp. 101–102), in the fragment that begins 'When I wanted to talk to her about Christianity . . . ,' he has removed irreverent allusions to confession, Eucharistic theophagy and the Christian religion in general, and also to the anti-Spanish black legend relative to the conquest of America." Zavala y Zamora, *Oderay*, 50–51.

37. "the unfortunate effects of extreme sensibility."

38. "the sincere desires of their daughters." Rodriguez also insinuates that the anonymous novel may not even be a real translation. A second subtitle of the book calls it a translation of an "anécdota inglesa," but as Rodriguez points out, some scholars question whether or not these advertised translations really were translations, and if they were, how accurate these translations might be. Rodriguez, "El discurso narrativo," 1434–35. My attempts to find the original English text have not proven successful so far.

39. "Oh! I will overcome, I will crush this feeling." *Amelia*, 17.

40. "the arrow of a savage." *Amelia*, 66.

41. "It was discovered that Carlos's injury, which Amelia had sucked, was poisoned: this is one of the atrocious actions of the barbarism of the American savages." *Amelia*, 102.

42. "bring back to life for me a loved wife . . . yes, you seem to me to be sensible." *Amelia*, 120.

43. "The Dictionary of Sensibility" hypertext project contains a list of terms associated with the genre, and instead of defining them, cites passages from a wide variety of works in which the terms are used in context. See Corey Brady

et. al., "The Dictionary of Sensibility" (http://www.engl.virginia.edu/enec981/dicitionary/intro.html).

44. *Amelia*, 123.

45. "the hand of those perfidious [Europeans] is that which has shot the poisoned arrow that now snatches your wife from you." *Amelia*, 126.

46. White, *Tropics of Discourse*, 193–94.

47. Weber, *Bárbaros*, 91.

48. Michelle Buchanan, "Savages, Noble and Otherwise, and the French Enlightenment," *Studies in Eighteenth-Century Culture* 15 (1986): 97.

49. Rueda, *Cartas sin lacrar*, 266–75.

50. García Garrosa argues that the religious fanaticism of Valladares contrasts strongly with the open and more tolerant attitude of other writers, and states that a clear contrast would be *Oderay*, "con la cultura y la religión indígena, que consideran más cercanas a la naturaleza, retomando así el tópico rousseauniano del buen salvaje frente a la sociedad corruptora." "with the indigenous culture and religion, considered closer to nature, returning in this way to the Rousseauian topic of the Noble Savage confronting corrupting society." María Jesús García Garrosa, "*La Leandra*, novela moral," *Anales de la Literatura Española de la Universidad de Alicante* 11 (1995): 135. Alvarez Barrientos also compares the representation of natives in the same novels, concluding that the natives' rites are considered on the same level as other religions in *Oderay*, and proclaiming *Oderay* innovative because of its message of toleration and tolerance. Alvarez Barrientos, *La novela del siglo XVIII*, 306.

51. "Within a short while accompanied by two others, an Indian whose appearance inspired veneration, came into the room. Her white coloring, different from all the others, which was dark, her fine skin, large black eyes, that all fit with the other parts of her face and body in coming together to make for a beautiful woman." Valladares y Sotomayor, *La Leandra*, 2: 168–69.

52. Ellingson, *Myth of the Noble Savage*, 127.

53. "how inhuman and horrible the religion that our compatriots practiced seemed to us, and about which María had already made us comprehend the absurdity of its ceremonies, the barbarism of its rites, and the cruelty of its precepts, all informed by the common enemy, supported by the superstitious priests and believed by the ignorant and barbarous people." Valladares y Sotomayor, *La Leandra*, 2:279–80.

54. Rueda, *Cartas sin lacrar*, 273.

55. Christopher Fox notes that some thinkers in the Enlightenment equated traveling in space with traveling in time, and that "the Others they encountered were earlier versions of themselves. It is in the Indians' 'present condition that we are to behold, as in a mirour, the gestures of our own progenitors,' claimed Adam Ferguson." Christopher Fox, "Introduction. How to Prepare a Noble Savage: The Spectacle of Human Science," in *Inventing Human Science: Eighteenth-Century Domains*, eds. Christopher Fox, Roy Porter, and Robert Wokler (Berkeley: University of California Press, 1995), 16.

56. Short sleeved outer dress and a shawl, considered everyday wear.

57. "Ladies, . . . in the Churches of this Island, such unacceptable adornment is not allowed. If my fellow islanders were to see you with half of your heads uncovered, hair so curled, and so full of flowers, with so many ties to secure the loose ends, plumes, ribbons, and other knickknacks whose names I do not know, and those, according to what I heard you call them last night, curlers, but which I would call rollers to pull in the most uncooperative locks: if they were to see you, I say, with those fallen tresses or big curls that cover your bosom, with uncovered throats, parts of your shoulders, and even more, they would be so horrified, that you would fear dreadful consequences. And, truth be told, that fashion, does it seem to you that it's proper and decent enough in which one would present oneself in the house of God, where He really and truly is as He is in heaven?" Valladares y Sotomayor, *La Leandra*, 2:351–53.

58. "Oh, goodness mother, I am going off to ready myself in the style that the Governor has prescribed, so as to go to mass in Church; which really should be with grand modesty in one's dress and with the greatest tenderness in one's heart." Valladares y Sotomayor, *La Leandra*, 2:354–55.

59. "Let's suppose that your friend has become the bloody remains of the cruelty of some Indian, who during the insurrection, entered the temple, took him to his home and who is barbarously filling his stomach with the flesh of your compatriot; which is just what I presume" Valladares y Sotomayor, *La Leandra*, 2:194.

60. "I firmly believe that someone who kills one's enemies, and dies confessing the Law of God, will achieve eternal life." Valladares y Sotomayor, *La Leandra*, 2:286.

61. Of this episode, María Jesús García Garrosa writes that the tone and attitude of the stories of Eduardo and Camilo and the story of María are designed to reflect "otro de los temas centrales de esta novela: la defensa-panegírico de la religión cristiana y sus preceptos." ("another of the central themes of this novel, the panegyric defense of Christianity and its precepts.") García Garrosa, "*La Leandra*, novela moral," 134.

62. White, *Tropics of Discourse*, 193–94.

Church, State, and Modernization: English Literature as Gentlemanly Knowledge after 1688

SIMON DURING

This paper belongs to the under-developed sub-discipline, "the historical sociology of literature," by which I mean that it considers literature as a social institution with specifiable material interests, organizational structures, and social functions rather than simply as a body of writing. But a caveat needs to be entered at once. The moment I am concerned with, the long eighteenth century, is, of course, when the term "literature" came to cover not written knowledge available to the literate in general but the kind of writing produced specifically by men and women of letters—and, in particular, imaginative writing.

From the sociological perspective, this change of "literature's" denotation is a consequence of a mutation of social function that the literary field underwent across the century.[1] To put a familiar case succinctly: literature became less centered on polite learning, including classical scholarship, and more centered on sympathetic imagination and the suspension of disbelief. At the same stroke, it also claimed a greater role in moral education. As it thereby extended its capacity for social agency and engagement, new readerships, particularly among women, were created alongside new genres and hierarchies of genres. By the time of Walter Scott's death in 1832, realist prose fiction had become dominant.[2]

This restructuring of the literary world is usually understood through categories like commercialization, political liberalization, secularization, domesticification, the emergence of the Habermasian public sphere, and the feminization of literary life—categories that can be grouped together under the head of "modernization."[3] While the modernization model cannot be discounted (in fact the relation between liberty, commerce, and the increase of the "trade of writing" was often adduced at the time), I want to argue that that model is inadequate to describe the conditions under which the literary world underwent transformation.[4] Indeed over the past twenty or so years a rather different account of eighteenth-century social and intellectual history has appeared in the scholarship of historians like J.C.D. Clark and J.G.A. Pocock.[5] Here the period is not analyzed as anticipating a modernized future but as imbricated in its pasts. In Clark's case particularly, if rather polemically, eighteenth-century England becomes a "confessional state" in which political differences remain primarily expressions of religious differences, and church/state relations are key to social, cultural, and intellectual formations.[6] A secular polity cannot be assumed. In a similar spirit, a series of recent studies have made the case that the Anglican religion played a more significant role in public life and attracted wider support and participation than had been recognized by earlier historians, undercutting accounts which present the period as primarily governed by the modernizing forces just mentioned.[7]

These revisionist accounts, whose impulse has indubitably been conservative but whose insights need not be contained within conservativism, have only been spottily absorbed by literary historians, and when they have been so absorbed, have often lapsed into only partly persuasive arguments that particular writers were more closely connected to Jacobitism than previous scholarship had supposed.[8] Yet they do allow us to inquire into the degree to which the transformation of literature's social function and status in England can be understood as an—admittedly highly-mediated—effect of the shift of relations between church, market, and state after 1688. More particularly they can provide the terms though which we can understand how a new literary formation came into being from within the older, only partly secularized concepts and institutional structures of polite learning. Such a revisionist account can also help us understand how older forms of literary production and knowledge responded to mutations in the literary field, whose "modernization" cannot effectively be understood macrologically as the smooth transformation from one set of structures and conditions into another but rather as the outcome of continual local frictions and exchanges between older and newer formations, both themselves under constant transformation. This essay presents itself as an account of two moments in which newer, secular formations energetically brushed against older, non-secular ones—and vice-versa.

Church-State Relations

To this end it is necessary to point to the church/state relations that are most relevant to the locations where old and new literary formations interacted with particular intensity. The 1688 English revolution put in place a quasi-confessional (*pace* Clark) state in which the established church retained important privileges but which tolerated other confessions, despite severe formal (if consistently obviated) civil penalties against those outside the Anglican fold.[9] At a more abstract level, once the church was detached from and subordinated to the state under the terms of the 1689 settlement, sovereignty was no longer securely legitimated by religion. These new state-church relations were passionately experienced as and through division, oppression, and efforts at reconciliation.[10] A series of negotiations between the established church and the state in the period immediately after the deposition of the Stuart regime led both to a structural connection between the rural clergy and the oppositional Tory grouping as well as widespread sympathy for the small break-away group of clergy, the so-called non-jurors, who could not accept the terms of the revolutionary settlement (the breaching of apostolic succession and the overthrow of divine right of kings) and who later refused to sign oaths of allegiance to new monarchs in 1701 and 1715.[11] A slow reconnection between the church hierarchy and state administration during the post 1714 period of Whig hegemony, although threatened by anti-clerical acts like the Quaker Tithe and Mortmain Bills of 1736, reached its apogée under last years of the Walpole and Pelham administrations. This was a remarkable feat since the Whig hegemony was also consistently supported by the dissenting churches largely in response to the continuing threat of Jacobitism and the high church interest.

During this period the Anglican clergy became increasingly professionalized, increasingly absorbed into state politics and increasingly drawn from filiative chains within the elite (in the latter half of the century about half of all clergymen were the sons of clergymen).[12] In many rural parishes, clergymen, not least through their sermons and their role as educators, were uncontested intellectual leaders, controlling channels for the dissemination of political and ethical discourse. The church's strong presence within the education system, not least through its influence in the universities, allowed it to select and recruit talented youth: the careers of

Edmund Gibson, Richard Hurd and Thomas Percy stand as examples: all became bishops though they were born into plebeian families. [13]

The American Revolutionary War marked a break within this structure since it effectively shunted the Dissenters along with the Anglican low church into political opposition. The founding of the republican state in North America enabled a certain transference of the dissident spirit from religious non-conformity to secular political radicalism at home.[14] And from the 1780s, the Hanoverian church-state alliance began to dissolve, in part because the church was no longer a central organ of social control; in part because the promise of toleration was reneged upon (the elder Pitt's rejection of the repeal of the Test and Corporation Acts in 1787 was a pivotal event in this regard); and in part because the church had become less and less connected, affectively and discursively, to large segments of the population, riven as it was by competition from evangelical 'new birth' Christianity on the one side and skepticisms and deisms on the other.[15] By the second decade of the nineteenth century, conservative intellectuals, facing an increasingly commercialized literary institution, echoed old ecclesiastical social theory by calling for a new, stronger church-state alliance to resist democratization and industrialization, with Coleridge's *Constitution of Church and State* (1830), written against Irish Catholic emancipation, leading the way.

Literature, thought of as written polite learning, was largely if decreasingly shaped within the structures that comprise this history, mainly because the Anglican church remained the largest and richest single institution engaged in intellectual production over the period.[16] For heuristic purposes, it is possible to divide literary production over the period into two blocs. The first, aimed at the marketplace, disseminated practical information, discipline, and various kinds of readerly excitement. In the mid-century, this bloc was dominated by market-attuned book-trade businessmen who turned away from collaborative enterprises and instead concentrated on distribution (export) marketing and the development of new formats (especially periodicals), primarily pitching their wares towards discretionary consumers from the middling ranks.[17] The second was produced from within the gentlemanly world at whose intellectual and material center lay the established church: it was Burke who was to say that "European civilization" was formed by two forces, "the spirit of a gentleman and the spirit of religion" and like many of his genteel contemporaries, Burke did not think of these two spirits as separable.[18] The English universities are to be included in this second bloc, since they effectively formed part of the established ecclesiastical apparatus.[19] Like market-oriented writing, gentlemanly, churchly literature was internally various, although it was often produced for selection mechanisms that intermittently governed professional entry and advancement within the church. It was characteristically aimed at maintaining the Episcopate's intellectual legitimacy and social power despite schisms within the church itself. Theological, devotional, scholarly, and pedagogic writing poured from the presses, with sermons being a staple of the publishing industry through the period. This bloc also covered more discretionary forms of learning as produced by writers supported by the Anglican church and in particular by relatively leisured and intellectually trained members of the country clergy. Local antiquarianism and natural philosophy were at the forefront here.

Alongside these two main blocs we can add two more: print primarily of professional interest to lawyers and medical practitioners; and the printed intellectual production of those groups outside or on the margins of the established church, namely republicans, dissenters, and especially in the period from about 1689 to about 1740 and from the other side of the political spectrum, the non-jurors. These groups have occupied recent scholarly attention to a degree that is incommensurate with their significance at the time, not least because women had more license to participate in print culture among dissenters and republicans than among Anglicans (although the key women intellectuals in the immediate Restoration period were Tory royalists (such as Aphra Behn and Mary Astell), and also because rational Dissent in particular figures so prominently in the genealogy of secular radicalism, not least through the sponsorship of the dissenting academies.[20] This is not at all to deny that these minor blocs were also important to eighteenth-century literary culture, nor to claim that they were isolated from the two mainstreams.[21]

In the end, commercial literature possessed most energy, and certainly that was where the genres that would come to dominate the literary world were developed, in part because it too provided a relatively welcoming environment for women to participate.[22] But we should not think of the gentlemanly literature of the orthodox as undynamic over the period, nor, indeed, as outside of commercial play, given that a significant proportion of the capital which supported intellectual life over the period was channeled through the church and those associated with it. Indeed it would be an error to think of the market-oriented and gentlemanly-ecclesiastical blocs except as engaged in constant, often mutually-supportive interaction and exchange. The two blocs often combined forces in educational writing in which both the church and the market had an interest. Moreover, the gentlemanly bloc routinely called upon the market bloc just to get its writing into print, even where it sought to subvent the booksellers through subscription or self publishing (hence the key role of intellectually-engaged printers like William Bowyer, Samuel Buckley, Samuel Richardson, John Nichols, and William Sandby). Several of the most prominent authors in the market for imaginative writing were clergymen: Laurence Sterne, Edward Young, Richard Graves, and Charles Churchill, to name just four of the more popular. Ecclesiastical careers could also be built on market-orientated scholarship, as in the case of Thomas Newton, bishop of Bristol, one-time fashionable London preacher, and editor of the bestselling, standard edition of Milton. A successful commercial enterprise like Edmund Cave's *Gentleman's Magazine* could come to prominence by promoting a competition (first prize £50) for the best poem on a religious topic, as it did in 1734.[23] And more importantly still, clergymen were crucial to the characterology of the dominant market-oriented genre—the sentimental-realist novel. Parson Adams, Yorick, the Vicar of Wakefield, Elizabeth Inchbald's Catholic priest Dorriford in *A Simple Story,* and Jane Austen's Edmund Bertram in *Mansfield Park* come immediately to mind. And this is to leave aside more complex interactions such as the role of Anglicanism and Tory mysticism within the conceptual and ethical structure of a novel like Samuel Richardson's *Clarissa*.[24]

At this point we can turn to two particularly revealing intersections between the market and the gentlemanly-ecclesiastical literary blocs. The first is John Nichols's prodigies of labor and print output from the middle of the 1770s to the 1820s, of which the finest fruit was his monumental nine-volume *Literary Anecdotes* with its eight-volume sequel, *Illustrations of Eighteenth-Century Literary History*, (the last volumes of which were, admittedly, edited by Nichols's son.)[25] These books provide a significant amount of the information that allows us to map the period's literary history to this day, even though they can be understood as a rebuke to the transformations within the print culture of their time. The second, from the heart of the gentlemanly ecclesiastical bloc, is the writing of a group of authors closely associated with William Warburton, bishop of Gloucester, sometimes known as the Warburtonians. As we shall see, this group developed some of the concepts that would become central to secular art-literature.

John Nichols and *Literary Anecdotes*

Nichols was primarily a printer. He had been apprenticed to the Bowyer firm in the 1750s, whose then proprietor, William Bowyer the younger, was a non-juror who played a significant part in bringing Tory and non-juring scholarship and polemic into print from the 1720s, but who also had lucrative contracts with the Whig-dominated House of Commons.[26] We can take the 1721, two-volume folio edition of Charles Leslie's self-published *Theological Works* (a source of much subsequent anti-liberal political theology) and the 1732 fine, illustrated edition of Theodore Bathurst's Latin translation of Edmund Spenser's *The Shephearde's Calender* as prestigious expressions of the firm's interests at that time.[27] But those interests ranged widely, and included important books in Welsh and monuments of book production such as William Cheselden's astonishing osteological atlas, *Osteographia*, whose illustrations of pathological skeletal anatomy seem (in this context) to belong not just to medical science but to ideology, invoking as they do the human 'mortification' that so underpins contemporary absolutist theories of sovereignty. Finally, and tellingly, the print shop produced a number of books on the history of printing and typography, an expression of a cult of the book which seems to have been particularly intense in this political-religious grouping.[28]

In 1766 Nichols became Bowyer's partner and controlled the shop from the mid-seventies when he purchased a share of the *Gentleman's Magazine*, whose editor he became. In addition to his work as a printer and magazine editor, he compiled a series of books mainly aimed at keeping the literary culture of the first half of the century in circulation. Many of these transposed into print manuscripts, letters, and papers that he had personally acquired. Indeed many relied on information solicited by him either via the correspondence columns of the *Gentleman's Magazine* or privately. Such books included an edition of Swift's minor works; Steele's letters; Benjamin Hoadly's sermons and pamphlets; Francis Atterbury's writings and papers; documents around Hogarth's life; and of course the *Literary Anecdotes* and *Literary History*. The "anecdote" genre was well established in the later eighteenth century, examples being William Seward's *Anecdotes of Some Distinguished Persons* (1795–97); Richard Gough's *Anecdotes of British Topography* (1768) and the more widely known *Anecdotes of English Painting* (1762–71) by Horace Walpole. In effect, the genre consisted of works that collected together fragments of information or recollection, whether transmitted orally, in manuscript, or in print, without organizing them either as history or as biography. Certainly it possessed little of the essayistic and reflective quality later ascribed to it by Isaac Disraeli.[29]

Nichols's contribution to the genre began as a record of the books printed by the Bowyer firm—it was first published under the title *Anecdotes of William Bowyer*. Nichols listed Bowyer's publications in chronological order and added biographical information about their authors in footnotes that could stretch across pages, drowning the body of the text. Later volumes of the *Anecdotes* and the *Literary History* extended the range of this feat of memorialization by elaborating on what had become a key feature of the *Gentleman's Magazine*—the obituary. They are effectively collections of extended death notices and literary remains addressed to an uncertain posterity.[30] It was if Nichols were trying to ensure that the lived world of post-1688 gentlemanly polite learning would be transmitted into a future in which it was being displaced by the modern literary institution. Indeed, although quite successful as a booktrade entrepreneur, Nichols was entrenched in the fading literary bloc: his firm failed to keep pace with contemporary booktrade developments such as the separation of retail, distribution, publishing, and printing arms, or the emphasis on fiction.[31] The paucity of fiction printed by the Bowyer firm is striking: leaving aside exceptional cases such as the second edition of *Robinson Crusoe* (demand for that book was so strong that much of the London trade become involved in printing it), only one novel is listed in its ledgers up until the 1740s, the little-known *Rosalinda: a Novel* (1733).

Nichols himself was probably not politically partisan: perhaps he even began as a Whig, and he is on record as an admirer of Richard Steele. But his publishing enterprises are unambiguously Tory in their interests and range: thus one of his partners in producing the *Literary Anecdotes,* and more especially its sequel, was the Tory politician and lawyer, George Hardinge, Queen Charlotte's attorney and the notorious defender of those charged with property damage in the 1791 Birmingham "King and Country" riots against Joseph Priestley. Nichols's Tory inclination was encouraged by the Bowyer firm's being so entrenched in the non-juring networks during his halcyon period from about 1720 to 1740, but he shared it with his readership (both for the *Gentleman's Magazine* and for his various document compilations) who largely belonged to the country gentry and particularly the country clergy, a group that began the century linked to Toryism and ended it as evangelicals or as Burkean conservatives awaiting the Anglo-Catholicism to come, as we shall see in regard to the Warburtonians.[32] Furthermore Nichols's feats of memorialization and retrieval can be twinned with the radical sentimentalism of novelized clergymen like Yorick and Parson Adams, since both are expressions of the slow ecclesiastical displacement from the emergent social sectors of the time—urban commerce and secular professionalism—as well as political interests bound to these sectors.

At any rate what Nichols retrieves from the Bowyer archive in the first volumes of his magnum opus *Literary Anecdotes* is a literary institution very different from that organized by successful book trade contemporaries such as the Robinsons, John Murray, James Lackington, Henry Coburn, and William Lane. He recovers a world dominated by learned, productive clergymen, clustered in families and often suspicious or contemptuous of the Whig hegemony as well as (in the early period) non-juror scholars who remained outside the state-sanctioned church. For him, their contribution constitutes what the period's literature *was*. The resonant names include Hilkiah Bedford, Joseph Bingham, Thomas Brett, Thomas Carte, Edmund Chishull, William Cole, Jeremy Collier, Thomas Deacon, Henry Dodwell, Elizabeth Elstob, Zachary Grey, George Hickes, Samuel Jebb, William Law, Thomas Smith, John Urry, and Thomas Wagstaffe, most of whom have been forgotten by literary history, despite Nichols's efforts, as has, indeed, the literary field of which they were ornaments.

In addition to the ordinary classical fare of polite learning, the writers memorialised by Nichols produced pioneering research on oriental languages and Hebrew in extension of an interest in "primitive Christianity" and patristic history dating back at least to Archbishop Laud's time.[33] They also made important inroads into knowledge of what would later come to be called the Anglo-Saxon dialect, although not so much to recover a tradition of English liberty but of a religious England not yet divided by the Reformation.[34] The Bowyer shop authors also printed masses of sermons and pamphlets combating Arianism, Socinianism, and Latitudinarianism. And they put into print a vast array of topographical and local historical information (sometimes original, sometimes transcribed from records and manuscript archives, sometimes reprinted), occasionally out of self-interest since rural clergymen could increase their income from tithes and glebes by retrieving lost and ancient rights from parish records. As Jeremy Gregory puts it, "parochial income could only be properly collected if the incumbent had a good grasp of local history."[35] Finally the firm printed some of the natural philosophy that was flowing from the Church through this period, although given the political nature of its networks, less than many of its competitors.

This literary production, like Nichols's own, was allied to the accelerated institutionalization of literary knowledge across a number of spheres. That is to say, Nichols was remembering but also participating in a process by which writing of all kinds joined the public sphere in an organized fashion so as to attract new forms of sociability and display. The gentlemanly-ecclesiastical bloc here helps to create polite learning as a public institution and utility. Examples of this process include the donation of large collections of printed and manuscript materials to libraries, with the Tory politician Robert Harley making the most ostentatious contribution. The professionalization of librarianship and record keeping was important too, with Andrew Ducarel, the Lambeth librarian under Secker's patronage playing a particularly important role, along with Thomas Astle, indexer of the Harley manuscripts and rationalizer of state-record keeping. At the same time formal associations of antiquarians were developed with the prestigious Society of Antiquaries (1717) at their head. Semi-formal scholarly clubs such as the Spalding Gentleman's Society also helped archives find their way into the public sphere—for instance, one of its members, the clergyman and antiquarian Samuel Pegg, appointed Nichols his literary executor, thereby transmitting another trove of dialect and Anglo-Saxon remains into print.[36] Less formally still, this gentlemanly, Tory institutionalization of public knowledge spread into the expanding popularity of book collecting itself, since collecting was at the time at least a semi-public activity entwined in the formal and semi-formal gentlemanly associations of scholarship and librarianism as well as the market, and was exposed to notice through widely advertized sales and book auctions. We can say, then, that the gentlemanly-ecclesiastical literary bloc helped develop the modern institution of literature despite its (qualified) opposition to that institution's means and purposes, and despite its products' failure to survive in cultural memory.

At the level of cultural politics, the Tory ethic that sounds through Nichols's enterprises can now be seen to resonate with later *dissident* intellectual groupings that helped constitute the modern literary institution. Although the intense scholarly activity of Nichols and the Bowyer printshop drew upon the productive labors of rural parsons, although it helped create literature as a public resource and helped secure the genealogy of eighteenth-century literary history, it nonetheless operated at a remove from full participation in sanctioned citizenship. It expresses a social alienation, which, in its more radical forms, respected the supernaturally-legitimated sovereignty that the 1688 revolution had overthrown. Once the 1689 constitution and its principles became all but unassailable, those grounding principles of Anglican and non-juring politics—"passive obedience" and "non-resistance"—can be understood as early theorizations of elite internal exile that finds little hope even in the politics of "patriot" identity and recognition, let alone in commercialized culture. Later, these habits of retreat from the apparatuses of state and commerce would be shared by many alienated literary intellectuals, as they produced avant-gardes within literary worlds in which, however, the remnants of old gentlemanly-ecclesiastical bloc played no important role.

The Warburtonians

From a certain point of view, it may seem that the non-juring and Tory networks that provide the bulk of the material in the first two volumes of Nichols's *Literary Anecdotes* stand at the opposite end of the spectrum of ecclesiastical-gentlemanly learning from that occupied by the Warburtonians. After all, William Warburton himself is an ornament of J.G.A. Pocock's "conservative enlightenment," and, as a self-ascribed "religious deist," he was a chief spokesman of the established church's Whiggish and rationalist wing.[37] He came to prominence after the publication of the first edition of his *Alliance of Church and State* in 1736 (augmented edition in 1766), in which he offered a legitimation for the actually existing English church-state relation on pseudo-Lockean philosophical grounds. There he argued that relations between the English church and English state were implicitly based on a contract with similar philosophical force to the prehistorical social contract between a sovereign and his people. The church and state were conceived of as two separate sovereign "societies," each possessing distinct corporate personalities and wills, which must necessarily enter into contractual agreement with one another since only the church can provide sufficient sanction for state law (through its promise of immortal life), while only the state can provide the force and legal structure that assures the church's survival. By this account, the state has no right to interfere with religious belief yet must insist upon the fundamental principles of natural religion. Only these principles can sanction the oaths which provide, so Warburton supposes, the necessary foundation of civil society.

In the end, Warburton's argument was a functionalist one that emphasizes the church's use to the state more than the inverse.[38] Indeed, in the context of 1736—the year *The Alliance* was written—its policy implications were those of conservative Whiggism. After all 1736 was an important year for church-state relations. The repeal of the Test and Corporation Acts was discussed in Parliament (and was decisively rejected in 1739, being put off the political agenda for almost half a century as a result); the Mortmain Bill passed that year made it harder to bequeath property to the church and thus liberated capital for the market; Lord Chancellor Hardwicke (one of Warburton's patrons) delivered a judgment in the case of Middleton v. Croft, "which effectively exempted laymen from the jurisdiction of the Church, thus definitively asserting the supremacy of statute over canon law;" and the Tithe Bill made it easier for Quakers to avoid paying tithes.[39] Warburton's book was an intervention into this welter of legal and governmental activity, which can be seen as rejecting Walpole's Mortmain and Quaker's Tithe Bills while buttressing Whiggish political theory. In these terms it paved the way for Pittite and post-1760 Tory governments to come, under which Warburton's career was secured.

Warburton's position within the gentlemanly-ecclesiastical intellectual bloc is characterized by the authority that he personally achieved and by the particular balance between what we, from within the current cultural organization, can recognize as its literary as well as its theological elements. In regard to the first, there is no doubt that despite a reputation for arrogance, Warburton was widely acknowledged as having achieved a pre-eminent position on the mid-century British intellectual scene.[40] Warburton's work was translated and discussed on the Continent, including by Lessing, Herder, Mendelssohn, Voltaire and Rousseau. At home, he gathered a circle of younger clergymen disciples/dependents, among whom the most notable were Richard Hurd, John Brown (of *Estimate of the Manners and Principles of the Times*), Thomas Balguy, William Mason, and, in the next generation and at one remove, Thomas Percy (of the *Reliques of Ancient English Poetry*). These members of the Warburton connection were aligned more loosely and occasionally to a wider, mainly Cambridge-based circle, many of them clerics, including Thomas Gray, Conyers Middleton, William Whitehead, Thomas Warton, and Richard Farmer.

Warburton attained this position through a particularly complex set of achievements and alliances which involved theological, social, literary, and political engagements largely aimed at securing patronage. To put this in slightly different, but still summary terms, Warburton's position was a complex, composite construction, drawn together from disparate (indeed *opposing*) elements, which probably by a mix of strategy and contingency, enabled him to connect to the central cultural and political logics of the period between the fall of the Court Whigs (1756) and the American Revolutionary War. It was a position that enabled his followers to occupy (or turn down) positions of authority in the first decades of George III's reign. And (at least from the perspective of the inner Warburton circle) one of its implicit objectives was to defend the Anglican church's privileged status in relation to the state: see for instance the debate between rational dissent and Thomas Balguy after the latter had offered a very tight version of the Warburtonian line on church authority in 1769 and once again in response to the 1772 Feathers Tavern petition.[41] The church's privileged relation to the state could, so Warburtonians hoped, support the transference of religious/political institutional and intellectual hegemony onto a wider cultural authority over public opinion, especially in the domains of taste and morals. This latter aim becomes apparent, for instance, in the letters sparked by Hurd's reading Francis Atterbury's *The Rights, Powers and Privileges, of an English Convocation* (1700) in 1760, in which Hurd and Warburton discussed the possibility of resuscitating Convocation, and in which it becomes clear that they conceived of Convocation as a censoring body, allied to the state, against free thought and licentiousness.[42] Or to take another instance, in his *Dissertation on the Rise of Poetry and Music* (1763), John Brown called for a revivication of the old role of the bard as a "useful servant of the State" with a role in setting norms for manners and customs.[43]

At the heart of Warburton's position lay his institutional power: he was himself a minor patron (he established, for instance, the Warburton Lectures designed to bring young divines to London notice) and, more to the point, was a conduit through whom others could find more important patrons. But he was also bound to his allies by complex codes of friendship and honor, partly derived from idealized courtly and militarisitic norms of gentlemanly conduct in lieu of strong patterns of solidarity among the Anglican clergy. This code lies behind the intense personal loyalty among this group as well as the bitterness with which supposed insults and slights were attacked. It's given ironical expression in Richard Hurd's reply to a critique by the learned clergyman, John Jortin, of Warburton's interpretation of Virgil in a 1755 pamphlet entitled, "On the Delicacy of Friendship" and its negative side is shown in Warburton's falling out with Samuel Richardson following a slight against Pope in *Clarissa*.[44]

The Warburtonians also held an identifiable if reactive intellectual position, whose core elements can be listed quite simply. They deployed Lockean rationalism to defend the quasi-confessional state against seven main formations: dissent especially in its Calvinist varieties; evangelicalism; high church Toryism; low church Arianism; Shaftesburyian moral naturalism and its associated aestheticism; neo-classicism and the predominance of the classical over the Christian heritage; and free-thought. We can concentrate on the last of these: if Warburton's career began with his tract on church-state relations, it was consolidated by the publication of the first volume of a long theological treatise, *Divine Legation of Moses Demonstrated on the Principles of a Religious Deist* (1737–41) which established his reputation, at least among centrist Anglicans, as the victorious champion of orthodoxy against freethinking deism. Indeed the book's argument is only persuasive within conceptual structures within which Enlightenment rationalist deism met Protestant Christianity.

Warburton argues that both the Jews's special protection by Divine Providence and the truth of Christian revelation can be ascertained by the Jews having a strong social morality without any doctrine of future rewards or punishments, and by Moses's having failed to disseminate the concept of eternal life among his people. Today that seems a stunningly counter-intuitive claim. What made it seductive at the time was its turning two of the freethinking deists's main historicist arguments against them: that the Old Testament did not mention the afterlife, and that pagan priestcraft was "accomodating" or esoteric—that is, that pagan priests did not publicly reveal their personal scepticism so that they might maintain their power over the superstitious populace. Hence Warburton is able to claim that Moses did not engage in priestcraft precisely because he was a genuine "prophet" granted genuine revelations from God. He did not have to promulgate "mysteries" because he knew that God was actively intervening in the world on behalf of the Jewish people. He could remain confident in his (typological) dissemination of religious truth if not fully cognizant of Christ's capacity to redeem mankind. The tortured argumentation here is a sign of the problem that post-Lockean/Newtonian divines faced as they attempted to balance rationalism and revelation basically by mapping out the borders between those moments in history in which God appeared and those in which he was absent and where "natural" processes were maintained.

On one side of this position, Hume lay in wait, whose *History of England* Warburton thought spelled "the end of all pretence of religion."[45] On the other stood those who resolutely rejected reason as a buttress for religion, like William Law (who wrote the most cogent attack on *Divine Legation* from the high church side). For the Warburtonians, God's presence (through prophecy and miracles) was mainly confined to the era before Christ's death (Richard Hurd in his sermons confined it more narrowly still to the period of the Gospels themselves), although God continued to use nature to warn and reward mankind. But God was also present in certain established church rites: Warburton, for instance, joined the pamphlet war against Benjamin Hoadly, who in his *Plain Account of the Lord's Supper* (1735), had argued that the eucharist was merely an edifying act of remembrance of Christ's redemptive suffering without efficacy for future salvation.[46]

Warburton's project, however, fell outside certain of the political interests and values connected to the Whig cause, not least when it approached the border between polite letters and theological dispute. Warburton had forged a literary career for himself from the beginning. He had begun it attached to the circle around Lewis Theobald under the patronage of the shady Whig financier, Sir Robert Sutton.[47] But in 1738, he formed a friendship with Pope after jumping to the poet's defence against Jean-Pierre de Crousaz's *Examen de l'Essai de Monsieur Pope sur l'Homme* which accused the *Essay on Man* of Leibnitzean deism. It was an apposite moment, since 1738 was, in Christine Gerrard's words, "'the *annus mirabilus*'" of Pope's opposition career."[48] Warburton's defense of Pope, though no doubt attuned to political nuances and certainly distancing him from Walpole's policies, was primarily literary-theological, and probably in part motivated by Warburton himself having come under attack for deism after the publication of *Divine Legation's* first volume, most vociferously by William Webster, a high church Anglican clergyman and editor of *The Weekly Miscellany*, part owned by William Bowyer.

After Warburton's pamphlet came to his notice, Pope seems to have welcomed Warburton warmly into his life because he felt the need of ecclesiastical support to buttress his claims to Christian orthodoxy, from which, as was posthumously publicly to be revealed, his friend and patron, Henry St John, Lord Bolingbroke, had lapsed. Warburton quickly took advantage of his warm welcome: Pope introduced him to the rich and philanthropic Ralph Allen (Warburton married his niece, and Allen's house, Prior Park, became Warburton's home) as well as to William Murray (later Lord Mansfield), a lawyer with a Whig power-base but persistently linked to Jacobitism. Warburton's new connections also led him to the Court Whigs, and at last to William Pitt who promoted Warburton to a lucrative bishopric in 1760. During Pope's lifetime, Warburton had influenced him in choosing targets for the last version of *The Dunciad*, and upon Pope's death, Warburton was named Pope's literary executor and was bequeathed Pope's copyrights.

Warburton assiduously promoted his Pope connection: he went onto produce an posthumous edition of Pope's works that controversially pushed their sense into Warburtonian channels. Warburton's official portrait (now in the National Portrait Gallery) depicts him with a medallion of Pope in the background, as if Pope were the inspiring genius of his life and work.[49] He formed a bond with Pope's publisher, John Knapton, and through him with Knapton's printer, none other than William Bowyer, whose London office served as Warburton's London postal address for many years, despite a sometimes difficult relation between the two men. The Bowyer connection led to Warburton's own literary remains becoming an archive drawn upon for later volumes of John Nichols' *Literary Anecdotes*.[50] And on occasion Warburton transferred Pope's mantle onto his own disciples, as when he encouraged John Brown to write a critique of Shaftesbury's deism, a project that Pope had earlier recommended to Warburton himself; when he introduced his own followers to patrons met through the Pope/Allen circle; and when he recommended William Bowyer to Richard Hurd (and vice versa), so that Bowyer came to print one of Hurd's early self-published works. Through that connection John Nichols was employed by Hurd and was able to collect materials for Hurd's biography, published first in Nichols's *History of Leicestershire* and then in *Literary Anecdotes.*[51]

The Pope/Warburton alliance also produced its own intellectual energy. In particular, Warburton and his disciples took up Pope's patriot critique of luxury and the leveling, vulgarizing, feminizing effect of commercial interests on national taste and energy, and channeled them into the new social settings and discursive channels of the Seven Years' War period, with John Brown's 1757 *Estimate* being the key text in this move.[52] But the Warburtonian position contained two limiting internal tensions, each played out both on institutional and intellectual terrains: that between politics and the church and that between literature and religion.

The tension between politics and religion can be quite quickly passed over for our purposes. Warburton and later Hurd were involved in politics since they were called upon to offer weakly Providential spiritual legitimations of the administrations to which their patrons were linked. It is this particular binding of religion to politics that marks the Warburtonians out from Hoadly and Thomas Herring, the dominant Whig ecclesiastical intellectuals of the previous generation. Thus, as a young divine Warburton in 1745 delivered a series of sermons which deemed the Jacobite invasion "unnatural," and on November 29, 1759, the day appointed for a public thanksgiving for British victories against the French, he preached a sermon at Bristol, which (in line with Warburtonian limited Providentialism) made the claim that God knew that Britain was the "sole remaining Trustee of Civil Freedom, and so of the great Bulwark of Gospel Truth," as Robert Ingram puts it.[53] Somewhat similarly, Richard Hurd delivered a series of sermons between 1776 and 1786 on the occasion of national events in which George III's policies were identified with the will of God. In his "Sermon before the House of Lords on the General Fast Day in 1776 on Account of the American Rebellion," the American revolt is seen as a criminal outrage against a "law and order" sanctioned by both God and George III; as the result of a fanatical attachment to "theory" against morality (in terms that pre-empt Burke on the French Revolution); and finally, as divine retribution for the growth of irreligious rationalism and luxury.[54] A similar logic is at work in Hurd's invocation of George III's sacral presence in his 1786 sermon to the House of Lords on the anniversary of Charles I's execution or "martyrdom":

> Have we that reverence of just authority, not only as lodged in the persons of inferior magistrates, or in the sacred person of the supreme Magistrate, but as residing in the

> LAW itself (in which the public will, that is, the whole collective authority of the State is, as it were, concentered)—Have we, I say, that ingenuous and submissive respect for this authority, which not only reason and religion, but true policy, and every man's proper interest requires?[55]

Here, in a characteristic mix of appeals to supernature, reason, and interest, it is as if the old doctrine of divine right has been transferred from the monarch (as in traditional Toryism) or the constitution (as in traditional Anglican Whiggism) to the state itself, in a move which belongs to the emergence of a new Toryism from out of the intermingled ashes of Jacobitism and Court Whiggism.

In this context, it is barely surprising that the Warburtonians set themselves against the push for parliamentary and administrative reform. Warburton (along with his patrons Lord Mansfield and Charles Yorke) was one of the leading agents in having John Wilkes removed from parliament—the excuse being Wilkes's role in writing a pornographic parody of Warburton's own edition of Pope's *Essay on Man*. By contrast, there were rare occasions in which Warburton's understanding of the church's authority over souls had political implications at odds with certain strong interests of the ruling caste. In 1766 he gave an influential sermon to the Society for the Propagation of the Gospel in Foreign Parts on the relation between colonialism and Christianity, which may well have influenced the famous (if reluctant) judgment against the legality of slave-owing in England by his patron and friend Lord Mansfield, a few years later, since both came down against on the notion that a slave could be deemed simply *property*.[56]

Yet Warburton was also tempted to dismiss the political scene in its entirety on very different terms, as in this letter written privately to Hurd in 1759:

> This as you truly say, is an age of real darkness: or, at least, of *false lights*. For what else are all the national advantages gained by spreading slaughter and desolation round the world. However it is much better to *win*, by this bad means, than, as in former bad administrations, to lose. I will venture therefore to congratulate you, even as a philosopher, on these late *glorious successes* in this annus mirabilis. And though I begin to think with Bolingbroke,

> *this earth may be the bedlam of the universe*, yet I think the great genius who presides in our consels, may be called the sage master of this mad-house, who directs their unmeaning extravagances to useful and salutary purposes.[57]

The "sage master" presiding over the secular madhouse is the elder Pitt, who was about to appoint Warburton to a bishopric, but the drive to repudiate the whole socio-political scene stands out from a passage like this. It is an esoteric message, intended for elect intimates only. In his younger disciples, however, the will to social non-participation and the blanket condemnation of the public worlds of politics and commerce becomes more open, fervent, and consequential. It is clearly expressed in Hurd's "Dialogue on Retirement" (where Hurd's spokesman for the choice of opting out of public life is the seventeenth-century royalist Abraham Cowley), and in Hurd's interest in the pastoral as a literary genre at the beginning of his career, as he reconciled himself to taking up an isolated rural parish in Thurcaston, Leicestershire. It also appears in the everyday retreat from public life through the musical aestheticism cultivated by the younger Warburtonians, especially by William Mason who was one of the first to import a pianoforte (in 1755) into Britain.[58] This turn away from the public world, slowly to reconnoiter a new kind of bourgeois private life, can also be recognized in Hurd's more pastoral (in the ecclesiastical sense) sermons which, striking a very different note from that of Hurd's public-occasion sermons, present critiques of the passions that drive hegemonic sociability (emulation, the love of fame, honor) while preaching humility, interior spirituality, and retreat from the rewards of the world. Reading these sermons, tinged as they are by quietism, it is possible to see how Hurd and Warburton became such ardent fans of Rousseau's *Julie* on its publication in 1760: there's a real flow across from their esoteric spiritualizing and privatizing Christian ethic, dismissive and fearful of the public world, to a Rousseauian domestic sentimental primitivism—Fénelon no doubt being their common ancestor.[59]

Now to the second internal tension in the Warbutonian's intellectual project: that between literature and religion, which can be more concretely described as a tension in the alliance between polite taste and learning on the one side and the clerical profession on the other. Warburton was on record as discouraging, indeed attempting to forbid, his clerical protégés from pursuing creative writing on the ground that, as Hurd put it, the profession was a "sacred one" and that its business "lay elsewhere" than literature.[60] Warburton also admonished clergymen outside his sphere of direct influence for their literary writings, most famously Laurence Sterne, and he could put his case very forthrightly. In his report to Hurd about his discussions with Mason when Mason was pondering a clerical career in 1754, Warburton presents his reasoning as a functionalist revision of a traditional high church program (in this instance, that of his antagonist, William Law):

> I found him [i.e. Mason] yet unresolved whether he should take the Living. I said, was the question about a mere secular employment, I should blame him without reserve if he refused the offer. But as I regarded going into orders in another light, I frankly owned to him he ought not to go, unless he had a *call*: by which I meant, I told him, nothing fanatical or superstitious; but an inclination, and, on that, a resolution, to dedicate all his studies to the service of religion, and totally to abandon his poetry. This sacrifice, I said, I thought was required at any time, but more indispensable so in this, when we are fighting with infidelity pro aris et focis.[61]

Despite this admonition, Mason did take orders without jettisoning poetry. And in general, the younger generation of Warburtonians were more literary than Warburton himself. It is true that Hurd gave up writing poetry as he gained preferment (though he still cultivated serious literary interests and passions and published editions of Addison and Cowley), but John Brown, for instance, wrote plays for the London stage, attracting both Warburton's and Hurd's disapproval as a result.

The institutional reason for encouraging the laying aside of literary interests was that, given the pressures both of free-thought and evangelicalism, the orthodox Anglican clerical profession required its members' full attention. Yet, somewhat ironically, it was partly in response to these pressures on the clergy that Richard Hurd sketched out a innovative (and neglected) theory of literature in a series of essays written between 1755 and 1765: "On the Idea of Universal Poetry," "On the Provinces of the Drama," "A Discourse on Poetical Imitation," and "Letters on Chivalry and Romance." They present few, if any, wholly original concepts and they are not as fully worked out or coherent as, for instance, Edmund Burke's 1757 essay on the sublime (which Hurd would seem to have influenced), but as a whole, and in relation to the institutional position from which they were written, they articulate a critical theory that helped ground the modern idea of literature.

Thus, in one of the earliest of his literary-theoretical contributions, "On the Idea of Universal Poetry" (1755), Hurd's basic move is to define poetry's main purpose as the giving of pleasure.[62] This was a radicalization of the definition of literature formulated in John Brown's *Essays on the Characteristics* (1751) which creates the category "pure poetry" to describe that form of writing wholly in the service of imagination unlicensed by reason (and according to Brown, for that reason primarily committed to "simplicity"). Brown develops this concept in a critique of Shaftesbury's aestheticising of virtue, which also led him to articulate an early argument for what became the Benthamite "greatest happiness" principle. Yet Brown's stance draws upon theological utilitarian political theory (Tillotson's, Hoadly's and Joseph Butler's) since for him, utilitarianism requires religious backing to be effectively transmitted—that is, the greatest happiness principle has to be calculated with immortal life in mind.[63] It is because religion and reason both involve calculation of utilities that poetry can be freed from, and independent of, both.

In Hurd's essay, certain consequences of Brown's move are explored in more detail. The deceptively simple claim that poetry primarily involves pleasure now decisively breaks with the rhetorical and ethical models of literature that dominated Renaissance humanism and neo-classicism. It also breaks with the critical problematic of figures like John Dryden and John Dennis, as well as that sketched out by Warburton himself in his preface to volumes three and four of Samuel Richardson's *Clarissa*. At the same time—and this is once again its basic point—this definition hardens the division between religion and poetry ("poetry" here means, to all intents and purposes, literature as we moderns categorize it in contradistinction to polite learning). We can state this conceptual structure in its simplest terms: poetry as defined as productive of pleasure is being removed from the public world of professional Anglican practice, which now needs stronger weapons of defense and stronger principles of authority. But defining poetry as primarily aimed at pleasure is also extraordinarily liberating: it frees literature from moral duties as well as from responsibilities to rhetorical precedent. Indeed it enables literature to become something like autonomous. Thus in "On the Idea of Universal Poetry," Hurd begins to sanction what he calls a "licence of representation, which we call *fiction*" as well as a liberation of style itself: "The *style* is, as it were the body of poetry; *fiction*, is its soul."[64] Literature becomes the expression of "something in the mind of man, sublime and elevated, which prompts it to overlook all obvious and familiar appearances, and to feign to itself other and more extraordinary; such as correspond to the extent of its own powers, and fill out all the faculties and capacities of our souls." It is in the service of restless imaginative drives that literature is drawn to "pagan fable" and "gothic romance." At the same time, literature's search for pleasure means that poetry aligns itself with rhythm, rhyme and music (a theme which will be taken up by John Brown in his *Dissertation on the Rise of Poetry and Music*). Indeed for Hurd the most recent mode of imaginative literature— realist prose fiction— which disarticulates the music of language from that imaginative liberation whose vehicle is romance, is a sign of the contemporary vitiated taste that was condemned most forcefully by Pope and Brown.

Of course this account of "poetry" as primarily imaginatively liberating and pleasurable stands against the project I described above: the transference of authority from the state and church to the domain of taste as a whole. This contradiction was lived out in a number of ways. For instance, while the Warburtonians discouraged literary pursuits by clergy, they also encouraged churchmen to maintain and extend their secular scholarship and command of polite learning, once again the better to resist deistic and evangelical currents and (esoterically) to shore up their social status. And individual Warburtonians struggled to avoid the responsibilities of the higher ranks of church office in order to protect that leisure in which they could be literary, according to their own lights. Hurd turned down the archbishopric of Canterbury and Balguy the bishopric of Gloucester. The terms of this struggle were spelled out in Mason's sonnet to Hurd on his taking up a less onerous bishopric earlier in his career (Lichfield and Coventry in 1775):

> Still let my HURD a smile of candour lend
> To scenes that dar'd on Grecian pinions tow'r,
> When "in low Thurcaston's sequester'd bower,"
> He prais'd the strain, because he lov'd the friend:
> There golden leisure did his steps attend,
> Nor had the rare, the well-weigh'd call of Power,
> To those high cares decreed his watchful hour,
> On which fair Albion's future hopes depend.
> A fate unlook'd-for waits my friend and me;
> He pays to duty what is Learning's claim,
> Resigning classic ease—for dignity;
> I yield my Muse to Fashion's praise or blame.[65]

Mason thinks of leisure as golden, and power as an oppressive weight: he hopes that Hurd, as a bishop, will continue to attend to and enjoy Mason's own experiments in revivifying ancient Greek dramatic forms for the modern stage (in useless resistance to fashion's control of contemporary taste) even as he applauds Hurd's giving up learning and classical *otium* for dignity in order to protect "fair Albion's future hopes," a protection of the nation-state which is simultaneously ecclesiastical, cultural, and political. The sonnet form that Mason chooses is already coded in this situation: despite the publicity given to it through Richardson's *Sir Charles Grandison* (1753), it is something of a coterie taste, emblematic of the imaginative freedom (and love of Italian Renaissance poetry) allowed to these gentlemanly clergymen scholars only as a problem, a tension, in what is not quite yet in the modern sense their "private" time.

* * *

This essay has argued that key sectors of the eighteenth-century literary field can be understood in terms of triangulated relations among the Anglican church, the state, and the market during a period when literature underwent profound changes as an institution. It makes this case to demur from those who believe that the period is most intelligible through narratives of modernization on the one side, or of the privatization of religious belief on the other. Here the gradual modernization of literature is not conceived as a smooth process of transformation in which the old polite learning gave way to new forms of market-orientated imaginative writing. Rather it is presented as an uneven mutation of a segmented field, in which some innovations (like the Warburtonian theory of literature) first appear in non-secular resistance to forces of transformation and secularization themselves.

But in conclusion I want to break with historical sociology for a moment to ask a more classically humanist question: what value do literary projects like those of the Warburtonians and the Nichols printshop have today, belonging as they do to a world and a structure of literary and intellectual life that have vanished, suggesting only slight continuities with our own? Are projects like these now culturally inert? And I think that the argument outlined above does help us answer a hesitant "no" to that. To take the first of my two cases here: as I have argued, Nichols's enormous labors of memorization, retrieval, and preservation can be conceived of as reaching back to the non-juring intellectual world in which the Bowyer firm first made its mark—that is, to a theo-political collectivity that refused to sign on to a Whiggish, liberal order. That refusal (and the Tory/Anglican political ethics of non-resistance and passive obedience to which it adhered) retains a force today for those of us in the humanities who are often in the business of trying to breath life into cultural and literary remnants whose public interest and value is disappearing into oblivion. But in the end the value of

Nichols's literary labours, like that of the Warburtonians's anticipation of a literature wholly given up to an autonomous imagination, is not to be found in what we share with them or what use-value they retain for us, including their use as evidence for re-narrativizations of literary history such as in this essay. Rather it's to be found precisely in their otherness, their strangeness, which historical sociology can also help us specify and recognize. It is the mute chill of death and mortification that emanates from them that makes them dangerous (if easy) to forget.

NOTES

1. My understanding of "literature"'s change of denotation has been most influentially articulated by Raymond Williams, most succinctly in his entry for "Literature" in *Keywords: A Vocabulary of Culture and Society* (London: Fontana, 1976), 152–53. Perhaps the most careful and extensive account of this change is Clifford Siskin's in *The Work of Writing: Literature and Social Change in Britain, 1700–1830* (Baltimore: Johns Hopkins University Press, 1998).

2. Siskin, *The Work of Writing*, 11.

3. For useful summaries of recent understandings of the mutation of literature's meaning and extent in terms like these, see George Justice, *The Manufacturers of Literature: Writing and the Literary Marketplace in Eighteenth-Century England* (Newark: University of Delaware Press, 2002), 20–27, and Paul Keen, *The Crisis of Literature in the 1790s: Print Culture and the Public Sphere* (Cambridge: University of Cambridge Press, 1999), 1–22. This kind of analysis begins with Ian Watt's classic account of the "rise of the novel."

4. See Alok Yadav's useful remarks on how commerce, liberty, and the republic of letters were often understood in Britain as co-dependent in his *Before the Empire of English: Literature, Provinciality and Nationalism in Eighteenth-Century Britain* (London: Palgrave, 2004), 69–72. Voltaire's *Philosophical Letters* is especially important in disseminating this understanding of these relations.

5. See J. C. D. Clark, *The Language of Liberty, 1660–1832: Political Discourse and Social Dynamics in the Anglo-American World* (Cambridge: Cambridge University Press, 1994); *Samuel Johnson: Literature, Religion, and English Cultural Politics from the Restoration to Romanticism* (Cambridge: Cambridge University Press, 1994); and *English Society, 1688–1832: Ideology, Social Structure, and Political Practice During the Ancien Regime* (Cambridge: Cambridge University Press, 1985). See also J. G. A. Pocock, "Post-Puritan England and the Problem of Enlightenment," in *Culture and Politics from*

Puritanism to the Enlightenment, ed. Perez Sagorin (Berkeley: University of California Press, 1980), 91–112.

6. See Jeremy Black, "Confessional State or Elect Nation?," in *Protestantism and National Identity: Britain and Ireland, c.1650–c.1850*, eds. Tony Claydon and Ian McBride (Cambridge: Cambridge University Press, 1998), 53–74, for a discussion of the issues involved in categorizing eighteenth-century England as a confessional state.

7. See John Walsh, Colin Haydon, and Stephen Taylor, eds., *The Church of England, c.1689–c.1833: From Toleration to Tractarianism* (Cambridge: Cambridge University Press, 1993), and W. M. Jacob, *Lay People and Religion in the Early Eighteenth Century* (Cambridge: Cambridge University Press, 1996).

8. See, for example, Clark, *Samuel Johnson* and Ian Higgins, *Swift's Politics: A Study in Disaffection* (Cambridge: Cambridge University Press, 1994). For a critical account see Robert Folkenflik, "The Return of the Jacobites and Other Johnsonian Topics," *Eighteenth-Century Studies* 33.2 (2000): 289–99. Also see Howard Erskine-Hill, "Literature and the Jacobite Cause: Was There a Rhetoric of Jacobitism?," in *Ideology and Conspiracy: Aspects of Jacobitism, 1689–1759,* ed. Eveline Cruickshanks (Edinburgh: John Donald Publishers, 1982), 49–70.

9. The recent historiography somewhat exaggerates the openness of the British state in relation to those outside the Anglican fold. Certainly intellectual and religious countercultures remained outside the mainstream, in part because the universities and, with some exceptions, the legal profession remained out of reach for Dissenters and Roman Catholics and because, as I am arguing here, Anglicanism had such intellectual and cultural reach and power. For a good example of recent thinking about this issue, see Paul Langford, *Public Life and the Propertied Englishman, 1689–1798* (Oxford: Clarendon Press, 1991), 72–90.

10. See Walsh, et. al., *The Church of England* for an excellent overview of the Anglican church in the period. The political attack on Anglicanism early in the century is described in J. A. I. Champion, *The Pillars of Priestcraft Shaken: The Church of England and Its Enemies, 1660–1730* (Cambridge: Cambridge University Press, 1992).

11. G. V. Bennett's *The Tory Crisis in Church and State, 1688–1730: The Career of Francis Atterbury, Bishop of Rochester* (Oxford: Clarendon Press, 1975) and the first chapter of F. C. Mather's *High Church Prophet: Bishop Samuel Horsley (1733–1806) and the Caroline Tradition in the Later Georgian Church* (Oxford: Clarendon Press, 1992) both provide accounts of this moment.

12. An account of ecclessiastical professionalization in the period appears in Geoffrey S. Holmes, *Augustan England: Professions, State and Society, 1680–1730* (London: G. Allen & Unwin, 1982).

13. It was difficult for ambitious intellectuals and scholars working around the universities to remain unordained: the career of John Taylor, son of a barber, noted Greek scholar, one-time Cambridge University librarian, editor of Lysius (printed by William Bowyer, who also acted as Taylor's London agent), one-time advocate of Doctor's Commons, and author of *Elements of Civil Law* is instructive in this regard. His resistance to taking orders was well known (he feared the politics involved) but the lure of lucrative preferments available by virtue of his scholarly fame was, in the end, too much for him. For a description of Taylor's career, see David MacKitterick, *A History of Cambridge University Press,* 3 vols. (Cambridge: Cambridge University Press, 1992–2004), 1:128. For the careers of plebeian-born bishops, see Paul Langford, *A Polite and Commercial People: England 1727–1783* (Oxford: Oxford University Press, 1989), 262–63.

14. See Colin Bonwick, *English Radicals and the American Revolution* (Chapel Hill: University of North Carolina Press, 1977), 199–215; and James E. Bradley, *Religion, Revolution, and English Radicalism: Nonconformity in Eighteenth-Century Politics and Society* (Cambridge: Cambridge University Press, 1990), 121–58.

15. See J. E. Cookson, *The Friends of Peace: Anti-War Liberalism in England, 1793–1815* (Cambridge: Cambridge University Press, 1982), 12–16, and James J. Sack, *From Jacobite to Conservative: Reaction and Orthodoxy in Britain, c.1760–1832* (Cambridge: Cambridge University Press, 1993), 46–50, for a discussion of the breakdown in relations between Dissent and the government in the 1780s. For slightly different accounts of the increasing distance between the church and plebeian cultures see E. P. Thompson, "Patrician Society, Plebeian Culture," *Journal of Social History* 7 (1974): 382–405, and *Customs in Common* (London: Merlin Press, 1991), 49–55.

16. This statement is not based on hard evidence, since no research exists that quantifies the various sources of money for literary and intellectual production in the period. But leaving private patronage aside, in terms of scale the Anglican church had no real competitor as a unified institution producing knowledge and discourse until at some point in the last decades of the eighteenth century commercial booksellers began to fund knowledge production for the market on what was probably a comparative scale (a market which itself partly rechannelled church incomes). For work on the general imbrication of the Anglican church with the larger society, see Clark, *English Society*, 161–73; William Gibson, *The Church of England 1688–1832: Unity and Discord* (London: Routledge, 2001), 148–81; and Jacob, *Lay People and Religion*. For the importance of the church to intellectual life, see B. W. Young, *Religion and Enlightenment in Eighteenth-Century England: Theological Debate from Locke to Burke* (Oxford: Clarendon Press, 1998), 6–7, and Jeremy Gregory, "Anglicanism and the Arts: Religion, Culture and Politics in the Eighteenth Century," in *Culture, Politics, and Society in Britain, 1660–1800*, eds. Jeremy Black and Jeremy Gregory (Manchester: Manchester University Press, 1991), 82–109.

17. The best brief summary of those publishers who turned to fiction in the period is to be found in James Raven, *British Fiction: 1750–1770* (Newark: University of Delaware Press, 1987), 35–42. For shifts in the publishing industry more generally, see Raven, *Judging New Wealth: Popular Publishign and Responses to Commerce 1750–1800* (Oxford: Oxford University Press, 2001), 1–60.

18. Edmund Burke, *Reflections on the Revolution in France,* ed. Frank M. Turner (New Haven: Yale University Press, 2003), 67.

19. Almost all clergymen had degrees from Oxford and Cambridge, and all those who worked at these universities were required to sign on to the 39 Articles. Many fellows only stayed at the University until they were awarded livings, and the colleges controlled many livings themselves. See G. V. Bennett, "University, Society and Church, 1688–1714," in *The History of the University of Oxford, vol. 5: The Eighteenth Century*, eds. L. S. Sutherland and L. G. Mitchell (Oxford: Oxford University Press, 1984), 359–400.

20. A good summary of women's moral writing is to be found in Kathyrn Sutherland, "Writings on Education and Conduct: Arguments for Female Improvement," in *Women and Literature in Britain, 1700–1800,* ed. Vivien Jones (Cambridge: Cambridge University Press, 2000), 25–46. Two more detailed but very informative case studies of women's relation to dissenting print cultures are to be found in Paula McDowell's "Enlightenment Enthusiasms and the Spectacular Failure of the Philadelphian Society," *Eighteenth-Century Studies* 35.4 (2002): 515–33, and Barbara Taylor, *Mary Wollstonecraft and the Feminist Imagination* (Cambridge: Cambridge University Press, 2003). It is important to recognize that, despite the Anglican church being a profoundly masculinist organization, women could and did play a significant role in its printed output: in the mid- and late-eighteenth century the contributions of Hannah Chapone and Hannah More stand out as examples. See Anne Stott, *Hannah More: The First Victorian* (Oxford: Oxford University Press, 2003).

21. Joseph M. Levine provides a study of Hickes in *The Battle of the Books: History and Literature in the Augustan Age* (Ithaca: Cornell University Press, 1991), 374–86.

22. A huge and varied literature exists on women's role in eighteenth-century commercial print culture. Two excellent recent contributions are *Women, Writing, and the Public Sphere: 1700–1830*, ed. Elizabeth Eger (Cambridge: Cambridge University Press, 2001), and Paula McDowell, *The Women of Grub Street: Press, Politics, and Gender in the London Literary Marketplace 1678–1730* (Oxford: Oxford University Press, 1998).

23. Carl Lennart Carlson, *The First Magazine: A History of the Gentleman's Magazine* (Providence: Brown University Press, 1938), 214 *ff.*

24. On this subject, see Margaret Anne Doody, "Richardson's Politics," *Eighteenth Century Fiction* 2.2 (1990): 113–26; Robert A Erickson, "'Written in the Heart': Clarissa and Scripture," in *Passion And Virtue: Essays on the Novels of Samuel Richardson*, ed. David Blewett (Toronto: University of Toronto, 2001), 170–201; Lois A. Chaber, "Christian Form and Anti-Feminism in *Clarissa*,"

Eighteenth Century Fiction 15.3 (2003): 507-38; Jerry C. Beasley, "*Pamela* and *Clarissa:* Fiction as Devotional Literature," in *Novels of the 1740s* (Athens: University of Georgia Press, 1982), 134–56; Rosemary Bechler, "'Triall by What Is Contrary': Samuel Richardson and Christain Dialectic," in *Samuel Richardson: Passion and Prudence*, ed. Valerie Grosvenor Myer (London: Vision Press, 1986), 93–113. A somewhat different view on Richardson's Anglicanism is to be found in my forthcoming essay, "Is *Clarissa* a Religious Novel? Why does it matter?"

25. For the most recent scholarship on Nichols see James M. Duitz, *The Works of John Nichols: An Introduction* (New York: AMS Press, 1968).

26. Printing history information on the Bowyer shop is available in K. I. D. Maslen, *An Early London Printing House at Work: Studies in the Bowyer Ledgers* (New York: Bibliographical Society of America, 1993). See also "Slaves or Freemen? The Case of William Bowyer, Father and Son, Printers of London, 1699–1777," in *Writers, Books, and Trade: An Eighteenth-Century English Miscellany for Willam B. Todd*, ed. O. M. Brack Jr. (New York: AMS Press, 1994), 145–55. Bowyer did not become involved in printing Jacobite political polemics and reportage as did Jacobite printers like Nathaniel Mist, Francis Clifton, and John Matthews, the last of whom was executed for printing seditious libel in 1719 (even though Bowyer did employ Mist's son).

27. For information on Leslie, see Robert Cornwall, "Charles Leslie and the Political Implications of Theology," in *Religious Identities in Britain, 1660–1832*, eds. William Gibson and Robert. G. Ingram (London: Ashgate, 2005), 28–42. For a study of the intellectual culture of the non-juring movement more generally, see Cornwall, *Visible and Apostolic: The Constitution of the Church in High Church Anglican and Non-Juror Thought* (Newark: University of Delaware Press, 1993).

28. See in particular Joseph Ames's *Typographical Antiquities* (1749).

29. See Isaac Disraeli, "Literary Anecdotes," in *Curiosities of Literature,* 3 vols. 14th ed. (London: E. Moxon, 1849), 3:300–303.

30. It is no accident, however, that the Bowyer shop had printed John Le Neve's list of obituaries in *Monumenta Anglicana* (1717) and elsewhere, nor that it had printed Samuel Jebb's *Bibliotheca Literaria,* an annual record of the "labour of the learned" which ceased publication in 1724.

31. A good account of the differences between "old" and "new" bookselling modes is to be found in Patricia Hernland, "Three Bankruptcies in the London Book Trade, 1746–61: Rivington, Knapton and Osborn," in *Writers, Books and Trade*, 77–123. Knapton and Rivington were very involved in what I am calling the "gentlemanly-ecclessiastical block" of the literary field.

32. A good sense of the readership can be drawn from Arthur Sherbo's *Letters to Mr. Urban of the Gentleman's Magazine, 1751–1811* (Lewiston, NY: Edwin Mellen Press, 1997). Seven of the eleven most regular correspondents to whom Sherbo draws attention were ordained Anglican clergymen.

33. See Peter N. Miller, "The 'Antiquarianization' of Biblical Scholarship and the London Polyglot Bible (1653–57)" *Journal of the History of Ideas* 62.3

(2001): 463–82.

34. See J. A. Cochrane, *Dr. Johnson's Printer: The Life of William Strahan* (Cambridge, MA: Harvard University Press, 1964), 13–21, for an excellent summary of the London printing trade at the time. Anglo-Saxon was expensive to print and sets of Anglo-Saxon print were uncommon. The Bowyer firm, however, owned a set, and could thus play a significant triage role in book production in this area.

35. Jeremy Gregory, *Restoration, Reformation, and Reform, 1660–1828: Archbishops of Canterbury and Their Diocese* (Oxford: Oxford University Press, 2000), 157. The most developed project of this sort was Andrew Ducarel's incomplete *Repertory of the Endowments of Vicarages of all the Dioceses of this Kingdom.* See John Nichols, *Literary Anecdotes of the Eighteenth Century; Comprizing Biographical Memoirs of William Bowyer, Printer, F. S. A. and Many of His Learned Friends; an Incidental View of the Progress and Advancement of Literature in This Kingdom During the Last Century; and Biographical Anecdotes of a Considerable Number of Eminent Writers and Ingenious Artists; with a Very Copious Index*, 6 vols. (London: Printed for the author, by Nichols, son, and Bentley, 1812), 1:388–89.

36. See Nichols, *Literary Anecdotes*, 1:1–162, for the Spalding Society.

37. For an account of Warburton, see J. G. A. Pocock, "Clergy and Commerce: The Conservative Enlightenment in England," in *L'eta dei lumi. Studi storici sul settecento europeo in onore di Franco Venturi*, ed. Raffaele Ajello, et. al., 2 vols (Naples: Jovene, 1985), 1:523–62. The secondary sources on Warburton from which I have drawn most are Arthur William Evans, *Warburton and the Warburtonians: A Study in Some Eighteenth-Century Controversies* (London: Oxford University Press, 1932); B. W. Young, *Religion and Enlightenment in Eighteenth-Century England: Theological Debate from Locke to Burke* (Oxford: Clarendon Press, 1998), 167–212; and Robert G. Ingram, "William Warburton, Divine Action, and Enlightened Christianity," in *Religious Identities in Britain,* 97–117. Warburton is the villain of Leslie Stephen's *History of English Thought in the Eighteenth Century* (New York: Harcourt, Brace and World, 1962), in an account which is, nonetheless, well worth reading.

38. Warburton's account of church and state relations shares much with the ancient Roman one in Montesquieu's *Considérations sur les causes de la grandeur des Romains et de leur décadence* (1734).

39. Langford, *A Polite and Commercial People*, 92.

40. Warburton's arrogance seems to have partly been in imitation of his models, themselves enemies, the Cambridge Whig scholar Richard Bentley and Alexander Pope of the *Satires*, who both maintained the hard abusive rhetoric of the early-modern republic of letters.

41. In the Feathers Tavern petition, senior Anglican clergy requested a repeal of the Test Acts. For rational dissent's response to Balguy see Joseph Priestley, *Considerations on Church-Authority, Occasioned by Dr. Balguy's Sermon on That Subject; Preached at Lambeth Chapel, and Published by Order of the Archbishop* (London, 1769); and Anthony Page, *John Jebb and the*

Enlightenment: Origins of British Radicalism (Westport: Praeger, 2003), 114–18.

42. Richard Hurd, *The Early Letters of Bishop Richard Hurd, 1739–1762*, ed. Sarah Brewer (Rochester: Boydell & Brewer, 1995), 359–61. The Lower House of the Convocation, the church's representative body, had been suspended in 1717 under George I, a key moment in the church's loss of autonomy; this intensified the Jacobitism of figures like Francis Atterbury.

43. John Brown, *A Dissertation on the Rise, Union, and Power, the Progressions, Separations, and Corruptions of Poetry and Music* (London, 1763), 222. For Brown's (neglected) contribution to eighteenth-century intellectual life see William Roberts, *A Dawn of Imaginative Feeling: The Contribution of John Brown (1715–66) to Eighteenth-Century Thought and Literature* (Carlisle: Northern Academic Press, 1996).

44. See T. C. Duncan Eaves and Ben D. Kimpel, *Samuel Richardson: A Biography* (Oxford: Clarendon Press, 1971), 329–30.

45. William Warburton, *Letters from a Late Eminent Prelate to One of His Friends* (London, 1809), 207.

46. See Guglielmo Sanna, "How Heterodox was Benjamin Hoadly?," in *Religious Identities in Britain,* 62–63, for a good account of this controversy which I here paraphrase.

47. Under a ruling by Lord Hardwicke, Sutton was expelled from Parliament for insider stock trading and lying: Warburton wrote a pamphlet in Sutton's defence.

48. Christine Gerrard, *The Patriot Opposition to Walpole: Politics, Poetry, and National Myth, 1725–1742* (Oxford: Clarendon Press, 1994), 47; see also Walsh, et. al., *The Church of England,* 33.

49. See William K. Wimsatt, *The Portraits of Alexander Pope* (New Haven: Yale University Press, 1965), 339–40.

50. See Donald W. Nichol, *Pope's Literary Legacy: The Book-Trade Correspondence of William Warburton and John Knapton with Other Letters and Documents, 1744–1780* (Oxford: Oxford Bibliographical Society, 1992), for the details of Warburton's relation to the booktrade.

51. See Nichols, *Literary Anecdotes*, 1:600–01, where Nichols describes his personal intimacy with Hurd. Some letters between Nichols and Hurd are printed here too: Hurd reads the first version of the *Literary Anecdotes* and advises Nichols against turning author.

52. It's ironical that, from an intellectual-historical point of view, this critique of luxury (itself ancient) first took its characteristic eighteenth-century form in a Catholic and French text, Fénelon's *Télémaque* (1699).

53. Ingram,"William Warburton," 114–15.

54. Hurd, "A Sermon preached before the House of Lords in the Abbey Church of Westminster on Friday, December 13, 1776, being the day appointed by Authority for a General Fast, on account of the American Rebellion," in *The Works of Richard Hurd, D.D., Lord Bishop of Worcester.* 8 vols. (London: T. Cadell and W. Davies, 1811), 8:3–16.

55. Hurd, "A Sermon, preached before the House of Lords, January 30, 1786; being the Anniversary of King Charles's Martyrdom," in *The Works of Richard Hurd,* 8:50.

56. My sense of the Mansfield judgment owes much to my conversations with Chris Brown on this matter.

57. Warburton, *Letters from a Late Eminent Prelate*, 220.

58. John William Draper, *William Mason: A Study in Eighteenth-Century Culture* (New York: New York University Press, 1924), 288–89.

59. See Hurd, *The Early Letters of Bishop Richard Hurd,* 368 *ff,* for Hurd on *Julie*.

60. Hurd, *The Early Letters of Bishop Richard Hurd,* 300.

61. Warburton, *Letters from a Late Eminent Prelate*, 125.

62. I discuss Hurd's literary theory in a little more detail in a forthcoming essay, "Mimic Toils: The Conditions of Possibility of Historical Reenactments," in *Rethinking History*.

63. See John Brown, *Essays on the Characteristics* (London, 1751), 19, for the definition of pure poetry. See also Draper, *William Mason*, 139. For the importance of public happiness to Hoadly, see his 1708 sermon, "The Happiness of the Present Establishment," in *The Works of Benjamin Hoadly,* 3 vols., ed. John Hoadly (London: Printed by W. Bowyer and J. Nichols and sold by R. Horsfield, 1773), 2:109–17.

64. Hurd, "On the Idea of Universal Poetry," in *The Works of Richard Hurd,* 2:11.

65. Nichols, *Literary Anecdotes,* 1:488.

That "Blunderbuss of Law": Giles Jacob, Abridgment, and Print Culture

JULIA RUDOLPH

Giles Jacob has been recently described as "the most prolific author of self-help legal manuals."[1] He is well known as the author of the enormously influential eighteenth-century *New Law Dictionary*—a text that reached a sizable audience not only in Britain but also in colonial America where it was "the most widely used English law dictionary" and could be found in the libraries of many colonial lawyers, including the most prominent.[2] The *New Law Dictionary* was probably Jacob's most successful work, but it was only one among the many practical legal, political, and literary works he produced in the first few decades of the eighteenth century. Jacob, like some other notable early eighteenth-century compilers of law, published a large number of texts on conveyancing, Chancery practice, local courts and officers, military, commercial, criminal, and constitutional law, as well as his law dictionary.[3]

Moreover, while legal writing was Jacob's primary occupation and contribution, poetry, satire, and literary biography were also a part of his published work. As the author of *The Poetical Register: Or The Lives and Characters of the English Dramatick Poets: With an Account of Their Writings*, Jacob is known among literary scholars for his role in a controversy concerning the reputations of John Gay and Alexander Pope.[4] Attacked and immortalized in Pope's *Dunciad* as "the Scourge of Grammar" and the

"Blunderbuss of Law," Jacob's reputation as the chief example of the incivility of the eighteenth-century common law has persisted. His work is often regarded by modern scholars of both law and literature as exemplary of an inferior English legal literature copiously produced in the early eighteenth century. This proliferating legal literature has generally been denigrated by modern scholars, who unfavorably compare it with the more "substantive" and "systematic" legal treatises of William Blackstone or Geoffrey Gilbert. Indeed, most scholars have set up a dichotomy between this practical, inductive, descriptive legal literature and a rational, analytic legal literature, and through this contrast the practical legal literature has remained an object of scorn rather than an object of study.[5]

Neither a Gilbert nor a Blackstone, Giles Jacob is, then, generally ridiculed as a hack. Yet as this essay will argue, Jacob should be understood as exemplary, in a more fundamental sense, of an evolving discourse of English common law. Jacob's law books are representative of the ways in which these early eighteenth-century abridgments, students' books, and legal handbooks effectively met new demands of legal education, contributed to broader traditions of humanist and Enlightenment writing, and took part in a burgeoning eighteenth-century print culture. Works like Jacob's law books developed in close relationship to manuscript commonplace traditions, and these texts must be understood within the context of legal education and the ways in which students and practitioners were taught to confront and master the sources of the law. These practices in education and in print—the ways in which these new printed books organized all this information of the law—must also be seen in the context of Enlightenment encyclopedic traditions. The law book authors, like encyclopedia-makers, were dealing with the problem of knowledge management or "information overload," and in response to this problem the learning of the law was systematized, alphabetized, and organized. As Ann Blair has explained, in the early modern period a "perception of an overabundance of books fueled the production of many more books, often especially large ones, designed to remedy the problem," and the recognition of the usefulness of these compilations and reference books was increasingly widespread.[6] If we look at Jacob's law books in these contexts we will no longer see simply what scholars have characterized as the emblematic texts of an inferior literature, often linked to a more general decline of common law in this age of reason, commerce and politeness.[7] Instead we will come to a deeper understanding of the relationship between English common law and Enlightenment cultures.

Learning and Commonplace Books

A notable expansion in legal publication began in the mid-seventeenth century, in part a consequence of the disruptions suffered by the Inns of Court, and of the movements toward law reform, during the civil wars and Interregnum.[8] This expansion built upon an already significant increase in the publication of law books which coincided with the advent of printing and accelerated from the 1590s onward.[9] Many examples exist of abridgments, tables, dictionaries, collections of cases and statutes, works on conveyancing, and on pleading and practice that were first published in the seventeenth century and used and valued well into the eighteenth century. The authors of the early eighteenth-century practical legal literature self-consciously relied upon the work of earlier abridgments; they continued the tradition initiated by the first compilers, Nicholas Statham and Anthony Fitzherbert, and perpetuated by later contributors such as William West or William Style.[10] The volume of law publications showed no sign of diminishing but rather seemed to increase in the eighteenth century. This publication boom was one response to the new difficulty of being educated in the law: with the decline of the Inns of Court in the late seventeenth and early eighteenth centuries self-education and apprenticeship became increasingly important.[11] And the law student was not only expected to read the law but also to compose a legal commonplace book, a practice that took on particular significance now with the scarcity of other methods of study or forms of legal note-taking.

Giles Jacob's education in the law, and his subsequent profession as legal author, are indicative of these developments. Unlike some other prominent legal authors, Jacob did not matriculate at one of the declining Inns nor was he called to the bar; rather he engaged in extensive reading and self-education, and served as an apprentice to an "eminent attorney" and as a steward and secretary to a prominent political official.[12] Jacob's legal education was clearly fairly typical, and it enabled him to understand what kinds of practical texts would be most helpful to the young lawyer. In fact Jacob asserted, in the preface to his text *The Statute Law Common-plac'd*, that his own failure to prosper in the practice of law made him peculiarly well equipped "to do some Service to others, at least in assisting their Memories, if not improving their Judgments, by reducing the several Branches of the Law to a proper Bounds, freeing them from a Confusion of Method, and perfecting what I find little more than begun by my industrious Predecessors."[13] The success of his early guides to court keeping and to the statutes, Jacob often claimed, led many practitioners and publishers to request further editions and this in turn encouraged him to compile other legal texts.

The difficulty of autonomous legal training was often acknowledged by Jacob and others. In his *Statute Law Common-plac'd* and *The Student's Companion: Or the Reason of the Laws of England* Jacob contributed to a fairly large contemporary advice literature dealing with the challenge of legal commonplacing.[14] Such advice to prospective lawyers was part of an important tradition of instruction in commonplacing that had developed in early modern Europe. As Ann Moss has shown, the commonplace book first fully emerged in Renaissance Europe although it was founded upon earlier ancient and medieval precedents. Detailed guidance as to the organization and content of such notebooks was articulated in the sixteenth century by major figures like Desiderius Erasmus; Erasmian examples were taught and extended in printed commonplace books throughout the sixteenth century, and these humanist educational reforms influenced English and Continental lawyers as much as they affected theologians and students of the arts.[15] Methods of commonplacing were also articulated in the seventeenth century by scholars such as John Locke, who took part in debates over practices of commonplacing and the authority of quotation. The advice literature on note-taking for law students contributed to these debates, and indicates some of the intersections between the explosion in print and the commonplace book, especially in terms of the impact of print on manuscript practices.

In the introduction to the second edition of *The Student's Companion*, for example, Giles Jacob offers the following advice:

> After a Treatise is fully read over, ask your self the Question, *What Knowledge you have gained thereby?* Do this immediately, and the Answer conceived in your Mind, instantly pen down under Heads, just as the subject Matter presents it self to you, and afterwards more methodically, on comparing the same with the Book, and referring to the Pages where it is to be found, in the Way of Alphabet; (and if the Treatise be large, and your Memory treacherous, it will be necessary to make Remarks as you proceed, or at the End of every Chapter). Then peruse these heads often, and when you have gone through all the Books, reduce the several Alphabets in a general *Common Place-Book*, without which no Man can be a thorough Lawyer.[16]

Jacob's emphasis is on detail and diligence, reflection and immediacy. The insistence upon rigorous work and persistence echoes a common earlier humanist refrain about the labors of scholarship.[17] Eighteenth-century authors of advice like Jacob also echoed John Locke's emphasis, in his *New Method of Making Common-Place Books*, on the function of the commonplace book as a repository or home-made reference book even more than its function as an aid to memorization.[18] The commonplace book was to be a collection of sources available to the young lawyer as much as it was to be a learning tool.

Jacob here also, obliquely, acknowledged the likely mistakes the inexperienced student would make. Frustrations and missteps, and the high stakes involved for the student compiling a legal commonplace book, were frequently noted by contemporaries.[19] Jacob's remedy was this proposed two-step method of note-taking. The study of law was not for the weak or faint of heart, Jacob also warned, and in undertaking this course of reading and note-taking "it is necessary that [the student] should pursue his Study with as great Diligence as his Strength of Constitution will permit." Jacob introduced the theme of manliness and potency by claiming that some men (including himself) can "read through a thin Folio in a Day," but for most men this was too taxing —"too Violent for the Body and Mind"—and it would lead to confusion rather than education.[20] Like other advisors, Jacob emphasized the material context of reading; he recognized the impact of the page, the labor required to decipher and record its meaning, on the content of the text. The best course to follow, Jacob and others agreed, was one of steady application, careful reading and copious note-taking.

Much of the advice literature insisted that the law student must read the original texts written by important authors like Sir Edward Coke, Christopher St Germain or Sir John Fortescue, but abridgments of these authors' texts as well as of writs, pleading, cases, statutes, and many other areas of the law, were also acknowledged and recommended. The eminent lawyer and author Roger North was an exception here, as he sternly advised "that a student must have a care of dealing in abridgments, indexes and common places, all of which are his enemies."[21] But most agreed with the sage judgment expressed by Matthew Hale in his preface to Henry Rolle's massive abridgment—a text and preface well-known throughout the eighteenth century—that abridgments "were published for the help and benefit of students, not to abate their industry." Indeed, Hale insisted that such books were a current necessity: "Whereas at this day the books of the law are grown very many and very large, so that many will not have the patience to read them all, the student will in this book have a considerable abstract and collection of most that is material in them."[22] The increasingly numerous abridgments and student handbooks were regarded as an aid and a model for the commonplace book. In composing his law commonplace book the student often copied the alphabetical headings employed in such abridgments. Printed and standardized sets of titles for commonplacing were also readily available for purchase, or, if the student were fortunate enough, he could follow the titles passed down by a trusted friend or experienced practitioner.[23]

Clearly a close relationship existed between student commonplace books and printed practical texts, like these abridgments of law. Indeed the abridgments initially developed out of students' and practitioners' commonplace books, and these manuscript practices continued to have a reciprocal influence upon print.[24] Although the early eighteenth-century abridgments worked within a printed genre which originated in the late fifteenth and sixteenth centuries, they also quite self-consciously drew upon the ongoing development of manuscript practices—unsurprisingly, since the legal commonplace book was an increasingly important tool for dealing with the profusion of knowledge and print.

Giles Jacob signaled his indebtedness to the commonplace tradition in his *Student's Companion* by manipulating the familiar image of the commonplace writer as a bee harvesting nectar from multiple flowers. He asserted that he was laying out a new path of legal knowledge, but also admitted that he was "obliged to our greatest Writers on the Subject for some of my choice Flowers of Reason."[25] Jacob also offered tribute to the manuscript tradition in the titles as well as in the content and structure of his *Statute law Common-plac'd* and his *Common-law Common-placed.* His abridgments and handbooks organized the material of the law under typical commonplace headings. Like other compilers, Jacob often followed an alphabetical organization, with topical headings and explanatory subheadings introducing the content of enumerated cases, statutes, and other records. In most legal commonplace books information was similarly presented in short paragraphs, or sometimes in enumerated points, under heads or titles.[26] Among the many extant examples of alphabetically-organized commonplace books, title parameters typically range from "acceptance" or "annuitie" to "warrantie," from "abjuration" to "woode," or from "administration" to "will." The interrelationship between print and manuscript is evident in the tendency for early eighteenth-century commonplacers to begin with "abatement" and end variously with "writs," "wreck," or "words"; this was likely due to the increasing influence of eighteenth-century abridgments by Jacob, Knighley D'Anvers, and William Nelson, or the earlier abridgments of William Hughes and William Sheppard, which opened with "abatement" as their first term.[27]

Printed abridgments were sometimes multi-volume and, like many manuscript notebooks, each volume opened with a table of contents or heads while the concluding volume offered an index of cases.[28] William Nelson's three-volume *An Abridgment of the Common Law*, for example, employed such headings as "abatement" through to "entry" in volume one, "error" to "profit" in volume two, and "prohibition" to "writs" in volume three. Within each topic, cross-references to other relevant or related entries were often noted, and citation of the source for each entry was inserted at the end of each paragraph or printed in the margins of the page.[29] These abridgments looked familiar to the reader, with commonplace headings across the top of the page, enumerated points below, and marginal citations throughout. Readers of the abridgments not only were guided and constrained by this format, but also helped to perpetuate these structures through their notes and commonplace books.[30]

These mutual influences between the commonplace book and the printed law book in their content, general format, and even in the specific layout of the page, shaped author, reader, and publisher practices. Although it is clear that the abridgments developed out of student commonplace books, it has been less well understood why greater numbers of these practical texts like Jacob's were published in the eighteenth century and what kinds of impact they had on the commonplace tradition or on legal education more generally. Perhaps the new and increasingly common printed books were meant not only as models and supplements but even as replacements for those "home-made" law books. These abridgments might be seen as the precursors to modern "Gilberts" or "Nutshells"—cram books students use today, useful for avoiding the more rigorous training involved in following a course of legal study and compiling a legal commonplace book for oneself.[31]

Or it is possible that they were seen as useful reference books or textbooks that one could annotate or use as a template for one's own notebook. Quite a few surviving examples of interleaved and annotated abridgments seem to indicate that these books were used *as* commonplace books, books that could be turned into a hybrid between textbook and notebook, reminding us of the instability of the text "written" by an author.[32] Not only slightly older titles, like Henry Rolle's *Abridgment*, but also newer titles like D'Anvers' *A General Abridgment of the Common Law* served this function. And it was not only folio volumes, with their wide margins for composition, that doubled as notebooks: quarto volumes like Samson Euer's *Doctrina Placitandi* were also annotated and interleaved with folio pages for note-taking.[33] These manuscript annotations appear as enumerated points, as references to cases, statutes, decrees, and maxims of the common law; they appear in the margins and on interleaved pages that mirror the printed text. These traces of reading were themselves read and used and valued by successive generations of readers, passed from owner to owner well into the nineteenth century, giving further indications of the intersections between manuscript and print, and between composition and consumption. These interleaved texts give us a real sense of the intertwined practices of reading and writing, and they alert us to the impact a text might have on its reader. It is also notable that this practice of interleaving and transformation was advocated for other essential texts, like Blackstone's *Commentaries*, well into the nineteenth century.[34]

Abridgment, Dictionary, Encyclopedia

Legal commonplace books are, then, one key to understanding that proliferation of legal texts, and they serve as an important context for reading the abridgments and other examples of the practical legal literature. Giles Jacob's works on law, like the rest of the law books produced by Nelson, D'Anvers, Matthew Bacon, John Lilly and others, were conceived of as reference works and repositories, and as a means of collecting, selecting, and often condensing the learning of the common law. [35] This was the sense in which they were "practical" books, to be used selectively in study and practice for the retrieval of information. But many of these law books were also intended to be used in their entirety, as coherent books to be read, not just consulted. The important insights into intentionality and authorship that scholars like Richard Yeo and Roger Chartier have brought to bear on the analysis of eighteenth-century dictionaries, libraries, and encyclopedias are also relevant here: the law books, too, "promised to replace other books, condensing knowledge . . . [and] they were conceived as having a structure or design, planned by an author."[36] These books were intended to provide instruction in an area of the law—or in the case of the larger abridgments, in the entirety of the common law—not only for students and novices but also for experienced practitioners who needed help in confronting the burgeoning literature of the law. The books' headings, sub-headings and cross-references were among the means used by eighteenth-century compilers of encyclopedias and by authors of law abridgments in order to convey the *unity* of their work. These methods enabled authors to combine the ease of alphabetical organization with the coherence of thematic or systematic exposition. Alphabetical organization afforded help in the process of selection, and simplicity in the categorization of material. But the use of cross-reference, and the advocacy of "systematic reading" in the law books, like the new encyclopedias, indicates that these volumes were also envisioned as systematic and coherent classifications of knowledge.[37]

Thus the abridgments not only drew upon older commonplace traditions but also participated in a long-standing encyclopedic tradition. Like other examples of "encyclopaedism" these law books shared a "passion for systematic classification of knowledge" expressed in "large-scale collection projects" and attempted "comprehensive coverage of particular disciplines."[38] These law books were produced during an eighteenth-century "age of encyclopaedias," along with John Harris's *Lexicon Technicum* or Ephraim Chambers' *Cyclopaedia*, and they shared some of the newer goals and concerns of that burgeoning genre.[39] Jacob, D'Anvers, Nelson, and Bacon, like the compilers of encyclopedias and dictionaries, experimented with the ordering of knowledge and reflected on the usefulness of their texts.[40] These and other abridgments that followed varied in their level of detail and subdivision of information but they all played a role in the formation of a legal "encyclopedic vision"—proposing not just one but a select number of texts "containing the collective knowledge of a community which might be put together again if all the other books were lost."[41] Moreover, all of these books were commercial enterprises, the law books as much as the encyclopedias, "a stunning example of how the trade in knowledge was judged to be worth large capital investment."[42] Written in the vernacular, and organized alphabetically, all of these books aimed to educate and communicate with an audience that was broader than the one for the older Latin encyclopedias, or Latin and Law-French texts.

One interesting example is Giles Jacob's *Every Man his Own Lawyer*. Although ostensibly a more popular and general law book, this text was a fairly robust survey of main points of legal process and personnel, estates, marriage and inheritance, and even of constitution and statute. Information that appeared in Jacob's other works was also included here, fitted for readers "of every capacity" and with the hope expressed that such information might have a beneficial effect on the prosecution of suits.[43] In an "Age of Inquiry into Things," as Jacob put it, knowledge can be organized and communicated in such a way as to be advantageous to an inquiring public but also "[afford] a very just Instruction" to legal professionals.[44] Jacob often defended his methods, and defended his abridgments, for their accessibility, clarity, and ease of use; in so doing his arguments repeated the claims made for collections or "libraries" in other fields.[45] Another notable feature of this and many others of Jacob's books is its size: printed in octavo format, these texts may have been conceived of as portable surveys of legal practice. Much like other respected law books, such as William Hawkins' *An Abridgment of the First Part of my Lord Coke's*

Institutes or Robert Gardiner's *Instructor Clericalis*, the goal was portability and usefulness.[46] A good number of the newer abridgments were published in quarto or octavo, and some of the older titles appeared in this smaller format as well. Such portable books "were another form of 'library' produced by the book trade."[47] These libraries, or bibliotheques, like the encyclopedias and dictionaries, were a form of response to the proliferation of print and the problem of collection. As Roger Chartier explains, these portable texts "had a counterpoint in the eighteenth century in a vast number of equally popular small, concise and easily handled volumes named *extraits, esprits, abreges, analyses*, and so forth."[48]

By contrast, the numerous collections of case reports published at this time were usually, although not exclusively, produced in folio volumes. Giles Jacob's folio edition of the reports of Chief Justice Holt is one example, and it provided yet another venue for Jacob's defense of collection and abridgment. Here Jacob hearkened back to the great books of Roman law, comparing a proposed abridgment to a digest of the common law that would contain the collective knowledge of the legal community:

> To write a compleat Abridgment of the Common Law, may justly, at this Time of Day, be thought a Work too extensive for any one Person to undertake. Such a Work, or rather a *Digest* of our Laws, is worthy of a *Juncto* of the first Men in the Profession; of an English *Tribonian* and his Fellows. When that shall be effectually performed, the seeming Contradictions of the Reports shall be reconciled, and those Cases shall be thrown aside which have been denied by later Authorities, and upon better Reasons: And then the recorded *Dicta* and *Responsa* of *Hale*, *Holt*, and *Lee*, will be written down for Text-Law; as in the *Roman Digest* we find those of *Paulus*, *Ulpian*, and *Papinian*.[49]

Jacob's proposal sounded similar to the eighteenth-century encyclopedic projects of Harris, Chambers, and others. It even anticipated later encyclopedias, like the third and subsequent editions of the *Britannica*, in suggesting this "Juncto" of multiple authors.[50] Jacob's reference to Roman law appears misleading, however, since he was not calling for an institute in the accepted sense of a systematic and analytic treatise or textbook of law. But his divergence from the Institutionalists is deliberate and instructive. Jacob adhered to eighteenth-century notions about reasoning through examples, comparisons, and juxtaposition, and he endorsed that combination of the alphabetical and thematic organization of information. In Jacob's mind the *dicta* and *responsa* of jurists would become text law still recorded as cases and arguments rather than in treatise form; analysis of law would remain inductive, rules and reasons would be derived from cases and remedies. Until such a complete abridgment or digest was possible, Jacob added, case reports and lesser abridgments like his own remained useful.

The volume of reports that followed Jacob's proposal is a large reference work, more than seven hundred folio pages arranged alphabetically from "abatement" to "writs," with extensive tables of titles, cases, and principal matters appended at the front and back. Jacob's *New Law Dictionary* is similarly large and aimed to be even more comprehensive than his other works. This dictionary is most like the work of Chambers and Harris and other encyclopedists both in terms of its layout (small print in double columns in two volumes of unpaginated folios), and in terms of its attempt at accessibility and communication with a wide audience. But Jacob produced narrowly topical as well as such broadly comprehensive works organized both alphabetically and non-alphabetically. He experimented with different methods of communicating information and quite often presented the same material in different formats, explicating the same writs, statutes, and cases in his multiple texts. He wrote for lawyers, local officers, merchants, students, clerks, stewards—and for poets, playwrights, and gentlemen of taste. Jacob's literary works were similarly varied and included essays, memoirs, plays, and poems as well as the *Poetical Register*, a broad anthology of collective biography in two volumes.[51] The *Poetical Register* betrays that same concern with the organization of knowledge; here, Jacob takes part in an "ordering of the arts" that has been described as a product of an Enlightenment interest in a history of the arts and in standards of taste and genre.[52] Jacob's *Poetical Register*, his *Law Dictionary*, and his many comprehensive abridgments and guides to the law share similar concerns, and may even have been influenced by a contemporary philosophical analysis of the intersections between language, knowledge, and civility.[53] Perhaps it was the multiple venues for reflection, and the comparisons naturally to be made among his own varied works, that led Jacob to question and experiment with the organization and communication of knowledge.

This variety should also serve as encouragement to us to read early eighteenth-century legal literature within those contexts of encyclopedia, bibliotheque, and commonplace book. These contexts allow us to come to a different assessment of the quality of these texts and a better understanding of common law thought in the era before Blackstone's treatises and Bentham's reforms. Eighteenth-century common law, both its literature and practice, has often been criticized as inaccessible and pedantic. It has been ridiculed as incoherent, a confused jumble of precedents, procedures, technicalities, and writs—a form of legal reasoning antithetical to reason and principle. The works of Giles Jacob and the rest of the practical legal literature of the early eighteenth century have always seemed to confirm that view. The analysis of law in these texts remained inductive, with rules and reasons derived from cases and remedies, and presented through alphabetical commonplace headings, subheadings, and the practice of cross-referencing. But this legal reasoning through examples, comparison, and juxtaposition is not *only* representative of a particularistic, inductive, "common law mind." These reading and writing practices are also illustrated by the Enlightenment encyclopedias and are also part of a broader Enlightenment interest in the management and cogent expression of knowledge. Inductive logic—looking at what information one does have, gathering and organizing that knowledge—was *also* a part of Enlightenment projects.

Those broad Enlightenment goals of critique and definition, of sweeping away the past and articulating abstract ideals, were certainly different from the common law's aims in the eighteenth century. But they were also intimately connected to common goals of containing, and making coherent, vast amounts of learning. And by the same token, Giles Jacob was surely a "blunderbuss of law" and early eighteenth-century common law texts were surely voluminous, difficult, technical, and arcane. But they were also a part of commonplace and humanist traditions of scholarship, and part of new Enlightenment approaches to the mastery, communication, and progress of knowledge.

NOTES

Portions of this article were presented at meetings of the American Society for Eighteenth-Century Studies, the American Society for Legal History, and the Workshop in the History of Material Texts at the University of Pennsylvania. The author would particularly like to thank David Ibbetson, Peter Stallybrass, and the anonymous readers for this journal for their many helpful comments.

1. David Lemmings, *Professors of the Law: Barristers and English Legal Culture in the Eighteenth Century* (Oxford: Oxford University Press, 2000), 67 n.18.
2. Gary L. McDowell, "The Politics of Meaning: Law Dictionaries and the Liberal Tradition of Interpretation," *The American Journal of Legal History*

3.44 (2000): 261. McDowell is citing Leonard Levy, "Origins of the Fifth Amendment and its Critics," *Cardozo Law Review* 19 (1997): 854.

3. Jacob was indeed the most prolific, producing dozens of law texts including, for example, *The Compleat Court Keeper* (London, 1713); *A Review of the Statutes both Ancient and Modern* (London, 1713); *The Accomplished Conveyancer* (London, 1714–15); *The Modern Justice* (London, 1716); *A Catalogue of Writs and Processes* (London, 1717); *Lex Mercatoria* (London, 1718); *Lex Constitutionis* (London, 1719); *The Statute Law Common-plac'd* (London, 1719); *The Student's Companion: Or, the Reason of the Laws of England* (London, 1725); *The Common Law Common-placed* (London, 1726); *A New Law Dictionary* (London, 1729); *The Compleat Chancery Practicer* (London, 1730); *City Liberties: Or the Rights and Privileges of Freemen* (London, 1732); *Every Man his Own Lawyer: Or a Summary of the Laws of England* (London, 1736); *Law Grammar* (London, 1744). Most of these and Jacob's other texts were reprinted in later editions.

4. J. McLaverty, "Pope and Giles Jacob's *Lives of the Poets*: The *Dunciad* as Alternative Literary History," *Modern Philology* 83.1 (1985): 22–32; Pat Rogers, *Grub Street: Studies in a Subculture* (London: Methuen, 1972), 288–89; Matthew Kilburn, "Jacob, Giles (bap. 1686, d. 1744)," *Oxford Dictionary of National Biography* (Oxford; Oxford University Press, 2004) <http://www.oxforddnb.com/view/article/14565>. The couplet in Pope's *Dunciad* is: "Jacob, the Scourge of Grammar, mark with awe,/ Nor less revere him, Blunderbuss of Law."

5. See, for example, W.S. Holdsworth, *A History of English Law*, 12 vols. (London: Methuen, 1924), 6:574; J.H. Baker, *An Introduction to English Legal History* (London: Butterworths, 2002), 190–91; A.W.B. Simpson, "The Rise and Fall of the Legal Treatise: Legal Principles and the Forms of Legal Literature," *University of Chicago Law Review* 48. 3 (1981): 632–79. Note that Simpson argues for the absence of published legal treatises in England (with a very few exceptions) from the age of Littleton to the age of Blackstone. See also Michael Lobban, "Blackstone and the Science of Law," *The Historical Journal* 30. 2 (1987): 313.

6. Ann Blair, "Reading Strategies for Coping with Information Overload ca. 1550–1700," *Journal of the History of Ideas* 64.1 (2003): 12, 22–23; Richard Yeo, *Encyclopaedic Visions: Scientific Dictionaries and Enlightenment Culture* (Cambridge: Cambridge University Press, 2001), preface.

7. In addition to the works of Holdsworth, Baker, and Simpson cited above see, for example, David Lemmings, *Gentlemen and Barristers: The Inns of Court and the English Bar* (Oxford: Clarendon Press, 1990), and Lemmings, *Professors of the Law*.

8. For a discussion of changes in legal education, see J.H. Baker "Readings in Gray's Inn, Their Decline and Disappearance," in *The Legal Profession and the Common Law, Historical Essays*, ed. J.H. Baker (London: Hambledon Press, 1986), 35–37; Alan Cromartie, "The Rule of Law," in *Revolution and Restoration: England in the 1650s*, ed. John Morrill (London: Collins & Brown, 1992), 55–

69; Wilfrid R. Prest, *The Inns of Court under Elizabeth I and the Early Stuarts, 1590–1640* (Totowa, N.J.: Rowman and Littlefield, 1972); Prest, "Law Reform and Legal Education in Interregnum England," *Bulletin of the Institute of Historical Research* 187 (2002): 112–22; Nancy L. Matthews, *William Sheppard: Cromwell's Law Reformer* (Cambridge: Cambridge University Press, 1984).

9. See Simpson, "Rise and Fall," 636, 639; David Ibbetson "Legal Printing and Legal Doctrine," *The Irish Jurist* 35 (New Series 2000): 345–46; Richard J. Ross "The Commoning of the Common Law: The Renaissance Debate over Printing English Law, 1520–1640," *University of Pennsylvania Law Review*, 146. 2 (1998): 329–461. A similar proliferation of medical literature took place in this period. See, for example, Mary Fissell and Roger Cooter, "Exploring Natural Knowledge: Science and the Popular," *The Cambridge History of Science, Volume 4: Eighteenth-Century Science*, ed. Roy Porter (Cambridge: Cambridge University Press, 2003): 146–51, and Fissell, *Vernacular Bodies: The Politics of Reproduction in Early Modern England* (Oxford: Oxford University Press, 2005).

10. Anthony Fitzherbert, *La Graunde Abridgment*, 3 vols. (London, 1514–16?); Nicholas Statham, *Abridgment* (Rouen, 1488?); William Style, *Regestum Practicale: Or, the Practical Register, Consisting of Rules, Orders and Observations Concerning the Common-Laws and the Practice thereof* (London, 1657); Edmund Wingate, *An Exact Abridgment of all the Statutes* (London, 1642).

11. Lemmings, *Gentlemen and Barristers*, 95–108.

12. Jacob, *Compleat Court Keeper*, iii–vi; Kilburn, "Jacob, Giles (bap. 1686, d.1744)."

13. Jacob, *Statute Law Common-plac'd*, A3 verso. In this preface the rhetoric of Jacob's request for patronage includes not only the usual claims for the modesty of his performance but also alludes to the hardships Jacob faced in his training and practice: "I think it consistent with my Duty to make an Apology for my very great Presumption in prefixing the Names of the Right Honourable the Lord Chancellor the Judges (the Ornaments of the Law, and Distributers [sic] of Justice) in the Front of this small Performance; and it would be wholly unpardonable, were it not to implore a *Protection*, which a Person bred to the Law, by a Train of Misfortunes may otherwise want." A3 recto.

14. This advice literature included texts such as William Fulbecke, *Directive or Preparative to the Study of the Law* (London, 1600); William Phillips, *Studii Legalis Ratio, or Directions for the Study of the Law* (London, 1675); Matthew Hale, "Lord Hale's Preface to Rolle's Abridgment," in Francis Hargrave, *Collecteana Juridica: Consisting of Tracts Relative to the Law and Constitution of England*, 2 vols. (London, 1791; reprint Littleton, CO: Fred B. Rothman & Co., 1980), 1:263–82; Roger North, *A Discourse on the Study of Laws* ([written c.1709] London, 1824); "Lord Chief Justice Reeve to his Nephew," Hargrave, *Collecteana Juridica,* 1:79–81; Thomas Wood, *Some Thoughts Considering the Study of the Laws of England* (London, 1727); Nathaniel Cole,

"A Prescription for Educating a Barrister, 1736," in Lemmings, *Professors of the Law*, 341–45.

15. See Ann Moss, *Printed Commonplace-Books and the Structuring of Renaissance Thought* (Oxford: Oxford University Press, 1996), chapters 5–7; Ann Blair, "Humanist Methods in Natural Philosophy: The Commonplace Book," *Journal of the History of Ideas* 53.4 (1992): 541–42; Richard Ross, "The Memorial Culture of Early Modern English Lawyers: Memory as Keyword, Shelter and Identity, 1560–1640," *Yale Journal of Law & the Humanities* 10 (1998): 270–80.

16. Jacob, Introduction to *The Student's Companion* (London, 2nd edn. 1734), vi–vii. The first edition of 1725 did not include an introduction.

17. Blair "Information Overload," 16.

18. John Locke, *A New Method of A Common-Place Book*, in *The Posthumous Works of John Locke* (London, 1706), 316–24. Locke's text was first published in French as "Nouvelle methode de dresser des recueils" in Le Clerc's *Bibliotheque Universelle et Historique* (Amsterdam, 1686). For Locke's methods and influence, see also Michael Hoeflich, "The Lawyer as Pragmatic Reader: The History of Legal Common-Placing," 55 *Arkansas Law Review* (2002): 97; Moss, *Commonplace Books*, 278–79; Blair "Information Overload," 21; G.G. Meynell, "John Locke's Method of Common-Placing, as Seen in His Drafts and His Medical Notebooks, Bodleian MSS Locke D.9, f.21 and f.23," *Seventeenth Century* 8 (1993): 245–67.

19. Matthew Hale, "Preface to Rolle's Abridgment," 277–78; North, *Discourse on Study of Laws*, 26–27.

20. Jacob, *Student's Companion*, vi.

21. North, *Discourse on Study of Laws*, 19, here referring by name to the abridgments by Anthony Fitzherbert and Robert Brooke; he later repeats the caution, and warns against other specific texts such as the abridgment by Edmund Wingate.

22. Hale, "Preface to Rolle's Abridgment," 279–80.

23. Ross "Memorial Culture," 281–82; Holdsworth, *History of English Law*, 6:601, notes the first such list of titles published by Samuel Brewster of Lincoln's Inn, "An Alphabetical Disposition of all the Heads Necessary for a Perfect Commonplace" (1680, 1681). See also Michael Hoeflich on the importance of such "canonical" lists of headings to the formation of an "interpretative community of legal professionals." Hoeflich, "Lawyer as Pragmatic Reader," 103.

24. John D. Cowley, *A Bibliography of Abridgments, Digests, Dictionaries and Indexes of English Law to the Year 1800* (London: Quaritch, 1932), xxxix; Richard Yeo, "A Solution to the Multitude of Books: Ephraim Chambers's *Cyclopaedia* (1728) as 'the Best Book in the Universe'," *Journal of the History of Ideas* 64.1 (2003): 63–65.

25. Jacob, *Student's Companion*, v.

26. Two good examples of commonplace books that presented information as a series of numbered points are: Free Library of Philadelphia, Hampton L. Carson Collection, John Strange Commonplace Book, MS LC.14.86; Inner

Temple Library, London, Barrington Collection, Law Commonplace Book, MS 68.

27. Columbia Law Library, New York, NY, Singleton Collection, Legal Commonplace MS 36, Legal Commonplace eighteenth-century MS 37; Harvard Law Library, Cambridge, MA, Special Collections, Commonplace c.1800 MS 1262, Commonplace after 1736, MS 1273, Lawyer's Commonplace Book ca. 1750, MS 4091. William Hughes, *The Grand Abridgment of the Law Continued* (London, 1660–63); William Sheppard, *A Grand Abridgment of the Common and Statute Law of England* (London, 1675); Knightley D'Anvers, *A General Abridgment of the Common Law, Alphabetically Digested under Proper Titles* (London, 1705–27); William Nelson, *An Abridgment of the Common Law* (London, 1725–26). Jacob adhered closely to these usual headings from abatement to writ in his *Common Law Common-placed* and *Review of the Statutes* among other works. Others of his texts are organized alphabetically but begin and end with specifically relevant terms; for example his *Modern Justice* begins with "affray" and ends with "wrecks."

28. Readers sometimes added their own indices to printed books, just as in commonplace notebooks such indices were not only prepared by the initial compiler but also added by later owners. One example of a manuscript that includes indices prepared both by the initial compiler and a later owner is Free Library of Philadelphia, Carson Collection, Crumwell Deth Commonplace, MS LC.14.80. A commonplace book that includes a handwritten index to a printed book, William Scroggs, *The Practice of Courts-Leet and Courts-Baron* (London, 1701), may be found in Inner Temple Library, Barrington Collection, Law Commonplace Book Containing Table to Scroggs etc., MS 60; another eighteenth-century law commonplace includes an alphabetical table of abbreviations for the works cited within the manuscript, Inner Temple Library, Barrington Collection, MS 68. See also Hoeflich, "Lawyer as Pragmatic Reader," 100.

29. Compare the abridgments with examples of commonplace books that employed a good deal of this kind of cross-referencing within the text, such as Columbia Law Library, Singleton Collection, MSS 36 and 37.

30. See Roger Chartier on the "activity of reading" in *The Order of Books*, trans. Lydia G. Cochrane (Stanford: Stanford University Press, 1992), 23.

31. Brian Simpson asserts that "To this day the case class system only works in the American law schools because students make use of various commercially produced summaries of the law, 'nutshells', 'Gilberts', and the like, which serve to redress the disorderly confusion of the case book from which it is pretended that they learn the law." A.W.B. Simpson, *Leading Cases in the Common Law* (Oxford: Clarendon Press, 1995), 7.

32. Chartier, *Order of Books*, 9–10.

33. Examples of annotated and interleaved copies of Rolle's *Abridgment* may be found in Inner Temple Library, Misc. MSS, Rolle's Abridgment MS Notes by Baron Price, MSS 125–30, and in Biddle Law Library, University of

Pennsylvania, KH/KD 295 R64 1668; an extensively annotated and interleaved copy of Samson Euer's *Doctrina Placitandi* (London, 1677) may be found in the library of Judge Henry Singleton, Columbia Law Library, Singleton Collection, MS 43. The library catalogue of Judge Martin Wright indicates that he owned a number of annotated and interleaved texts, including "four volumes of D'Anvers *Abridgment* (1701) with manuscript notes." Inner Temple Library, Barrington Collection, Catalogue of Sir Martin Wright Library 1769, MS 63.

34. As Michael Hoeflich points out, William Wright's *Advice on the Study of Law* (London, 1810; Boston, 1811) suggests that students have a copy of Blackstone interleaved for note-taking. Hoeflich is mistaken, however, in regarding Wright's approach as unusual. Hoeflich, "Lawyer as Pragmatic Reader," 109. Compare also Richard Yeo's suggestion that for some, less scholarly, readers, Chambers's "*Cyclopaedia* functioned as a ready-made commonplace book." Richard Yeo, "Encyclopaedism and Enlightenment" in *The Enlightenment World*, eds. Martin Fitzpatrick, Peter Jones, Christa Wold and Ian McCalman (New York: Routledge 2004), 360.

35. John Lilly, *The Practical Register: or A General Abridgment of the Law* (London, 1719); Matthew Bacon, *A New Abridgment of the Law* (London, 1736–66). The first three volumes written by Bacon, but published anonymously, appeared between 1736 and 1740; Bacon died before completing the fourth volume and later volumes were complied by other authors. Cowley, *Bibliography of Abridgments*, lx–lxiv; Holdsworth, *History of English Law*, 12:169–70.

36. Richard Yeo, "Encyclopedic Knowledge," in *Books and the Sciences in History*, eds. Marina Frasca-Spada and Nick Jardine (Cambridge: Cambridge University Press, 2000), 210. See also Chartier, *Order of Books*, 64–66.

37. For analysis of the goals and intentions of the new encyclopedias, see Yeo, *Encyclopaedic Visions*, xiii, xv, 12, 16–27, 110–115;Yeo, "Encyclopaedic Knowledge," 215–21; Yeo, "Encyclopaedism and Enlightenment," 357–59. Here too the abridgments and encyclopedia demonstrate a connection with the commonplace book: Ann Blair avers that "sophisticated thematic indexing or commonplacing which cross-referenced and systematically compared material in related categories could bring material together in new ways, highlighting contradictions and interconnections and potentially yielding new insights." Ann Blair, "Annotating and Indexing Natural Philosophy," in *Books and the Sciences*, 73.

38. Yeo "Encyclopaedism and Enlightenment," 350.

39. John Harris, *Lexicon Technicum: or an Universal English Dictionary of Arts and Sciences* (London, 1704); Ephraim Chambers, *Cyclopaedia: or an Universal Dictionary of Arts and Sciences* (London, 1728).

40. Giles Jacob offers this kind of reflection in his preface to *A Report of all the Cases Determined by Sir John Holt Knt. From 1688 to 1710* (London, 1738), ii–iii. The attribution of this edition of reports to Jacob is made in Charles C. Soule, *The Lawyer's Reference Manual of Law Books and Citations* (Boston: Soule and Bugbee, 1883), *The Catalogue of the Hampton L. Carson Collection: Illustrative of the Growth of the Common Law*, 2 vols. (Boston: G.K. Hall, 1962),

and repeated, for example, in the online catalogues of the Harvard and Columbia University Law Libraries. Other examples of this kind of self-conscious reflection may be found in Nelson, *Abridgment of the Common Law*, preface; D'Anvers, *General Abridgment*, "To the Reader"; Matthew Bacon, *A General Abridgment of Cases in Equity* (London, 1732), iii; Bacon, *The Compleat Arbitrator*, (London, 1731), iii–v.

41. Yeo, *Encyclopaedic Visions*, 3.

42. Yeo, "Encyclopaedism and Enlightenment," 354.

43. Jacob, *Every Man his Own Lawyer*, vi. By contrast the preface to *The Attorney's Pocket Companion*, 2 vols. (London, 2nd edn., 1733) warned against expanding popular knowledge of law (here directed against recent legislation passed to end the use of law Latin) because of the danger that it would lead to frivolous and expensive lawsuits.

44. Jacob, *Every Man his Own Lawyer*, v–vi.

45. Compare Jacob's statement with the statement of Gabriel Naudé in his *Advis pour dresser une Bibliotheque* (1627) quoted by Roger Chartier: "In the first place they save us the trouble of seeking out an infinite number of highly rare and curious books; secondly, because they leave space for many others and give relief to a Library; thirdly, because they condense for us in one volume and commodiously what we would have to seek with much trouble in several places; and finally, because they bring with them a great saving, being certain that it requires few testons . . . to buy them than it would require ecus if one wanted to have separately all the [works] that they contain." Chartier, *Order of Books*, 65–66.

46. William Hawkins, *An Abridgment of the First Part of my Ld Coke's Institutes* (London, 1711), iii–iv; Robert Gardiner, *Instructor Clericalis* (London, 1693). Jacob claims that a book like his *Grand Precedent*, for example, will be "particularly useful as an itinerant Library or Office." Giles Jacob, *The Grand Precedent: Or, the Conveyancer's Guide and Assistant* (London, 1716), A2 verso.

47. Chartier, *Order of Books*, 68.

48. Ibid. One indication of the prevalence of these small volumes may be found in the sale catalogue of the library of the eighteenth-century lawyer, William Carr, where the list of "practical" law books in octavo owned by Carr runs for four pages. Daniel Browne, *A Catalogue of the Libraries of the Honourable William Carr, of Lincoln's-Inn, . . . And of the Reverend Mr. John Herbert* (London, 1721), 21–25. Compare also the multiple editions of Thomas Basset, *A Catalogue of the Common and Statute Law Books of this Realm* (London, 1671–1730), and "A Complete Catalogue of Law Books Published since 1700," in *A New and Correct Catalogue of all the English Books Which have been Printed from the Year 1700 to the Present Time* (London, 1767).

49. Jacob, *Report of all the Cases Determined by Sir John Holt,* ii–iii.

50. Yeo, *Encyclopaedic Visions*, 183.

51. See Giles Jacob, *The Poetical Register:Or the Lives and Characters of the English Dramatick Poets. With an Account of Their Writings* (London,

1719); *An Historical Account of the Lives and Writings of Our Most Considerable English Poets, whether Epick, Lyrick, Elegiack, Epigrammatists, Etc.* (London 1720). Both volumes were reissued in 1723.

52. See McLaverty, "Pope and Giles Jacob," 24; John Brewer, *The Pleasures of the Imagination: English Culture in the Eighteenth Century* (Chicago: University of Chicago Press, 1997), chapter 11; Lawrence Lipking, *The Ordering of the Arts in Eighteenth-Century England* (Princeton: Princeton University Press, 1970).

53. Note, for example, Jacob's emphasis on legal knowledge and "politeness" on the first page of the preface to his *Common Law Common-Placed*: "The Great and Commendable Learning of the Laws of one's Country, if rightly considered, is equal with any other Learning, even the Politest of the most flourishing Kingdoms, tho' it is not commonly so accepted; as it points out to us Justice between Man and Man, and the Means that secure all Men from Injustice; And if Knowledge, in general, is to be estimated by the Difficulty in its attaining, that of the Law, beyond any other, merits our Approbation." See also Mc Dowell, "Politics of Meaning," 268–70.

Forging Literary History: Historical Fiction and Literary Forgery in Eighteenth-Century Britain

ANNE H. STEVENS

In his article "History's Greatest Forger: Science, Fiction, and Fraud Along the Seine," historian of science Ken Alder purports to have discovered a letter in a French archive by Denis Vrain-Lucas, a notorious nineteenth-century forger who made a fortune selling letters he claimed to have discovered in a hitherto-unknown casque of papers by such luminaries as Galileo, Alexander the Great, and Mary Magdalene (all written in French!). By creating his own invented letter to serve his larger intellectual purposes, Alder revisits Vrain-Lucas's acts of forgery, employing the familiar eighteenth-century framework of the discovered manuscript in order to muse theoretically on the nature of historical knowledge, and call for "a more expansive view of what counts as a credible account of the past." Both Alder the supposed translator of this letter and his alter-ego Vrain-Lucas discuss the creative element present in all acts of historical reconstruction. In his "translator's" introduction, Alder argues,

> If a narrow descriptive facticity cannot exhaust the plenitude of nature, why should the plenitude of the human past be more easily encompassed? Yet many historians continue to represent the past in as positivist a mode as any scientist, and they continue to do so using literary technologies—

> both forms of writing and the presentation of evidence—that historians borrowed back from the natural sciences in the nineteenth century.

Speaking in the voice of Vrain-Lucas defending his acts of forgery within his invented letter, Alder makes a related point: "Only when historians are obliged to work between the documents and fill in the gaps—for there are always gaps—do the imaginative faculties become engaged in storytelling, and only then can we paint the true picture of an age."[1]

Alder characterizes the dominant mode of contemporary historiography as positivistic, exhibiting a "narrow descriptive facticity" that misses the forest for the trees, ignoring larger truths about the past in favor of antiquarian details. In contrast to this scientific attitude towards the past, Alder celebrates the historian's work as an artistic endeavor, likening it to both literature ("storytelling") and the visual arts ("paint the true picture of an age"), in a manner reminiscent of postmodern theorists of historiography such as Hayden White and Paul Ricoeur. In reaction to positivistic, scientific models of historical investigation, many postmodern critics react skeptically, doubting the possibility of actually recovering the past on its own terms.[2] Alder's work of historical fiction couched as forgery, in contrast, takes this skepticism and channels it in a much more optimistic, even celebratory, direction in regards to the creative and imaginative dimensions of historical reconstruction.

In this essay, I wish to explore a similar dialectic of historical positivism and skepticism in eighteenth-century Britain. Over the course of the century, but particularly in the second half, new and more scientific standards of historical investigation developed, with practitioners expressing a greater confidence about their ability to know the past. During these years, a series of monumental achievements in historiography appeared: David Hume's *History of England* (1754–62), Edward Gibbon's *Decline and Fall of the Roman Empire* (1776), and William Robertson's *History of Scotland* (1759), to name just three of the most celebrated. As part of this increased interest in the past and increased optimism about the ability to understand earlier historical periods, a range of new types of writing about the past proliferated, such as antiquarian studies, social and cultural history, literary history, universal history, and conjectural history.[3] While the study of history was developing much more rigorous standards of investigation and historical works were among the bestselling titles of the century, a strain of historical skepticism was gaining force, often finding expression in the writings of the very same people who were doing the confident historical investigation. This philosophical skepticism is perhaps most dramatically illustrated in the writings of major historians such as Hume and Robertson.[4] The works of these philosophical historians were steeped in skepticism about both individual historical details and the possibility of achieving any kind of historical certainty.[5]

While many eighteenth-century historians such as Hume expressed skepticism about their own historical investigations, other writers celebrated the imaginative dimension of historical investigation, à la Alder. These imaginative manifestations of historical skepticism took the form of historical fictions and literary forgeries, both of which flourished in the late eighteenth century. My essay will survey a few examples of the historical forgeries and historical fictions of the late eighteenth century, placing them in the context of this dialectic of positivism and skepticism. In particular, I will examine some of the ways in which both modern scholars and eighteenth-century practitioners have connected those phenomena. Both literary forgery and historical fiction as practiced in the second half of the eighteenth century depend upon another of the age's notable intellectual developments, an emergent literary historicism: the idea that literature has a history, part of and parallel to a larger cultural history, and that literary style is a product of its historical moment, which can be reconstructed through scholarly analysis. As literature comes increasingly to be valued as a repository of history in the later eighteenth century, both literary forgers and historical novelists experiment with this new valuation, depositing their own interpretations of the past into new imaginative works.

While Hume famously called his own time "the historical age," it is no coincidence that the eighteenth century was also certainly the golden age of historical forgery. In recent years the phenomenon of literary forgery has attracted the attention of a number of scholars, including Paul Baines, Nick Groom, and Ian Haywood.[6] Eighteenth-century forgery is most often associated with its most famous practitioners, the paired figures of Thomas Chatterton and James Macpherson, although there were many other notorious forgers throughout the century. The eighteenth century is also widely regarded as the period in which the field of literary history came into its own, taking on many of its recognizably modern features.[7] Anthony Grafton, among others, has explored the reciprocal relationship between literary forgers and literary scholars: "For 2,500 years and more, forgery has amused its uninvolved observers, enraged its humiliated victims, flourished as a literary genre, and, most oddly of all, stimulated vital innovations in the technical method of scholars."[8] The phenomena of literary forgery and literary history are dialectically linked: as scholars evince an increasing interest in the past and confidence about their investigations, forgers prey upon this interest by creating new documents meant to pass for historical artifacts.

Many of the milestones in both the history of literary forgery and the development of English literary history cluster around the 1760s and early 1770s. James Macpherson inaugurated the decade and his series of Ossian poems with *Fragments of Ancient Poetry* in 1760. Thomas Percy published his monumental ballad collection *Reliques of Ancient English Poetry* in 1765. The previous year, Horace Walpole's *The Castle of Otranto* appeared, neither an act of forgery nor a literary history but a Gothic novel that borrows liberally from both genres, especially in its prefatory material. Although his Rowley forgeries were not published until several years after his death in 1770, in 1769 Thomas Chatterton famously and notoriously sought Walpole's opinion of his manuscripts, while debates about the authenticity of the Rowley poems appeared throughout the decade of the 1770s. And in 1774, the first volume of Thomas Warton's *History of English Poetry*, the first English literary history, was published. The synchronicity and interconnectedness of notorious literary forgeries and groundbreaking literary histories becomes apparent by looking at the controversies surrounding Chatterton and Macpherson in particular. The greatest literary historical minds of the day, including Percy, Warton, Hugh Blair, Samuel Johnson, and Thomas Tyrwhitt, were all involved in debating the authenticity of these texts, and one byproduct of these debates was that they helped to develop more sophisticated critical principles of textual analysis and literary history. Both defenders and detractors of Chatterton and Macpherson based their arguments on a sense of literature as a repository of information about social and cultural history, alternately pointing out, for example, the historicity or the anachronisms of the texts' language, style, and subject matter.

A good deal of the recent scholarly literature on forgery has focused on the creative rather than the criminal dimensions of the act, or on the conjunctions between the two, as in Ken Alder's exploration of the mixed motivations of Denis Vrain-Lucas. In his 2001 book *Faking Literature*, for example, K. K. Ruthven uses a poststructuralist framework to examine and to celebrate forgery: "We ought to revalue literary forgery as an antinomian phenomenon produced by creative energies whose power is attested to by the resistance they engender in those who feel compelled to denounce and eradicate it." Forgeries, he contends, "exhibit a carnivalesque irreverence towards the sanctity of various conventions designed to limit what is permissible in literary production."[9] A version of this "carnivalesque irreverence" can be seen in Patricia Highsmith's 1970 novel *Ripley Under Ground*, where the main character, Tom Ripley, becomes enmeshed in a complex scheme of art forgery. He defends his actions, arguing that "an artist does things naturally, without effort. Some power guides his hand. A forger struggles, and if he succeeds, it is a genuine achievement."[10] Though Ripley's championing of forgery as a form of artistic achievement and his refusal to distinguish between the authentic work of art and the copy sound seductively postmodern, even Baudrillardian, it is important to note that he not only celebrates the creative aspects of forgery but also commits identity theft and multiple murders.

My point here is not to express outrage over the "crimes of writing" of past centuries, but merely to articulate a reluctance to embrace a completely relativistic attitude towards truth.[11] A distinction should be made between forgery as a crime intended to deceive for profit and glory and the use of gestures of forgery for rhetorical effect or in order to mimic or recreate the style of another era, even though a Macpherson or Chatterton blurs those very boundaries.[12] In the first camp I would place the real Vrain-Lucas selling his forged letters to the credulous scholar Michel Chasles, in the second, Ken Alder inventing a new letter by Vrain-Lucas as a way of commenting upon historiography.

In *The Making of History*, Ian Haywood delineates a similar movement from outright forgery to the employment of the gestures of forgery in the transition from the poetry of Chatterton and Macpherson to the historical novel as practiced by Sir Walter Scott. For Haywood, "their aims were the same: the literary making of the past."[13] This is a tremendous leap to make from Macpherson's and Chatterton's forgeries in the 1760s to the Waverley Novels (1814–1832) on the basis of a common motivation to "make" history. But I agree with Haywood that there is a connection between literary forgery and historical fiction. Both are imaginative attempts to reconstruct the past, borne of a skeptical reaction to increasingly scientific attitudes towards history. In between these two points I would like to propose a number of moments in literary history that can be seen as intermediate steps between Macpherson and Scott, which I will explore in the remainder of this essay.

One line from forgery to historical fiction can be traced from Macpherson as an alleged folklorist, collecting fragments of ancient poetry, to Scott's work as a literary antiquary and ballad collector in his first publication, *The Minstrelsy of the Scottish Border* (1802). Scott's antiquarian background informs the construction of his novels, particularly in his use of antiquarian paratextual matter such as footnotes and multiple scholarly and pseudo-scholarly prefatory framing devices, while the debate over the authenticity of the poems of Ossian figures prominently in the plot of his novel *The Antiquary*.

Over the last several decades, Scott has been demoted from his traditional place in literary history as the inventor of the historical novel. Katie

Trumpener, one of the key figures in Scott's demotion, puts it succinctly: "Most of the conceptual innovations attributed to Scott were in 1814 already fully established commonplaces of the British novel."[14] In a similar way, he is not the first to connect historical fiction and literary forgery. In fact, some of the earliest English novels that employ historical settings play with this connection between fiction and forgery. Walpole famously and influentially began the preface to the first edition of *The Castle of Otranto* in the voice of an antiquary:

> The following work was found in the library of an ancient catholic family in the north of England. It was printed at Naples, in the black letter, in the year 1520. How much sooner it was written does not appear. The principal incidents are such as were believed in the darkest ages of christianity; but the language and conduct have nothing that savours of barbarism.[15]

Although he confesses his authorship in subsequent editions, in the first edition Walpole employs a framing device that masks his novel as a much more ancient work, just as Macpherson and other forgers had done. And at least initially, some readers took the preface at its word. Even the *Critical Review*, for example, leaves the question of the text's authenticity open for debate:

> The ingenious translator of this *very curious* performance informs us it was found in the library of an ancient catholic family in the north of England . . . . Whether he speaks seriously or ironically we neither know nor care. The publication of any work, at this time, in England composed of such rotten materials, is a phenomenon we cannot account for.[16]

Although the reviewer dismisses *The Castle of Otranto* as trash, he does not definitively state that it is a work of fiction, as later reviewers did. Instead, he dismisses the question of the text's authenticity as both unanswerable and irrelevant.

Walpole uses the discovered manuscript topos with much more pronounced and unambiguous irony in his later and less celebrated *Hieroglyphic Tales*: "The Hieroglyphic Tales were undoubtedly written a little before the creation of the world, and have ever since been preserved, by oral tradition, in the mountains of Crampcraggiri, an uninhabited island, not yet discovered."[17] Here Walpole parodies the discovered manuscript convention by carrying it to an absurdist and paradoxical extreme—the text, written before the creation of the world, has been preserved by oral tradition, and on an uninhabited island, no less. Near the end of his preface, the author describes his next project:

> I will not detain the reader longer from the perusal of this invaluable work; but I must beseech the public to be expeditious in taking off the whole impression, as fast as I can get it printed; because I must inform them that I have a more precious work in contemplation; namely, a new Roman history, in which I mean to ridicule, detect and expose, all ancient virtue, and patriotism, and shew from original papers which I am going to write, and which I shall afterwards bury in the ruins of Carthage and then dig up, that it appears by the letters of Hanno the Punic embassador at Rome, that Scipio was in the pay of Hannibal, and that the dilatoriness of Fabius proceeded from his being a pensioner of the same general.[18]

Walpole takes on the persona of a not-very-subtle forger for his collection of outrageous tales, anarchically clearing a space for his fantastic and boundary-pushing narratives by casting doubt upon the validity of traditional historical narrative. In this way he deliberately yokes historical forgery and historical fiction, casting both in an ironic and absurdist light.

The ironic depiction of historical forgery in the *Hieroglyphic Tales* builds upon the skepticism that became much more pronounced in Walpole's thinking on historical matters in the 1760s and 1770s. Walpole's major work of historical scholarship in this period (which led to his complete break with the Society of Antiquaries), *Historic Doubts on the Life and Reign of King Richard III* (1768), had tried to demonstrate through the example of the reputation of Richard III how received historical wisdom can be built upon flimsy and partisan foundations. He begins the work with an expression of extreme historical skepticism:

> So incompetent has the generality of historians been, for the province they have undertaken, that it is almost a question, whether, if the dead of past ages could revive, they would be able to reconnoitre the events of their own times, as transmitted to us by ignorance and misrepresentation. All very ancient history, except that of the illuminated Jews, is a perfect fable.[19]

Walpole casts doubt upon received historical truths, such as the portrait of Richard III as a tyrant and a monster that Shakespeare helped to solidify in the minds of the English, and chooses not to replace these notions with any new historical certainty: "All I mean to show, is, that though he may have been as execrable as we are told he was, we have little or no reason to believe so."[20] Thus in both his serious critical work and his fantastic fictions Walpole gives voice to a strong strain of historical skepticism, leading to both the debunking of historical commonplaces and the inauguration of a new vogue for historical fictions.

One of Walpole's novelistic heirs, Sophia Lee, draws upon another set of historic doubts for her immensely popular historical novel *The Recess, or, A Tale of Other Times* (1783–85), which tells the story of two fictional daughters of Mary, Queen of Scots. Forgery pervades her work: she borrows her subtitle from Ossian and frames her tale as a discovered manuscript à la Chatterton. The historical uncertainties that make her fiction possible surround a number of ambiguous events in the life of Mary, Queen of Scots and in particular a set of possibly forged papers, the casket letters, which implicated her in adultery, conspiracy, and the murder of her second husband, Lord Darnley.[21] In the opening paragraph of her advertisement to the novel, Lee employs the convention of the discovered manuscript in order to leave the door open for a fictional reimagining of the past:

> Not being permitted to publish the means which enriched me with the manuscript from whence the following tale is extracted, its simplicity alone can authenticate it. —I make no apology for altering the language to that of the present age, since the obsolete stile of the author would be frequently unintelligible. —A wonderful coincidence of events stamps the narration at least with probability, and the reign of Elizabeth was that of romance. If this Lady was not the child of fancy, her fate can hardly be paralleled; and the line of which she came has been marked by an eminent historian, as one distinguished alike by splendor and misery.[22]

Here Lee coyly plays with issues of authenticity and fictionality. She cannot supply readers with information regarding the origins of her manuscript, but instead wants them to judge it on its style and emotional effect. She raises the possibility that the manuscript is invented a number of times, calling her heroine perhaps "the child of fancy," and highlighting the "romance" of the story. But she also suggests that in the sixteenth century history itself resembled romance, as anyone familiar with the dramatic and improbable events of Mary's life would attest. By using the language of fiction ("probability," "fancy," "romance") Lee transfers doubts about the authenticity of the casket letters onto Lee's own invented manuscript. In other words, since the evidence indicting Mary may very well be a fiction, Lee counters with her own fictional exoneration of Mary, which she then presents in the guise of a discovered manuscript of questionable authenticity. While Walpole dramatically and anarchically connects historical fiction, forgery, and skepticism, casting "historic doubts" on any positive understanding of the past, here Lee performs a similar but more localized gesture, suggesting that "romance" is the only certainty we are left with when examining Mary's biography.

Almost twenty years after *The Castle of Otranto*, the *Critical Review* became more skeptical about the discovered manuscript convention:

> She talks indeed of an obsolete manuscript, and of the wonderful coincidence of history; but these are subterfuges which no longer surprise or deceive us. It is new; it is instructive; it is highly interesting; and we wish that this new mode of writing were more frequent. We are more affected with even the pretended memoirs of the counsellors and generals of Elizabeth, than with Sir Charles Beverley or Colonel Belville; and if costume is properly preserved, may be often instructed by them.[23]

Juxtaposing the *Critical*'s assessments of *The Castle of Otranto* and *The Recess* we can see an evolution of their criteria of judgment. In the former case, the reviewer declares himself unable to ascertain whether the work is published from an authentic manuscript or not, but dismisses the work as trash in any case. In the latter review, the subterfuge of the discovered manuscript no longer has any currency except as an empty novelistic gesture; however, the status of the novel has risen.[24] The reviewer praises the novelty of the work and particularly the inherent interest in seeing the private lives of historical personages as opposed to the Sir Charles Beverleys and Colonel Belvilles of the contemporary novel.

Following the examples of Walpole and Lee, dozens of historical novelists used the convention of the discovered manuscript to introduce their narratives, turning it into one of the age's great novelistic clichés. Though the language of these prefaces is often by-the-numbers, a few popular novelists engage with the intersections of the burgeoning field of literary history, Enlightenment skepticism, and literary forgery in surprising and thought-provoking ways. One of the more interesting examples of this can be found in *The Jesuit; or, the History of Anthony Babington, Esq. An*

Historical Novel (1799) by Mrs. F. C. Patrick. In the preface she claims her book is not a work of fiction but a modernization of an old manuscript. She assures readers of her veracity by reference to a recent forgery controversy:

> Rejoice with me, then, good and amiable reader, that I was present at the very first opening of the chest which contained the famous Shakespearian Manuscripts; which, in spite of Mr. Ireland's assertions, and the manifold proofs of old spelling, moth-holes, mutilations, &c. (which we must not suppose were brought forward without a thorough conviction, on Mr. Ireland's part, that *we*, the ignorant herd, would be satisfied with them) some independent geniuses have hitherto cavilled at and disputed, nay even positively denied, that the Plays were Shakepeare's . . . . I protest, in the sincerity of my heart, they are as genuine as the manuscript I am now introducing; and, I believe, no impartial critick will attempt to prove that mine is not so.[25]

Patrick refers here to one of the most outrageous examples of eighteenth-century forgery, W. H. Ireland's Shakespeare manuscripts. In 1796, three years before *The Jesuit* was published, Ireland's Shakespearean forgery *Vortigern and Rowena* was laughed off the London stage. By saying that her manuscript is as genuine as Ireland's, then, Patrick is comparing herself to a recently disgraced forger, a national joke. Like Walpole in his preface to the *Hieroglyphic Tales*, Patrick brings up an obvious forger in order to satirize the staleness and utter improbability of the discovered manuscript convention. In the process, she also connects her type of imaginative historical re-creation with Ireland's, linking forgery and historical fiction as two versions of the "modern antique." Several years later, Ireland himself turned novelist, putting his experience as a creator of historical forgeries to more respectable uses by producing among other texts a historical novel, *The Catholic, An Historical Romance*, a fictionalized account of the Guy Fawkes affair that partakes of Patrick's anti-Catholic fervor.[26]

A more tangled relationship among literary history, historical mimicry, and historical fiction can be found in Helen Craik's novel *Henry of Northumberland, or the Hermit's Cell* (1800). In the preface, Craik describes how, while visiting at a friend's house, she discovers a chest of papers:

> Amongst the number was a manuscript, much torn and defaced; which, on perusal of the contents, I found bore a strong similitude to the principal events mentioned in the modern and very beautiful poem of the "Hermit of Warkworth."

> It appeared to be a simple, unadorned matter of fact journal of some occurrences relative to the noble family of the Percys during the reigns of Henry IV. and V.[27]

"The Hermit of Warkworth" was a long ballad-imitation in three "fits" by Thomas Percy.[28] Today the poem is most frequently remembered as the target of Johnson's caricature of ballad simplicity:

> I put my hat upon my head
> And went into the Strand.
> And there I met another man
> Whose hat was in his hand.

But in its day, "The Hermit of Warkworth" was critically and commercially successful, going through three editions in 1771 alone and included in later editions of Percy's *Reliques*.[29]

Both Percy's poem and Craik's novel take place in fifteenth-century England, during the reigns of Henry IV and V. The narrative of Craik's three-volume novel contains considerably more incident than Percy's poem. As befits the scope of a novel, Craik begins her story with the infancy of her hero, Henry Percy (son of Hotspur), while Thomas Percy begins his narrative when Henry is a young man, in love with the fair Lady Eleanor Neville. As Percy's poem begins, and two-thirds of the way through the first volume of Craik's novel, the couple has been separated in the midst of a storm and are reunited in a hermit's cell near Warkworth Castle in Northumberland. The hermit shares his tale with the pair, the long interpolated "Hermit's Tale," which Craik adapts very closely from "The Hermit of Warkworth." Bertram, the friend of Percy's grandfather the first earl of Northumberland, loves Isabel. When she is kidnapped, he goes in search of her, and in the process of rescuing her he mistakenly murders her and his brother, who was aiding her escape. Bertram then retreats from the world to become the titular hermit. Bertram's narrative takes up most of Percy's poem, which ends with five brief stanzas detailing Henry and Eleanor's marriage and Henry's restoration to favor with Henry V. In contrast, Craik's novel pays considerably more attention to the story of Henry and Eleanor. After the hermit's story, Percy shares his own story of his adventures in Scotland. A large portion of the third volume of *Henry of Northumberland* concerns Percy's journeys to Florence, Bologna, and Milan. Like "The Hermit of Warkworth," however, the book ends with the protagonists' marriage and Percy's restoration to favor.

Like many novels of this time, *Henry of Northumberland* employs chapter epigraphs, often drawn from English poets like Shakespeare, Pope, and Goldsmith. Besides these conventional choices, quite a few of the chapters take their epigraphs from "The Hermit of Warkworth," so that Percy's poem functions as an intertext and shadowy presence throughout the novel. This symbiosis between ballad imitation and historical novel highlights the tangled connections between these two characteristic late eighteenth-century phenomena. To trace the path of literary circulation, a literary historian, Thomas Percy, collected and annotated ballad literature. Then he published a modern ballad imitation, "The Hermit of Warkworth," complete with critical and prefatory material that mimicked his scholarly work.[30] A couple of decades later, Helen Craik's *Henry of Northumberland* borrows much of its narrative and historical color from Percy's poem. A number of details from the poem migrate directly into the novel, such as the "dried fruits, and milk, and curds" that constitute the hermit's fare as well as several historical and biographical footnotes that Craik copies verbatim into her text. In her preface, she ironically claims to have discovered and modernized an old manuscript whose narrative resembles Percy's poem. She further blurs the line between fact and fiction throughout her narrative. For example, the novel opens with the first Earl of Northumberland in his castle waiting for intelligence from the Battle of Shrewsbury. A messenger arrives with news:

> "The King," pursued Bardolp, "is mortally wounded, and Prince Henry slain by the conquering arm of your son; both the Blunts fell by the hand of Douglas; young Prince John, Westmorland, and Stafford, only secured their safety by a timely retreat from the field of battle; and Monmouth's worthy favourite, Sir John Falstaff, is prisoner to my Lord your son; as are likewise many more of greater rank and merit."[31]

It's within the realm of possibility that Craik includes an overtly fictional character in her catalogue of historical figures as a sly comment upon the imaginative dimensions of any act of historical understanding, echoing the sentiments of her novelistic forebears Walpole and Lee. Or perhaps to view it in that way would be merely to project modern critical concerns back onto Craik's eighteenth-century novel. As Alder has contended, however, every act of historical creation involves an imaginative leap and an act of projection.

The novels I have briefly glanced at in this essay illustrate some of the ways in which literary forgery and historical fiction are connected as two skeptical reactions to the increasing scientific orientation of historiography in the eighteenth century. As a more positivistic approach to history develops in the second half of the century, in reaction to and alongside it there develops a skeptical, doubting attitude towards this confidence, which manifests itself in works as diverse as Ireland's *Vortigern and Rowena* and Craik's *Henry of Northumberland.* These novels also highlight some of the ways in which the high and the low, popular and scholarly writings interact in this period. Just as *Libra,* Don DeLillo's historical novel about the Kennedy assassination, bridged the gap between high theory and popular fiction by embodying the academic historical skepticism of the 1980s (while linking it to JFK conspiracy theories), so too the historical novels of the late eighteenth century suggest the pervasiveness and popular dissemination of skeptical attitudes towards historical certainty.

NOTES

This article began as a paper at the 2006 ASECS conference in Montreal, in a session on "Writing Literary History" organized by Ruth Mack. Much of my research was conducted while attending a 2005 NEH Summer Seminar organized by Stephen Behrendt at the University of Nebraska, Lincoln. I would like to thank Jeff Rufo, Will Kenton, Michael Rotenberg-Schwartz, and Philip Rusche for their comments on an earlier draft of the manuscript.

1. Ken Alder, "History's Greatest Forger: Science, Fiction, and Fraud along the Seine," *Critical Inquiry* 30 (2004): 703, 702, 707–08.

2. On the skeptical attitude towards the past see, for example, Mary Poovey, "The Structure of Anxiety in Political Economy and *Hard Times*," in *Knowing the Past: Victorian Literature and Culture*, ed. Suzy Anger (Ithaca: Cornell University Press, 2001), 152: "A past 'event' only manifests itself as meaningful to the present reader through, and in the terms provided by, the interpretive response it occasion. . . . The way we delineatc the beginning and ending of a text or an event—the way we identify the 'text' or the 'event' itself—derives from our present sense of its meaning *in relation to our own interpretative categories*, which exist to make the past meaningful to us now." We can only know the past, Poovey contends, by imposing our present terms upon it; we cannot know it on its own terms.

3. See Mark Salber Phillips, *Society and Sentiment: Genres of Historical Writing in Britain, 1740–1820* (Princeton: Princeton University Press, 2000).

4. I explore Hume and Robertson's skepticism and its relation to the novel more fully in my article "Sophia Lee's Illegitimate History," *The Eighteenth-Century Novel* 3 (2003): 263–91.

5. For an influential though now dated account of the skeptical turn in eighteenth-century historiography, see Hayden White, *Metahistory: The Historical Imagination in Nineteenth-Century Europe* (Baltimore: Johns Hopkins University Press, 1973) , esp. 48: "By the last quarter of the eighteenth century, this ambivalence had been transformed into Irony, which expressed itself in a historical epistemology that was Skeptical in the extreme and in an ethical attitude, generated by Skepticism, that was manifestly relativistic."

6. On literary forgery in general and eighteenth-century forgery in particular see Joseph Rosenblum, *Practice to Deceive: The Amazing Stories of Literary Forgery's Most Notorious Practitioners* (New Castle, Del.: Oak Knoll Press, 2000); John Whitehead, *This Solemn Mockery: The Art of Literary Forgery* (London: Arlington Books, 1973); Paul Baines, *The House of Forgery in Eighteenth-Century Britain* (Aldershot: Ashgate, 1999); K. K. Ruthven, *Faking Literature* (Cambridge: Cambridge University Press, 2001); and Ian Haywood, *The Making of History: A Study of the Literary Forgeries of James Macpherson and Thomas Chatterton in Relation to Eighteenth-Century Ideas of History and Fiction* (London: Associated University Presses, 1986). Most recently, Margaret Russett's *Fictions and Fakes: Forging Romantic Authenticity, 1760–1845* (Cambridge: Cambridge University Press, 2006) has charted new terrain in this field, exploring the connections, among other things, between the notion of forgery and the rise of the novel.

7. For a classic and a recent discussion of the development of literary history in the eighteenth century, see René Wellek, *The Rise of English Literary History* (Chapel Hill: University of North Carolina Press, 1941) and Phillips, *Society and Sentiment.* On the related topic of the development of an English literary canon see Jonathan Brody Kramnick, *Making the English Canon: Print-Capitalism and the Cultural Past, 1700–1770* (Cambridge: Cambridge University Press, 1998) and Trevor Ross, *The Making of the English Literary Canon: From the Middle Ages to the Late Eighteenth Century* (Montreal: McGill-Queen's University Press, 1998).

8. Anthony Grafton, *Forgers and Critics: Creativity and Duplicity in Western Scholarship* (Princeton: Princeton University Press, 1990), 5.

9. Ruthven, *Faking Literature*, 3, 4.

10. Patricia Highsmith, *Ripley Under Ground* (New York: Vintage, 1992), 66.

11. See Susan Stewart, "Scandals of the Ballad," *Crimes of Writing: Problems in the Containment of Representation* (Oxford: Oxford University Press, 1991), 102–31.

12. In the same way, most teachers of literature would probably want to make a distinction between celebrated acts of literary plagiarism, such as Laurence Sterne's liberal borrowings from his source material in *Tristram Shandy*, and a student cutting and pasting a term paper from the Internet.

13. Haywood, *The Making of History*, 161. On Scott, history, and fiction, see also Avrom Fleishman, *The English Historical Novel: Walter Scott to Virginia Woolf* (Baltimore: Johns Hopkins University Press, 1971), Georg Lukács, *The Historical Novel,* trans. Hannah and Stanley Mitchell (Lincoln: University of Nebraska Press, 1962), Everett Zimmermann, *The Boundaries of Fiction: History and the Eighteenth-Century British Novel* (Ithaca: Cornell University Press, 1996), James Chandler, *England in 1819: The Politics of Literary Culture and the Case of Romantic Historicism* (Chicago: University of Chicago Press, 1998), Ina Ferris, *The Achievement of Literary Authority: Gender, History, and the Waverley Novels* (Ithaca: Cornell University Press, 1991), and Harry Shaw, *The Forms of Historical Fiction: Sir Walter Scott and His Successors* (Ithaca: Cornell University Press, 1983), among many other works.

14. Katie Trumpener, "National Character, Nationalist Plots: National Tale and Historical Novel in the Age of *Waverley*, 1806–1830," *ELH* 60 (1993): 687.

15. Horace Walpole, *The Castle of Otranto: A Gothic Story*, ed. W. S. Lewis (Oxford: Oxford University Press, 1996), 5.

16. Review of *The Castle of Otranto*, *Critical Review* 19 (1765): 50–51.

17. Walpole, *Hieroglyphic Tales* (San Francisco: Mercury House, 1993), 7.

18. Walpole, *Hieroglyphic Tales*, 10.

19. Walpole, *Historic Doubts on the Life and Reign of King Richard the Third* (London: J. Dodsley, 1768), iii. I read his comment about "the illuminated Jews" ironically. By calling all ancient history a "fable" except for the Hebrew Bible, Walpole implicitly suggests that the Bible too may be filled with "ignorance and misrepresentation."

20. Walpole, *Historic Doubts*, 2. For an entertaining fictionalization of Walpole's doubts, see Josephine Tey, *The Daughter of Time* (New York: Macmillan, 1951).

21. On the casket letters in the eighteenth century, see Jayne Elizabeth Lewis, "Mary Stuart's 'Fatal Box': Sentimental History and the Revival of the Casket Letters Controversy," *The Age of Johnson* 7 (1996): 427–73, and Colin Kidd, "The Ideological Significance of the *History of Scotland*," in *William Robertson and the Expansion of Empire*, ed. Stewart J. Brown (Cambridge: Cambridge University Press, 1997), 122–44.

22. Sophia Lee, *The Recess; or, a Tale of Other Times*, ed. April Alliston (Lexington: University Press of Kentucky, 2000), 5.

23. Review of *The Recess*, *Critical Review* 55 (1783): 233–34.

24. As late as 1784, however, reviewers were not yet completely jaded by the discovered manuscript convention, as evidenced in a review of William Godwin's Ossian-inspired novel *Imogen* in the October 1784 *Critical Review*: "Whether this be really a translation from the Welsh, and the original of great antiquity, as the editor affirms, it is impossible for us to determine without farther evidence. But we do not hesitate to pronounce that it abounds with tender sentiments, pleasing description, and an innocent simplicity of manners" (58: 312).

25. Mrs. F. C. Patrick, *The Jesuit; or, the History of Anthony Babington, Esq. An Historical Novel*, 3 vols. (Bath: R. Cruttwell, 1799),1: vii–viii.

26. See W. H. Ireland, *The Catholic: An Historical Romance* (London: W. Earle, 1807). The similarity of their novels and particularly their virulent anti-Catholicism raises the possibility that Patrick and Ireland may have been acquainted.

27. Helen Craik, *Henry of Northumberland, or the Hermit's Cell: A Tale of the Fifteenth Century*. 3 vols. (London: Minerva Press, 1800), 1: x–xi.

28. See Thomas Percy, "The Hermit of Warkworth," *Reliques of Ancient English Poetry* (Philadelphia: Porter and Coates, 1873).

29. See Nick Groom, "*Fragments, Reliques,* and MSS: Chatterton and Percy," in *Thomas Chatterton and Romantic Culture*, ed. Nick Groom (New York: St. Martin's, 1999), 192–93.

30. To further complicate matters, novelist Sophia Lee published a long narrative poem modeled on "The Hermit of Warkworth." See Lee, *A Hermit's Tale: Recorded by His Own Hand, and Found in His Cell* (London: T. Cadell, 1787).

31. Craik, *Henry of Northumberland*, 1:8.

"All beautiful in woe": Gender, Nation, and Phillis Wheatley's "Niobe"

JENNIFER THORN

The Scotsman John Gabriel Stedman's praise of Phillis Wheatley, in his 1796 *History of a Five Years Expedition*, exemplifies the association of Latin with poetry, and both with full humanity, that has persistently framed the reception of Phillis Wheatley's classically-inflected poetry. Having discussed, in successive preceding paragraphs, "the Languages of the African Negroes" and their singing, "like that of some birds, melodious but without Time," Stedman turns to Wheatley. Race seems to trump all other possible measures of identity as he makes his transition from Surinamean "Black People" to the Bostonian Wheatley: "these People are not Divested of a Good Ear, and Even of Poetical Genius, . . . when they have had the Advan[ta]ge of Education," the paragraph begins. Wheatley is proof: "a black Girl Call'd Phillis Wheatley who was a Slave at Boston in New England . . . even learn'd the Latin Language And Wrote 39 Elegant Pieces of Poetry on different Subjects, which were Published in 1773."[1] Tellingly, Stedman's examples of "Blackness" are all slaves, even as some are implicitly more fully human than others. Surinamean slaves, representing "uncivilized" blackness, evince a pleasing but animalistic musicality in the ways they speak and sing; Wheatley, as "civilized" blackness, evinces full humanity in the ways she reads Latin and writes "Elegant" poetry.

Stedman's elevation of Wheatley's Latin against Surinamean singing would seem to serve ably as additional evidence for Henry Louis Gates's influential argument that the Enlightenment valorization of literacy as a crucial marker of civilization undergirded European denigration of Africans as uncivilized and fit for domination.[2] But to read Wheatley's epyllion "Niobe in Distress for her Children, Slain by Apollo" in the context of the differences between British and American attitudes toward Latin poetry at the time of the poem's composition is to be made less comfortable with the view that the classical allusions in Wheatley's poetry figured unambiguously and simply as beneficial, as proof of the intelligence and humanity of Africans. That Wheatley pursued, with "Niobe," elevation-by-association is made evident in the poem's full title, "NIOBE in Distress for her children slain by APOLLO, from Ovid's Metamorphoses, Book VI, and from a view of the Painting of Mr. Richard Wilson." To date, the poem has not been read in relation either to Ovid's "Niobe" in the form in which Wheatley would have been most likely to have encountered it, the 1719 compilation edited by Samuel Garth, or to the Welsh Wilson's 1760 *The Destruction of Niobe's Children*, which made his career. In the belief that this context illuminates the poem, as the poem also illuminates this context, I attempt such a reading here.

Even as Wheatley's lengthy title seems to court approval as a humble imitator, her subtle rendition of "Niobe" marks her as a bold innovator. Though, as I hope to show here, eighteenth-century America and Britain differed markedly in their estimation of the relation of the classics to national well-being, the measure of value for both was the classics' putative effects on young men–their utility, or lack thereof, in instilling ideal masculinities intimately related to national self-definition. This context makes significant Wheatley's selection of Ovid and "Niobe," a tale of female rivalry in which fecundity is imagined as a measure of female claim to divinity and devotion. Wheatley's rendition of the tale emphasizes its moral, an approach that aligns her with America's often moralizing response to the classics. At the same time, the moral that she finds differs starkly from the prevalent early American assumption that the classics instilled effeminacy and immoral ambition in the young.

Wheatley's relation to her English readership is similarly complex. Having failed to find an American publisher, Wheatley adapted the original manuscript of *Poems on Various Subjects, Religious and Moral* in pursuit of London publication; this goal prompted the addition of the volume's several classically-inflected poems.[3] Less fully discussed to date are the ways in which Wheatley negotiated the competing claims of Britain and America through her subtle self-definition in relation to the classics. Aligning herself with the classics, Wheatley aligned herself, in important ways, with England—with its abidingly high estimation of the classics, familiarity with which marked gentility and class standing. At the same time, her emphasis upon the morality of Niobe's story marks a departure from the English tendency to use classical references to test and reward familiarity with literary tradition, a valuation of "the classics" as an enabler of the display of cultural capital that significantly de-particularizes the texts that constitute it. That is, where American moralists read the classics in effect serially, asking, "what does this particular narrative model for our young?," English aestheticists generally figured the classics as a whole greater than its parts, an allusive web that, in theory, only the legitimately privileged could negotiate. Wheatley is like the English in her matter-of-fact turn to the classics, and like Americans in her interest in "Niobe" as a moral tale. She is unlike the English in her moralism, and unlike Americans in the nihilism of the "Niobe" she tells; and the bleak morality of her "Niobe" is suggestively related to the particularities of her situation as a young woman enslaved in the North.

Wheatley launched "Niobe" into an American readership newly unsure of the moral or patriotic appropriateness of the classics for American education, and a British readership that, in contrast, understood the classics through the lens of aesthetic theory. Though Ovid lost, as Virgil and Horace gained stature in eighteenth-century England, the value of the classics per se stood secure. Indeed, the debate between the Ancients and the Moderns attests to the pervasive sense that the Ancients must be known, even if knowledge of their greatness was sometimes deemed most useful as it enabled Moderns to supercede it. In contrast, the 1770s and 1780s saw intensified scrutiny of English-derived, traditional curricula by self-styled American patriots, doubtful of the applicability of English models to new American situations, even as the avid classicism of some, like Jefferson and Adams, continued unabated.[4] Ovid in particular was criticized, in mid- to late-eighteenth-century America, as improbable, useless, and immorally illustrative of the open and unpunished pursuit of power and sensual gratification. Both of these self-consciously nationalistic contexts make it significant that the poem by Wheatley that most totally relies on classical precedent should be drawn from the *Metamorphoses*, indeed, should be the story of Niobe, describing the fate of a semi-divine woman who refuses to bow down to a goddess arguably no more divine that she is herself. I will argue here that reading the poem in the context of American and British responses to Ovid and Wilson in the era in which Wheatley wrote and first published "Niobe" clarifies both the poem's ambivalence and its innovation, both of which return us to necessary reexamination of the ways that

American and English responses to the classics were pervasively framed in terms of gender ideals and their relation to national identity.

"Prodigious hurt": Wounded American Boys and the Classics

In 1769, John Wilson, the Latin master at the Friends' Latin School of Philadelphia, resigned his prestigious position and left the field of education, declaring that he had come to see the teaching of classical mythology as inimical to Christian morality. His letter of resignation vividly conveys his condemnation of American schools for their exposure of the Christian boys in their charge to "the shocking Legends and abominable Romances of the worst of Heathens." It is "surprizing [and] monstrous" that American schoolboys should

> be obliged to be Pimps of the detestable Lusts of Jupiter & Mars, attend the thefts and Villainy of Mercury, or follow Aeneas on his Murdering Progress, while the Actions and Sufferings of the great and worthy Propagators of our Holy Religion that Succeeded the Apostles are totally hid from their Eyes. Is Bacchus preferable to Ignatius, Apollo to Origin, or will Helena and Clytemnestra yield an affecting Instruction or warm our Hearts with the Love of Virtue like the Virgin Martyrs & Heroines of Christian Story? [5]

Wilson's rejection of his own classical education reflects a religiously-derived sense of adult obligation to the young that sharply differentiates the two groups' characteristic modes of perception. Where experienced adults know how to extract value from the unrealistic and immoral plots of classical mythology, boys cannot but identify with the villains whose amours and "Villainy" are regularly rewarded there. Though this kind of adult concern for childish credulity is to be found in eighteenth-century England—Johnson's *Rambler* No. 4 is a *locus classicus*—the genres so debased were typically chivalric romance and fairy tales, and rarely classical mythology.

Wilson resigned his post at the beginning of a period of intense American scrutiny of the effects of classical education on the younger generation of boys whose adult conduct might vindicate the Revolution and, thereafter, sustain the project of nation-making. Near the end of that period, Anthony Benezet, like Wilson a Quaker anticlassicist and abolitionist, criticized the classics in terms that both echo and extend Wilson's assertion that classical mythology forces boys to identify with villainy. In a 1783 letter to John

Pemberton, a Quaker merchant and itinerant preacher, Benezet asserted "the prodigious hurt done by those romantic and mad notions of heroism etc which are early implanted in the tender minds from the use of those Heathen Authors Ovid, Virgil, Homer, etc, which they are generally taught." Here again boys are figured as helplessly susceptible to damage-by-reading. Classical "heroism" implants vice: it "nourishes the spirit of War in Youth" and is "diametrically opposite to our Christian teaching." "[M]y concern," Benezet states, "is absolutely to avoid our Youth spending their time in classical studies, the chief tendency of which is, to find the corrupt passions of the Human heart."[6] The following year, in a letter to Robert Pleasants, one of Virginia's most noted Quaker abolitionists, Benezet reiterated his view that the study of Latin and Greek lured boys away from piety, instilling in them a "tendency to wed to the world, and beget an enmity to the cross." Benezet singles out Ovid, Virgil, and Horace as especially "opposed to our Religious Profession," expressing the wish that "such a knowledge of the English Language [might be] taught in our Schools, as may make the use of the learned languages unnecessary."[7]

The mid- to late eighteenth-century American questioning of the value of the classics rested upon the assumption that formal education could and should shape young men to an ideal American masculinity: active, masterful, disciplined, and useful. Thus Thomas Paine criticized the classics as inculcators of passivity in the boys who drudged through them. National pride led him to support the replacement of classical with scientific study in American schools: "I have no notion of yielding the palm of the United States to any Grecians or Romans that were ever born."[8] Patriotism of a similarly gendered sort also prompted Jonathan Boucher's critique of the place of the classics in American education. Boucher, a Tory and Anglican minister who ran the boarding school in Maryland attended by George Washington's stepson, John Parke Custis, lamented the loss of civic promise he saw in "an abundance of men, of liberal, generous, and cultivated minds, lost and undone by the habit, first acquired at school, of reading only classics."[9] The patriot and printer William Bradford, who valued cultivated conversation highly enough to found, in 1754, Philadelphia's London Coffee House, expressed his view in 1774 that pre-Revolutionary America had no need of poets, except perhaps those who, like the seventh-century BC poet Tyrtaeus, wrote poems promoting war.[10] The architect Benjamin Latrobe imagined, in a letter of 1798, a brighter world for boys in which "Terence, Phaedrus, Ovid, and other poets, from whom no one ever learned a single useful fact, should be rejected." He could "much sooner make a perfect botanist than a good Greek scholar" of the average "boy ten or twelve years old," he wrote, "and I am sure the botanist would be happier, healthier, and less agitated by false notions of glory and honor than the exposition of Homer."[11] A similar preference for the practical and physical informs William Livingston's opposition to the kind of education that he himself had received at Yale. Livingston, an attorney and future representative of New Jersey at the Constitutional Convention, asserted the urgent, and highly physical, needs of the colonies in a 1768 letter:

> [w]e want hands . . . more than heads. The most intimate acquaintance with the classics, will not remove our oaks; nor a taste for the *Georgics* cultivate our lands. Many of our young people are knocking their heads against the Iliad, who should employ their hands in clearing our swamps and draining our marshes. Others are musing, in cogitation profound, on the arrangement of a syllogism, while they ought to be guiding the tail of a plow.[12]

All of these leaders fear the deformity of American boys by the classics, a nationally-crippling transformation of natural physical strength and civic usefulness to effeminate passivity and irrelevance.

The lawyer and Connecticut Wit John Trumbull, whose knowledge of Latin and Greek had gained him admission to Yale at the age of 7, lamented in similar terms the ruinous effect of the classics on young boys, who "plodding on in one dull tone, / Gain antient tongues, and lose their own." The first book of his satiric *Progress of Dulness*, describing young Tom Brainless's non-education at Yale in these terms, appeared in 1773, the same year as Wheatley's *Poems on Various Subjects*. Trumbull turns to the training of American females in coquetry in the poem's second part, criticizing Harriet Simper's education "in Folly's school." "Learning is call'd our mental diet, / That serves the hungry mind to quiet," Trumbull declares; girls deserve education as much as do boys, and need to know, for the sake of those they will influence in their capacity as wives and mothers, more than "[t]he arts of dancing and of dress."[13] The poem's third and final section intensifies its portrait of the classically-trained male as a stupid, effeminate wimp: here Tom Brainless, finally a clergyman, is married off to the aging Harriet Simper, her beauty lost, her coquetry having failed to secure her a husband and provider. He marries her in compliance with his friends' expectations, believing those who tell him that she will make a suitable clergyman's wife; he courts her in laughably outdated dress; and he performs the duties of the marriage bed only to comply with the Biblical injunction to multiply.[14] This marriage of effeminate male incompetence and selfish female superficiality is cast as a suitably ironic punishment for both the classically-trained Tom Brainless and the fashionable Harriet Simper: both young people comply with the deluded prescriptions of their elders and are rewarded with social approval, national irrelevance, and personal unhappiness.

Tom Brainless reads the classics as part of his training in pathetic conformity; Harriet Simper reads *Pamela* as part of her training in enervating consumerism. Tom Brainless's reading, reflecting his deference to learned convention, might have led him to encounter Ovid's *Art of Love*. Seeking titillation, Harriet Simper might well also have encountered some form of it, as is suggested by the attitude to Ovid evident in the 1784 pamphlet *Lessons for Lovers; With Some Tender and Pathetic Anecdotes, Taken from Real Life*, by Ovid Americanus, whose pseudonym implies the association of Ovid not with "the classics" but with amorous titillation. John Wilson worried that the classics "obliged" boys "to be Pimps of the detestable Lusts of Jupiter & Mars," teaching them immorality and violence. *Lessons for Lovers* contains "Lusts" aplenty, though they are neither inspired by reading nor depicted as especially "detestable." Though the first "lesson" focuses on the tumble into attraction of a young couple and their response to the pregnancy that ensues, its main protagonist is neither young lover, but instead the woman's loving father. When Anna, weeping, faces her father with the news of her pregnancy, she is likened to "weeping Niobe in grief," a reference that seems to associate the name Niobe narrowly with tearful supplication for forgivenness: Anna "pray'd the Gods to give relief, / And cast a pitying eye on heav'n / In hopes her fault would be forgiv'n."[15]

Anna seeks forgiveness for pregnancy from her loving and eventually forgiving father; Ovid's Niobe seeks and does not receive mercy from a spiteful goddess who has murdered Niobe's seven sons as punishment for an imprudent vaunting of her fecundity. As if anticipating Susannah Rowson's *Charlotte Temple*, published in London in 1791, Ovid Americanus gives its readers the sentimental pleasure of contemplating paternal pain:

> Then see the wounded parent sigh,
> The glistening tear stand in his eye,—
> The trembling lip–the faultring tongue–
> The heart with sharpest tortures wrung;
> The wordless torrent of distress,
> That more than language can express— . . .
> 'To think how tenderly I rear'd
> Your infant years!–this the reward!—
> Oh! ANNA, ANNA! did you know
> But half my feelings and my woe–'[16]

It is ironic that a tale referencing Ovid's "Niobe" should include so dominant a sentimental father, and no mother.[17] *Lessons for Lovers* thus displaces women from the heart of what is, in the original Ovid, a homosocial story of female rivalry and maternal suffering.

The pleasures that Ovid Americanus offers his readers are clearly not intertextual: indeed, *Lessons for Lovers* is the more enjoyable as its readers are the more ignorant of Ovid and of Niobe. "Ovid" works as a kind of brand name, promising both salaciousness and a polite cover for it. In this pitch to both frank appetite and superficial good taste, Ovid Americanus is of a piece with the liberalizing "climate for consuming luxuries and patronizing art and architecture" noted by David Bjelajac: throughout the first three quarters of the eighteenth century, he writes, "Ordinary, middle-class Americans . . . beg[a]n to emulate their aristocratic superiors in purchasing luxuries that would distinguish them from the propertyless poor."[18] This cultural use of superficial references to classical texts to mark and celebrate aspirations of upward mobility extended to affordable engravings like the William Woollett engraving of Richard Wilson's *Niobe* that it is likely Wheatley saw, rather than the original painting that she references in the full title of "Niobe." The relevance of this context to our appreciation of Wheatley's choice of "Niobe" as subject matter as she pursued the publication in London that had eluded her in Boston is compounded by the fact that she was herself such a "luxury," such a marker of status, as a slave in an era in which American uses of the classics not infrequently took the shape of bestowing upon slaves "classical" names like Juba and Cato.

Stedman praises Wheatley's familiarity with Latin and the "Elegan[ce]" of her poetry: fundamental to the market for classically-inflected art, be it for the elite or the masses, is the association between the two. *Lessons for Lovers* demoted Niobe in favor of paternal tears, a marginalization of the eponymous heroine that also characterizes Richard Wilson's *The Destruction of Niobe's Children*. Wilson places a tiny, statue-like Niobe in a darkly moody landscape; the sky and trees are made more emotive than she. Wilson's Niobe signifies not morally, as a choice-making character, but intertextually, as a means of demonstrating insider knowledge. Here again, knowledge of the classics is associated with privilege; and here again, an outsider, the Welsh Wilson, defied expectation in asserting his right to represent "the classics."

"The good breeding of poetry": Joseph Addison and Richard Wilson

The writers involved in the translations of *The Metamorphoses* that were most widely available in England in the mid to late-eighteenth century did not share John Wilson's perception that the classics were unsuitable, even dangerous reading for sincere Christians. Thomas Tickell's praise of Addison in his "Preface" to the 1721 edition of his works presumes the value not only of the classics, but of the early exposure to them that was the mark of an aristocratic upbringing:

> An early acquaintance with the Classics is what may be called the good breeding of Poetry, as it gives a certain gracefulness which never forsakes a mind that contracted it in youth, but is seldom or never hit by those, who learn it too late. He [Addison] first distinguished himself by his Latin compositions, [. . .] and was admired as one of the best authors of the Augustan age.[19]

Here the classics enable intellectual display that differentiates the genteel from the vulgar, an attitude equally definitive of the painting career of Richard Wilson. Addison's discussion of Ovid in the *Spectator* typifies the complexity of eighteenth-century deference to the classics in ways that are equally evident in Wilson's turn to "Niobe." Even as Addison appreciates, in *Spectator* No. 417, the ways that Ovid "describes a Miracle in every Story, . . . and shews Monster after Monster, to the end of the *Metamorphoses,*" he deems Ovid's heroic poetry "affected and unnatural" in its themes in *Spectator* No. 279.[20] In his poem "To Mr. Dryden," Addison's admiration of Dryden's classicism rests upon Dryden's ability to defer to precedent respectfully in order to supersede it, an achievement that accrues glory for contemporary Britain:

> Thou mak'st the beauties of the Romans known,
> And England boasts of riches not her own . . .
> Thy copy casts a fairer light on all,
> And still out-shines, the bright original.
> Now Ovid boasts th'advantage of thy song,
> And tells his story in the British tongue . . . .
> Then will thy Ovid, thus transform'd, reveal
> A nobler change then he himself can tell.[21]

Deference to the classics is the necessary prerequisite to trumping them; ease with Latin enables putting the Latin poets in their place.

The complexity with which Dryden entwines learned deference to classical tradition with competitive aggression also characterizes his equally paradoxical articulation of the relation of imitation to originality in his preface to *Troilus and Cressida.* He casts his openly appropriative use of Longinus in the play as respectful, even ethically necessary homage: "We ought not to regard a good imitation as theft; but as a beautiful Idea of him who undertakes to imitate, by forming himself on the invention and work of another man." The modern writer "forms himself" self-consciously on precedent, a verb that suggests a self-subordination belied by Dryden's further elaboration of the process of imitation: the writer who imitates "enters into the lists like a new wrestler, to dispute the prize with the former Champion." Paradoxically, the very aggression that would, in effect, throw precedent to the mat also elevates it to heroic stature: "Those great men whom we propose to our selves as patterns for our imitation, serve us as a Torch, which is lifted up before us, to enlighten our passage; and often elevate our thoughts as high, as the conception we have of our Author's Genius."[22] Thus the highest artistry reflects the most confident and sustained knowledge of precedent, an "imitation" that enables and, ironically, defines "originality."

"Imitation" of this subtly aggressive sort was the guiding principle of Richard Wilson's career, and it was "imitation" that pushed him to his innovative approach to "Elegance." A founder of the Royal Academy and occasional dinner partner of Samuel Johnson, he grew up in genteel poverty in Wales. Educated at home, he was so deeply immersed in the classics that even late in life, Wilson recited, for his companions' pleasure and his own, "passages from Horace's original Latin *ex tempore*–a feat of truly remarkable erudition, even for the eighteenth century."[23] This pride in gentility deeply shaped Wilson's career; he dedicated himself to proving both that the English could paint classical landscapes as well as the revered Italian and French, and that artists could be the social equals of the nobly born. He was able to afford this vocation only because the classical landscapes that he made in hopes of old-style patronage sold extremely well as engravings, eagerly purchased by the middling classes on both sides of the Atlantic. By the end of his career in the 1790s, Wilson received more commissions from print-sellers than from private individuals. Given its seclusion on the estate of the Duke of Cumberland, it is highly unlikely that Wheatley actually saw the Richard Wilson *Niobe* that she cites in her title. Instead, she probably saw one of the many prints of the 1761 engraving of Wilson's *Niobe* made by William Woollett, who was later made famous by his engraving of Benjamin West's 1771 *Death of General Wolfe*. It is doubly ironic that Wheatley occludes the picture she actually saw. First, by citing Wilson, she seems to "form[] [her]self on the invention and work of another man"—to claim inspiration not obsequiously, but assertively, "disput[ing] the prize"—a fitting valorization of an "originality" very like that which characterizes her particular reading of Niobe.

In addition, that Wheatley, a female slave resident in Boston, claims relation to Wilson in many ways defies his own elitist approach to classical landscape. His dependence on middling-class consumers of engravings of his works notwithstanding, Wilson sought, and believed in, old-style patronage throughout his career. He desired, in his classical paintings, to be inaccessible to the bourgeoisie, implanting allusions desirably understood only by the elite. This coexistence, in Wilson, of affirmation of hierarchy and dependence on the democratization of taste that came with global capitalism is the more pointedly ironic for the source of Wilson's income in his old age. Wilson's late-life poverty was eased only by his inheritance of a small estate in Wales from a younger brother who had immigrated to America and become a wealthy tobacco merchant. Thus Wilson, typically of his elitist era in valorizing the classics and knowledge of Latin, was able to offer us the paintings that made this view plain only because of the economic base provided by the work of printmakers and slaves.

Wilson displayed his 1760 *The Destruction of Niobe's Children* (fig. 1) in the first showing of the Society of British Artists, a group he helped to form in pursuit of respectability for British painting. Wilson's *Niobe* was purchased by the Duke of Cumberland and attracted a great deal of attention–so much so that twenty years later, Joshua Reynolds made Wilson's *Niobe* an exemplar of the improper placement of figures in his fourteenth *Discourse on Art*. David Solkin notes that "Wilson's commitment to the cause of achieving social respectability for his chosen profession" was especially evident in *Niobe*, which "secured Wilson's reputation as an artist in the Grand Style."[24] The painting's popularity reflected not only its visual qualities, however theorized by contemporaries, but also the efficacy of its function as, in Solkin's words, a "thinking man's parlour game," which "flattered his own intellectual capacities—and those of his public as well."[25] The two central figures in the painting directly evoke a sculptural rendition of Niobe shielding her youngest daughter that was a standard destination in the Grand Tour. Painting *Niobe*, the Welsh Wilson made a bid against the odds for the legitimacy of British landscape painting in an era when Claude, Lorain, Poussin, and their followers dominated the field. It is thus a final irony to see the enslaved American Wheatley asserting the

Figure 1. *The Destruction of Niobe's Children,* Richard Wilson, 1714–1782, 1760. Yale Center for British Art, Paul Mellon Collection

humanity and dignity of Africans in her reference not to the engraved version of the painting she is most likely to have seen, but to the painting *Niobe*, firmly housed in the home of the Duke of Cumberland throughout the eighteenth century. Both poem and painting challenge nationalized claims to exclusivity of value–Italians, ancients, English–and signify specifically to audiences involved in their own nationalized self-definition.

"The vengeance of the skies": Destructive Mothers and the Singularity of "Niobe"

Of Wheatley's classically-inflected poems, "To Maecenas" has received the most perceptive attention as, in Paula Bennett's words, "an authentic re-vision of a classical original, Horace's ode to his patron, Gaius Maecenas."[26] Other classically-inflected poems, including "An Hymn to the Morning" and "An Hymn to the Evening," rely less deeply on the Latin texts they reference; because they affirm the inevitable punishment of evil, they support John Shields's sense that Wheatley's classicism was readily and totally absorbed within her Christianity.[27] This seemingly Christian assurance of divine order, omnipresent in Wheatley's many elegies, is best exemplified by "On Recollection," which opens with an invocation of Mneme and the nine muses and follows Mneme, memory, as she travels through "Phoebe's realms, fair regent of the night" to bring dreams to mortals.[28] The poem's final stanza identifies the primary value of memory in prompting repentance, imagining an angry and punitive god, certain chastiser of wrongdoing:

> Of Recollection such the pow'r enthron'd
> In ev'ry breast, and thus her pow'r is own'd.
> The wretch, who dar'd the vengeance of the skies,
> At last awakes in horror and surprize,
> By her alarm'd, he sees impending fate,
> He howls in anguish, and repents too late. (lines 41–46)

Memory enables learning: evil may be perpetrated by those heedless of divine omnipotence, but inevitably dreams, recalling past misconduct, bring grief and repentance. "[W]rath divine" awaits all but the "holy [and] upright heart" (lines 50, 48). This classically-inflected presentation of the inevitable and just "vengeance of the skies" corresponds entirely with the Christian order evoked in the biblically-inspired "Goliath of Gath," the only other epyllion that Wheatley wrote besides "Niobe." In stark contrast to the unremedied injustice of "Niobe," "Goliath of Gath" assures readers that God will always strengthen the arm of the underdog and punish the unjust: "there's a God, who governs all below / . . . / And to our pow'r consigns our hated foes" (lines 163, 167).

Wheatley's treatment of Niobe is unique in relation both to her own oeuvre to the translations available in her day.[29] Where both her pious elegies and her classically-inflected pastorals presume divine infallibility and redemption after death, "Niobe" offers heavenly compensation neither for a goddess' jealous slaughter of a rival's children nor for that rival's petrification of grief. Throughout Wheatley's oeuvre and especially in her many elegies, death is represented as a blessing, the longed-for gateway to "yon bright regions" of heavenly reward for virtue; "Niobe" renders it simply as "the gloomy mansions of the dead" (line 136). In addition, Wheatley's "Niobe" differs greatly from the Niobe found in the translation of the *Metamorphoses* most widely available throughout the eighteenth century in both England and America, the 1717 compilation edited by Samuel Garth; Samuel Croxall, who translated *Aesop's Fables* in 1722, adding extensive Christian morals of his own devising, translated book 6, in which the Niobe story is told. Croxall casts Niobe as inexcusably arrogant and justly punished as a bad mother, where Wheatley's Niobe errs primarily in failing to gauge accurately the power of profoundly unjust gods. "Beautiful in woe," she learns from her grief and is turned to stone not as divine punishment (as in the version of the story told in the *Iliad*, book 24) but as a consequence of her own psychological state–a fidelity to the original Ovid that even such important contemporary critics as Vincent Caretta and David Solkin have missed.[30] Wheatley quotes Niobe's response to the terrible news of her sons' murder: "Why is such privilege to them allow'd? / . . . / Dwells there such mischief in the pow'rs above?" (lines 165, 167)– an indictment of the legitimacy of the gods' supremacy that the poem does not finally contradict. This prolongation of grief and anger, reminiscent of the defiant rejection of "normal mourning" in terms of which Jahan Ramazani has characterized the modern elegy, is unique in Wheatley's oeuvre and, indeed, rare in her moment—a "modern" refusal of consolation necessarily related to the gendered particularities of the Northern slavery that so profoundly shaped Wheatley's life and career, to which I turn shortly.[31]

Wheatley deemphasizes Ovid's ascription of Niobe's hubris to her genealogy (she is a granddaughter of Tantalus), locating her error instead in the linked failures of perception: she recognizes neither her children's value nor her rival's immense power: "Beyond descriptions beautiful she moves / Like heav'nly *Venus*, 'midst her smiles and loves" (lines 57–58): Niobe exults in her divine genealogy, her wealth, her power, her marriage to Jove's son Amphion, and her fourteen children. When the prophetess Manto urges the women of Thebes to worship Latona, Niobe "shakes her graceful head with stern disdain" and tells them that Latona's power is an illusion. Their faith is "madness," and their prayers will not be heard.

> Proudly she turns around her lofty eyes
> And thus reviles celestial deities:
> 'What madness drives the *Theban* ladies fair
> To give their incense to surrounding air?
> Say why this new sprung deity preferr'd?
> Why vainly fancy your petitions heard? (lines 61–66)

Niobe then reminds them of Latona's vulnerabilities, asserting her own greater claim to divinity and worship as "an empress with a goddess join'd." To this point, Wheatley has presented Niobe's claims to worship as not without merit: her rival is indeed frail, and her genealogy and wealth are indeed great. Only now, as Niobe asserts that her fecundity exempts her from the "frowns of fortune," does Wheatley present Niobe's self-perception as logically flawed: "What if indignant she decrease my train / More than *Latona*'s number will remain?" (lines 81–82).

Importantly, Wheatley gives this portrait of an inadequately appreciative mother, one who uses her children as pawns in assertions of her own identity and worth, only after a stanza directly addressing Niobe and endorsing her proud delight in her children. This address, entirely of Wheatley's devising, names her maternal arrogance sympathetically, softening the fatal confrontation of the fifth stanza:

> Wherever, *Niobe*, thou turn'st thine eyes,
> New beauties kindle, and new joys arise!
> But thou had'st far the happier mother prov'd,
> If this fair offspring had been less belov'd:
> What if their charms exceed Aurora's teint,
> No words could tell them, and no pencil paint,
> Thy love too vehement hastens to destroy
> Each blooming maid, and each celestial boy.
> (lines 29–36)

Latona is shamed by Niobe's assertion that to have two children is to be as good as childless, and it is through her children that she exacts revenge on her more fertile rival. Enraged, Latona urges her twin children, Phoebus (Apollo) and Phoebe (Diana), to take revenge; they slaughter Niobe's seven sons.

Wheatley's Niobe loves her sons totally and is so devoured by grief that even her enemy feels for her: "She weeps, nor weeps unpity'd by the foe" (line 176). She falls on their bodies, and she speaks words that Wheatley quotes, making us shared auditors of her admission of near-defeat:

> On each pale corse the wretched mother spread
> Lay overwhelm'd with grief, and kiss'd her dead,
> Then rais'd her arms, and thus, in accents slow,
> 'Be sated cruel *Goddess*! with my woe;
> If I've offended, let these streaming eyes,
> And let this sev'nfold funeral suffice:
> Ah! take this wretched life you deign'd to save,
> With them I too am carried to the grave.
> Rejoice triumphant, my victorious foe,
> But show the cause from whence your triumphs flow?'
> (lines 177–86)

Blinded by grief, Wheatley's Niobe concedes Latona's superior power, begging that Latona take her life, too–she's as good as dead, she says, if her sons are dead. This grief-stricken admission of defeat immediately yields to one final defiant boast: her seven daughters mean she is still more fertile than her rival, Niobe cries out. Predictably, Latona then has her twins slaughter Niobe's seven daughters. Stunned by the enormity of her loss, Niobe gradually turns to stone, a transformation that is presented not as divine punishment but as an extension of her psychological state. Niobe finally becomes literally what her pain makes her figuratively: stone, but stone that continues to cry.

Samuel Croxall's "Niobe," which is of course a translation rather than a response to the original, opens as Ovid does, with a look back at the story of Arachne that immediately precedes "Niobe." The moral of both stories, in Croxall's words, is that it is a mistake "Vainly above the Gods [to] assum[e] a State."[32] The assertion of this predictive moral is followed by an itemization of the reasons for Niobe's pride, in terms that urge negative judgment of Niobe.[33] Her children inspire this "Dame" with "vain Ambition"; she is "conceited" and ruled by "tow'ring Fancy." In Wheatley's Niobe, Amphion, Niobe's husband, despairs and commits suicide in a couplet, bringing to four lines the totality of the poem's attention to him as a father or actor of any kind; Croxall gives three lines and greater sympathy to this suicide. Wheatley's Niobe wonders why her father-in-law Jove hasn't immediately exacted revenge for the murder of his grandsons and suicide of his son; Croxall weakens Niobe's case by occluding Jove entirely. Croxall also erases Niobe's suffering over her sons' bodies; his Niobe is almost immediately "the miserablest Object seen," a thing so stripped of vitality that her later petrification cannot seem a loss.[34]

Wheatley urges sympathetic attention to Niobe, "all beautiful in woe," in terms that both extend and qualify Peter Coviello's attention to the ways that "[in] the era of the nation's founding . . . the matter of affect and its place in civic life became the source of a remarkable degree of contention and volatility."[35] Coviello reads several of Wheatley's poems against Jefferson's famous assertion of black inferiority in his *Notes on the State of Virginia*, suggesting that ironically and implicitly, Wheatley and Jefferson agree that the capacity to feel right is an important measure of fitness for citizenship. In the *Notes*, Jefferson denigrates Wheatley by name, saying that though "religion" can produce a poet like her, blacks are incapable of true poetry because they grieve only fleetingly. "Niobe" would seem exactly to coincide with Coviello's concerns and arguments were it not for the fact that Niobe's capacity to feel gets her nowhere: the lessons that she receives in grief and in her nature as a mother humanize her, and this new understanding is prelude not to empowerment but to living death. Even as we come to pity "The Phrygian queen, all beautiful in woe," our feeling—our identification—teaches not enlightenment but impotence. The chastened rebel whose "streaming eyes" will never stop flowing has, if anything, better reason to believe in her own superiority to the gods who thwart her. Niobe's skepticism is both contained and intensified by her own monumentalization, a process crucially informed by her identity as a mother. Suffering is not redemptive in "Niobe": "Why vainly fancy your petitions heard?" (line 66).

Wheatley's "Niobe" demands attention in relation to an American ideal of her day, Republican motherhood, and a practice, the surprisingly understudied anti-reproductivity of the Northern slavery, that so profoundly shaped her life. This "family slavery," in William Piersen's phrase, imposed formidable obstacles to reproduction: those bondsmen who labored most faithfully for their owners discovered that full integration into their master's family usually precluded the development of independent black families for themselves. Loyalty to the one naturally conflicted with the time and responsibility demanded by the other. The tension between family slavery and slave families ultimately fractured both institutions and gave the lie to the so-called civilizing mission of Christian bondage.[36] As Jacqueline Jones notes, "under [these] conditions, a slave woman's value increased in direct proportion to her experience as a childless houseservant."[37] The fecundity that was valued by Southern slaveowners was loathed by their Northern counterparts; as Edgar McManus concludes, "[n]ext to superannuated blacks, women with a record of fecundity were least in demand. That a slave birth technically increased the owner's capital did not offset the personal inconvenience of sharing living space with unwanted children." McManus cites advertisements from New England newspapers of the 1760s and 1770s in which a young slave woman is offered for sale though she is "not known to have any failing but being with child, which is the only cause of her being sold"; others convey the wish of masters to give away slave babies free of charge.[38]

In Wheatley's "Niobe," what women are, first and foremost, is reproductive and angry. Impossible as it may be to ascribe definitively any biographically-inflected intentionality to the reading of Wheatley's poems, the intensity of her rendition of "Niobe" as a tale of wrongly valued reproduction resonates suggestively against her situation as a slave, barred both from association with other slaves and free blacks and from the establishment of her own family until after her masters' deaths and her own emancipation. Wheatley's life situation also gives the lie to the alleged universality of her era's ideal of Republican motherhood, by which women were relegated to the domestic sphere to raise their sons to republican devotion to nation. That a female slave, whose status as slave in the North mandated her non-reproductivity, should write so movingly about a competition between powerful goddesses over their relative fecundity, ironizes their equation of female worth with reproduction, even as it sympathizes intensely with the reduction of a former mother to childlessness that is the poem's primary plot.

Julie Kipp has argued that the late eighteenth-century British preoccupation with motherhood differ sharply from those found in the early eighteenth century in that the later period pushes mothers into a fatal double bind: here, it is the most loving who are most murderous. In the works that she considers by authors including Horace Walpole, Matthew Lewis, Charlotte Smith, Sophia Lee, and Mary Wollstonecraft, maternal love of children is invariably destructive, whether as a sign of unstable and infectious mothers' need of expert control or as an indictment of an unjust world that twists even mother love into fatality.[39] Because "Niobe" focuses more centrally on rival mothers than on mothers and children, Kipp's model might seem not to apply to it. For both the victorious Latona and the punished Niobe, children are props, extensions of maternal will; Latona's children are her agents of murder, and Niobe's receive her punishment. Still, Wheatley's Niobe shares with other gothic and proto-gothic texts the despairing suggestion that maternal love is so devouring that to embark upon it at all is to face annihilation within it. Perversely, Niobe's children would be alive were they "less belov'd," less worthy of boasting; and in Wheatley's "Niobe," as in the gothic, readers are reinforced in an anti-Enlightenment, and anti-Christian sense of injustice on a scale beyond remediation.

Our first "sight" of Niobe is of a queen–a term by which Wheatley characterizes Niobe fully five times in the poem–who is lovely and grief-stricken. Wheatley's Niobe is dignified in defeat: "less haughty than before," she is "strangely chang'd!–yet beautiful in woe." The last lines of this first verse restate her declared topic: she wants "to show / The Phrygian queen, all beautiful in woe." Repeating this phrase, Wheatley emphasizes Niobe's beauty: what is its specific nature? The Philadelphia printer William Spotswood, whose 1790 *Metamorphoses* was the first post-war translation of the text in America, praises Ovid for the catharsis that he prompts by depicting the fall of one who begins so high: she enjoys "an honourable marriage, the dominion over a mighty kingdom, and a numerous offspring. . . . All these are on purpose contrived to make her fall appear the greater; nor does the poet himself suffer us to overlook a circumstance of so great weight."[40] This traditional framing of Niobe clarifies Wheatley's somewhat different project in making suffering "beautiful" above all in its meaninglessness: nothing is learned, no social benefit accrued, no divine order affirmed, by Niobe's suffering and petrification.

Wheatley's use of Ovid appeals to English complacency about the value of the classics as the basis of "good breeding." She sent her "Niobe" into an American readership that worried about the potentially anti-Christian and effeminizing impetus of classical literature, a moralizing concern that coexisted with eager consumption of classically-inflected consumer goods. Wheatley seems to value "Niobe" precisely for the undermining of certainty that American readers feared; the grief of her protagonist, a defiant and accidentally murderous mother, is "beautiful," above all, in its intensity and its futility. At the same time, simply by reading "Niobe" in moral terms, Wheatley differed from her English readers, who valued the classics primarily in aesthetic terms and for the ways that they were associated with gentility and status. This intersection of political, moral, and aesthetic frameworks for reading both the meaning of Wheatley's career and her individual poems suggests the necessity of contextualizing historically and locally the association of "literacy" with both Latin and the achievement of full humanity that is evident in John Gabriel Stedman's praise of Phillis Wheatley as exemplum of literate black humanity. As we have seen, Richard Wilson's classicism let him continue to affirm his own elitist gentility, even as these pretenses were materially enabled by the sale of prints to the masses and by his tobacco-trading brother's wealth. He worked, throughout his career, to assert the right of the British to "classical" landscapes dominated by Italian and French painters, a nationalizing impetus that occludes his status as a Welshman. That is, Wilson's oeuvre shored up a hierarchy of values by which class status was marked by knowledge of Latin, gentility by Englishness—a hierarchy for which he, a middling-class Welshman, was an unlikely poster child. Making this argument, I urge awareness of the ways that seemingly binary oppositions hide divisions within each alleged pole: a spectrum of associations, positive and negative, of Latin with status. The contexts I have described for the composition and consumption of Wheatley's "Niobe" also allow us to reexamine the critical reception of Wheatley's Latin: the ahistorical unselfconsciousness of the still dominant association of her classical allusions with racial self-hatred and/or oppression.

"An especially awful, virtually absurd set of lines by Ms. Wheatley": June Jordan's condemnation of Wheatley's "Niobe" is of a piece with the imperative that drives her pioneering assertion (published in 1985) of the "miracle" of Wheatley's poetic career: she looks at Wheatley in pursuit of a self-created slave poet, "compelled" to "the labors of her poetry" neither by her owners' "extraordinary kindness" nor by "the wealth of white men's literature with which she found herself quite saturated . . . with no choice in the matter" but by her unquenchable poetic nature.[41] As was the case with many analyses of Wheatley in this era of her rediscovery, Jordan blames Christianity and the western canon for estranging Wheatley from authenticity and anger, finding evidence only of false consciousness in the piety and classical allusions that fill her verse. Jordan's dedication to, and formulation of, racial integrity also inform her disapproval of Wheatley's elegies as "the verse of good girl Phillis ever compassionate upon the death of someone else's beloved"; only "Thoughts on the Work of Providence," with its "incisive and unmistakeable" celebration of natural creation, qualifies as real poetry.[42] Its success, however, resonates only weakly against the poems that Jordan wishes Wheatley had written, poems of "vernacular praise to Senegal, precise to slavery, and therefore accurate to the secret wishings of her lost and secret heart."[43]

Jordan's politicized aesthetics have been recently contextualized by Henry Louis Gates as part of the movement, between Wheatley's mid-eighteenth-century and Jordan's late-twentieth century America, "from a situation where Phillis Wheatley's acts of literacy could be used to demonstrate our people's inherent humanity and their inalienable right to freedom, to a situation where acts of literacy are stigmatized as somehow acts of racial betrayal."[44] Gates imagines the Boston worthies who corroborated her composition of the poems being published under her name:

> [T]here, perhaps gathered in a semicircle, would have sat an astonishingly influential group of the colony's citizens determined to satisfy for themselves, and thus put to rest, fundamental questions about the authenticity of this woman's achievements. Their interrogation of this witness, and her answers, would determine not only this woman's fate but the subsequent direction of the antislavery movement, as well as the birth of what a later commentator would call a new species of literature,' the literature written by slaves.[45]

Gates imagines this audience manifesting its skepticism that a black girl could have written the poems she hoped to publish in book form by asking, "'Who was Apollo?' 'What happened when Phaeton rode his father's chariot?' 'How did Zeus give birth to Athena?' 'Name the Nine Muses.'"[46] That such a cross-examination did not literally take place in this way undermines Gates's argument in one way; it is also undermined in its presumption of the singularity of Wheatley's treatment.[47] Though without a doubt her youth, race, and status as a slave made more likely, even crucial the prefatory attestation of her authorship placed in her *Poems on Various Subjects* when it appeared in 1773, many white women in eighteenth-century America had to undergo similar scrutiny. For example, before Martha Wadsworth Brewster's *Poems on Divers Subjects* could be published in 1757, she had to undergo a cross examination that included extempore versification, within a strict time limit of only minutes, of a passage from Scripture.[48] That is, the skepticism with which Wheatley's literacy and, with it, claim to full humanity was met reflected not only attitudes toward her African origins and status as slave but also hostility toward women's literary production.

Even as Wheatley's lengthy title seems to court approval as a humble imitator, her innovative rendition of "Niobe" marks her rather as a bold innovator. It is Wilson who is the imitator, and proudly so. Wheatley's "Niobe" focuses on women in ways that intersect importantly with her era's relegation of education to elite males, its nationalizing elevation of motherhood, and its denial of that ideal to Northern slaves, explicitly barred from forming their own families. Wheatley's classicism in "Niobe" enables perhaps her sharpest expression of anger and grief, her boldest portrait of selfish and cruel superiors. Only by reading the situation of the classics in her era can we overcome the biases that mar revisionist attention to Wheatley; only by broadening our pursuit of her works' racial import to include close attention to nation and gender can we appropriately situate her in her transatlantic moment and appreciate her achievement.

NOTES

1. John Gabriel Stedman, *Narrative of a Five Years Expedition against the Revolted Negroes of Surinam*, ed. Richard Price and Sally Price (Baltimore: Johns Hopkins University Press, 1988), 515–17.

2. Henry Louis Gates, "Introduction," *"Race," Writing, and Difference*, ed. Henry Louis Gates, Jr. (Chicago: University. of Chicago Press, 1986), 1–20; Gates, *The Signifying Monkey: A Theory of Afro-American Literary Criticism* (New York: Oxford University Press, 1988), especially chapter 4, "The Trope of the Talking Book"; Gates, "Critical Remarks," in *Anatomy of Racism*, ed. David Theo Goldberg (Minneapolis: Minnesota University Press, 1990), 319–29.

3. Kirstin Wilcox has compared the proposed Boston edition to the actual London edition in order to argue that revisions and additions that characterize the latter enabled the repackaging of "[t]he local prodigy of Boston" as "an accomplished woman of letters" ("The Body into Print: Marketing Phillis Wheatley," *American Literature* 71. 1 [March 1999]: 18).

4. Meyer Reinhold notes that the era of debate was also one of increasing familiarity with the classics: "it is . . . probable that never since antiquity were the classics, in one form or another, read by a greater proportion of a population" (*Classica Americana: The Greek and Roman Heritage in the United States* [Detroit: Wayne State University Press, 1984], 24).

5. Cited in Carl J. Richard, *The Founders and the Classics: Greece, Rome, and the American Enlightenment* (Cambridge MA: Harvard University Press, 1994), 223–24.

6. Cited in George S. Brookes, *Friend Anthony Benezet* (Philadelphia: University of Pennsylvania Press, 1937), 389–90.

7. Cited in Reinhold, *Classica Americana*, 122.

8. "African Slavery in America," published March 8, 1775 in the *Pennsylvania Journal* and the *Weekly Advertiser*; the following month, Paine and others established the first anti-slavery society in America. Cited by Reinhold, *Classica Americana*, 126.

9. Cited by Reinhold, *Classica Americana*, 25.

10. "[T]his does not seem the proper time for poetry, unless it be such as Tyrtaeus wrote." William Bradford to James Madison, 17 October 1774, in *Papers of James Madison*, ed. William T. Hutchinson and William M.E. Rachal (Chicago: University of Chicago Press, 1962), 1:126; cited in Reinhold, *Classica Americana*, 37.

11. Benjamin Latrobe to Ferdinand Fairfax, Esq., 28 May 1798 ("Thoughts on the National System of Education"), in *The Journal of Latrobe* (New York: D. Appleton, 1905), 72, 71.

12. Cited in Reinhold, *Classica Americana*, 36.

13. John Trumbull, *The Satiric Poems of John Trumbull*, ed. Edwin T. Bowden (Austin: University of Texas Press, 1962), 35, 81.

14. On this he rigg'd him in his best,
And got his old grey wig new-drest,
Fix'd on his suit of sable stuffs,
And brush'd the powder from the cuffs,
With black silk stockings, yet in being,
The same he took his first degree in . . .

. . . .

The Priest then bow'd in sober gesture
And all in scripture terms addrest her;
He'd found for reasons amply known,
It was not good to be alone,
And thought his duty led to trying
The great command of multiplying . . .
(Trumbull, *Satiric Poems*, 96–97)

15. Ovid Americanus, *Lessons for Lovers; With Some Tender and Pathetic Anecdotes, Taken from Real Life* (Philadelphia, 1784), 13.

16. *Lessons for Lovers*, 13.

17. For readings of Wheatley's use of sentimentalism as legitimating of her rhetorical authority, see Annie Finch, "Phillis Wheatley and the Sentimental

Tradition," *Romanticism on the Net* 29–30, February-May 2003; and Astrid Franke, "Phillis Wheatley, Melancholy Muse," *New England Quarterly* 77 (2004): 224–51.

18. David Bjelajac, *American Art: A Cultural History* (Upper Saddle River, NJ: Prentice Hall, 2005), 76, 77.

19. Thomas Tickell, Preface to *The Works of the Right Honourable Joseph Addison, 1721*, in *The Miscellaneous Works of Joseph Addison*, ed. A.C. Guthkelch, 2 vols. (London: G. Bell, 1914), 1:xliii–xiv, cited in Suzanne Gippert, *Joseph Addison's Ovid: An Adaptation of the Metamorphoses in the Augustan Age of British Literature* (Sankt Augustin: Gardez Verlag, 2003), 10.

20. *Spectator* No. 417 (June 28, 1712) in *The Spectator*, ed. Donald F. Bond, 5 vols. (Oxford: Clarendon Press, 1965), 3:565–66; *Spectator* No. 279 (January 19, 1712) in *The Spectator*, ed. Donald F. Bond, 2:588.

21. "To Mr Dryden," in Samuel Johnson, *The Works of the English Poets, With Prefaces, Biographical and Critical.* (London: J. Johnson et al., 1810), 8:494.

22. *The Works of John Dryden*, ed. Edward N. Hooker, H. T. Swedenberg, et al., 20 vols. (Berkeley: University of California Press, 1956–1984), 13:228.

23. David Solkin, *Richard Wilson: The Landscape of Reaction* (London: Tate Gallery Publications, 1982), 12–13. For related discussions of the ideological significance of Wilson's innovative approach to landscape, see also "Nobleness and Grandeur: Forging Historical Landscape in Britain, 1760–1850," brochure by Olivia Horsfall Turner to accompany exhibit at the Yale Center for British Art, January 27–April 24, 2005; and John Barrell, *The Political Theory of Painting from Reynolds to Hazlitt* (New Haven: Yale University Press, 1986), 340–41.

24. Solkin, *Richard Wilson*, 16.

25. Solkin, *Richard Wilson*, 61.

26. Rather than grouping "To Maecenas" with Wheatley's classicist poems, Paula Bennett places it within a group of poems that assert "Wheatley's project of self-redemption–that is, her legitimation of her right to practice her vocation" ("Phillis Wheatley's Vocation and the Paradox of the 'Afric Muse,'" *PMLA* 113. 1 [1998]), 64.

27. John C. Shields, ed., *The Collected Works of Phillis Wheatley* (New York: Oxford University Press, 1988), 250.

28. Phillis Wheatley, *Complete Writings*, ed. Vincent Caretta (New York: Penguin, 2001), line 12. All references to Wheatley are to this edition.

29. Arguing from a different context, Emily Stipes Watts also characterizes Wheatley's Niobe in terms of defiance (*The Poetry of American Women from 1632 to 1945* [Austin: University of Texas Press, 1977], 38). John C. Shields also sees Wheatley as innovative in her sympathy for Niobe (*The American Aeneas: Classical Origins of the American Self* [Knoxville: University of Tennessee Press, 2001], 222–23).

30. Solkin asserts that "Ovid's narrative ends with her being turned into stone by the gods," a plot that characterized Homer's rendition of the story of Niobe, but not Ovid's (*Richard Wilson*, 60). The same confusion of variants

characterizes Caretta's explanatory note to Wheatley's "Niobe": "At last taking pity on her, the gods themselves performed the funeral services, and Zeus turned Niobe into a weeping statue" (Wheatley, *Complete Writings*, 182).

31. Jahan Ramazani asserts that the modern elegy presents grief as "resistant to the standard elegaic salves, prolonged and complicated by guilt and ambivalence" in *The Poetry of Mourning: The Modern Elegy from Hardy to Heaney* (Chicago: University of Chicago Press, 1994), 5.

32. A.D. Melville's 1986 translation renders this more neutrally:

> She took no warning from the punishment
> Of her compatriot to give the gods
> Their proper place and moderate her tongue.

Ovid, *Metamorphoses*, trans. A.D. Melville (New York: Oxford University Press), 1986, 125.

33.
> Her Husband's Fame, their Family's Descent,
> Their Pow'r, and rich Dominion's wide Extent,
> Might well have justify'd a decent Pride;
> But not on these alone the Dame rely'd.
> Her lovely Progeny, that far excell'd,
> The Mother's Heart with vain Ambition swell'd:
> The happiest Mother not unjustly styl'd,
> Had not conceited Thoughts her tow'ring Fancy fill'd.

Ovid's Metamorphoses, in Fifteen Books. Translated by Mr. Dryden, Mr. Addison, Dr. Garth, Mr. Mainwaring, Mr. Congreve, Mr. Rowe, Mr. Pope, Mr. Gay, Mr. Eusden, Mr. Croxall, and other Eminent Hands (London, 1727), 3rd. ed. 1:208–209.

34.
> And she, who toss'd her high disdainful Head,
> When thro' the Streets in solemn Pomp she led
> The Throng that from *Latona*'s Altar fled,
> Assuming State beyond the proudest Queen;
> Was now the miserablest Object seen:
> Prostrate among the clay-cold Dead she fell,
> And kiss'd an undistinguish'd last Farewel.
> Then her pale Arms advancing to the Skies,
> Cruel *Latona*! triumph now, she cries.
> My grieving Soul in bitter Anguish drench,
> And with my Woes your thirsty Passion quench;
> Feast your black Malice at a Price thus dear,
> While the sore Pangs of sev'n such Deaths I bear.
> Triumph, too cruel Rival, and display
> Your conqu'ring Standard; for you've won the Day.
> Yet I'll excel; for yet, tho' sev'n are slain.
> Superior still in Number I remain.

(Croxall, *Ovid's Metamorphoses*, 1:214–215).

35. Peter M. Coviello, "Agonizing Affection: Affect and Nation in Early America." *Early American Literature* 37. 3 (2002): 440. Julie Ellison discusses a similar strategy of paradox in *Cato's Tears and the Making of Anglo-American Emotion* (Chicago: University of Chicago, 1999): "Wheatley maneuvers expertly between the attraction of Anglo-American political and religious ties and revolutionary patriotism, drawing on her slave status to speak as an expert witness on liberty" (20–21).

36. William D. Piersen, *Black Yankees: The Development of an Afro-American Subculture in Eighteenth-Century New England* (Amherst: University of Massachusetts Press, 1988), 36. Piersen also notes the significance of the low rate of reproduction of blacks relative to whites: Rhode Island statistics from the 1755 census and Connecticut statistics from the 1774 census "suggest[] over a 30 percent lower ratio of children to women among blacks than among whites" (19). For a related discussion of the nearly insurmountable obstacles to marriage and reproduction that were the correlate of slavery in New England, see Joanne Pope Melish, *Disowning Slavery: Gradual Emancipation and 'Race' in New England, 1780–1860* (Ithaca: Cornell University Press, 1998).

37. Jacqueline Jones, "Race, Sex, and Self-Evident Truths: The Status of Slave Women during the Era of the American Revolution," in *Women in the Age of the American Revolution,* ed. Ronald Hoffman and Peter J. Albert (Charlottesville: University Press of Virginia, 1989), 315.

38. Edgar McManus, *Black Bondage in the North* (Syracuse: Syracuse University Press, 2002), 38. *Continental Journal* (Boston), 1, 8 March 1781, cited in McManus, *Black Bondage*, 38. *New England Weekly Journal*, 15, 22 November 1731; 25 February 1733/4; 4 January 1737; 19, 26 July 1737; 6 June1738; *Boston Gazette*, 25 June 1754; *Boston Newsletter*, 26 June 1760. Cited in McManus, *Black Bondage*, 37–38.

39. Julie Kipp, *Romanticism, Maternity, and the Body Politic* (New York: Cambridge University Press, 2003). Kipp's reading of Romantic-era representations of motherhood is especially relevant to my argument here in her attention to the regularity with which motherhood, whether portrayed sympathetically or punitively, carries with it a "sense of the ultimate inscrutability of the natural world, the operations of which often defy logic" (56).

40. P. Ovidii Nasonis *Metamorphoseon libri X. Or, Ten select books of Ovid's Metamorphoses; with an English translation, compiled from the two former translations, by Davidson and Clarke; a prosody table and references, (after the manner of Mr. Stirling) pointing out, at one view, the scanning of each verse; and Davidson's English notes* (Philadelphia, 1790), 25–26.

41. June Jordan, "The Difficult Miracle of Black Poetry in America, or Something Like a Sonnet for Phillis Wheatley," in *On Call: Political Essays* (Boston: South End Press, 1985), 92, 90–91.

42. Jordan, "The Difficult Miracle," 93, 92.

43. Jordan, "The Difficult Miracle," 92.

44. Henry Louis Gates, Jr., *The Trials of Phillis Wheatley: America's First Black Poet and Her Encounters with the Founding Fathers* (New York: Basic

Civitas Books, 2003), 84.

45. Gates, *Trials*, 6–7.

46. Gates, *Trials*, 29.

47. As Kirstin Wilcox has noted, there is no evidence for this scene, so vividly imagined by Gates; see "The Body in Print," 10.

48. Sharon M. Harris, ed., *American Women Writers to 1800* (New York: Oxford University Press, 1996), 311. For discussion of the skepticism that greeted female authorship in colonial America, see also Pattie Cowell, *Women Poets in Pre-Revolutionary America, 1650–1775: An Anthology* (Troy, NY: Whitston Publishing, 1981).

"This Rhapsodical Work": Object-Narrators and the Figure of Sterne

HILARY ENGLERT

It is conventional wisdom within literary studies today that Laurence Sterne possessed a unique narrative method, one which provoked wide, if largely unsuccessful, imitation. Modern critics have been vigilant to differentiate the most celebrated of modernist and postmodern authors—the true heirs to the legacy of Sterne—from those profit-seeking, coattail-riding hack-writers who, shortly following the publication of the first installment of *Tristram Shandy*, began to shadow the fashionable novelist in great numbers. As Alan B. Howes has documented, it was on behalf of this critical effort, in the context of the early twentieth-century rehabilitation of Sterne's literary reputation, that the term "Sternean" was first mobilized. After nearly a century and a half of critical disfavor, which itself followed a brief but intense period of vogue, Sterne emerged in the 1920s as an icon—in Leslie Stephen's formulation, "perhaps the greatest artist in the language."[1] In dubbing Sterne's brand of humor "Sternean" in 1921, Thomas Seccombe sought both to credit Sterne with inaugurating a tradition and to sharpen the distinction between this newly exalted artist and his lowly impersonators. Sterne's "Shandean . . . portraits," contends Seccombe, "stand out like chefs-d'oeuvre in a large gallery of uninspired replicas and other fifth-rate compositions."[2] More recent scholars have closely guarded the Sternean pedigree against imposters and pretenders.

Take, for instance, Roger D. Lund's indignant response to Malcolm Bosse's suggestion that Charles Johnstone's 1760 *Chrysal; or the Adventures of a Guinea* be understood as distinctively modern in its formal design and experimental in its narrative disorder. Lund flatly rejects Bosse's characterization, contending that this novel, which he suggests is more accurately likened to a "modern supermarket tabloid," is "less modern than merely muddled" and that its structural discontinuity "derive[s] less from Sternean sophistication than . . . from haste and clumsiness."[3]

Late eighteenth-century critics, too, resented the Sternean striving that they attributed to the writers of these "uninspired replicas," many of which, like *The Adventures of a Guinea*, feature sprawling narratives told from non-human perspectives.[4] A 1781 piece in the *Critical Review* dismisses another object-narrated novel, *The Adventures of a Hackney Coach*, as a "flimsy performance" in which it is impossible to trace any of the "marks of taste and genius which so eminently distinguished the truly original writer whom our author seems ambitious of imitating."[5] This work is cast as a "servile copy of Sterne" by a "pretender to literary fame," seeking to "spin out" his book with disconnected materials joined by sudden Shandean transitions: to "fill it up as well as he can with something which he has ready cut and dried for the occasion."[6] The same year, Helenus Scott anticipates just this critical treatment of her own rambling *The Adventures of a Rupee* when, in her preface, she archly distinguishes it from the "affected and foolish productions" of "the insignificant and ignorant imitators of Sterne," a gesture presumably designed both to poke fun at the critical discourse around Sterneana and to establish a potentially profitable link to the celebrity novelist.[7]

Eighteenth-century reviewers' efforts to fortify and police the boundary between this high source and his mean imitators betray the vulnerability of that boundary to attacks from both directions. While the *Critical* avails itself of the monument of Laurence Sterne to denigrate recent novelistic production, only a generation earlier Sterne had been routinely accused of the same shoddy compositional methods and narrative incoherence now associated with his inferiors. In fact, Sterne's celebrated experimental narrative techniques may well have been influenced by his contemporaries. If later-century object-narrators mobilize Shandean devices, tricks, and trappings, if they playfully invoke Sterne in their prefaces and advertisements, it is also the case that for a full decade before the publication of the first two volumes of *Tristram Shandy*, object-narratives had explored their own place within an increasingly commercialized print culture with features later elaborated and popularized by Sterne: among them, the direct address to both critics and readers, the taxonomizing of readers, the authorial self-consciousness, the inscription of the scene of writing, and digressive reflections on the process of novel-writing and on the literary marketplace. Indeed, several recent critics have identified the early object-narrated novel as a concrete textual predecessor of Sterne. Thomas Keymer, for instance, treats *Tristram Shandy* as a now privileged, but typical, example of mid-century popular fiction, which he characterizes both by its unruly narrative structures and by its interest in the relationship between authorship and publication, and, as he puts it, "the overdetermination of both by the forces of literary commodification."[8] Keymer has argued that, in his major works, Sterne, a "voracious reader of new fiction," made use of a repertoire of mid-century tropes, narrative strategies, and formal techniques common in popular fiction that preceded him.[9] He points to *Tristram Shandy*'s indebtedness to the mock-autobiographical, for instance, a now forgotten fictional subgenre, which "use[s] autobiographical form as a convenient receptacle for miscellaneous matter," typically resulting in what he calls "a vigorous farrago of tales and digressions."[10]

It is in these explicit terms that critical reviewers condemned the increasingly popular object-narrated novels of the second half of the century. The subgenre is consistently described as an expedient vessel, a sort of crude disposable packaging in which disparate materials are presented. Another piece in the *Critical Review* in 1781, for instance, calls this fictional mode "a convenient method to writers of the inferior class, of emptying their commonplace books, and throwing together all the farrago of public transactions, private characters, old and new stories, everything in short, which they can pick up."[11] Writers of object-narrated novels are cast as literary scavengers, indiscriminately borrowing content from presumably unauthorized "old and new" sources, compiling heaps of scraps and fragments and passing them off as coherent works. The reviewer characterizes this process as "making up a book," implicitly distinguishing it from the processes of authorship in a way that raises important questions about the nature of literary production, property and value, questions that had fueled both public and legal debate for decades.

As much as Keymer's characterization of the mock-autobiographical resonates with complaints against the slack, episodic organizational framework underwritten by the object-narrator device, it also echoes mid-century response to the narrative design of the early volumes of *Tristram Shandy*. A few months after the publication of the first installment of the novel, a satirical pamphlet titled *The Clockmakers Outcry Against the Author of the Life and Opinions of Tristram Shandy* dismisses Sterne as the "tagger of a really contemptible *farrago*."[12] In the same formulation used later to protest the *Hackney Coach*'s Sternean derivativeness, this written attack casts *Tristram Shandy*'s chief distinction, its digressions, as "flimsy imitations" of Jonathan Swift. Sterne's writing process is described as joining or patching together—that is, "tagging"—incongruous, extraneous, borrowed pieces to form a padded whole that "turns out but a mere wild-goose chace. . . . What he descants upon Gravity [for example] is far from new, and therefore no way interesting: it helps to eke out the two volumes, as do an hundred other adventitious articles not naturally arising from the subject."[13] The appearance of volumes three and four a year later was registered as a straining, cynical extension of a commercial project that had run its course. Owen Ruffhead in the *Monthly Review* lodged his complaints with Shandy himself: "Mr. Tristram, you are dull, *very dull.* Your jaded Fancy seems to have been exhausted by two pigmy octavos, which scarce contained the substance of a twelve-penny pamphlet; and we now find nothing new to entertain us."[14] Later volumes were consistently decried as stale continuations of a tired formula, bloated with recycled humor and bits of borrowed learning. Even *A Sentimental Journey*, whose publication in 1768 arguably revived Sterne's reputation, was vulnerable to the charge of swelling. An unsigned review of that work in the *Critical* asked indignantly: "who does not see that this character of La Fleur is pieced out with shreds which Mr. Yorick has barbarously cut out and unskillfully put together from other novels?"[15]

If Sterne evokes inimitability for contemporary critics and late eighteenth-century reviewers, then, his name generated more complex, sometimes contradictory resonances for readers and writers earlier in the century. Far from an indisputable sign of originality, during the '60s and '70s, the name of Sterne was just as likely to signify the instability of the borders still being drawn between rigorous narrative license and slapdash compositional practice, between legitimate imitation and copying, between literature and hack-work, writing and marketing, respectable publication and institutionalized piracy. Unparalleled in his celebrity and hailed as an original genius, Sterne was also persistently accused of incoherence, affectation, ephemerality, pandering to the market, inflating his works with extraneous materials, and improper borrowing, the last of which charges culminated in his reputation as a flagrant plagiarist during the last years of the century.

Moreover, conflicted response to the formal design of Sterne's works was bound up with the controversial material forms in which they appeared and reappeared for decades. Sterne's narrative peculiarities, born of, in Robert Mayo's characterization, "his interest in humors and oddities, 'characters' and episodes, and significant moments of experience," lent themselves to the magazine tradition of reprinting detached episodes and literary fragments.[16] Immediately following each book-form installment of *Tristram Shandy*, passages were excerpted and sent into wide circulation by the periodicals. The *Sermons* and *A Sentimental Journey* received the same treatment, resulting in a handful of narrative scraps that, according to Mayo, "quickly became established as repertory pieces" making a succession of appearances in the "town and country magazines" and later in a number of popular miscellanies and collections of Sternean "beauties."[17] The serialization of *Tristram Shandy* and the unrelenting republication of excerpts from all three of Sterne's major works throughout the remainder of the century cast suspicion on the integrity of both the writer and the work, even as it extended the power, range, and fame of both.

Sterne's significance to the object-narrative as a subgenre of the novel, then, is not one of simple literary influence or indebtedness. Rather, the loose narrative structure, the digressions and interruptions, the sudden transitions and semi-autonomous sketches and episodes associated with Shandeanism, the serial publication of *Tristram Shandy*, and the rampant magazine and miscellany redactions before and after his death combine to create a picture of literary culture in which the object-narrative had a secure place. This is a picture that complicates evaluative distinctions taken for granted by contemporary literary history. Indeed, it is a picture that complicated the emerging doctrine of proprietary authorship—with its chief values, the originality of the artist and the organic unity of the work—in light of which the object-narrative came to be discredited. During a period in which the ethical, aesthetic, and legal categories governing copyright, commercial publication, and professional writing were under construction, the figure of Sterne represents a tethering together of conceptual elements and compositional practices, the separation of which would be all but complete by the end of the century.

Object-narrated tales and novels share with the works of Sterne a narrative method that both explores and exploits the realities of a new market for literature as popular entertainment. In referring to *Tristram Shandy* as a "rhapsodical work" mid-way through volume 1, Sterne identifies this method.[18] If current connotations of rhapsodical include the enthusiastic or musical, however, the term named a less exalted kind of performance in eighteenth-century usage. Citing the appearance of the word in *Tristram Shandy* to exemplify its obsolete meanings, the OED defines rhapsodical in relation to a literary work as "consisting of a medley of narratives" and "fragmentary or disconnected in style." Likewise, the obsolete meanings of rhapsody include "a literary work consisting of miscellaneous or disconnected pieces." The 1767 bug-narrated *The Ants*, subtitled *A Rhapsody*, playfully advertises the link between its narrative method and Sterne's commercial success in an elaborate prefatory account of its passage from manuscript to print.[19] The narrator of the preface, the work's fictional editor, describes its fictional author as having failed in his efforts to publish his work, which is declined by a local bookseller who dispenses this advice: "if you had employed half the time this work cost you, in writing a romance or a novel in the modern way, or composing something in the Shandean stile, I could have . . . published your copy with credit and advantage to myself."[20]

The joke here, of course, is that *The Ants* is composed in what has, by the year of its publication, become well-known as the "Shandean stile," especially in its extension of the tradition of the object-narrative as a collection of miscellaneous reflections, incidents and episodes. Recognizable as the brand of a distinct class of mid-century fiction, the rhapsodical operated on the margins of acceptable literary practice. In referring to Sterne as among the "authors who wrap themselves up from the ken of our comprehension in rhapsodical obscurity," *The Clockmakers Outcry* castigates both the rhapsodical method per se and Sterne's recourse to it.[21]

The 1760 *Transmigrating Soul; or, an Epitome of Human Nature* aligns non-human narration, structural discontinuity, and the increasingly disreputable practices of literary production associated with both when the narrator offers to inform the gentle reader of "the grand motive of [its] writing this rhapsodical chapter."[22] Indeed, he confesses: " —I was somewhat desirous to fill up a page or two, but being at this juncture a little deficient in point of matter, I thought the above would serve extremely well to lengthen my book."[23] Book 2 of this novel opens with "An address to the reader, which he may either peruse, or take a leap over, agreeable to his fancy."[24] While this is evidently available to us as a joke about the conventionality of paratexual materials, not to mention as a playful echo of *Tristram Shandy*'s frequent exhortations to the reader to move on, go back, or skip ahead, there is also a way in which it is perfectly frank. Like many object-narratives, *Transmigrating Soul* is comprised of a collection of equivalent, interchangeable chapters, any of which the reader may choose to skip, skim, or read out of order. As the narrator explains, this is a narrative structure conditioned by the market : "I consider it as a sign of false judgment, as well as ingratitude, in any author, who is dependant on the public, not to diversify his works with morsels of literary matter to suit every tooth."[25]

Indeed, the morsels of literary matter constituting the typical object-narrative represent a remarkable degree of generic and discursive variety. As Christopher Flint notes, "a single tale [in this mode] may incorporate satire, allegory, anatomy, picaresque, scandal chronicle, roman à clef or secret history, news, propaganda, autobiography, moral tale, sentimental romance, Aesopian fable, spy novel, travelogue, and imaginary voyage."[26] Moreover, rather than the rationally unfolding progression of events that constitutes a developmental plot, the object-narrative consists of an accumulation of discrete character sketches, scenarios, incidents or fragments of incidents with no necessary relation to one another. Many—*The Adventures of a Goose-Quill* (1751) and *The Adventures of a Pen* (1795), for instance—reproduce scraps of the poems, receipts, and epistles for the composition of which they have been pressed into service by their possessors.[27] Others contain interpolated bits of verse or prose from other sources. The 1780 *Adventures of an Air Balloon*, for instance, which is narrated by an aerial vehicle that documents the dialogue and interaction of its passengers, recounts the ride of "a celebrated Historic, Dramatic, and Miscellany Writer, *and a Poet*" who arrives with a poem, *The Rape of the Smock*, which he forgetfully leaves behind in the vehicle.[28] Reproduced in its entirety, this two-book poem is the 1717 satire of Alexander Pope's *Rape of the Lock* by Giles Jacob, one of the dunces featured in Pope's 1728 *Dunciad*. *The Adventures of a Pen* reprints an array of previously appearing snatches of text, including a letter, which it cites, from the "Story of Edward and Maria," an epistolary tale that appeared in an American magazine four years earlier.

The narrative conceits of this subgenre reinforce their motley, episodic construction. Because the parameters of the object-narrated tale are dictated by the object's perspective and because the object's passage through the world is dependent not on its own will or agency but on the contingencies of exchange, episodes are frequently abruptly suspended rather than concluded, and strung together haphazardly. Likewise, the device of the transmigrating spirit to which most of these narratives make recourse, both facilitates and figures the rhapsodical effect. The object-narrator is conventionally a spirit or demon, or a human soul, condemned to occupy a series of objects or bodies as a form of karmic punishment. Untethered to any one material incarnation, these fictional observers enjoy an exaggerated mobility and capacity to shift perspective that might accommodate a limitless series of encounters, transactions and narrative episodes.

These formal features of the eighteenth-century rhapsodical object-narrative announce its relationship to the increasingly commercialized literary field of the period. As Christoper Flint has demonstrated, the kinship between this subgenre and *Tristram Shandy* is most palpably evinced in the narrative structure of both, a narrative structure which figuratively "reproduce[s] the endless circulation of text in modern print culture."[29]

Flint's focus is on the ever increasing production of books—intact print objects—and their seemingly feverish circulation among readers. Yet his insight here might be extended to other dimensions of literary circulation represented by these narratives, specifically the mobility of the incorporeal work through material incarnations: periodical redaction and, later in the century, republishing in volumes of beauties, gleanings, excerpts, and fragments. Novels narrated by animated objects, identified pejoratively as "picaresque miscellanies" nearly seventy-five years ago by J.M.S. Tompkins, may be best understood in their complex figuration of magazine and miscellany publication.[30]

If, as Liz Bellamy notes, the discursive variety and "diffuse structure" of these works render them "reminiscent of the periodical journalism of the early eighteenth century," the historical basis of the connection is quite concrete.[31] From its first incarnations, this narrative mode enjoyed close ties to the world of periodical entertainment. As much as it draws on the generic traditions of picaresque satire, the secret history, and the spy narrative, the object-narrative also can be traced to the conventional modes of eighteenth-century magazine fiction categorized by Robert Mayo: specifically, the mock-heroic and mock-sentimental tale, the satirical adventure story, the dream vision or dream allegory, and the oriental tale.[32] Moreover, many tales featuring story-telling objects took their "original" shapes in parts published serially by magazines like the *Lady's*, the *London*, the *Gentleman's*, and the *Royal*, among them the adventures of a mirror, a quire of paper, a gold ring, a pen, a shilling, a sopha, a stage coach, a louse, and a bedstead.[33] While periodical publication offered itself as a logical venue for this kind of episodic fiction early in the century, by mid-century a novel form in this mode had emerged around a series of conventions designed to reinforce its ties to the pleasures, values, and in some cases, the vices and embarrassments associated with magazine fiction. The worldly object-narrator of *Memoirs and Interesting Adventures of an Embroidered Waistcoat* (1751), for instance, urges its amanuensis to take down its tale, speculating that "some of the magazines will sufficiently reward [him] for a Detail of [the] story."[34] In the same vein, the one-volume *The Adventures of a Black Coat* (1760) constructs the literary field in which it appears as an "age of *Magazines* and *Chronicles*," in which "the *Cacoethes Scribendi* hath infected the town so much, that almost every *shop*, or *workroom*, harbours an author."[35] While these works were published as books, they, like their mid-century fellows, are allied in a variety of ways to a magazine tradition: they are constructed on a logic of seriation, narrative accumulation, and piecemeal assembly; their prefaces routinely thematize the material conditions of their production, distribution and reception in the context of the periodicals; and many of the metaphors suggested by the particular objects they feature underscore links to the culture of redaction and reprinting.

One such metaphor is mobilized by the narrator of *The Adventures of a Embroidered Waistcoat* who, on its self-representation, is "as wonderful and as replete with Matter as most Part of our late Novels."[36] The embroidered coat offers a familiar figure for the fabric of a sprawling narrative, woven of many threads of different colors, thicknesses, and qualities. Not surprisingly, perhaps, the figure of the coat—specifically, the harlequin's coat—is consistently used by contemporary reviewers to describe Sterne's rhapsodical narrative design. The *Monthly Review* in 1767, for instance, submits that Sterne's "real prototype" is "Harlequin," quipping that "so motley a performance [as *Tristram Shandy*] can only be denominated the PANTOMIME of literature."[37] Years earlier, in response to the publication of *Sermons of Mr. Yorick*, Owen Ruffhead objected to the indecency of attributing pious works to an "assumed character" derived from an "obscene Romance." In an unsigned review for the *Monthly*, he bemoans that the "solemn dictates of religion" should "be conveyed from the mouths of Buffoons and ludicrous Romancers" who "mount the pulpit in a *Harlequin's coat*."[38] To be sure, these critical comments refer most immediately to Sterne's extravagance, affectation, impropriety, and self-promoting buffoonery, his equivocation between imitation and originality, and his penchant for disguise. Yet they also provide a ready figure for the organizational structure of his major works and for the modes of publication with which they came to be associated, specifically seriation, the printing of detached episodes in the magazines, and the reprinting of excerpts, beauties, and reparatory pieces within the miscellanies.

Yorick's Skull; or College Oscitations, a collection of Shandean fragments and commentary on Sterne published in multiple editions during the 1770s, is framed by a prefatory explication of this metaphor: "a miscellany may very justly be compared to harlequin's jacket, which is generally made up of shreds and remnants of different colours, so disposed as to amuse the eye with a kind of regular variety."[39] While the explicit point made here concerns the entertainment value of this particular timely miscellany, the figure of the harlequin's jacket subtly marks out an affinity between Sterne's motley productions and those of the miscellany. In its elaboration of this metaphor, the preface to *Yorick's Skull* revalues the implications of its vehicle and recuperates the design of the miscellany—and, by implication, that of the rhapsodical narrative—in the name of pleasure: "the pantomime itself is not a bad emblem of this unconnected kind of writing; for the changes are sometimes so quick and wonderful, that we are surprised to find ourselves, conveyed, in the space of a few minutes, through palaces, groves, cities, and cottages, variously entertained, either with the grandeur, simplicity, bustle, or retirement, of every scene, in its distinct succession."[40] No longer a figure for flimsiness or fraudulence as it had been for the *Monthly Review*, "pantomime" now signifies the breathless wonder and excitement borne of variety, speed, and the unanticipated shift in perspective: "a MISCELLANEOUS writer has this considerable advantage over all others, that he can prevent his subject becoming dull and insipid, by changing it whenever it begins to be tedious and displeasing to him."[41]

In extrapolating reading habits from the structure and design of seventeenth- and early eighteenth-century literary anthologies, Barbara Benedict argues that such works afforded precisely the virtues outlined by *Yorick's Skull*, for readers, who, she suggests, "skipped between unconnected items rather than either shifting between different sorts of literature or engaging in long stints of reading."[42] Indeed, she specifically opposes this reading practice to the strategies necessitated by "single-narrative prose or poetic works."[43] The popularity of the rhapsodical narrative throughout the second half of the eighteenth century suggests that this tradition of reading survived the early modern anthologies at the heart of Benedict's study, even as the material forms conditioning this reading changed.

Reflecting on this persistence, Benedict submits that "the novel as a genre . . . most evidently [took] over many of the cultural functions of the literary anthology" toward the latter part of the century.[44] Much prose fiction published in inexpensive volumes during the second half of the century established continuity with the timely miscellanies by recasting its structures as novelistic plot, albeit non-developmental, non-teleological, episodic, plot. Likewise, she speculates that the "fad for [reprinting in compilations] severed scenes of sentiment from other works like Laurence Sterne's *Tristram Shandy* . . . influenced the form of the novel during this period."[45] As the case of Sterne exemplifies, fictional episodes and fragments detached from their "original" contexts were routinely reprinted in periodicals and compilations during the century. Robert Mayo charts a number of individual pieces "making the rounds" of up to eleven different publications, and reappearing in magazines and miscellanies as what he calls "resurrections" and "ghostly revisitations," metaphors that evoke the circulating objects and transmigrating sprits whose adventures are increasingly narrativized throughout the century.[46]

As professional authorship came to be defined against the practices of compilation (recall Justice Hailes's complaints in the 1773 piracy case *Hinton v. Donaldson* against "tasteless compilers' . . . ransacking [and] plundering" to produce their "monthly hashes of literature," which they pass off as "entire[ly] new") and as the conventions of the novel as an elevated genre began to be codified to the exclusion of earlier models of long prose narrative, it may be that writers of fiction sought to combine the increasing legitimacy and putative integrity of the novel form with the pleasures of the magazine and miscellany traditions.[47] Like the anthology or the magazine, the object-narrated rhapsodical novel is framed, in Leah Price's construction, as "an aggregate of modular parts rather than an indissoluble whole."[48] Designed as though to facilitate extraction, its structural looseness and variety of matter deliver a kind of already excerpted effect, which, when coupled with the thematic of social and economic circulation, suggests an allied relationship to the culture of reprinting. In offering a steady stream of delectable, detachable narrative episodes and fragments without the belabored connective tissue, this kind of narrative could accommodate a reader forced or inclined to stop and start, to be repeatedly interrupted and thrown back into the text, however briefly. Appearing in small, cheap editions or disposable periodicals, most novels featuring object-narrators were of the class of popular literature meant to be carried about, on journeys and on the person, handed from one reader to another, or carelessly left behind for the next reader. The "plots" of these texts not only accommodate but figure this kind of readerly intermittence, this "disconnected dipping and skipping" in Barbara Benedict's formulation: episodes give way to one another with egregious abruptness; the linearity of the plot is never offered as the organizing principle of the narrative; interchangeable characters come and go without ceremony as though modeling the disposableness that characterizes the text itself.[49]

Many of the objects featured in object-narrated novels are designed to contain or cover characters as a means of facilitating their mobility, and by extension, their adventures. The story-telling figures at the heart of these narratives, in other words, paradoxically combine perpetual movement with complete enclosure. The embroidered waistcoat conditions polite social exchange; the blackcoat ensures safe movement through the streets. The several balloons, the stage coach, and the hackney coach shelter people as they are propelled into motion and dialogue.[50] Even the slippers, shoes, and wig fit snugly over, on, or around the extremities of their wearers who make use of them in transit or in company.[51] From articles of apparel to street and aerial vehicles, narrating objects function as forms into which bodies or parts of bodies might be inserted, removed, substituted for one another. Christopher Flint's insight that the story-telling particle of matter that narrates Tobias Smollett's 1769 *Adventures of an Atom* transgresses "all boundaries of human containment, yet is one of the most contained things on earth" may be applied to object-narrators more generally.[52] At the same time, these objects narrativize histories of their own possession by the spirits who inhabit them, and their chains of custody and containment by the people whose tales they tell. Spirits inhabiting vehicles tell the stories of their passengers; animated garments tell the tales of their wearers. It is dynamic form that gives voice to content in these novels, assorted content derived from chance encounters and then patched together. Boundaries between insides and outsides, owners and objects, possessions and the possessed are crossed and blurred, redrawn, and crossed again.

It may be that the excitement and meaning of these narratives is to be found in the permeability of the boundary between form and content, in the metaphorical suggestion not merely that a text's packaging might have as much to say about it as its story, but that the process of packaging—and repackaging, excerpting, redaction, reprinting—might both engender and animate that story. Even as the narrative trajectories of these vehicles and coats and slippers and shoes are those of wear and tear, tattering and deterioration, it is nonetheless their utility as objects that guarantees their circulation and their circulation that keeps them vital.

The quire of paper that tells its tale serially in the *London Magazine* in 1772 forcefully articulates this double bind.[53] This is an allegory of textual production and circulation, excerpting and extraction, fragmentation and reprinting within hack-culture. While in the form of fine cambric, bits and pieces of the material narrator are "pilfered," "filtche[d] from its abundance," "snipped by scissors," "cribbed," and "hacked and tortured into a multitude of strange little forms, with no small skill and contrivance."[54] Indeed, the protean non-human narrator, who continually refers to its "mutilated" condition, is rendered a "wretched, dirty fragment, full of rents," collected by a rag-man, thrown in "under the loads of [other] miscellaneous tatters," sold to a paper-maker, and finally reincarnated as the very page in the "fashionable magazine" lying in the reader's hands.[55]

In a compelling discussion of speaking objects in eighteenth-century literature, Christopher Flint reads this story as "convey[ing] the essential poverty of textual embodiment, [its narrator] portraying its destined conversion into a printed book as a terrifying unalterable condition."[56] Flint cites this piece as an instance of the object-narrative's general lament over the loss of authorial control and status in "an overpopulated print culture."[57] For him, the speaking object, which he traces back to Jonathan Swift's 1704 *A Tale of the Tub* and Charles Gildon's 1709 *The Golden Spy*, dramatizes "the mechanical and alienated nature of modern writing," and "Adventures of a Quire of Paper" dramatizes this alienation by representing the condition of print as engendering a loss of identity[58]. But if Flint is right in suggesting that "the power to tell stories is compromised by the subjection of the storyteller to systems of social, economic, and material exchange that delimit its identity" in these narratives, we must also recall that these systems of exchange condition the very possibility for these tales to be told.[59] Far from simply bemoaning its fragmentation or ephemerality, the quire of paper repeatedly gives voice to its desire to continue moving through the world, changing shapes, meeting up with bits of itself here and there. It is not all textual embodiment that worries the narrator of this tale. Rather, as Flint himself points out, the quire of paper fears "the permanence of *book form*" insofar as this would "cut [it] off forever from being united to [its] other widely scattered and wretched parts, in [its] original form."[60]

This is a peculiarly counter-intuitive fantasy – read allegorically, it suggests that it is only through participation in the culture of magazine and miscellany excerpting and reprinting that the quire of paper may sustain a relationship to its original form. As Jonathan Lamb has noted, it is the possibility of a break in the circuit of exchange that represents the greatest annoyance to story-telling objects: "Gildon's coin protests against the injustice of being held by a miser . . . Helenus Scott's rupee complains bitterly when it is immobilized in a pawnbroker's shop; an anonymous pin resents being placed in a miser's hoard; an ostrich feather is outraged when it is lodged in a warehouse and subsequently exhibited in a collection of New World curiosities."[61] And the quire of paper expresses dread at the prospect of being contained in the static form of a book. Just as the reprinting of the fragment or detached episode extends the life of, even revives, a flagging literary piece (however much it may also be said to have contributed to its mutilation), the perpetual circulation of these objects is the only alternative to their annihilation. These texts suggest, then, that the soul of literary culture is located in exchange, that literary meaning takes shape at the zones of contact and interaction between people, between texts, and between people and texts, and not inside of the heads of sovereign geniuses or of static volumes.

In other words, not only were the notions of "authorial" identity and prerogative, the loss of which Flint sees mourned in these pieces, at their most unstable during this period, but they were surely not assumed by the writers of late-century object-narratives. A distinction must be drawn between the authorial self-conception of early-century figures like Gildon and Swift, whose works plainly articulate concerns about the debasing effects of the commercialization of literary culture, and that of most of the later-century writers of rhapsodical narratives. While these earlier figures were no doubt highly conscious of and frequently ambivalent about their shifting relationship to the literary marketplace, later-century writers of popular fiction were, in Mark Blackwell's formulation, "resigned to their role as laborers turning out print-based consumables in response to the demand—the fashions—of a specific time and place."[62] Theirs was a popular fictional subgenre that belonged to a culture of literary production and exchange against which proprietary authorship was in the process of being defined. Its close connections to practices of compilation—including cooperative or collaborative compositional strategies, interpolation of borrowed passages, formulaic adherence to conventions, and unbridled reprinting—would, by the end of the century, disqualify it from consideration as serious, respectable literature. Its writers were surely conscious of their increasingly subordinated status within the literary field. As such, they may well have sought to expose the inadequacies of emerging discourses of literary property and professional authorship in the name of their own contributions to literary culture cast as the culture of entertainment.

Sterne's works were legible in this register during his lifetime in a way that has been obscured by the twentieth-century celebration of his seminal genius. His most renowned novel and his most notorious, the work responsible for countless "stupid imitations" and "modern Shandy-like pages," might be read as a sustained inquiry into the phenomenon of dubious, displaced, and shifting origins.[63] Indeed, *Tristram Shandy* thematizes its own construction in episodes, digressions, and interruptions that weave in and out of the narrative account of its author's questionable origins, the completion of which it endlessly defers. This novel is anything but fixed – the narration moves backwards and forwards, following tangents and detours, accommodating interpolated and borrowed passages, and calling on any number of outside forces to set itself "a-going, and make the world run mad after it."[64] This is a tale highly conscious of the process by which it is spun, and ridden with scenes that playfully raise topical suspicions about that process, and about the materials that might make it up, only to make light of those suspicions.

Take for example the much discussed found-sermon scene of *Tristram Shandy*'s volume 2, an episode featuring a peculiarly mobile text, which Homer Obed Brown has read as a paradigm for the novel itself, "a figurative repetition of the text as a whole."[65] When Uncle Toby is suddenly struck with an errant thought of the "great *Stevinus*"—the inventor of "the celebrated sailing chariot . . . of such wonderful contrivance and velocity"—Corporal Trim is beckoned to fetch and "look into" a book by this author for a closer account of his nautical machine. Unable to "spy aught of a sailing chariot in it," Trim jokingly throws the book open and gives it "a good sound shake." To the company's surprise, what falls out of the leaves of the volume is the manuscript of a sermon, later revealed to have been penned by the parish Parson Yorick: "There is something fallen out," Trim declares, "but it is not a chariot, or any thing like one . . . 'tis more like a sermon,—for it begins, with a text of scripture, and the chapter and verse;—and then goes on, not as a chariot,—but like a sermon directly."[66]

Part of the gag here is that the sermon goes on very much like a chariot: not only is it designed to put its bit of scripture back into circulation, but as a novelistic device, it functions as a vehicle for the real substance of the episode. As J. Paul Hunter points out, "no reader who navigates chapter xvii remembers much about the sermon as such."[67] The scene's interest lies in the sermon's interruptions, the confusion and dialogue engendered by and surrounding the sermon, not the sermon itself. Moreover, this scrappy little work has an uncanny way of breaking out of its textual boundaries, having been in the extra-novelistic world both preached and published by Sterne in 1750 and then reprinted by him under the name of Yorick in 1766.[68] Trim's "drolling" suspends the notion of the book as the pure, still, incorporeal emanation of its author's mind and invites the reader to confront the book's material dimensions and its function as a container and vehicle for other works. The sermon episode conditions the interpolation of a text (the sermon is reproduced in the form of Uncle Toby's dramatic reading), but it also figures the practice of interpolation within novelistic production and perhaps the compiling of detached episodes in the magazines and miscellanies. More to our point, as a pious work spun out from a holy text and later plagiarized by a "certain prebendary" of the cathedral of York, this fallen manuscript plays havoc with the distinction between sanctioned (indeed, sanctified) borrowing and illegitimate textual appropriation.[69]

The episode ends with an account of the accidents and exchanges that mark the sermon's movement through the world following its discovery by the Shandy family, a journey whose wretchedness and expansiveness rival those of the quire of paper's adventures:

> Ill-fated sermon! Thou wast lost, after this recovery of thee, a second time, dropp'd thro' an unsuspecting fissure in thy master's pocket, down into a treacherous and tatter'd lining,—trod deep into the dirt by the left hind foot of his Rosinante, inhumanly stepping upon thee as thou falledst;—buried ten days in the mire, —raised up out of it by a beggar, sold for a halfpenny to a parish-clerk,—transferred to his parson,—lost for ever to thy own, the remainder of his days,—not restored to his restless MANES till this very moment, that I tell the story.[70]

After a history of loss, discovery, and again loss—that is, having fallen through the worn pocket of its author's garment (his coat, perhaps?)—abuse, exchange, plagiarism, and unauthorized duplication, the material object of the sermon is imagined reunited with its spirit (its "MANES") in this postscript. Here, Sterne playfully explores the relationship between rhapsodical literary production and circulation and the emerging notion of the literary object as incorporeal property. In this context, the itinerant sermon indeed offers itself as a paradigm, not merely for the novel that contains it, but for the figure of Sterne more generally. Bound up as he was with the conventions and compositional practices of what was to become a debased subgenre, Sterne constructed—and sustained—a campaign on behalf of his singularity, originality, and ingeniousness at least as powerful as his reputation for borrowing, swelling, and compiling.

In a review of the first two volumes of *Tristram Shandy* in the *Annual Register*, Edmund Burke rehearsed what had become a common complaint about popular fiction of the day: "the story is in reality made nothing more than a vehicle for satire on a great variety of subjects."[71] Undeterred, Sterne appropriated the metaphor in a private letter announcing his intention to begin the fifth volume: "I care not a curse for the critics—I'll load my vehicle with what goods *he* sends me, and they may take 'em off my hands, or let them alone."[72] Tethering a proprietary author's insistence that his work is inspired to an avowal of the rhapsodical implied by the vehicular metaphor, Sterne plays again with the border between originality and borrowing. It is this sort of exchange that allows us to restore Sterne to his place within the mid-eighteenth-century literary field. Here he emerges as the rhapsodical writer he clearly was—a figure with an acute sense of the impact of a work's material forms on its cultural elevation or debasement and the importance of manipulating those forms. The contemporary monumentalization of Sterne has served to mystify the literary field in which he worked by evacuating precisely the compositional practices and commitments that he shared with the writers who are now available to us merely as his imitators—practices and commitments only now recognizable to us as the hallmarks of corrupt cultural production.

Like the eighteenth-century anthologist, the object-narrator is, in Leah Price's terms, "an amanuensis rather than a creator . . . represent[ing] a community instead of expressing a self."[73] It is this sense of community that self-consciously defines the object-narrative: it is a commodity—an object of exchange—circulating within the commercial world, but it has a kind of agency, too, in its capacity to produce emotional and ideological effects on individual selves and on social dynamics. If Sterne was careful always to express an elaborated self, he was no less conscious that wide, on-going, constantly renewed circulation, reprinting, and retailing—far from debasing a work—would increase its legs, body it forth, and in turn extend its cultural power.

NOTES

1. Sir Leslie Stephen, *Hours in a Library*, 4th ed. (London: G. P. Putnam's Sons, 1919), 130–63.

2. Thomas Seccombe, *The Age of Johnson* (1928), 179–88; reprinted in Alan B. Howes, *Sterne: The Critical Heritage* (London: Routledge and Kegan Paul, 1974), 36.

3. Roger D. Lund, *British Novelists, 1660–1800*, vol. 39 part 1 of *Dictionary of Literary Biography*, ed. Martin C. Battestin (Michigan: Gale Research Company, 1985), 293–300.

4. Consigned to relative obscurity for most of the twentieth century, the object-narrative (alternately termed the it-narrative or circulating narrative) has recently received significant critical attention as a distinct literary form. Important essays include Jonathan Lamb, "Modern Metamorphoses and Disgraceful Tales," *Critical Inquiry* 28 (2001): 133–66; Christopher Flint, "Speaking Objects: The Circulation of Stories in Eighteenth-Century Prose Fiction," *PMLA* 113 (1998): 212–26; Aileen Douglas, "Britannia's Rule and the It-Narrator," *Eighteenth-Century Fiction* 6.1 (1993): 65–82. Books that contain protracted discussion of the mode include Deidre Lynch, *The Economy of Character: Novels, Market Culture, and the Business of Inner Meaning* (Chicago: University of Chicago Press, 1998); Liz Bellamy, *Commerce, Morality and the Eighteenth-Century Novel* (Cambridge: Cambridge University Press, 1998); Markman Ellis, *The Politics of Sensibility : Race, Gender and Commerce in the Sentimental Novel* (Cambridge: Cambridge University Press, 2004); Laura Brown, *Fables of Modernity: Literature and Culture in the English Eighteenth Century* (Ithaca: Cornell University Press, 2003). See also *The Secret Life of Things: Animals, Objects, and It-Narratives in Eighteenth-Century England*, ed. Mark Blackwell (Lewisburg: Bucknell University Press, 2007). For a partial list of primary works see Richard K. Meeker, "Bank Note, Corkscrew, Flea and Sedan: A Checklist of Eighteenth-Century Fiction," *Library Chronicle* 35 (1969): 52–57.

5. *Critical Review* 51 (1781): 286, 287.

6. *Critical Review* 51 (1781): 287.

7. Helenus Scott, *The Adventures of a Rupee: wherein are interspersed various anecdotes Asiatic and European* (London, 1781), ix. On the Sterne industry and the phenomenon of Sterneana in the eighteenth century, see J. C.

T. Oates, *Shandyism and Sentiment, 1760–1800* (York: Cambridge Bibliographical Society, 1968).

8. Thomas Keymer, *Sterne, the Moderns and the Novel* (Oxford: Oxford University Press, 2002), 3, 17.

9. Keymer, *Sterne*, 59.

10. Keymer, *Sterne*, 65, 64.

11. *Critical Review* 52 (1781).

12. *The Clockmakers Outcry Against the Author of the Life and Opinions of Tristram Shandy* (London, 1760); reprinted in Howes, *Critical Heritage*, 67–68.

13. *Clockmakers*; reprinted in Howes, *Critical Heritage*, 67, 69.

14. Owen Ruffhead, *Monthly Review* 24 (1761): 101–16; reprinted in Howes, *Critical Heritage*, 122.

15. *Critical Review* 25 (1768): 181–85; reprinted in Howes, *Critical Heritage*, 198.

16. Robert Mayo, *The English Novel in the Magazines: 1740–1815* (Oxford: Oxford University Press, 1962), 325.

17. Mayo, *Magazines*, 336, 337.

18. Laurence Sterne, *The Life and Opinions of Tristram Shandy, Gentleman* (New York: The Modern Library, 2004), 27.

19. *The Ants; A Rhapsody* (London, 1767).

20. *Ants*, x.

21. *Clockmakers*; reprinted in Howes, *Critical Heritage*, 69.

22. *The Transmigrating Soul; or, an Epitome of Human Nature* (London, 1760), 70.

23. *Transmigrating*, 70–71.

24. *Transmigrating*, 67.

25. *Transmigrating*, 129.

26. Flint, "Objects," 219.

27. *The Adventures of a Goose-Quill* (London, 1751); J. Hunt, *The Miscellany: Containing The Cottage; or Winter Evening's Amusement. The Adventures of a Pen. and A Poem on Death* (London, 1795).

28. *The Adventures of an Air Balloon* (London, 1780), 73.

29. Flint, "Objects," 215.

30. J.M.S. Tompkins, *The Popular Novel in England* (1932; reprint, Lincoln: University of Nebraska Press, 1961), 47.

31. Bellamy, *Commerce*, 125.

32. Mayo, *Magazines*, 38.

33. For a full list, see Mayo, *Magazines*, 442–553.

34. *Memoirs and Interesting Adventures of an Embroidered Waistcoat* 2 vols.(London, 1751), 1:5.

35. *The Adventures of a Black Coat* (London, 1760), ix–x.

36. *Waistcoat*, 2:6.

37. Ralph Griffiths (unsigned), *Monthly Review* 36 (1767): 93–102; reprinted in Howes, *Critical Heritage*, 181.

38. Owen Ruffhead (unsigned), *Monthly Review* 22 (1760): 422; reprinted in Howes, *Critical Heritage*, 77.

39. William Combe, *Yorick's Skull; or, College Oscitations, with Some Remarks on the Writing of Sterne, and a Specimen of the Shandean Stile* (London, 1774), 12.

40. Combe, *Skull*, 12–13.

41. Combe, *Skull*, 13.

42. Barbara Benedict, *Making the Modern Reader: Cultural Mediation in Early Modern Literary Anthologies* (Princeton: Princeton University Press, 1996), 20.

43. Benedict, *Making*, 20.

44. Benedict, *Making*, 176.

45. Benedict, *Making*, 179.

46. Mayo, *Magazines*, 256, 229.

47. James Boswell, *The Decision of the Court of Session upon the Question of Literary Property in the Cause of Hinton against Donaldson* (Edinburgh, 1774); reprinted in *The Literary Property Debate: Six Tracts, 1764–1774,* ed. Stephen Parks (New York: Garland, 1975), 6. On the emergence of professional authorship in the eighteenth century, see Mark Rose, *Authors and Owners: The Invention of Copyright* (Cambridge, MA.: Harvard University Press, 1993); Mark Rose, "The Author as Proprietor: Donaldson v. Becket and the Genealogy of Modern Authorship,"*Representations* 23 (1988): 51–85; and Martha Woodmansee, *The Author, Art, and the Market: Rereading the History of Aesthetics* (New York: Columbia University Press, 1994). On the elevation of the novel as a genre, see William Beatty Warner, *Licensing Entertainment: The Elevation of Novel Reading in Britain, 1684–1750* (Berkeley: University of California Press, 1998).

48. Leah Price, *The Anthology and the Rise of the Novel from Richardson to George Eliot* (Cambridge: Cambridge University Press, 2000) 24.

49. Benedict, *Making*, 18.

50. Susan Smythies, *The Stage-Coach* (London, 1753); *The Sedan: A Novel: In Which Many New and Entertaining Characters Are Introduced* (London, 1757); *The Adventures of an Air Balloon* (London, 1780); Dorothy Kilner, *The Adventures of a Hackney Coach* (London, 1781).

51. *The Secret History of an Old Shoe* (London, 1734); *The History and Adventures of a Lady's Slippers and Shoes. Written by Themselves* (London, 1754); *The Genuine Memoirs and Most Surprising Adventures of a Very Unfortunate Goose-Quill: With an Introductory Letter to Mrs. Midnight's Tye-Wig* (London, 1734).

52. Flint, "Objects," 218.

53. "Adventures of a Quire of Paper," *London Magazine* (August 1779): 355–58; (September 1779): 395–98; (October 1779): 448–52.

54. "Adventures of a Quire," *London Magazine* (September 1779): 396, 397, 398.

55. "Adventures of a Quire," *London Magazine* (September 1779): 397, 398; "Adventures of a Quire," *London Magazine* (October 1779): 448, 449.

56. Flint, "Objects," 219.

57. Flint, "Objects," 218.

58. Flint, "Objects," 219.

59. Flint, "Objects," 221.

60. Flint, "Objects," 219; "Adventures of a Quire," *London Magazine* (October 1779): 451, emphasis mine.

61. Lamb, "Metamorphoses,"155.

62. Mark Blackwell, "Hack-Work: It-Narratives and Iteration," in *The Secret Life of Things: Animals, Objects, and It-Narratives in Eighteenth-Century England*, ed. Mark Blackwell (Lewisburg: Bucknell University Press, 2007), 189.

63. Walter Scott, *Miscellaneous Prose Works of Sir Walter Scott* (1834); reprinted in Howes, *Critical Heritage*, 372; Ralph Griffiths, *Monthly Review* 32 (1765): 20; reprinted in Howes, *Critical Heritage*, 3.

64. Sterne, *Tristram Shandy*, 11.

65. Homer Obed Brown, "Tristram to the Hebrews: Some Notes on the Institution of a Canonic Text," *MLN* 99.4 (1984): 731.

66. Sterne, *Tristram Shandy*, 84.

67. J. Paul Hunter, "Response as Reformation: *Tristram Shandy* and the Art of Interpretation," *Novel* 4 (1971): 134.

68. Hunter, "Response," 133.

69. Sterne, *Tristram Shandy*, 102.

70. Sterne, *Tristram Shandy*, 102.

71. Edmund Burke, *Annual Register* 3 (1760): 247; reprinted in Howes, *Critical Heritage*, 106.

72. Sterne to John Hall-Stevenson, June 1761, *Letters of Laurence Sterne,* ed. Lewis Perry Curtis (Oxford: Clarendon Press, 1935, 1967), 140; reprinted in Howes, *Critical Heritage*, 127.

73. Price, *Anthology*, 68.

Contributors to Volume 37

Shane Agin is Assistant Professor of French at Duquesne University. He is currently co-editing, with Diane Berrett Brown, a collection of essays on sex education in eighteenth-century France and completing a book on the development of Diderot's aesthetic thought.

Tony C. Brown is Assistant Professor of English at the University of Minnesota, Twin Cities. Currently an NEH Fellow at the Huntington Library, he is completing a book manuscript entitled "Beside History: Rethinking the Primitive in Aesthetics, Literature, and Historiography."

Simon During is Professor of English at The Johns Hopkins University and also holds a position as Professorial Fellow of the School of Culture and Communications at the University of Melbourne. His books include *Foucault and Literature* (1993), *Patrick White* (1996), and *Modern Enchantments: The Cultural Power of Secular Magic* (2002). He is editor of the widely used textbook, *The Cultural Studies Reader*, now in its third edition (1993, 1999, 2007). His current work explores intersections among literature, politics, and religion in Britain between 1688 and 1914.

Hilary Englert is Assistant Professor of English at New Jersey City University where she teaches British literature and gender studies. She is currently completing a book manuscript on the relationship between eighteenth-century literary property discourse and the conventions of popular fiction, entitled *Foraged Fiction: Locating Literary Value in the Eighteenth-Century Novel.*

Ana Hontanilla is Assistant Professor of Spanish at the University of North Carolina in Greensboro and the author of *Good Taste, Imagination and Virtue in Eighteenth-Century Spain* (Madrid: Iberoamericana, forthcoming).

Mark R. Malin is Associate Professor of Spanish at Randolph-Macon College in Ashland, Virginia. His research interests include eighteenth- and nineteenth-century prose, and the Spanish epistolary novel of these periods.

He currently serves as an at-large member of the Ibero-American Society of Eighteenth-Century Studies. His recent projects include work on sentimentalism in the late eighteenth-century novel, and the representation of natives and the influence of Cervantes and *Don Quijote* in the same period. His critical edition of Estanislao de Cosca Vayo's 1827 epistolary novel *Voyleano, o la exaltación de las pasiones* has been accepted for publication by the Grupos de Estudios del Siglo XVIII.

Frank Palmeri is Professor of English at the University of Miami. He is the author of *Satire in Narrative* (1990) and *Satire, History, Novel: Narrative Forms, 1665–1815* (2003), and editor of *Humans and Other Animals in Eighteenth-Century British Culture* (2006). He is currently working on the afterlife of Enlightenment conjectural history in nineteenth-century social sciences, as well as on the eclipse and reemergence of satire in the long nineteenth century (1790–1910).

Stuart Peterfreund is a Senior Associate Dean and Professor of English at Northeastern University. He has been a Dibner Fellow in the History of Science and Technology at MIT and a Summer Seminar Fellow in the Social History of Science at Harvard. A founding member and past president of the Society for Literature, Science, and the Arts (SLSA—formerly the Society for Literature and Science [SLS]), he has published extensively in seventeenth-, eighteenth-, and nineteenth-century social history of science. His most recent books are *Shelley among Others: The Play of the Intertext and the Idea of Language* (2002), and *William Blake in a Newtonian World: Argument as Art and Science* (1998). His current project, on which the essay appearing in this volume is based, is a study of natural theology from Bacon to Darwin.

Suzanne R. Pucci is Professor of French at the University of Kentucky. She specializes in eighteenth-century studies, questions of representation, and relations between early modern and contemporary culture. She has published *Diderot and a Poetics of Science* (1986), and *Sites of the Spectator: Emerging Literary and Cultural Practice in Eighteenth-Century France* (2001). She is co-editor of *Jane Austen and Co.: Remaking the Past in Contemporary Culture* (2003); editor of *Diderot in the Wake of Modern Critical Thought* (special issue of *L'Esprit Créateur*, 1984); and co-editor of *Esthétiques de l'intime/Esthetics of Intimacy* (2004). Her articles on Marivaux, Diderot, Beaumarchais, Montesquieu, and Molière have appeared in edited collections and journals, including *Yale French*

Studies, Eighteenth-Century Studies, Mosaic, The Eighteenth Century: Theory and Interpretation, and the *Stanford French Review.*

Julia Rudolph is Assistant Professor of History at the University of Pennsylvania. She is author of *Revolution by Degrees: James Tyrrell and Whig Political Thought in the Late Seventeenth Century* (2002), and editor of *History and Nation* (2006). She is currently at work on a study of legal culture during the early Enlightenment in England.

Anne H. Stevens is Assistant Professor of English at the University of Nevada, Las Vegas. She has published articles in *Critical Inquiry*, *The Eighteenth-Century Novel*, and elsewhere, and is currently completing a book project entitled *Antiquarian Romances: Historical Fiction Before Scott.*

Jennifer Thorn is Assistant Professor of English at Colby College and editor of *Writing British Infanticide: Child-Murder, Gender, and Print, 1722–1859* (2003). She has published articles on Eliza Haywood and reproductivity, Haywood and race, and race and early translations of the *Arabian Nights Entertainment.* She is at work on a book tentatively entitled *Phillis Wheatley, Grief, and Gender.*

Editorial Readers for Volume Thirty-Seven

DAVID ARMITAGE / History / Harvard University
ELISABETH ARNOULD-BLOOMFIELD / French / University of Colorado, Boulder
JEAN BLOCH / French / Royal Holloway University of London
GAIL BOSSENGA / History / College of William and Mary
FRANCES BOTKIN / English / Towson University
REED S. BROWNING / History / Kenyon College
JORGE CAÑIZARES-ESGUERRA / History / University of Texas, Austin
ARIANNE CHERNOCK / History / Boston University
TITA CHICO / English / University of Maryland
MITA CHOUDHURY / History / Vassar College
LUCIA HELENA COSTIGAN / Spanish and Portuguese / Ohio State University
RACHEL COWGILL / School of Music / University of Leeds
SCOTT DALE / Spanish / Marquette University
AILEEN DOUGLAS / English / Trinity College, The University of Dublin
TIMOTHY ERWIN / English / University of Nevada, Las Vegas
ANITA GUERRINI / History / University of California, Santa Barbara
REBECCA HAIDT / Spanish / Ohio State University
CHRISTOPHER HENDRICKS / History / Armstrong Atlantic State University
RUTH HILL / Spanish / University of Virginia
KRISTINE IBSEN / Spanish / University of Notre Dame
THOMAS E. KAISER / History / University of Arkansas, Little Rock
CATHERINE KAPLAN / History / Arizona State University
HEIDI KAUFMAN / English / University of Delaware
JASON M. KELLY / History / Indiana University—Purdue University, Indianapolis
DAVID KUCHTA / Maine Women Writers Collection / University of New England, Westbrook
LOWELL LINDGREN / Music and Theater Arts / MIT
MARK MALIN / Spanish / Randolph-Macon College
ROBERT MARKLEY / English / University of Illinois, Urbana
ROBERT MAYER / English / Oklahoma State University
GARY MCDOWELL / Jepson School of Leadership Studies / University of Richmond

ASECS Executive Board 2007–2008

For information about the
American Society for Eighteenth-Century Studies, please contact:
ASECS
P.O. Box 7867
Wake Forest University
Winston-Salem, NC 27109-7867
Telephone: (336) 727-4694
Fax: (336) 727-4697
E-mail: asecs@wfu.edu
Web Site: http://asecs.press.jhu.edu

American Society for Eighteenth-Century Studies

Patron Members 2007–2008

Hans Adler
Janet Aikins
Paul Alkon
Emily Anderson
Mark S. Auburn
Paula Backscheider
James G. Basker
Barbara Becker-Cantarino
Barbara Benedict
Oliver Berghof
R. Bernasconi
Kevin Binfield
Theodore E.D. Braun
Fritz Breithaupt
Peter M. Briggs
Michael Burden
Joseph A. Byrnes
Susan Carlile
Julie Choi
Michael Conlon
Brian A. Connery
E. Heckendorn Cook
Kevin L. Cope
Brian Cowan
Margaret Mary Daley
Jenny Davidson
Joan DeJean
Robert DeMaria
Julia Douthwaite
William F. Edmiston
Liisa Erickson
Robert A. Erickson
Roger J. Fechner
Jan Fergus
Riikka Forsstrom
Bernadette Fort
Christopher Fox
Robert Glen
Scott Gordon
Sayre Greenfield
Monika Greenleaf
Joan R. Gunderson
Phyllis Guskin
Mark Haag
Knud Haakonssen
Wolfgang Haase
Martha Hamilton-Phillips
Karsten Harries
Corrine Harol
Phillip Harth
Donald M. Hassler
Ruth Hill
Robert H. Hopkins
Robert D. Hume
Lynn A. Hunt
J. Paul Hunter
Catherine Ingrassia
Malcolm Jack
Margaret C. Jacob
Regina Mary Janes
Annibel Jenkins
George Justice
Sarah Kareem
Gary Kates
Michael Keevak
Shirley Strum Kenny
Thomas Keymer
Heather King
Charles A. Knight
David H. Koss
Thomas W. Krise
Susan Lanser
Meredith Lee
Nancy M. Lee-Riffe
Elizabeth Liebman
Devoney Looser
Robert P. MacCubbin
Aino Makikalli
Marie E. McAllister
Christie McDonald
George C. McElroy
Alan T. McKenzie
James C. McKusick
Donald C. Mell Jr.
John H. Middendorf
Eun Kyung Min
Dennis Moore
Anja Mueller-Muth
Melvyn New
Yvonne Noble
Mary Ann O'Donnell
John H. O'Neill
Frank Palmeri
Douglas Lane Patey
Virginia J. Peacock
Ruth Perry
Jane Perry-Camp
Stuart Peterfreund
R.G. Peterson
Adam Potkay
John Valdimir Price II
Ruben D. Quintero
Ralph W. Rader
John Radner
Bryant T. Ragan
Tilottama Rajan
Gary Richardson
John Richetti
James Rosenheim
Treadwell Ruml II
Roseann Runte
Peter Sabor
Carole Fungaroli Sargent
William C. Schrader
Steven D. Scherwatzky
Harold Schiffman
Volker Schroder
Norbert Schurer
Richard Sher
Eleanor F. Shevlin
John Shields
Kazuko Shimizu
Craig A. Simmons
John Sitter
Douglas Smith
Robert Louis Smith
Barbara Stafford
Ann T. Straulman
Susan Staves
Masashi Suzuki
Mika Suzuki
Ruud N.W.M. Teeuwen
Diana M. Thomas
Linda Troost
Randolph Trumbach
Raymond Tumbleson
Bertil Van Boer
David F. Venturo
Joachim Von der Thusen
Howard D. Weinbrot
Byron R. Wells

(Cont'd)

Patron Members 2007–2008 (Con't)

Betty E. White
J. Edmund White
Lance Wilcox
James A. Winn
Karin E. Wolfe
Larry Wolff
Servanne Woodward
James Woolley
Karin Wurst
William Zachs
Lisa Zeitz

Sponsoring Members 2007–2008

Joseph F. Bartolomeo
Thomas F. Bonnell
Martha F. Bowden
Leo Braudy
Noel Chevalier
Stephen P. Clarke
Brian Corman
JoLynn Edwards
A.C. Elias, Jr.
Robert A. Erickson
Liisa Erickson
Bim Erlenkotter
Clarissa C. Erwin
Daniel Timothy Erwin
David Fairer
Lisa Freeman
Anita Guerrini
Roger Hahn
Elizabeth Harries
Julie C. Hayes
Issac Kramnick
Lawrence Lipking
April London
Paul Longmore
Robert Markley
John McCarthy
R.W. McHenry
Patricia H. Michaelson
Ellen G. Miles
Jane Milling
Jessica Munns
Felicity Nussbaum
John C. O'Neal
George W. Poe
Melinda Rabb
Walter E. Rex
Albert J. Rivero
Betty Rizzo
Barbara B. Schnorrenberg
Frank Shuffelton
Julia Simon
Jeffrey Smitten
Dennis Todd
Deborah M. Valenze
Myron D. Yeager

Institutional Members 2007–08

American Antiquarian Society
Arizona State University
College of the Holy Cross, *Dinand Library*
Colonial Williamsburg Foundation, *John D. Rockefeller, Jr. Library*
Emory University, *Woodruff Library*
Florida Atlantic University, *Wimberly Library*
Folger Institute
Fordham University, *History Department*
Indiana University, *Kokomo Library*
Metropolitan Museum of Art, *Thomas J. Watson Library*
Newberry Library
Niedersaechsische Staats & Universitaets-Bibliothek
Northwestern University Library
Ohio State University Libraries
Omohundro Institute for Early American History, *Kellock Library*
Rutgers University, *Alexander Library*
Smithsonian Institute, *AA/PG Library*
Stanford University, *Green Library*
State University of Ghent
Sydney University, Fisher Library
Thomas Jefferson Memorial Foundation, *Research Center*
University of California, *Science Library*
UCLA, William Andrews Clark Memorial Library
University of California, Santa Barbara, *Division of Humanities & Fine Arts*
University of Evansville Library
University of Kentucky, *Young Library*
University of North Carolina, *Davis Library*
University of Notre Dame, *Keough Institute for Irish Studies*
University of Pennsylvania Libraries
University of Rochester Library
University of Texas at Austin, General Library
University of Victoria, *McPherson Library*
Washington University, *Olin Library*
Yale Center for British Art, *Reference Library*
Yale University, *Library*

Index

Every effort has been made to include references to all identifiable persons living before or during the long eighteenth century, as well as to often cited twentieth-century critics and commentators, and to provide a selective listing of relevant concepts and keywords. Readers may also wish to consult the endnotes of each essay for more comprehensive information.

A

B

C

D

K

L

M

N

O

P

Q

R

S

T

Z